CLASH OF THE CAPITAL SHIPS

CLASH OF THE CAPITAL SHIPS

FROM THE YORKSHIRE RAID TO JUTLAND

ERIC DORN BROSE

Naval Institute Press
Annapolis, Maryland

Naval Institute Press
291 Wood Road
Annapolis, MD 21402

Library of Congress Cataloging-in-Publication Data

Names: Brose, Eric Dorn, 1948– author.
Title: Clash of the capital ships : from the Yorkshire raid to Jutland / Eric Dorn Brose.
Other titles: From the Yorkshire raid to Jutland
Description: Annapolis, Maryland : Naval Institute Press, [2021] | Series: Studies in Naval History and Sea Power | Includes bibliographical references and index.
Identifiers: LCCN 2021026458 (print) | LCCN 2021026459 (ebook) | ISBN 9781682477113 (hardback) | ISBN 9781682477120 (ebook) | ISBN 9781682477120 (pdf)
Subjects: LCSH: Jutland, Battle of, 1916. | World War, 1914–1918—Naval operations, British. | World War, 1914–1918—Naval operations, German.
Classification: LCC D582.J8 B76 2021 (print) | LCC D582.J8 (ebook) | DDC 940.4/56--dc23
LC record available at https://lccn.loc.gov/2021026458
LC ebook record available at https://lccn.loc.gov/2021026459e

♾ Print editions meet the requirements of ANSI/NISO z39.48-1992 (Permanence of Paper).
Printed in the United States of America.

29 28 27 26 25 24 23 22 21   9 8 7 6 5 4 3 2 1
First printing

Maps drawn by Chris Robinson.

CONTENTS

MAPS

ACKNOWLEDGMENTS

Any book purporting to be a work of synthesis should begin by acknowledging those authors whose spadework forms the foundation for such a study. So, thanks go to the prodigious research accomplishments of the scores of historians whom I list in the introduction—with honorable mention needed here for the seminal sleuthing of Julian Corbett, Holloway Frost, Otto Groos, Arthur Marder, Andrew Gordon, James Goldrick, John Brooks, Gary Staff, Nicholas Jellicoe, Holger Herwig, Volker Berghahn, Michael Epkenhans, and Werner Rahn.

This work unfolded over the first five years of retirement solitude after ending my active teaching career in 2015. There were no seemingly endless months of archival research in foreign cities as with earlier publications, just stacks of library books to consult at home along with my personal holdings. It will come as no surprise, therefore, that *Clash of the Capital Ships* could not have been completed without the indispensable aid of many library and interlibrary loan staffs, mainly those of Drexel University, the University of Pennsylvania, Tulane University, and the New Orleans Public Library. I want to express similar gratitude to the graphics and cartographic expertise of Peter Groesbeck of Drexel and Chris Robinson of Annapolis, whose efforts made my book's maps possible. Many of the photos would not have surfaced, moreover, without Janis Jorgensen of the USNI archive rummaging through the photos held by the Naval Institute in Annapolis. And thank goodness for the Library of Congress. My acquisitions editor at the Naval Institute Press, Glenn Griffith, deserves a special salute for his faith in the worth of the project and unique ability in the midst of a leadership reshuffling at NIP as well as a global pandemic to guide things successfully to contract. Once production got underway and photos and maps were secured and finished, my study came under the careful scrutiny of Mary Hardegree. I have benefited from several good copy editors over the years, but none who tightened up and fine-tuned a manuscript of mine as expertly as she did. Special thanks for help big and small also goes to the late James Hornfischer of Hornfischer Literary Management, Frank Wilson of the *Philadelphia Inquirer*, and former SECNAV John Lehman.

Continuing on a personal note, I want to express gratitude to my wife, Faith Yvonne Sumner, who needs no introduction in the tragedy of war, having flown often-frightened soldiers into combat zones with her employer, World Airways, and then accompanied the happier, fortunate ones out again. She has helped me so much to write this history with a depth of feeling that would otherwise have been lacking.

Finally, thanks go skyward to my father, Robert William Brose (1918–93), lieutenant commander in the USS *Abner Read*, sunk by a kamikaze during World War II. Dad first sparked my interest in history when he gathered the family together for Sunday evening episodes of *Victory at Sea* in the early 1950s. He did not do this to celebrate war, however, for I shall never forget his reminding my brothers and me after we proudly proclaimed victory over neighborhood kids in a rather rough and tumble day of aggressive struggle that "war is not a game!" His hand came down hard on the dinner table, leaving no glass, plate, utensil—or us—unshaken. This was just one of so many important lessons.

None of the persons above deserves any share of the blame, of course, for the shortcomings of mine that probably remain in *Clash of the Capital Ships*.

Eric Dorn Brose
New Orleans

INTRODUCTION

The Battle of Jutland (aka Skagerrak), May 31–June 1, 1916, pitted against one another for the first time the two largest fleets of World War I—those of Great Britain and Imperial Germany. It would be the largest clash of capital ships in the history of modern naval warfare. At stake this day, and on the days of likely follow-up battles, was mastery of the North Sea, maintenance of Britain's strangling blockade of Germany, control of the English Channel, preservation of an uninterrupted supply and reinforcement of allied armies in France, holding open crucial material lifelines to Britain—even protecting the motherland from invasion. Arguably at stake, therefore, was the outcome of the Great War itself.

But why should any historian write another book about Great War naval encounters in the North Sea culminating with Jutland? One annotated bibliography listed 528 titles on this battle alone, and that was twenty-nine years ago (1992).[1] Obviously, that work does not include the spate of further works that appeared as the centennial of this naval showdown in 2016 drew near.[2] Although the subject is certainly a heavily traveled historiographical sea lane, the differing opinions among the latest, high-quality monographs warrant further discussion and synthesis. The argument for a revisitation strengthens given the wealth of valuable primary material that has surfaced in recent decades.[3] Furthermore, all these newer publications just about force us to brush off the dust of many decades, in some cases almost a century, from the older materials to reexamine these earlier primary and secondary sources for insights prompted by the newer books and articles—in other words, to allow the interaction

1

of old and new to synergize, and then to develop the conclusions that the evidence reveals in a new light.[4] This must be done, moreover, in a truly comparative fashion, for too many of the best works do not do complete justice to both the British and the German sides.[5] In short, we do, in fact, need a comparative–interpretive work of synthesis on the largest sea clash in history, then or since.

Clash of the Capital Ships is such a study, for it not only revisits this history based on much of the mass of extant evidence that a century of publication on the topic has unearthed, but also takes a stand on the most important bone-of-contention issues that Jutland/Skagerrak has generated. These battle controversies cannot be properly understood, however, without putting them in the causally related context of earlier developments in the northern naval war beginning in late 1914/early 1915. Several of the early chapters discuss the impact of the Royal Navy's defeat of Graf Spee off the Falkland Islands (December 8), Germany's retaliatory raid on Yorkshire (December 16), and Britain's blood revenge at Dogger Bank (January 24)—incidents not only closely related to one another but that also put their stamps on the bloodied battle face of May 31–June 1, 1916. Finally, the aftermath of the battle to 1918 is also revisited, particularly the lessons learned on each side and how they might have been applied to a narrowly missed second clash in August 1916.

All these topics relate inextricably to pivotal personalities on opposing sides: the commanders-in-chief (Cs-in-C) (Sir John Jellicoe and Reinhard Scheer); Scheer's predecessors (Friedrich von Ingenohl and Hugo von Pohl); and the battlecruiser chiefs (Sir David Beatty and Franz Hipper). I also examine the often troubled relationships among them, especially Jellicoe and Beatty on the British side, and Scheer and Hipper on the German. Furthermore, because, as one reader of my manuscript observed, World War I naval action demonstrates how circumstances like weather, military intelligence, and political leadership "can be so changeable and unreliable as to give all of the humans involved at sea mere supporting roles,"[6] it has been necessary to devote attention to those weather and secret intelligence factors as well as reexamine the role of top leadership: figures in the British Admiralty like First Lord Winston Churchill, First Sea Lord Sir John ("Jacky") Fisher, Sir Arthur Wilson, and Sir Henry Oliver; and, of course, Kaiser William II, his great fleet builder Alfred von Tirpitz, and others in the imperial entourage. My judgments attempt to give credit where due, but sometimes wax harsh. Unfortunately, many of these men, just like their army counterparts and, indeed, their compatriot nations, entered a struggle wanted by the blind many, understood with acute intuitive insight by the rare few, and known by next to none with a clairvoyance that foresaw "misfortune, much woe, no ray of hope, a sea of tears immeasurable."[7] In so many ways—tactically, operationally, strategically—it was a blind sail into the fog; in human terms, for thousands of persons, it was a disaster.

This introduction does not discuss every aspect of my interpretation of naval action in the North Sea from 1914 to 1918. These findings are spread over hundreds of pages of text and even more numerous, often chunky endnotes. Some hints about my leanings, however, are in order. On the British side, I enter into the "Beatty versus Jellicoe" historical feud jousting, for a variety of reasons, more for Jellicoe. His cautious but competent tactics at Jutland made victory possible, tactics spawned by his Fabian strategic leanings over the previous two years. British battlecruiser commander David Beatty, a hard-charger too eager for battle after Dogger Bank—a battle whose lessons (armor-piercing [AP] shell, gunnery, turret safety, etc.) remained largely oblivious to him and many others on the British side—also receives his due, however, including some recounting of the redeeming aspects of his cavalierly aggressive role in general, but also of his performance at Jutland, especially in the later stages of the battlecruiser duel before the main fleets engaged.

Largely rejecting only partially convincing recent attempts to rehabilitate the Admiralty, moreover, I pass a rather critical judgment on the sea lords. There would not be another Trafalgar in 1916 because of their questionable decisions and deplorable misuse of valuable intelligence. The lack of adequate armor-piercing shell until 1918, which factored negatively into the fighting at Jutland, must also be laid at their doorstep. None of this alters the fact, however—one disputed by the Germans for decades—that the British, as noted above, achieved a strategic victory at Jutland, albeit tactically a very costly one.

Indeed, compared to the Admiralty's shortcomings, German intelligence failures weighed heavier in the historical scales. Not only would secret British code-breaking techniques (exposing most every enemy operation) remain unknown to the German side, but—what is less appreciated in the literature—German Cs-in-C did not possess any kind of comparable intelligence enabling them accurately to predict British fleet movements or even pinpoint the exact naval base being used at any given time by enemy squadrons, bases stretching over hundreds of miles of coastline from the Channel to Scotland.

On the other hand, further review of the evidence warrants somewhat more lenient assessments (than found in previous works) of German figures like the Kaiser, who remains here a pitiable leadership figure buffeted by opposing factions and torn psychically as he gradually lost effective control of naval authority when "German eyes turned north" to the Skagerrak in 1915–16, but one who managed at times to exhibit more humane sensitivity—at least in this stage of the war—than seen in previous portraits. I also offer revised views on Tirpitz, who wanted to take gambles, to be sure, but not suicidal ones; as well as Ingenohl and Pohl, who did not exhibit the spinelessness Tirpitz's diatribes threw against them.

Scheer, whose faction took over in hostile fashion in early 1916 in reaction to the perceived unmanly failings of their predecessors, is also undeserving of some of the worst—mainly British—criticisms. In *Clash of the Capital Ships*, I offer glimpses into the very complex personality of this German C-in-C, insights that explain his "lion-in-lamb's-clothing" behavior in 1915, his bafflingly aggressive tactics at Jutland in 1916, as well as his attempt two months later to "win" again. Moreover, Scheer's top staffers, Adolf von Trotha and Magnus von Levetzow—one, von Trotha, more cautious when attacking, the other, von Levetzow, a more impulsive charger—would play significant supporting roles at the Skagerrak, interacting with and alternately dampening or stimulating the conflicting impulses of their Janus-faced commander.

Hipper, too, was complex, and certainly, like Scheer, no hero, "inconvenient" or otherwise.[8] His murderous coastal raid of December 16, 1914, and the debacle at Dogger Bank on January 24, 1915, tragedies for which he shared much of the blame, provide ample proof of that. Both of these actions, moreover, factored heavily into driving others, especially Scheer and the Tirpitzites, out to sea in search of further combat. The Skagerrak, finally, would offer only partial redemption for Hipper.

■ ▆ ■

I now turn back the clock to the approaching winter of 1914–15, not long after the Royal Navy's espionage-laden (and never adequately explained) destruction of Graf Maximilian von Spee's German East Asiatic Squadron off the Falkland Islands on December 8—in so many ways the ideal point of departure for the tragic events of December 16, 1914, in Yorkshire and January 24, 1915, off Dogger Bank.[9]

▪ 1 ▪

ENGLISHMEN'S HOMES

At Scarborough, on the coast of England abutting the North Sea, a rugged bluff rises three hundred feet from the beaches. Atop this imposing barrier, medieval architects had raised castle walls eighty feet high and twelve feet thick. By December 1914, warm weather had once again yielded to the brutal, bone-piercing chill that rules this spot from late autumn to spring, giving the sun as little chance of reaching the citadel as would-be invaders centuries ago. Peering reverently up to it from the waters they plied daily, Yorkshire fishermen saw the castle ruins looming ambiguously over the whitecaps, a rugged stone symbol of Great Britain's once-unconquerable might.

In 1914, the surrounding plateau and seaside area below had become a popular resort town and lost all military import. It got very busy in summer, keeping fishing trawlers constantly underway, but became much less frequented, with fewer out-of-towners to feed, when fall weather set in. Despite the changing season, the Grand Hotel, on the southern side of the bluff opposite the castle, still offered luxurious accommodations for some wealthy offseason guests.

Near the middle of the month, more tables than usual for this time of year began to fill for afternoon tea in the glass-fronted café with its spectacular seaward view. Around one table gathered popular actress Fay Lonsdale, booked locally for an upcoming holiday play, joined by her theatrical entourage.[1] The presence of these thespians was likely not the real buzz around the room, however, for naval news—the real excitement in a seafaring nation—had taken center stage across the breadth of British land.

Word of Vice Admiral Sir Frederick Doveton Sturdee's annihilation of Graf Spee's German East Asiatic Squadron off Port Stanley had reached the Admiralty days before, becoming two-day headlines. But this good news mixed with anxious tidings, for many said the German navy would be "coming out" soon to settle scores. The probability bordered on certainty, for as the days passed, the nervous victors of the Battle of the Falklands could not fail to hear the clarion cries for divine retribution echoing and careening from across the Channel.

■ ■ ■

Hotel guests in seaside towns and newspaper readers throughout the British Isles were not the only ones concerned about what move the Germans would make to avenge Graf Spee, a revered legend in Germany in his own time. Indeed, the same topic had energized the War Room inside the Admiralty's "Old Building" in London on a daily basis well before news from the Falklands broke.[2] Since the detaching of three battlecruisers on November 11 to confront Graf Spee—two of Britain's first, *Invincible* and *Inflexible*, to the South Atlantic, and the newer, larger, faster *Princess Royal* to guard near the new Panama Canal—nervousness had reigned in this secretive, officious structure regarding the increasing likelihood that the German High Seas Fleet, eager to exploit the weakened state of the Royal Navy, would steam into the North Sea, land somewhere on the coast north of the capital, and transform William Le Queux's fictional nightmare scenario, *The Invasion of 1910*, which still unnerved the public psyche of Britain, into terrible reality.

It was well known that Kaiser William had devoured the book, most assuming that he dreamed of invading Britain. During the autumn fighting in France, moreover, his armies drove on Calais as a potential staging area close to Dover; and when this failed, he gave consideration to alternative invasion contingencies (see map 1.1). General Sir Herbert Horatio Kitchener, Secretary of State for War, remained so convinced this invasion would occur on November 17 or 20 that he held defensive maneuvers in eastern England at Weybourne Hope with 300,000 men, the bulk of the twenty-five "Kitchener divisions" training for the Western Front.

Admiral Sir John Arbuthnot ("Jacky") Fisher, the irascible First Sea Lord of the Admiralty, Chief of Naval Staff, founder and inspirer of the modernized Royal Navy with its revolutionary "dreadnought" battleships and battlecruisers, thought the Germans were coming too; but when the best lunar and tidal conditions passed a few days later, he shifted his invasion expectations to the next days when there would be a waning moon and high tide at dawn—around December 8. Fisher's scenario

MAP 1.1. The North Sea Theater

became even more likely when on November 30, the British Minister in Copenhagen submitted a detailed report (compiled from British agents) about a large flotilla of troop transports the Germans assembled at Kiel, on the other end of the canal to Cuxhaven and Wilhelmshaven, the main bases of the German fleet. Apparently, Britain had only one week to ready its defenses.

The emergency necessitated urgent discussions by the so-called War Group, or "Cabal," as some in the navy called it. In the first chair sat First Lord of the Admiralty Winston Churchill, the civilian political head of the navy, worried that the long dark nights of late autumn would conceal the enemy and prevent detection of landing forces crossing the North Sea.[3] Fisher, Churchill's naval counterpart; Rear Admiral Sir Henry Oliver, the Chief of War Staff; and Admiral Sir Arthur K. Wilson VC, another old salt and close adviser, rounded out the War Group. While the buck stopped with Churchill, his decisions were always sifted through the advice of these men as well as the Commander-in-Chief of the Royal Navy in far off Scapa Flow, Admiral Sir John Jellicoe. On rare, especially controversial occasions, staunch navy opposition, either from Fisher or Jellicoe or both, could stymie the First Lord.

Opinions in the Cabal were sharply divided. The seventy-two-year-old Wilson, a retired admiral and himself First Sea Lord from 1910 to 1911, had come into the War Group when Fisher returned to the Admiralty in late October. Wilson rejected "the dream of most naval officers of a great sea fight in which by some means we are able to collect all our forces together and crush the Germans at one blow." Rather, Britain should counter the "object of the German main fleet" which was "to enable a [Spanish Armada–style] landing on the southeastern coast." It was mainly Wilson who had argued successfully against Jellicoe for a defensive dispersal of capital ships after German cruisers raided Yarmouth on November 3 (see chapter 2). Thirteen "predreadnought" battleships of the King Edward class (1902–7) and Duncan class (1899–1904) had been taken from "Grand Fleet" battle squadrons in Scapa Flow and Cromarty—missing sixteen big capital ships (including the three southbound battlecruisers), Jellicoe could barely restrain himself. Having assembled altogether twenty-six predreadnoughts along the coast from Rosyth to the Channel, squadron commanders had received orders "at the first sign of an enemy expedition . . . to attack it immediately."[4] Wilson, also the War Group's liaison with the Admiralty's decrypting team, and Oliver, former head of the Naval Intelligence Division (NID), remained hopeful that radio direction stations (using cross bearings and triangulation) and code-breaking efforts, both making progress, would facilitate disrupting the enemy near the coast.

Fisher, who did not respect Wilson, scoffed at the notion of these obsolete vessels—which he had once dubbed too weak to fight, too slow to run away—halting the Germans. Howard of Effingham and Francis Drake had put to sea with superior ships in 1588, but now even the powerful King Edward battleships, dubbed by common folk "the Wobbly Eight" because they steered erratically, were outdated. Better to stop the enemy invasion at sea with Britain's state-of-the-art vessels, even though the repeated sweeps into the North Sea ordered by the C-in-C took a toll on tired men and weary machines.[5] The First Sea Lord gave Jellicoe a much better chance while sweeping, moreover, than any advantage Wilson, Oliver, and their old ships would receive from NID. While out in late November, intelligence signaled that "all German flotillas" had been put at general quarters. Jellicoe expected a battle to destroy the invasion forces at sea, but nothing came of it, which did not surprise Fisher given the lack of an old moon and no dawning tide.[6]

Churchill had his own doubts about any naval-battle edge coming at this moment from British interception of German signals. Summarizing his thoughts at the time, he wrote later that "between collecting and weighing information and drawing the true moral there from is often an unbridgeable gap. Signals have been made, the wireless note of a particular ship is heard, lights are to be shown on certain channels at certain hours, ships are in movement, sweeping vessels are active, channels are buoyed, [and] lock-gates are opened. But what does it all mean?"[7] Churchill would no doubt have ended meetings like this with the upbeat remark that everyone, of course, should remain vigilant.

■ ▦ ■

As they caucused, Britain's newest capital ships anchored at Scapa Flow in the Orkney Islands and Invergordon near Cromarty off Moray Firth. Churchill had sent the modern portion of the fleet north in early August to avoid being trapped inside naval installations at Plymouth, Portsmouth, and other Channel towns, a move that would prove effective in blinding German commanders concerning their enemy's whereabouts. While older squadrons in Queenstown (Ireland) and the English Channel interdicted trade to Germany in their sectors, Jellicoe's warships and armed merchantmen (10th Cruiser Squadron) cut off Germany-bound traffic in the north, thus sealing tight a long-distance blockade meant gradually to economically debilitate Berlin's war effort.

Cromarty was more typical of British naval bases, with one approach channel through the firth. Around Invergordon's piers and German-style floating dry dock, Jellicoe currently stationed the rest of acting–vice admiral Sir David Beatty's squadron of fast, less heavily armored battlecruisers, now only four in number, and other light forces. Although the base earlier had no antisubmarine defenses, they were in place by mid-November.

Scapa Flow, on the other hand, was a very unconventional station. A vast 120-square-mile natural harbor surrounded by several of the southern Orkney

Islands, it could be accessed through three main channels between islands and numerous smaller sounds, all subjected to strong tidal currents and frequent storms that ruled out any possibility of having a floating dry dock. Alarmingly, by early December, precious little had been done to guard Jellicoe's nineteen dreadnought battleships there—two were refitting in England—against surprise attacks. The work of sinking block ships in the inlets and putting out booms supporting antisubmarine nets in the channels had gotten underway, but the C-in-C remained typically anxious.

John Jellicoe grew up in Southampton during the 1860s, the son of a mail packet steam captain and eventual superintendent of the line.[8] The busy life of a port city with its arrivals, departures, and cacophony of ships' bells and horns was as normal for him as the rising and setting of the sun. It was no departure from the norm, therefore, when he became a cadet on a navy training ship at the age of twelve (1872). As a teenage midshipman, he excelled at seamanship, navigation, gunnery, torpedoes, study endurance, and meticulous paperwork, all helping some years later (1884) to bring a diminutive young lieutenant with an engineer's cautious brilliance to the attention of the captain of the Royal Navy's gunnery school, Jacky Fisher. When the future First Sea Lord became Director of Naval Ordnance in 1889, he appointed Jellicoe as his assistant.

"Fisher had unrolled the carpet; Jellicoe stepped neatly along it."[9] By 1904, Fisher, the new First Sea Lord, had Captain Jellicoe by his side when designing the revolutionary HMS *Dreadnought*, an all-big-gun battleship bristling with ten 12-inch cannon. Promotions and fleet commands followed quickly: rear admiral, second-in-command, Atlantic Fleet, Gibraltar (1907); vice admiral heading the Atlantic Fleet (1910); second-in-command, Home Fleet (1912); and Second Sea Lord (1912) under First Sea Lord, Prince Louis of Battenberg. It was at this time, interestingly enough, that the retired Fisher predicted, misreading his far more prudent protégé: "if war comes in 1914, Jellicoe will be Nelson at Trafalgar."[10]

Jellicoe showed some of this promise at fleet maneuvers in July 1913. The game posited a German "Red Fleet" commanded by Jellicoe spearheading an invasion force across the sea to Britain. The Royal Navy's Number One outmaneuvered the "Blue Fleet" under then–C-in-C Sir George Callaghan, successfully landing the enemy between the Humber estuary and Newcastle-Tyne. Churchill, observing from Jellicoe's flagship, was so unnerved by the demonstrated distinct possibility of Britain's collective bad dream coming true that he called off the exercise—lest Germany's High Seas Fleet get ideas. In all likelihood, however, Churchill also knew at this moment that if war came, Jellicoe would replace Callaghan. When the Home Fleet, now dubbed the Grand Fleet, embarked on its first sweep into the North Sea from Scapa Flow on the morning of August 4—fourteen hours *before* Britain's ultimatum to Germany expired, in response to false reports from the British Embassy in Berlin that the German fleet was "coming out"—Jellicoe stood at the helm.

Once in charge of the Grand Fleet, Great Britain's usually phlegmatic master and commander worried incessantly about many things. Could a flotilla of German destroyers, or even a few submarines, penetrate Scapa Flow and launch a devastating, decimating torpedo attack? Gripped by such anxious thoughts earlier that autumn, he had shifted the entire fleet from Scapa Flow and Cromarty to the northern side of Ireland and western side of Scotland. However, when HMS *Audacious*, one of the newer dreadnoughts, hit a German mine and sank on October 28, and then the German navy raided Yarmouth on November 3, he moved the fleet back. Jellicoe's perception of vulnerability spiked again after reading a report that at least two U-boats had been in or near Scapa Flow while his squadrons swept into the North Sea (November 22–26).

On December 4, Jellicoe stayed busy aboard HMS *Iron Duke*, the Grand Fleet's flagship. He had sent the Admiralty an alarming missive about capital ship dispersal policies that "greatly handicap me in obtaining the crushing victory over the High Seas Fleet that is expected of me."[11] Jellicoe's assertive words reflected the apprehensive mood that subdued him of late. On the next day, winds outside shrieked and wailed, howled and groaned, assaulting the three squadrons of steel monsters on battleship row and rudely mocking the most powerful fleet in the world.[12] Inside, Jellicoe heard the menacing message. The gale force winds presently playing havoc with his squadrons had no doubt broken mines adrift in all directions of the North Sea, making the probability of another *Audacious*-type disaster so certain as to force cancellation of the next sweep scheduled for two days later. The storm also obliterated all booms and nets put in place thus far.

When news of the Battle of the Falklands broke on December 9–10, the previous days' storms had passed, giving way to Scapa Flow's normally turbulent weather. The Grand Fleet's dilemma, however, had intensified. Jellicoe agreed with the Admiralty that the Germans, wanting revenge, would come out soon before Beatty's three battlecruisers returned from the South Atlantic and the Caribbean. "The enemy," wrote Jacky Fisher, "will quite likely strike a blow at once to take off [embarrassing] attention from the Graf Spee affair." Or perhaps Berlin would postpone the attack until near Christmas, thought Jellicoe, "expecting the Britishers to be drunk." But like Fisher, he bemoaned the debilitating machinations of those around Wilson—had not the C-in-C shown in 1913 the difficulties of blocking an invasion force already close to British shores?[13]

But could the Grand Fleet fulfill the nation's expectation of a "crushing victory" far out in the North Sea? Indeed, terrible weather, threatening mines adrift, surprise destroyer or submarine raids on his bases, and sixteen capital ships swept from his command did not come close to constituting the greatest worries for a man who worried about everything because it would have been criminally negligent not to do so. For one thing, his counterpart, German C-in-C Friedrich von Ingenohl, had the luxury of bringing out his main force when all ships were seaworthy—less of a problem for him without the constant wear and tear on boilers, condensers, and turbines; the refitting; and the dry-docking that making sweeps and maintaining a long-distance blockade imposed on his enemy. For Jellicoe, these realities brought the dreadnought battleship balance—nineteen to fourteen at this time—too close to one-to-one for comfort. Worse still, qualitatively and technically, as fighting machines, he believed his foe's designs compared better. Furthermore, although he had no data on German shell quality, he had a backlog of worries about the deficiency of Britain's, especially at ranges above 10,000 yards. With the range of torpedoes lengthening beyond 10,000 yards, however, firing at 15,000 to stay safely away from torpedoes seemed to be a very dubious alternative because of shell failings at this range, but less troubling (due to those torpedo dangers) than his strong prewar preference for smashing the enemy at 6,000–8,000 yards. Such dead-end dilemmas would induce in Jellicoe a case of "the piles" (see chapter 6).

Torpedoes from enemy destroyers burgeoned into Jellicoe's greatest worry, in fact, when he considered the numerical odds in this category of vessels. To protect troop transports to France, the Admiralty had assembled forty destroyers (minus those refitting) in faraway Harwich, including all the latest M- and L-class models, and then shifted eight of Jellicoe's forty-eight older models (Acorn and Acasta classes) to guard 3rd Battle Squadron's "Wobbly Eight" at Rosyth, leaving Jellicoe in the far north, after the steady drain from refitting needs, with only thirty to thirty-five sub–state-of-the-art destroyers. The Admiralty had promised the Channel-guard Harwich Force to the C-in-C when major actions arose; but given the vast distance that separated the two bases, Jellicoe doubted whether these vessels could join his Grand Fleet in time for battle. Given the alarming prospect of facing eight German flotillas at sea—perhaps as many as eighty-eight "torpedo boats," at least a one-to-two disadvantage—he knew Germany's fast attackers could quite possibly overwhelm his own. Keenly aware of the difficulty and objections to turning away from the enemy in a fleet action—all guns are deranged or stopped; one does not lose, but neither does one win—Jellicoe knew that if facing such a menace, he nevertheless would have to do so. It is doubtful that Jellicoe ever learned the number of destroyers the Germans actually sent out with their capital ships—sixty to sixty-five—but these figures would also have alarmed him in 1914. Among German commanders, for that matter, the mystery of British destroyers, whose numbers and deployment were "not known to us,"[14] generated similar levels of anxiety.

Given the importance of the Royal Navy to Britain's national security, said Churchill, Jellicoe had become the only person on their side capable of losing the war in a single afternoon, a reality that did nothing to reduce his admiral's anxious preoccupation with how masterfully to play the bad hand he believed had been dealt him.

· 2 ·

DEATH NOTICES

The deciduous foliage had already fallen throughout the sprawling English-style wood that engulfed Schloss Heltorf. The ancestral estate of the Imperial Counts of Spee stood cold and motionless as if in an early winter wake, waiting and hoping for the redeeming rebirth of spring. Sadly, grievingly, the season had passed for the latest *Reichsgraf* and the two sons who would have succeeded him, all three victims of the misfortunes of war. Their nation waited for a different kind of redemption—the less-than-noble kind that only revenge could bring.

The death notice (*Todeszettel*) for the father and his sons kept to their Catholic traditions.[1] The right and left panels, respectively, of the black-bordered card were devoted to the sons, Otto and Heinrich: Christian Dietrich's painting of Jesus walking on the water, which hung in the boys' bedroom, and Ernst Deger's painting of Madonna and Child, which hung in the *Schloss* chapel where Heinrich and Huberta, the younger children, took their first communion in 1906. A painting of the Crucifixion was placed in the center for Graf Spee. Each panel was accompanied by a quote from the Bible. Below Graf Spee's panel appeared lines from 2 Timothy: "I fought the good fight, I finished the race, I kept the faith." While the widowed Countess Margarete did not intend to promote the idea of martyrdom with this image and these words—it had been her husband's wish that death, when it came, come at sea, and it had—there can be little doubt that his martyrdom, and the need to avenge it, was the message gotten by all Germans who revered the Count.

Still in its first year, World War I had already produced tragedies and terrible atrocities but also displayed chivalry, mercy, and a kind of innocence from the depravity usually surrounding wars that do not end quickly: notable examples being the humane treatment of civilians taken by Graf Spee's lone commerce raider in the Indian Ocean, SMS *Emden*; and the famous Christmas Truce on the Western Front that first December. The more admirable side of this ongoing conflagration was fading away rapidly, however, by the end of 1914. The determination of many in the German navy to put the English on notice that they would pay dearly for the death of Graf Spee, his sons, and his men reflected this vindictive emotion. Few in Germany—or Britain for that matter—felt the humbling metaphysical need to supplicate themselves before their God as human beings guilty of warring and destroying his creation. Instead, one heard the loud refrain, "*Gott strafe England!*" ("May God punish England!")

■ ■ ■

Vice Admiral Franz Hipper could often be found leaning on the railing of the flying bridge of his flagship battlecruiser, SMS *Seydlitz*, chain-smoking as usual. On this particular day in December, something had imparted a somber look onto his countenance as he stared trancelike past the forward 11-inch "Anna" turret, the wind-swept quarterdeck and bow, out past the mouth of the Jade River and Wilhelmshaven Roadstead, and beyond into the invisible infinity of the Helgoland Bight and the North Sea. Once the day's wire about the Falklands sea battle descended and circulated from the crestfallen Kaiser, soon reaching all the way down to the stokers, his thoughts seemed to be circling and recircling around the operational what-ifs of recent weeks, as if their history could only be remembered in the cloud-reflected sea-green blur of that far off spot. Graf Spee, his sons, and two thousand sailors had died. Two of the four ships that Hipper had once commanded, *Gneisenau* and *Leipzig*, were bloody, mangled, sunken wrecks. Like every captain who acquires a proprietary love for his ship, Hipper mourned these losses too. Subordinates like his chief of staff, Commander Erich Raeder (of World War II fame), knew when not to disturb Hipper. Although a naturally polite and good-natured leader, the chief occasionally lost his temper and "flew out of his skin," cursing in "true Bavarian dialect."[2] This could be one of those times.

Like many German officers in 1914 who had entered the navy in their teens, risen through the ranks, and finally attained flag status after decades of service and successive promotions, Franz Hipper had advanced into his fifties when war broke out.[3]

A shopkeeper's son, he hailed from the landlocked Munich region, where neither the tedious basics of Catholic grade school nor the uninspiring classical curriculum of a public gymnasium exerted as strong a pull as the violence-laden maritime adventures of novelist Frederick Marryat. The eighteen-year-old who donned the uniform of naval cadet in 1881 would remain something of an outsider as a Bavarian Catholic petty bourgeois in the empire's overwhelmingly Prussian-Protestant, aristocratic military establishment; but his knack for handling ships and navigating, his expertise in gunnery and other technical aspects of seamanship, and long years of hard work cleared a way upward as the 1890s drew on into the new century. He served a year as senior watch officer on a battleship with the Kaiser's brother, Prince Heinrich, three years as navigator of the Kaiser's yacht, and three years commanding five ships, including light cruiser *Leipzig* and armored cruiser *Gneisenau*.

Hipper also spent fourteen years in the torpedo boat service; and while this time definitely accelerated his upward mobility, it cemented his outsider status too. Somewhat like the hard-charging horse artillery, who were seen in the army as bizarre practitioners of "the secret science of the black collar" for their unusual mastery of speedy and lethal weaponry, the men of the torpedo boats were likewise dubbed "black comrades of the wild and daring chase."[4] Some of the newer 400–600-ton boats built for use with the High Seas Fleet reached speeds of 25–33 knots and unleashed (from three tubes) 17.7-inch torpedoes: submerged warheads that posed arguably a greater threat to warships than the 11- or-12-inch shells of Germany's dreadnoughts. Because the "torpedo crowd" came into command positions earlier than others in the navy, and their vessels were regarded by some as competitors of sorts to the massive battleships, the "Black Hussar" skippers were often resented or barely tolerated. "We officers of the torpedo section constituted a corps within a corps," recalled Naval Secretary Alfred von Tirpitz, the minister most responsible for pushing funding bills through parliament and building the German navy. "Our united spirit was everywhere recognized, but also envied and opposed."

In October 1911, Hipper became chief of staff to the Deputy Flag Officer of Scouting Groups (SGs), and in January 1912 advanced to outright Deputy Flag Officer of this sister reconnaissance unit to the three main battleship squadrons. The former landlubber and unprivileged outsider, now an uncomfortable insider with a determination to prove himself, became the Scouting Groups' Flag Officer in October 1913. This put him in command of Group I's three battlecruisers, *Von der Tann*, *Moltke*, and *Seydlitz*; Germany's latest upgraded heavy armored cruiser, *Blücher*; as well as Group II's torpedo boats and light cruisers.

Demonstrating the old "torpedo boat spirit" in one of his first fleet maneuvers as commander in May 1914, the new flag officer devised a novel tactic: the so-called battlecruiser breakthrough, which featured the big fast cruisers blasting their way through the enemy's destroyer and cruiser screens to determine the location of the opposing main fleet and open the way for the bigger ships. This daring and dangerous charge was but a variation of the "torpedo boat attack" that he had demonstrated as a younger officer in naval war games before an impressed Kaiser William II. Two years later at Jutland, Group I was ordered to make such an attack (see chapter 11), one so characteristic of their "Black Hussar" esprit.

When war came in early August 1914, Hipper stood ready to put practice into play, but no opportunities presented themselves. High Seas Fleet C-in-C Friedrich von Ingenohl also stood braced for action, urging his squadrons to stay "sharp and resolute for the day of the decisive battle (*Entscheidungsschlacht*)." The Royal Navy did not initiate a nineteenth-century style blockade close to the German coast, however, instead pulling their patrols back hundreds of miles and returning them to bases somewhere along the lengthy coastline from the Channel to Scotland—German intelligence knew "next to nothing," in fact, "about the presence of the [Grand Fleet's many squadrons]."[5] The High Seas Fleet maintained a defensive posture in harbor throughout the late summer and early fall, waiting for large-scale assaults that did not come. Only the Battle of the Bight on August 28, when Beatty's stronger British battlecruiser force lured three of Hipper's light cruisers to their destruction, temporarily altered this picture.

Stung to the core of his being by these minor losses, the Kaiser immediately sheathed his sword: "No advances until I give the order." With the sword, however, was also sheathed the emperor's usual forced bombastic demeanor, which gave way for now to what seems to have been his underlying meek and timid nature (see chapter 4). In keeping with this frail mindset, on October 6 he expressly forbade any unwise action against the larger British fleet. Defense was now the order of the day to guard the North Sea and Baltic coasts against the British and Russian navies.[6] Ingenohl was left with only three options: (1) hold back the main battleship squadrons and preserve them for *Der Tag*, "The Day" of a decisive sea battle against the British fleet; (2) however, this much-anticipated great day would have to wait for the enemy to be diminished in size prior to such a battle—usually a *sine qua non* for the Kaiser—by mining and submarine strikes coordinated with sorties of the Scouting Groups; or (3) keep the whole fleet absolutely inactive and intact, as the German diplomatic corps preferred—and more often than not the vacillating Kaiser too—then exploit it as leverage against Britain during any peace talks that might arise out of a war soon to end in victory, or worse, a stalemate that might necessitate a "Second Punic War" against the navy of Carthage-like England.[7]

■ ■ ■

There had been only three possibilities during the long autumn of 1914 for the kind of major action yearned for by Franz Hipper and the most aggressive faction of his top deck comrades. First, an invasion of Britain, which the authorities discussed seriously until mid-October when they put this plan on hold until army victories in northern France produced a favorable staging area, preferably near Calais. From late October to mid-November combat raged at nearby Ypres, Belgium, and a breakthrough to the Channel beckoned. For his part, allegedly, the emperor found it hard to wait for this breakthrough to the Channel ports. "The Kaiser's rage is directed entirely against England," reported several members of his entourage. "He is quite set on attempting a landing over there."[8] News trumpeted by the hawks about Graf Spee's smashing victory over a Royal Navy detachment at Coronel (off Chile) on November 1, which coincided with these hopeful preinvasion assaults at Ypres, found a more belligerent William seemingly ready to unsheathe his sword again (see below).

Over the second possibility, a battlecruiser bombardment of the British coast, in order to lure out and destroy a portion of Britain's larger fleet (i.e., defeat it "in detail"), raged a high-stakes struggle of scheming and intrigue within the divisive command structure of Germany's fragmented naval establishment—a military house much more badly divided against itself than Britain's hierarchical but often consensual decision-making chain. The main advocate of risking battle, Naval Secretary Alfred von Tirpitz, found himself in a difficult situation politically, for he sat outside a less action-inclined chain of command descending from the wobbly, inconsistent Kaiser to the Chief of the Admiralty Staff, Admiral Hugo von Pohl, to Ingenohl. Tirpitz had the right of access to the emperor, and this influence was certainly enhanced by the prestige he had earned pushing successive naval bills through parliament since the late 1890s, but the Naval Secretary possessed less advisory clout than the cunning head of the Kaiser's Privy Naval Cabinet, Admiral Georg von Müller, who had regular daily sessions with William. While doing what he could at Western Front Imperial Headquarters to encourage naval action against Britain, therefore, Tirpitz maneuvered a protégé of his, Rear Admiral Paul Eckermann, into the position of Ingenohl's chief of staff to embolden the C-in-C to strike the Royal Navy, even if only by engaging and defeating it in detail, the extreme most the Kaiser appeared likely to approve—but someway, somehow, Tirpitz wanted more than that, and kept working on the malleable emperor to that end.[9]

Few in the German navy could even dream about a career as successful as Ingenohl's.[10] Fifty-seven years old in 1914, he had served under Tirpitz in the Navy Office, headed a department in the Admiralty Staff, commanded the East Asiatic Squadron as well as a cruiser and battleship squadron in the High Seas Fleet before assuming command of this entire force in 1913. He had also commanded the Kaiser's yacht, been admitted as adjutant to William's entourage, and received eight special orders and decorations from the Kaiser. Fealty to his liege lord was going to factor immensely into his thoughts and actions.

This is not to say that Ingenohl—a former torpedo boat commander along with everything else—was a coward. After Beatty's battlecruisers sank three German light cruisers in the Battle of the Bight on August 28, he urged the Kaiser to let him use his fleet in similar operations against the British, whittling down their numbers until the quantitative odds drew even, a decisive battle could be risked, the blockade broken, and the war won. William's orders of October 6, however, made that possibility more remote. By October 24, when Tirpitz visited Ingenohl on fleet flagship SMS *Friedrich der Grosse*, the C-in-C's depression over the fleet's imposed inactivity, inability to contribute to the war effort, and the sagging morale of officers and seamen was so apparent that the Naval Secretary lost confidence in Ingenohl's "leadership qualities."[11]

The main defender of the Kaiser's seeming aversion to risking the fleet, Admiralty Staff Chief Pohl, remained consistently against committing the battlecruisers to action, for in all likelihood, to prevail against a smaller force plus guard against British reinforcements that might arrive unpredictably from bases along the coast—no one was certain exactly which bases the British used at any given time[12]—Germany needed to back up Hipper with all three main battleship squadrons. To Pohl, the likelihood of a disaster if the entire Royal Navy fell upon the smaller German fleet pitted him in a nasty feud with Tirpitz that autumn. Although the Admiralty Staff Chief did not completely doubt the genuineness of Tirpitz's aggressive stance, he thought the great fleet builder also pursued a vain personal agenda to prove the worth of his prewar construction programs before the war ended with nothing to show for his ships. The accusation had some merit.[13]

A November 3 mission to shell Yarmouth (see map 1.1) and destroy any retaliating forces failed to produce the victorious action desired by the Hotspurs, Tirpitz and Eckermann. They had put enough pressure on Ingenohl by October 28 that he perked up and approved the idea of the battlecruisers shelling the fortified town while the main fleet waited in support sixty miles beyond the Helgoland Bight, but only if the bombardment occurred at long range, for at short range (e.g., a mile or two) the flat trajectory of shells could easily propel them over the legitimate military targets into a hospital located behind the fort, causing what he regarded as scandalous consequences.[14] Privy Naval Cabinet Chief Müller undercut Pohl before the emperor and advocated the Tirpitz/Eckermann/Ingenohl proposal, in part to upstage his political rival, Tirpitz. A somewhat more upbeat Kaiser swung to their side and approved the sortie but insisted that the naval air station at Cuxhaven reconnoiter the North Sea to ensure that the Grand Fleet could not entrap the bulk of the German navy. Although not center stage at the moment, the cautious William, the player usually open to Pohl's views, had clearly not disappeared from the theater. On the day of the mission, Hipper's ships engaged light forces off the coast and departed without shelling the forts. The Scouting Groups and 1st and 3rd Squadrons (that had come out in support) steamed back to Wilhelmshaven having essentially accomplished nothing—except what Tirpitz and Eckermann had wanted to avoid, namely, the public perception throughout Germany that "the first operation of the big ships" had been "a spineless defeat."[15]

News of Graf Spee's defeat of Rear Admiral Sir Christopher Cradock at Coronel, which reached Berlin right after the Yarmouth raid, revived Ingenohl's spirits even more to the point of writing Tirpitz on November 9 "that someday, perhaps, we will succeed in bringing one part of the English fleet to blows" and be confident in the outcome after the East Asiatic's "wonderful victory" demonstrated that "we are not behind the English in gunnery."[16] He asked Müller for the Kaiser's permission to let Hipper bombard the Yorkshire coast. The battleship squadrons would provide North Sea support much farther than usual beyond the Helgoland Bight. In higher spirits since Coronel, and still hopeful about an Ypres breakthrough, the Kaiser, his bombastic persona ascendant, agreed, asking only to be informed as soon as the ships left Germany.[17]

Ingenohl ordered Hipper to draft the operational plan, which he finished on November 25.[18] While the coastal bombardment took place, two submarines would wait off the estuary of the Humber River to intercept enemy ships (thought to be there) exiting the river or hurrying north from the Harwich-Yarmouth area.[19] Further illustrating German concern about a threat from the south, light cruiser *Kolberg* would lay down a mine belt off Flamborough Head, several miles south of Scarborough, to block enemy squadrons that might come up there. The main fleet, meanwhile, would advance into the North Sea a few miles off the northern edge of the "South-Western Patch" (SWP), a shallow part of the southwestern Dogger Bank perfect for fishermen but not for the deep draft of huge capital ships. This rendezvous spot[20] lay a good 150 miles past the Terschelling-Horns Reef line marking the outer edge of the Bight,[21] beyond which the fleet could not go without the Kaiser's approval. Although the main fleet's waiting lair 130 miles east of Hipper ruled out close support—Ingenohl and Hipper appreciated this liability but considered it nearly impossible that William would approve positioning the battleship squadrons any closer to the coast—the risk seemed manageable to Ingenohl. The main fleet would wait until Hipper declared his mission accomplished.

The plan had its risks, of course, but even if enemy forces had put to sea on one of their periodic sweeps, or sortied from nearby bases, their forces would be threatened by submarines, mines, and torpedo boats—the plan called for seven of eight German destroyer flotillas to participate. Thus, the chances of defeating the Royal Navy in detail and improve the odds in the North Sea looked fair even if Ingenohl's battleship squadrons trailing Hipper had to engage. This latter eventuality seemed the most unlikely of the scenarios, however—no doubt a comforting consideration for Germany's anxious and stress-ridden fleet commander.

Ingenohl scheduled the mission for November 29 after a German submarine, the *U-27*, had reconnoitered the coast for the presence of mines through which the raiders would have to navigate. With the scouting underway, anxiety levels ticked up, however, after belated news of Jellicoe's late November sortie into the North Sea. Although still confident of his fleet's chances in a major engagement, Ingenohl began to have dread-ridden second thoughts about taking the main fleet so far into the North Sea that it could be "weakened by submarines and destroyers, perhaps without ever sighting the enemy fleet."[22]

He also worried that German naval codes had been compromised, making the likelihood of Jellicoe springing a trap with the entire Royal Navy greater still. That the fleet chief had doubts about such a vital security issue despite the disbelieving objections of Pohl indicates that the arguments of complaining Cassandras in the officer corps had made their way up to the highest level. As Hipper's Chief of Staff (COS) Raeder recalled sympathetically, "there were agitated suspicions in the fleet for a long time already [*in der Flotte war schon längere Zeit der Argwohn sehr rege*] that the English were in a position to decipher our wirelesses. . . . The cipher keys were therefore being changed frequently; for important operational wirelesses, even special exceptional ciphers were used." None of these precautions helped if the code itself had been cracked (see chapter 3), but that the code may have been broken was exactly the accusers' point, one which made continued issuing of orders by radio "inexplicable" (*unerklärlich*), especially with the ships in port making dispatches "by other means" (i.e., by hand) "easily done."[23]

That *Von der Tann*'s boiler pipes required overhaul presented a prudent—and convenient—reason for further hesitation. As concerns mounted, the jittery C-in-C postponed the mission indefinitely in late November, even though Hipper and Eckermann kept urging action to exploit the weakened state of the British fleet, which numerous reports indicated had detached battlecruisers to confront Graf Spee. Continued inaction, they warned, would tempt the British to send more ships south on this vengeful manhunt.[24] On December 8, Ingenohl sent the *U-27* out again to scout the Yorkshire coast, but this mission, like the first, offered no guarantee of action to follow.

There remained a third and final possibility for a potentially war-changing battle: a sortie of the battlecruisers and at least one battleship squadron to escort Graf Spee's East Asiatic Squadron safely back into Wilhelmshaven, bringing two additional armored cruisers, *Scharnhorst* and *Gneisenau*, and three light cruisers into the home fleet. This scenario, also pressed by Tirpitz and Hipper,[25] would have almost inevitably led to a clash against British squadrons deployed to block Spee's return. The annihilation of his squadron off the Falklands on December 8 hurled this dream of meaningful combat onto the scrap heap of wartime could-have-beens. Given the unlikelihood of an invasion of Britain after the enemy finally held at Ypres in November, only one option—coastal bombardment—remained alive.

■ ▦ ■

Even though vengeful emotions swelled up behind this option, it continued to arouse sharp opposition. Still against the notion of jousting with the Royal Navy, a faction centered around 1st Squadron Chief Wilhelm von Lans, known throughout the higher ranks of the German naval officer corps for his caution and prudence, argued that attacking "the English" would be madness, a fight for the sake of fighting, "like a boxing match at a parish fair."[26] They would only pursue battle once they had assembled sufficient strength; but that would probably not happen until after first letting the High Seas Fleet flounder all over the North Sea, easy prey for enemy destroyers and submarines. Lans and his many compatriots, all undoubtedly sobered still more by Britain's smashing Falklands victory, preferred to battle closer to home in the German Bight, where the Helgoland Fortress, minefields, and even the Baltic reserves of the older predreadnought 4th, 5th, and 6th Squadrons could supposedly help the main fleet achieve success. Making it harder for Ingenohl to resist such timorous arguments, he could reckon that Lans would certainly find the support of Pohl, the potential backing of Müller, and perhaps that of the "crestfallen" Kaiser too.

Tirpitz and Eckermann pushed from the other side to the annoyance of the C-in-C, who had grown steadily more tired of pressure from opposing factions, while also feeling micromanaged by perceived lesser talents from above.[27] The chief's COS reported that he and his staff had not given up on Ingenohl, who wanted to be more aggressive and overcome his nervousness. It was said that the fleet would go out if *U-27* reported affirmatively, but Ingenohl's timid side found reinforcement from Pohl, the Kaiser's lackey, whose submissiveness lamed Germany in wartime and who, wrote Eckermann, should receive "a steady dose of chloroform." All were pushing Ingenohl to act more independently and saw signs of progress, but they wished their chief "would start doing more of the pushing."[28]

Adding to this pressure, an angry Hipper and his COS, who had wanted to sortie to bring Graf Spee back safely, pressed for action if *U-27* returned with positive findings. Ingenohl's earlier qualms about potential civilian collateral damage during his raid did not resonate with them, for it was an unfortunate but obvious fact that doing one's duty in modern war, and especially in this war, went hand in glove with the indiscriminate slaying of soldiers and civilians alike. Germany must break the morale of the English people, and then their physical resistance would break too. If this bombardment prodded them to retaliate by pursuing madly to the Dogger Bank, the main fleet would crush them. Only a decision at sea would break the blockade.[29]

■ ◼ ■

On Monday afternoon, December 14, Ingenohl waited anxiously with Eckermann for Captain Wegener of the *U-27*, who had just returned from a six-day scouting mission.[30] The exhausted submarine skipper said that storms had destroyed his wireless antenna and delayed him over the Dogger Bank, blowing him off course and foiling a rendezvous with the picket boats that should have relayed his report. Present now, Wegener explained that from the Wash to Newcastle-on-Tyne he had seen no newly laid enemy mines obstructing coastal waters. Twelve miles farther offshore, he found the German-laid mine belts also intact. Importantly, a wide mine-free gap (that earlier in the war the Germans had left open) was still free of mines for the approach and exit of the raiding forces. This meant that the mission could proceed.

Orders went out immediately. The first, to the naval air station in Cuxhaven, read, "Request extensive reconnaissance by airship and airplane to the west, northwest, and north, December 15th and 16th; German forces at sea, leaving Jade at 0330, passing

Helgoland 0530; Ingenohl" (see chapter 3). Similar alerts were radioed to the lightships as well as the mine sweeping division. Lastly, Hipper received orders to make his final preparations before putting to sea before dawn on the morrow. That Ingenohl did not include the Kaiser in these communications exposed the fact that he had no intention of risking a veto by revisiting the subject with the unpredictable head of state, somewhat of a gamble from a nervous C-in-C unaccustomed to wagers.[31]

Evidently, Ingenohl had already decided to sortie if Wegener brought good news, for he had immediately responded to the skipper by ordering him to accompany Hipper to aid in navigating the mine-free gap. As Jacky Fisher had predicted (see chapter 1), the German chief, whose navy had suffered a devastating defeat, could not shrink from action and thereby evoke embarrassing censure from officers, seamen, or, indeed, from the whole Fatherland. Vice Admiral Reinhard Scheer, then commanding the latest predreadnoughts of 2nd Squadron, wrote later about the mood in the navy as all eyes had followed Graf Spee from his victory at Coronel to the costly defeat at the Falklands on December 8: "The news [from Coronel] lifted up our spirits in the fleet. Proud, confident, and thankful, we thought about these men, left to themselves alone out on the ocean's breadth, men who had brought honor and glory to our flag. Fate prevented them from seeing home again, but they who rest with their leader at the bottom of the ocean off the Falkland Islands gave us a brilliant example of heroism and attention to duty."[32] Although nerve-wracked by the lengthy decision process, Ingenohl would attempt to follow this example.

Thus, German naval command had decided to bombard Yorkshire. Gone were concerns that Ingenohl had considered important seven weeks earlier (when planning the Yarmouth raid) about the need to shell coastal military targets from long enough range for the steep declination of shells necessary to minimize the risk of hitting nearby civilian sites. Even at long range, and even with Germany's excellent marksmanship, there would obviously be risks. However, that an officer whose ingrained morality and respect for the values of civilization had earlier prevented him from countenancing short-range firing now issued such unqualified, anything-goes orders was telling, especially when considering that harmless, almost entirely touristy Scarborough was one of the targets (see chapter 3). Too many had died—also recently, and shockingly, in the Germany navy—to maintain assumptions and standards of legality and decency in war. There was undoubtedly suppressed guilt in Ingenohl's case, but English civilians had come nevertheless into the crosshairs—a fact, ironically, that would have revolted Graf Spee. The unstable, unpredictable, pathetically inconsistent, politically vulnerable, decision-averse Kaiser was not going to be pleased either.

■ 3 ■

TURNABOUT IS FOUL PLAY

At 0330 (3:30 a.m. German time) on Tuesday, December 15, Hipper's Scouting Groups slipped over the Jade River bar and out of harbor. The crisp cold night concealed these twenty-seven grey raiders from a slumbering, darkened Wilhelmshaven to the port side, several lightships near and far the only specks of illumination. All sailors had bathed and donned clean uniforms, including cloth name tags, standard procedure in the German navy to guard against infection should they become wounded, or misidentification should they die. Duty called. The Fatherland must be avenged.

Once all ships had cleared the river, passed through the minefield channels, and the wide bay, they fanned out into a defensive steaming formation in the Bight, the five big cruisers in line ahead—SMS *Derfflinger*, the newest German battlecruiser, had joined Scouting Group I—and the perimeter guarded by light cruisers and torpedo boat destroyers.

Four hours steaming brought them well past Helgoland, where the powerful force turned to port and headed northwest out of the Bight toward the northern side of the Dogger Bank (see map 1.1). One more hour brought first light, a moderate sea, and decent visibility. A Zeppelin on its reconnoitering run passed overhead to a succession of cheering sailors as, in one ship after another, the men spotted the flying silver monster.

Scouting Groups I and II of Hipper's flotilla (1st and 2nd SG) maintained a northwest course throughout the day. As the late-afternoon darkness of December 15 began

25

to descend around the task force, three light cruisers and all seventeen destroyers fanned out in front of the battlecruiser line, but only four miles ahead to maintain contact. Trailing the big cruisers steamed mine-laden light cruiser *Kolberg*. The sea was running rougher, the wind rising, and a heavier rain falling. Sailing dark and blind without radio signals to avoid detection, the raiders found it increasingly difficult to navigate toward the Dogger Bank, some eight hours away.

As time passed nervously to midnight and beyond, radio operators listened anxiously for hours to a beeping cacophony of British wireless signals, but Hipper stayed the course until, reaching the northern side of the Bank to avoid enemy fishing boats that might give them away, he turned west-southwest and closed on enemy shores.

Unknown to the Germans, British warships of significantly greater strength headed south from Scapa Flow, Cromarty, and Rosyth. At 0100 (midnight British time), the four light cruisers guarding the right forward flank of this flotilla were only an hour north of *Kolberg* at the end of Hipper's line—a night action had been narrowly avoided.[1] From the Flow came Vice Admiral Sir George Warrender's 2nd Battle Squadron (2nd BS), by itself a formidable force of six dreadnought battleships and four modern light cruisers. From Rosyth sailed Rear Admiral William Paken-ham's 3rd Cruiser Squadron (3rd CS) of four older armored (i.e., heavy) cruisers. And from Cromarty steamed four battlecruisers and seven destroyers under Vice Admiral Sir David Beatty.

■ ■ ■

David Beatty had advanced to his elite position in the Royal Navy in a most unortho-dox manner. His family background in the Anglo-Irish squirearchy explains much about him personally and also played a definite role in his rapidly unfolding career.[2] His great-grandfather fought at Waterloo and another ancestor raised a troop of cavalry that served with Wellington in Spain. His grandfather, also a squire, was longtime Master of the Foxhounds in County Wexford, while his father braved combat in the British cavalry in India before retiring to a life of horse-raising, polo, and steeplechases. Born in 1871, David joined the navy in 1884, in part to escape a turbulent life under his hard-drinking, tyrannical father and alcoholic mother, but his own personal liking for the fast-paced hunt, the rough ride, and the hard charge would carry over into naval action.

Indeed, the bravery, risk-taking, and willingness to seize the initiative he displayed in the Sudan campaign on the Nile in 1898 and the suppression of the Boxer Rebellion in

1900 brought him to the attention of military giants like Sir Herbert Horatio Kitchener and Jacky Fisher. The youngest captain in the navy in 1900, he became the youngest rear admiral in 1910. First Lord of the Admiralty Winston Churchill liked him too, snapping up Beatty as his naval secretary in 1911. When the flag of the prestigious battlecruiser squadron became vacant in 1913, it seemed easy for the ambitious forty-two-year-old to finesse "WC" into appointing him to command it. Knighthood and promotion to vice admiral—once again, the youngest to hold such high rank—followed in 1914.

War's outbreak meant departure from the Channel ports to a remote northerly lair at Invergordon and Cromarty. In October Jellicoe, ever cautious, pulled the Grand Fleet back to the west until the *Audacious* met her grisly end, which depressed Beatty: "The sad thing about these sinkings is that ships' companies go without striking a blow, without seeing the enemy, and without getting warmed up with excitement. Surely it is the most cold-blooded way of taking your departure from this world. However, we can get used to anything, I suppose, given time and experience."[3]

Jellicoe's apparent retreat, coupled with the enervating energy- and emotion-drain of sweeps and blockade patrols, took a further toll on Britain's naval cavalier. He complained subtly about the C-in-C's caution in a letter to his naval patron, Churchill, whom he suspected would sympathize: "The feeling is gradually possessing the fleet that all is not right somewhere . . . and [that] we are gradually being pushed out of the North Sea, and off our own particular perch. . . . The fleet's tail is still well over the back. We hate running away from our base and the effect is appreciable. We are not enjoying ourselves."[4] He added a pinch of the heroic horseman to the mix in letters to his wife, Ethel: "I would like to command a cavalry regiment for ten minutes in a rough and tumble. . . . I'd give up my battlecruisers if I could command one regiment of cavalry. Our lot is terribly irksome here. I have 5,500 men and four magnificent machines pining for something to do and we can do nothing. All our time is taken up avoiding submarines."[5]

November brought the squadron back to Cromarty, but the unacceptable circumstances of uneventful sweeps followed by day after day behind booms and antitorpedo nets did not change. "The anxiety of this sea life with the valuable machines and the valuable thousands of lives depending on you is very very great . . . and yet when we go out again, that same day or the next, we are filled with hope that perhaps this time the opportunity will come, and think of nothing else, and it never comes. Surely this is the hardest and most cruelly trying kind of warfare."[6]

The only effective antidote to this poisonous idleness and ineffectual activity—the only way out—would be a coded message from Jellicoe to raise steam, sally forth, and fight the good fight. A missive from the C-in-C on December 12 perked up the battlecruiser chief somewhat. They were to stay concentrated in harbor for a week, given the likelihood the Germans would come out before Britain's three battlecruisers returned from the South Atlantic and Caribbean. "Against our concentrated mass they stand no chance."[7]

Beatty got what he wished for during the night of December 14. The Admiralty contacted Jellicoe that German ships sailed for British shores. Jellicoe alerted squadrons at Rosyth and Invergordon to make ready. Beatty's ships pulled in torpedo nets and weighed anchors at 0500 (5:00 a.m. British time), only two and a half hours after Hipper left Wilhelmshaven.

■ ▣ ■

The Admiralty's special intelligence unit, located in and around Room 40 in the Old Admiralty Building, had received intercepts of Ingenohl's wireless messages to Cuxhaven Naval Air Station, the roadstead lightships, the mine sweeping division, and Hipper; and then alerted Henry Oliver, the First Sea Lord's Chief of War Staff and former Director of the Naval Intelligence Division (NID). Only in recent days had the Admiralty's decrypting staff made fairly good naval sense out of all these kinds of wireless intercepts.

"Room 40 OB," as this unit was called, did not exist in August.[8] As the records of encrypted messages began to accumulate during the first weeks of the war, however, Oliver sought the help of Sir Arthur Ewing, Chief of Naval Education. In early November, the man who replaced Oliver in NID when he joined Fisher's staff, Captain Reginald ("Blinker") Hall, joined the team. Together, Oliver, Ewing, and Hall assembled a group of specialists whose differing individual skills supported one another symbiotically: some knew German, but not the navy; some served in the navy, but knew no German; while only one, Commander C. J. E. Rotter, knew both as well as an extensive amount about codes and the ciphers that further scrambled codes, making them very difficult to understand—or impossible, as most Germans assumed.

None of this would have helped, however, without three seemingly incredible strokes of luck. In the course of October, Room 40 OB had acquired two of the three codes and cipher keys used by German vessels at sea. One had been seized by the Royal Australian Navy from a German merchant ship. Another was gathered from the German light cruiser *Magdeburg*, which had run aground near the Gulf of Finland and been captured by the allied Russian navy. The final batch came to Room 40 in the first week of December, fished out of the Channel by the patriotic skipper of a trawler whose catch included the lead metal box of a German destroyer that had followed procedure: stuffed the code/key book into the box and tossed it overboard, where it lay sunken for seven weeks. Ingenohl's signals of December 14 had been sent in all likelihood using three different codes, but now Room 40 could learn something from them all.

By December, messages like these got intercepted and recorded by a variegated system of radio receiver set operators of the Post Office, the Marconi Company, the Royal Navy wireless station at Stockton, and additional sites outfitted on the shore of the Wash that autumn as intercepts had piled up. Operatives telegraphed this stolen information over land lines to the Admiralty, where Rotter and his team decrypted them, Oliver's professors translated them, and others sorted out duplicates. Finally, Room 40's head analyst, Commander Herbert Hope, opined which intercepts seemed important enough to forward to Oliver, who in turn added his opinion about the general scheme of the enemy and passed them along to the special adviser without portfolio of the War Group, Admiral Sir Arthur Wilson, who gave them to Churchill.

Very remarkably, the entire process of decrypting, translating, and interpreting these wirelesses unfolded from early afternoon, when Eckermann sent them, to early evening when Wilson, who had read them an hour or so before Churchill, entered the First Lord's office. Hope and Oliver had concluded that the Germans merely planned some sort of exercise in the Bight, but Wilson thought the intercepts pointed to a potential sortie of Germany's SGs against Britain itself, and he convinced the others. That the messages mentioned only the Jade River and Hipper, and not the mouths of the Elbe, Weser, and the Ems where other squadrons were stationed, may have convinced Wilson that Ingenohl's orders applied only to Hipper. However, 1st and 3rd Squadrons—all fourteen of the High Seas Fleet's dreadnought battleships—also anchored at Wilhelmshaven. That Ingenohl's orders to the main fleet had not been intercepted did not mean that his dreadnoughts would not take part. Moreover, his intercepted wireless to the Cuxhaven Naval Air Station referred to "German forces at sea" (see chapter 2): a few words, sufficient to the wise, hinting at the possibility of a major sortie. So, another fact stands out, namely, that the fledgling nature of Room 40, combined no doubt with overwork, had limited Wilson's ability to respond to the enemy's operation.

Around 1900 (7:00 p.m.), Wilson knocked and entered Churchill's work room down the corridor from Room 40, asking that the War Group meet immediately. Within ten minutes, Fisher came to the War Room from his residence next door. Oliver hardly ever left this cavernous conference hall, its walls covered with numerous huge maps—in fact he slept there. After Fisher had his chance to read the decrypt, the time for tough decisions began.[9]

Wilson read the evidence to indicate an impending movement of German battlecruisers and perhaps an offensive of some sort that had time to reach British coasts. The enemy main fleet appeared not to be involved. Wagering that they would target Harwich or the Humber,[10] he recommended sending the Harwich Force to Yarmouth, putting predreadnoughts in the Channel on alert, and steaming Beatty's battlecruisers and one battle squadron from Scapa Flow southward with all dispatch. Although Fisher thought the entire Grand Fleet should mobilize, the others disagreed, worried more about losses to mines, submarines, and further depletion of ships' machinery than about an impending invasion. After all, the battleships of the High Seas Fleet itself would be needed for this. Furthermore, lunar and tidal conditions no longer favored a landing. And so Oliver drafted the orders to Jellicoe as Wilson had framed them (including rendezvous coordinates). After receiving them in the early minutes of December 15, Jellicoe objected that he thought it imperative to mobilize the entire Grand Fleet, arguing that the Admiralty should order the valuable light cruisers and destroyers at Harwich north to join him in winning what could be the decisive sea battle of the war. But Fisher did not press the matter—that he did not oppose a man like Wilson, whom he did not trust, strikes one as another remarkable thing. So Churchill prevailed at the Admiralty against the C-in-C. The only concession: adding 3rd CS. The Harwich Force, however, would not patrol only past Yarmouth.[11]

Over this decision hung a cloud of worrisome apprehension. In the course of their meeting it had become clear to Britain's naval brain trust that for the trade-off of possibly destroying a crucial part of the German navy, they were exposing home coasts either to a raid or perhaps a preinvasion preparatory, softening-up strike, which to them may have explained the rationale behind Germany's November 3 strike on Yarmouth. Indeed, nothing like this had occurred since 1667 when a Dutch fleet bombarded Sheerness, sailed up the Medway, and captured the flagship. But what was the alternative? Even if they sent the entire Grand Fleet and all other squadrons to guard four to five hundred miles of coastline, their concentration at the point the Germans chose would be too weak to prevail, as Jellicoe had proved in 1913. The Royal Navy's only option would have to be retaliatory in nature.

■ ◼ ■

The British battlecruisers and their destroyer escorts passed through the boom defenses of Cromarty during the predawn hours of December 15, adjusting their course at daylight in order to affect a rendezvous with Warrender's battleships and light cruisers. The sea had turned heavy, causing even the Fast Cats, *Lion* and *Tiger*, *Lion*'s sister, *Queen Mary*, and the oldest of the battlecruisers, *New Zealand*, "to roll and screw in a somewhat disquieting manner." The night and morning had been "quiet" in the radio room, so if the Germans were really at sea, they were not using wireless.[12]

At noon, now over one hundred miles east of Invergordon, the battle force from Scapa Flow came into view off the port bows of Beatty's destroyers. Warrender signaled his hunch: "I think raid probably Harwich or Humber." The British destination for first light on Wednesday the 16th, a coordinate chosen by the Admiralty twenty-five miles southeast of the Dogger Bank's South-Western Patch (SWP), looked good for intercepting ships heading toward Harwich or Humber—especially the latter—but also an ideally chosen spot on the seemingly unlikely off chance that invaders aimed for the Yorkshire coast Jellicoe himself had selected for landing sites during 1913 fleet maneuvers (see chapter 1). Warrender also informed Beatty that the Germans had exited the Jade "at daylight today" (i.e., 7:30 a.m. British time, December 15). Thus, Scapa Flow had muddied their prospects of destroying 1st and 2nd SG by missing Hipper's actual departure time (2:30 a.m. British time) by four or five hours. They probably believed, therefore, that they had time to catch Hipper as he approached, not as he retired. The Admiralty deserves much of the blame, however, for although the decrypt specifically mentioned 0330 (German time) for departure, the wire to Scapa Flow said rather vaguely that "good information just received shows German 1st Cruiser Squadron with destroyers leave Jade River on Tuesday morning early,"[13] which Scapa assumed meant "first light."

Jellicoe had carefully selected the course to this location so that his invaluable capital ships would stay far to the east of the coastal mines laid by both the Germans and the British. Warrender sailed confidently southward, knowing he could easily outgun Hipper. Only the shortage of destroyers worried him: "If Commodore [Reginald] T[yrwhitt's destroyer force from Harwich] does not join up, I fear enemy's destroyers only." Indeed, without Tyrwhitt, Hipper alone would outnumber Warrender seventeen to seven in torpedo boat destroyers.

With darkness falling at 1500 and the flotilla about sixty miles off Aberdeen, Pakenham's 3rd CS, northbound from Rosyth, approached off the starboard beam. For the remaining hours of night before reaching their blocking point, Warrender positioned Beatty's battlecruisers in the van five miles ahead of 2nd BS with the light cruisers five miles to starboard of Beatty—the cruisers that would miss Hipper's light cruiser *Kolberg* by an hour at midnight. The heavy cruisers sailed five miles to port of 2nd BS, the destroyers ten miles off Warrender's port flank and somewhat astern. That he stationed 3rd CS and all seven destroyers on the eastern flank indicated clearly that he anticipated Hipper coming out of the first light (or even before dawn) from the east. In fact, if Hipper had left port "at daylight," and if he had headed to the Humber or Harwich, British ships might have collided with German at about 0400.

Before dinner was served in the wardroom of *Lion*, Beatty "paid one of his rare visits and found everything full of hope and anticipation."[14] Apparently, the current mission and sense of impending action against the German navy had supplanted the usual old standby topic of conversation on occasions like this when the chief visited, namely, an indignant bristling at the Admiralty's "stupidity, ineptitude, swollen-headedness, pettiness, and narrowness of outlook."[15] Sailors always knew better than politicians or old seamen who had been kicked upstairs, but this time at least the sea lords seemed to have gotten the jump on the Germans.

■ ▪ ■

At this very moment, in the first blustery hours after sunset, the High Seas Fleet steamed out of the roadsteads of Wilhelmshaven and Cuxhaven and headed north, roughly the same course Hipper had taken many hours earlier. At 2000 (8:00 p.m. British time), the fleet flagship and two battleship squadrons rendezvoused near Helgoland with 2nd Squadron, eight of the newest predreadnought battleships under the command of Vice Admiral Reinhard Scheer, and then all turned west-northwest toward the SWP of the Dogger Bank.

On the western tip of Ingenohl's powerful armada came a twelve-mile wide advance guard, fourteen ships strong, spearheaded by armored cruisers *Roon*, *Prinz Heinrich*, and light cruiser *Hamburg*.[16] Trailing this screen by six miles sailed *Friedrich der Grosse* with 1st, 3rd, and 2nd Squadrons, twenty-two battleships stretched out imperially, west to east, for many miles. Six miles behind them at the eastern end of the line steamed a light cruiser and twenty-one destroyers. Guarding the entire north flank of the battleship squadrons, Ingenohl stationed five light cruisers (including *Hamburg* on the van's right side) and only three destroyers (with *Hamburg* up front). Reflecting his worries about British forces coming up from the south, however, on that side he placed a light cruiser and twenty-five destroyers (including the south side of the van).

For the first time these eighty-five warships represented more than a symbol of prestige and pride for the Kaiser and an impatient German public, for now, the High

Seas Fleet went battle ready into a combat zone. Indeed, only one fleet in the world existed which if fully concentrated could defeat this onrushing enemy, whose core of fourteen dreadnought denizens steamed in the dimly stern-lit darkness of night determined with God's blessing to "punish England."

By midnight (British time), Ingenohl had proceeded another fifty miles toward his prearranged guard position, still many hours away. Hipper, meanwhile, had almost navigated around the Dogger Bank. In the pitch-black rough seas, one of Hipper's torpedo boats, *S-33*, lost contact with the others and radioed light cruiser *Strassburg*: "Have lost touch. Course please."[17] The cruiser shot back: "Stop wireless." Learning of all this on the bridge of *Seydlitz*, Hipper snapped at his communications officer: "The fools will give us away!"[18] The admiral, chain-smoking again, started pacing angrily back and forth, cursing in Bavarian under his breath.

His force stayed the course, except for the now quiet (and quite lost) *S-33*, which had continued to steer to the southwest for two hours before giving up and turning back east, directly into the Dogger Bank. Nearing its center (thirty miles north-northeast of the SWP on the 55th Parallel) at 0400, December 16, *S-33* was astonished to see four British destroyers only a few hundred yards ahead. The alert skipper steered cleverly into their line, hoping that nighttime would conceal his identity. The ruse worked, and after a while *S-33* turned away to port, hopeful for a rendezvous with the High Seas Fleet, whose *avant garde* sailed about fifty miles to the southeast. He also broke radio silence again to report his sighting to an exasperated Hipper.[19]

The radio room operator on *Friedrich der Grosse* picked up *S-33*'s signal at 0421. A messenger took it to the admiral, reporting that one of their torpedo boats had sighted four enemy destroyers fifty miles off to starboard. Ingenohl thought for a moment.[20] Why was *S-33* so far behind Hipper? Had it stopped to inspect a fishing boat? Or had it reported the position incorrectly? Were enemy destroyers really so close to the northwest? Did their presence explain the heavy wireless traffic detected by his radio operators since leaving base? Finally, after no further reports of sightings, he ordered the course to remain the same.[21]

The news had disturbed the top man's rest. Why were four destroyers at sea in the middle of the night too far out for a coastal patrol? Blockaders probably patrolled much farther north of the Dogger Bank or farther south in the Channel. Could it be that enemy destroyer flotillas out led the whole Royal Navy, steaming unexpectedly from bases in the north, not from the south, to approach his starboard flank where he had only a handful of cruisers and destroyers, a nightmare scenario? Had the British managed somehow to compromise Germany's codes? These worries—like all fretting, more pronounced at night—reactivated a twitch that had bothered Ingenohl of late.[22]

Remarkably enough, S-33 had luckily and unknowingly threaded a needle through the five-mile gap between Beatty's battlecruisers ahead of Warrender's battleships, and on farther to pass behind Pakenham's armored cruisers and then reached these four destroyers, the first of two divisions of the 4th Destroyer Flotilla stationed ten miles beyond 2nd BS's port stern flank. At 0515, HMS *Lynx*, leading this 1st Division, spotted *V-155* to port, the leading German torpedo boat scouting ahead of the northern wing of Ingenohl's van. The entire British force had just crossed the German line of advance some twenty miles west of Ingenohl's flagship.

Lynx blinked the recognition signal to the interloper and, receiving an incorrect reply, gave chase and opened fire at five hundred dark and blurry yards. After a half hour, the three trailing destroyers of the 2nd Division joined this confusing nighttime action, which two additional German torpedo boats had joined along with *Hamburg*, the light cruiser of the German screen's northern wing, which had raced northwest to the muzzle flashes and gunfire. As the battle turned south—the outgunned British destroyers attempted to resume station off Warrender's port flank—the amazing accuracy of the German gunners, aided by *Hamburg*'s gunfire-synchronized searchlights, inflicted serious damage to *Lynx* and the second in line, *Ambuscade*, which had to limp toward home escorted by a third destroyer, *Unity*, a costly action that presaged similar British losses on the night of May 31, 1916 (see chapter 12). To the surprise of the British, however, when 2nd Division entered the fray shortly after 0600, *Hamburg* and her torpedo boats turned away. There were two dead and fifteen wounded on the British side, with similar wounded casualties on *Hamburg*, whose dangerous searchlights had been knocked out.[23]

Even more important operationally, Ingenohl had heard quite enough from the radio operators of the advance guard. Particularly worrisome, *V-155* had reported "being chased [by] ten enemy destroyers," highlighting for the anxious admiral the danger of nighttime action against enemy destroyers of uncertain (but apparently ever-increasing) number—reportedly ten now, not four. With 1st Squadron's dreadnoughts only an hour away, perhaps only fifteen miles from the van of a larger enemy fleet, prudence seemed to be the better part of valor—at least until dawn. At 0530, therefore, the admiral ordered, "Port turn by squadron, all steady on SE, all ahead full together." At 0620, once the entire High Seas Fleet headed to the southeast, including the screen, which had to be called back to take up station as rear guard, the C-in-C ordered, "Turn together by squadron onto heading E-SE-by-E, engines back one half."[24] From this position, easing slowly east-southeastward away from its rendezvous with Hipper (slightly northeast of the SWP), the High Seas Fleet could reverse course again and deal with the enemy.

■ ■ ■

Never a smooth sail, the western edge of the North Sea roiled in a near-gale tantrum during the predawn hours of December 16 as a threatening storm front advanced from the Yorkshire coast toward the Dogger Bank. Hipper's torpedo boat crews, normally so ready to mock landlubbers who complained of stormy weather that to veteran "black comrades" seemed only a moderate sea, were humbled before the fury of nature. Their masts bent and broke, their decks shipped two feet of water, and their torpedo tubes flooded and could not be fired. The sea also presented a danger to the light cruisers, which were nearly ten times larger. Slung in hammocks along gun decks outside large steel doors leading to the casemates, Hipper's 5.9-inch gun crews, who would shoot first at dawn, struggled with sea sickness too, even though the battlecruisers were five times larger than the light cruisers.

The storm certainly complicated things, for how could the bigger vessels carry out this mission if they could not see their targets on land? Light cruiser *Strassburg*, several miles off the coast by 0600, alerted Hipper, "Bombardment off shore not possible owing to heavy sea. Lights visible ahead. Coast not distinguishable. Cannot keep course owing to heavy sea. Turning east."[25]

Hipper caucused in the chart room of *Seydlitz* with COS Raeder and Flag-Captain Moritz von Egidy. The latter advised following the light forces back. Raeder disagreed. What to do? After campaigning all autumn for action of the sort that now beckoned, and given his still vibrant torpedo boat *esprit de corps*, Hipper could give only one answer. "Yes Raeder, we'll put this through. I'm not going to let down my command." "But the light forces," Raeder said before being interrupted. "Will be sent back to the main fleet," snapped Hipper. "Only the *Kolberg* will remain with us. She must get rid of her mines."[26]

At 0635 (6:35 a.m.), he signaled all the torpedo boats and the three light cruisers not needed for mining to reverse course. They turned out of the wind. The five big ships and *Kolberg* continued westward through a thirty-mile gap in the coastal minefields[27] and then split up: *Seydlitz*, *Moltke*, and *Blücher* headed north toward Hartlepool; while Hipper's newest battlecruiser, *Derfflinger*, went south to Whitby and Scarborough with *Von der Tann* and *Kolberg*.

These sites had been chosen for bombardment rather arbitrarily, for they represented the only towns of any size or significance beyond the minefield gap through which Hipper would also have to escape. Hartlepool and Whitby possessed targets of some military significance. Scarborough, on the other hand, had only a cavalry cantonment near town protected by a few obsolete field artillery pieces. Despite later assertions to the contrary, the German naval leadership knew about the legally and morally dubious aspect of this part of the mission.[28]

At 0806 on a rainy, misty, and bleak morning, *Derfflinger* and *Von der Tann* opened fire on Scarborough with secondary armament from one mile off shore, while *Kolberg* continued south ten miles to Flamborough Head to lay mines.[29] Down below, handling squads muscled powder charges and shells into hoists, while above, casemate gunners rammed payloads into recoiled barrels as had been done many times in prewar firing practice. "Revenge for the *Scharnhorst*" and "Revenge for the *Gneisenau*" they yelled—those who had served in the Far East especially loudly—as one shell followed another on its deadly path.[30] As the big ships streamed slowly south past the castle, starboard guns trained next on the Grand Hotel.

Still sound asleep in her suite, actress Fay Lonsdale (see chapter 1) awoke with a start when salvos cracked thunderously into the cold morning mist. After a few more loud booms, she hurried to her window. Lonsdale made out the blurry outlines of the passing ships, the gun flashes, and a second later, the deafening blasts. Just then, a projectile exploded in the café below, killing a waiter and two guests at breakfast and badly wounding several more. The concussion knocked her to her knees, and she instinctively and frantically scrambled on all fours under a table. More shells slammed into the hotel higher up one after the other, coming closer and closer to her makeshift shelter. One of the lucky ones, she made her way to safety in the hotel cellar.

The bombardment continued for thirty minutes. Residents and a few out-of-towners ran through the streets to points farther from the shore, especially the railroad station, where they crammed into empty cars. The enemy gunners "distributed their broadsides indiscriminately all over the town,"[31] hitting the castle walls and keep, the Grand Hotel and all other hotels on the bluff, three churches, the entire suburb of Falsgrave, where a wireless station was located, and more. At one home, a postman was just delivering mail to a maidservant when a shell landed, killing them both instantly. The crushed front of the house would be depicted in a famous recruiting poster depicting what once was "an Englishman's home." The town "had become a landscape of gaping holes, roofless houses, smashed timbers, scattered bricks, and broken glass."[32] Shockingly, seventeen civilians lay dead and ninety-nine severely wounded, bringing the brutality of war to doctors and nurses who had not imagined, except in a Le Queux-style invasion nightmare, that they would be facing such a gory challenge.

Derfflinger and *Von der Tann* finally left to fire on Whitby, where they missed a coast guard signal station, but inflicted four more civilian casualties. Meanwhile, *Seydlitz*, *Moltke*, and *Blücher* attacked Hartlepool, a more legitimate target defended by three 6-inch shore guns and a flotilla of two light cruisers, four destroyers, and a submarine.

Approaching the town still five miles out at 0745, Hipper's ships first encountered the destroyers on their patrol and opened fire. Three of the outgunned coastal guards wisely retired, but one, HMS *Doon*, charged bravely on what seemed like a hopeless torpedo run, getting within five thousand yards, firing, missing, and then turning away. Three of her sailors died and six suffered wounds. This day found the Royal Navy destroyer corps exhibiting astounding bravery and courage.

Although the shore batteries were similarly outmatched, they shot from point-blank range at huge objects, seemingly impossible to miss. The enemy raiders paid a heavy price, therefore, suffering considerable physical damage and losing eight sailors with an additional twelve being wounded, mostly on *Blücher*. The flat trajectory of the German naval guns, in contrast, meant that their aim at much smaller targets had to be extremely pinpoint-precise to avoid hitting something else. Although eight of the British defenders were killed and twelve were wounded, none of the guns had been silenced. The raiders succeeded, however, in mauling and running aground a light cruiser as it tried to exit the harbor. Four sailors got killed and seven were wounded.

Like Scarborough, the name of Hartlepool would be remembered largely for other reasons, however, due to the appalling loss of civilian life as German shells missed batteries and randomly pierced factories, churches, and homes, and killed refugees in the streets. One family, fleeing as their fellow countrymen had done in Scarborough, fell victim to a shell burst that killed a fourteen-year-old boy, an eight-year-old girl, a seven-year-old boy, and badly wounded the mother holding a baby, which was unscathed. Another projectile entered a home, killing the father, mother, and six children, but again sparing a baby. Five hotels, seven churches, ten public buildings, and three hundred houses lay in ruins. Eighty-six people had been killed and 424 were wounded.

Almost immediately, news of Scarborough, Whitby, and Hartlepool got out to a jolted and stunned British nation. One of the first to learn at 0830, Churchill had just started his day. "I was in my bath," he recalled, "when the door opened and an officer came hurrying in from the War Room with a naval signal which I grasped with dripping hand. 'German battlecruisers bombarding Hartlepool.' I jumped out of the bath with exclamations. Sympathy for Hartlepool mingled with what Mr. George Wyndham called 'the anodyne of contemplated retaliation.'"[33]

The retaliators soon contemplated in the War Room as they had two evenings earlier: Churchill, Fisher, Oliver, and Wilson. They sent the predreadnoughts at Rosyth to block the coast if Hipper fled north; and Tyrwhitt's flotillas to Yarmouth to reinforce Warrender's weak destroyer escort. Finally, they informed the ships already at sea about the raid. Two hours later, when the horrible news "magnified by rumor had produced excitement," Churchill met with the Prime Minister and War Cabinet and "was immediately asked how such a thing was possible." He produced charts showing the Admiralty's "contemplated retaliation" and the likely positions of the German ships now "within our claws."[34]

At 0930, Hipper rendezvoused with *Derfflinger* and *Von der Tann*. *Kolberg* joined them some minutes later, and they all reentered the minefield gap. The chief radioed Ingenohl that he had completed the operation, and then steamed, as his light cruisers and destroyers had done earlier, toward the main fleet, which waited, presumably, just north of the SWP, a spot Hipper would reach in midafternoon. The entire fleet could then return to base or destroy retaliatory elements of the Royal Navy.

■ ▪ ■

Light cruiser *Hamburg* and three torpedo boats turned away from the fray provoked by the British destroyers around 0600 (6:00 a.m.), joining armored cruisers *Prinz Heinrich*, *Roon*, light cruiser *Stuttgart*, and other destroyers in what now became a temporary rear guard.[35] Several minutes later, Ingenohl ordered the High Seas Fleet to steam southeast, and later east-southeast by east until daylight. Around 0700, HMS *Shark* and three others, all that remained of Warrender's destroyers, sighted the retreating German rear guard through the first rays of daylight glowing in the east. The three speedy vessels increased speed to 30 knots and opened fire at 4,000 yards.

Continuing the chase a few minutes later, they identified *Roon* and radioed the armored cruiser's position to Warrender's 2nd BS. German jamming efforts delayed the oft-repeated transmission, however, until 0730. Finally alerted, the British dreadnoughts altered onto a zigzag course to the east, while Beatty, still unaware of *Roon*, turned north to close Warrender, having searched in vain for Commodore Tyrwhitt southeast of the SWP.

At 0800, Beatty received a surprising message from Warrender: "Are you going after *Roon*?" Once *Shark*'s delayed wirelesses clarified the situation for Beatty, he turned to the northeast, increased to 24 knots, and spread his light cruisers out ahead. Simultaneously, Warrender's battleships reversed to the southwest to rejoin 3rd CS near the original block position below the SWP, where apparently they still anticipated the main threat. Although Warrender ordered Beatty "not to go too far on your proposed course,"[36] horses in the hunt do not stop eagerly—and Beatty wanted to catch his fox, which he assumed might be Hipper. By 0815, Beatty's flotilla got another signal from *Shark* that they were being chased by German forces. The enemy hunters had turned to attack at 0802, which prompted *Shark* to retreat toward Beatty's rapidly charging warships.

At 0820, however, the German cruisers, having heard no signal that their main fleet had turned back in support, reversed course to the east. Ingenohl had heard his rear guard report "enemy destroyers in sight." He also knew that Hipper had detached his light forces toward the main fleet much earlier, and that his battlecruisers would "follow after shelling complete." Based on Eckermann's known views as well as the postbattle reactions of many German officers,[37] historians need only a little imagination to depict the scene of disappointment and disbelief on the bridges of Ingenohl's command when he nevertheless decided against helping 1st and 2nd SGs, but rather to stay the eastward course for home.

Ingenohl's thought process is clear enough from the evidence. Throughout the planning stage for this mission, he had measured the element of risk as slight. It seemed more likely that the enemy would suffer losses from German submarines, mines, and torpedo boats, but now *his* command faced apparent peril. Sailing much further westward would perhaps have been hard to justify before the Kaiser: less so if nothing went wrong, but impossible if enemy destroyers and submarines penetrated his weak right flank, preyed on the battle squadrons, and then the Grand Fleet itself appeared and completed a rout. Such visions of disaster allowed something akin to panic to undermine the resolve of an already nervous commander. Thus, even though his own destroyers had more than enough fuel for a Wilhelmshaven-Britain round trip (as well as higher speed combat past the SWP), he grew fearful that they would run out. Extreme nervousness also made leaving 1st SG look acceptable. With the element of surprise on Hipper's side, Ingenohl conveniently convinced himself that his vice admiral would remain safe, an equally dubious decision with regard to leaving 2nd SG on its own too. Fortunately for the C-in-C, both of his choices appeared somewhat less unacceptable after disaster was averted.[38]

Even now, however, battle might have resulted, for Beatty's light cruiser van and lead battlecruiser (*New Zealand*) had gained almost ten miles on the escapees. The slower *Roon* probably had Beatty's ships in effective range as time ticked away to 0900, for visibility, although worsening, stayed passable near the SWP as the storm moved east. In a matter of minutes, the pursuers would open fire. If that had happened, could

Ingenohl, a man of honor, allow himself to abandon badly outgunned *Roon*, *Prinz Heinrich*, and several light cruisers and destroyers to their fate, ignoring potential losses to the High Seas Fleet similar to Graf Spee's nationally traumatic tragedy eight days earlier? As for Warrender, would he not also have raced northeast to the sound of the guns in support of Beatty, suppressing all worries about having a mere four destroyers?

These distinct possibilities evaporated around 0900, however, when Warrender and Beatty got delayed messages from the grounded light cruiser at Hartlepool and also heard from the Admiralty that the Germans had shelled the town. Both forces wheeled about and raced back toward the coast. Ironically, the signals reporting the Yorkshire Raid, which a woefully cataractic German intelligence system hoped would hurry a significant portion of the Grand Fleet to its destruction (from which nearby bases would they supposedly hurry, an empty Grimsby on the Humber?) had instead snatched two powerful dreadnought squadrons out of the open jaws of near certain defeat in detail. Churchill later claimed that Beatty would certainly have retired, exploiting his superior speed, if he had sighted the German battle squadrons about to engage him.[39] The First Lord may not have known Beatty as well as he thought, for news of the unfolding disaster in Yorkshire had still taken ten minutes to force its way into the mind of this maritime cavalier and compel him to change course. But even if Churchill's assessment of Beatty was right—he acted this way at Jutland, for instance (see chapter 10)—the limited visibility on this morning may have eliminated all possibility of escape as the German battleships emerged from the rain, surrounded, and pounced. Moreover, neither Beatty nor Warrender coming to his aid with only four destroyers could have outrun a fast torpedo-bearing wolf pack numbering seventy-five destroyers and light cruisers (including an eastward-scurrying 2nd SG). After a few additional hours, moreover, the capital ships of Hipper's 1st SG would have joined the fray with Jellicoe a day away.

■ ▆ ■

Shortly after 1000 (10:00 a.m.), having deduced that there must be a gap in the German-laid minefield, Jellicoe informed his forces of this and they sailed westward toward the opening. Beatty and the light cruisers steamed north of the SWP; Warrender, the armored cruisers, and four destroyers south of it.

At 1130, Beatty's light cruisers sighted to the southwest a portion of Hipper's retiring light cruisers and torpedo boats entering the SWP from the west and engaged. By late morning the terrible weather from Yorkshire had gotten this far to the east, which helped the German ships slip away to the south. They did not identify the enemy light cruisers or know that Beatty's battlecruisers sailed nearby. A stroke of good luck now aided the Germans, for rather than pursuing the enemy, the normally sharp British light cruiser commander, Commodore William Goodenough, apparently misinterpreting a badly worded signal from Beatty's flag-lieutenant, Ralph Seymour, turned back northward and disappeared from German sight to resume station in ahead of *Lion*.

The German light forces retreated right back into harm's way when exiting the southern end of the SWP. The right wing of Warrender's squadron spotted them at 1210 only 6,000 yards to starboard. Luckily for the badly outgunned Germans, the officer in charge of this battleship division, Rear Admiral Sir Robert Arbuthnot, abided by a time-honored tradition giving only the flag-commander the right to order fire and refused therefore to do so until Warrender commanded it. At this very moment of hesitation, the vulnerable German light cruisers and destroyers turned hard to port, escaped eastward into the squall, and disappeared from view. Incredibly, by surviving, 2nd SG had won this round of the match. At the time, however, no consolation came to disappointed, disgusted German officers in the distant main fleet listening to desperate signals from Hipper's light forces, which seemed destined in minutes to be destroyed.[40]

The order to turn away from "the gigantic silhouettes of the British super-battleships" rather than attacking them through the building storm had not come easily, however, and this decision added to the controversies stirred up on the German side. The initial thoughts of the sixteen destroyer captains who saw the massive smoke clouds and outlines of Warrender's six dreadnoughts, the latest activated models in the Grand Fleet, waxed unanimously aggressive, for naval prey like this formed the stuff of torpedo boatmen's dreams. But first impressions instantly yielded to the sobering reality of the near impossibility of attacking successfully. Assaulting into a squall and heavy-caliber enemy fire without Hipper's battlecruisers to support them, a 6,000-yard charge before reaching an advantageous firing position—assuming doused torpedo tubes were clear of seawater—could likely have been disastrous. An idea proposed by one torpedo boat commander to track the big ships for three hours until nightfall and then attack was also overruled as "hopeless"[41] by the senior light cruiser officer present, Captain Viktor Harder of *Stralsund* (captain of *Lützow* at Jutland).

The British also lost round two of the match. By 1300, Warrender's battleships had cleared the southern reaches of the Dogger Bank and steamed west toward the minefield gap. Beatty had reversed course to the east in order to maintain a block-ing position between Hipper and his base, a basic naval tactic. Both assumed that the big German cruisers must emerge somewhere near Beatty or 2nd BS. Indeed, Hipper, having cleared the minefields around 1100, sailed toward the rendezvous with Ingenohl, that is, on a potential collision course with 2nd BS. At 1139 Hipper received an alarming report when his light cruisers and destroyers reported their brief engagement with enemy light cruisers—Beatty's, as it transpired. Turning to one of the officers on the bridge, Hipper asked sharply, "Where is the main fleet?" He received a gut-punching reply, "Running into the Jade." His biographer and subordinate naval colleague, Hugo von Waldeyer-Hartz, recalled the admiral's reaction: "A real Bavarian oath burst from his lips and his staff knew that he would not fail to tell the Commander-in-Chief what he thought. Hipper never failed in frankness towards his superiors. For the moment he realized that he had only himself to rely upon. At top speed the battlecruisers swept forward [toward imperiled 2nd SG], whirling propellers churned the sea to foam."[42]

Hipper again started cursing in Bavarian at 1213 when his badly outnumbered light forces notified him about a British battle squadron south of the SWP. At 1244, having finally heard that his light forces had escaped danger, Hipper changed course and circled far to the northeast, barely missing being spotted by Warrender. Steaming some twenty-five miles above the SWP, he also swept around Beatty and made for home—without knowing, however, that Beatty sailed nearby (see chapter 5).

"Here again God helped us,"[43] Hipper wrote from the safety of the Jade, a slam at Ingenohl, who should have made God's help unnecessary. Worse, the C-in-C had missed a brilliant opportunity to destroy an important British battle squadron (2nd BS) and help to win the war. No one could fault Hipper's crews, on the other hand, for failing to execute their mission. God's will to punish England and her civilians had been fulfilled. At least as far as his own command was concerned, therefore, the lead article of the *Hamburg News* of December 17 offered considerable solace. The men of the German battlecruisers waxed proud "to have delivered the message to Great Britain with the thunderous voice of their guns that the spirit of the fallen and sunken of the Battle of the Falklands is alive and showing how terribly frightful it can be."[44] Indeed, their spirited, high-caliber "death notice" had been a frightening one.

· 4 ·

MIGHTY HASHES

Beatty's cruiser forces stayed at sea an extra day after failing to intercept Hipper. The Admiralty had finally called out Jellicoe in the afternoon of December 16 after a decrypt put Ingenohl off the Danish coast: coming out, they thought; going in, in fact. So, with nothing else to do, the C-in-C ordered firing exercises. The battlecruisers returned to Invergordon late on the morning of December 18.

The weather was passable for this time of year, which only served to deepen the collective depression among the officers and men, for passable weather two days earlier would certainly have spelled doom for enemy light forces, and in all likelihood have drawn Hipper to his doom as well. Intensifying the emotional strain, news had spread quickly among ships companies that "Jerry" had not only devastated Hartlepool, as the first signals reported, but also Whitby and Scarborough.

After Beatty's ships dropped anchor, colliers pulled alongside and the dirty, back-breaking, thankless task of coaling commenced. With fossil fuel dust blackening the air, supply boats approached with provisions, mail, and newspapers. British dailies spewed wrath and indignation at the depravity and outlawry of the Germans. The shooting of hostages and destruction of cities in Belgium, still fresh in everyone's memory, had been shocking enough, but now this?! The sailors who read the papers that morning found little consolation in the slamming of the Germans, however, for much of the press pointed angry fingers at their vaunted guardians of the high seas too, repeating over and over again the incredulous refrain, "Where was the navy?"

Crestfallen that evening over the opportunities missed during the mission, and acutely aware of the sagging morale brought on by the newspaper reports, Beatty, "more affected and perturbed than I ever saw him before or since," recalled Filson Young, "wrote a brief manifesto or message to his fleet, expressing his deep sympathy with them in their disappointment and inspiring them with his hope of an early retribution."[1] Ships' companies assembled on the morning of the nineteenth to hear their captains read this message.

Just as the returning British sailors did, all people who read newspapers, and many who did not, got caught up in the nasty postmortem of the German raid. The *Daily Chronicle* of London called it "an infamous crime against humanity and international law."[2] In an open letter to his constituents in Hartlepool, Sir Walter Runciman condemned it "as a colossal act of murder by ingrained scoundrels with results that will stamp them for all time as heinous polecats." In another open letter to the Mayor of Scarborough, Churchill branded Hipper's force the "assassin squadron" and the "Scarborough bandits. . . . The stigma of the baby-killers of Scarborough will brand its officers and men as long as sailors sail the seas."

But some publications pointed the finger the other way. The *Morning Post* and the *Globe* thought the First Lord of the Admiralty protested too much, "It is unwelcome to the English nation that the highest leader of the powerful, albeit silent English fleet throws around insults." A letter writer in the *Economist* described the limited military defenses of the towns that under the letter of international law made them "legitimate" targets, implying that they should have been better protected by the navy.

In London, the *Observer* and the *Times* sprang to the navy's defense, pointing out that it could never protect the whole shore, and that the mission of the fleet remained destruction of the enemy fleet, not to be parceled out enervatingly for the protection of every town, to which the *Northern Daily Mail* replied pithily, "No doubt the larger question of naval strategy must take precedence over the defense of particular towns, but at the same time, we may be permitted to hope that we are not to be made a target for German ships even in the interest of higher strategy."

For the Admiralty, the days after the raid proved extremely trying. With pressure mounting from the press as well as the cabinet in London, Churchill and his colleagues refused to play into German hands and disperse the fleet all along the coast. In a statement of December 17, they declared the enemy attack "devoid of military significance." While loss of life and damage to property may occur, "which is much to be regretted," coastal attacks "must not in any circumstances be allowed to modify the general naval policy which is being pursued." The Admiralty made no further detailed comment about the previous day's operation. They would "bear in silence the censures of our countrymen" in order to protect the secrecy of Room 40 intelligence.[3]

The Admiralty, however, made one surreptitious change in the disposition of the Grand Fleet. Beatty had long advocated moving his battlecruisers south to Rosyth on the Firth of Forth. They moored closer to the enemy there, and therefore stood a better chance of meeting Hipper's fast ships at sea, or even cutting them off from base. Fisher, on the contrary, had never liked Rosyth as an anchorage, saying he "hated" it, especially the "beastly [railroad] bridge, which if blown up, makes the egress very risky." But Churchill thought better, backed Beatty, the man he had advanced, and ordered him south on December 21. Jellicoe thought the shift ill-advised, writing to Beatty, the winner in this, with Fisher-like language: "I hate Rosyth. It is not my wish that you are there, merely the Admiralty's fear of a raid."[4]

Clearly, the events of December 16 had not improved relations between Churchill and Jellicoe, Jellicoe and Beatty, or within the War Group itself, but Fisher found ways to make things worse. To Jellicoe he complained about Arbuthnot thinking he had to wait for Warrender's order before opening fire as well as about Goodenough not pursuing enemy light forces. Within the War Group, Fisher would not have been able to stay silent about Wilson's expectation of twenty-six old battleships deterring the Germans. As he wrote later: "we said to them 'a la Chinois,' making great grimaces and beating tom-toms, 'If you come again, look out!' but the Germans weren't Chinese, and they came." At least he blamed himself for not listening to Jellicoe and letting him sail on the fifteenth. In the last analysis, all concerned had "made a mighty hash of it." Waxing more optimistic, Churchill looked to the future, confident that Room 40 intelligence, better visibility, and a more favorable turn of British fortune would spell doom for the Germans if they tried again. Indeed, shortly past noon Warrender and Hipper had sailed only twenty-eight miles apart, steaming direct for each other. If Hipper had stayed his course, even with poor visibility, he might have been destroyed or escaped directly into Beatty hurrying to the sound of the guns. "No use crying over spilt milk," responded Fisher more philosophically.[5] There was, however, one unknown—one that would not be known in Britain for some time—that would have significantly undermined Churchill's optimism: namely, that the entire High Seas Fleet had been present in the Dogger Bank endangering Beatty's four battlecruisers and Warrender's six battleships, 40 percent (ten of twenty-five) of Royal Navy dreadnoughts available in the North Sea (or in dry dock) in mid-December 1914.

The lessons Fisher drew from December 16 made him much more pessimistic than Churchill about the chances of avoiding another "hash" if the Germans came out again on Christmas Day, as Jellicoe thought they would. Indeed, the man who had reformed the Royal Navy after 1904, eliminating ships that were "too weak to fight and too slow to run away," and substituting for many of them the dreadnought battleships and battlecruisers of the modernized Royal Navy, knew he had only finished half of the job, for there were serious personnel issues that needed addressing. Upper class and tradition-bound, naval officers of the predreadnought era were "too often recruited by nepotism or influence" and dominated by a code of discipline "based on the principle of absolute, unquestioning obedience of, and subordination to, one's superiors." They looked above them for the next Francis Drake to defeat an Armada, and the next Horatio Nelson to win another Trafalgar, making them less capable than they should have been to show individual initiative. The Beattys and Jellicoes represented the new breed Fisher wanted, not the Goodenoughs who did not question orders, or the Arbuthnots who would not act without them. "I can't stand a fool however amiable," Fisher wrote Beatty, "and I don't believe that in war it is anything short of criminal to keep the wrong men in any appointment high or low . . . OLD WOMEN MUST GO!"[6] Arbuthnot, demoted from commanding an impressive dreadnought battleship division to older armored cruisers (1st CS) after the raid, was apparently the first outdated deficiency who "had to go."

As observed earlier, however, Fisher, for all his faith in the new C-in-C, had nevertheless misread him, for unlike the daring—dare one say Beatty-like?—Victor of Trafalgar, Jellicoe waxed more cautious and, given the wartime situation he faced, more responsibly prudent. Jellicoe's solution to the probably unreformable generation of hide-bound officers with whom he grew up, moreover, was not to retrain old dogs with new tricks by insisting on initiative and improvisation—again, more like Beatty—but rather, consistent with his leaderly circumspection, to control them from his talented top with a detailed manual of battle orders designed to leave tactically very little to question. Time would tell whether this didactic approach would benefit or detract from his legacy when first he faced Britain's Teutonic nemesis.[7]

■ ■ ■

On Christmas Day the entire Grand Fleet waited in the North Sea in the hope that Ingenohl could be baited into action and punished for the infamous "Scarborough Raid," as many in Britain like Churchill now dubbed it. The plan called for an attack on the Cuxhaven Naval Air Station with sea planes attached to Commodore Tyrwhitt's light cruisers and destroyers. If the High Seas Fleet exited its bases to destroy this weaker force, Jellicoe would close the trap. The Germans did not take the bait, which caused more disappointment, but some action did ensue.

On "First Christmas," December 25, three of Hipper's battlecruisers lay at anchor off the Jade with seven battleships. Ingenohl felt he had reason to anticipate a British attempt to sink block ships on the river bar. If Beatty struck again as he had on August 28, the embarrassing Battle of the Bight, Ingenohl did not want to lose again because his heavy forces could not sortie due to low tide inside the Jade.[8] But German intelligence, woefully behind Britain's, had it wrong: Jellicoe made no attempt to sink block ships.

That it was Christmas, however, perked up spirits. The mood among many of the seamen had markedly improved, moreover, because of the Yorkshire Raid. Most knew the big battle they wanted had not happened, but there had finally been action against—so the officers said—important British naval installations and coastal fortifications. On *Von der Tann*, the fleet's oldest battlecruiser, Captain Max von Hahn had also prepared a fitting Christmas Day celebration. That morning forty small Christmas trees, one for each mess, were being loaded aboard along with sacks of nuts, oranges, chocolates, a plentiful supply of schnapps, crate after crate of goose for roasting, and packages from home, which invariably contained more delicacies and booze. It was going to be a welcome deviation from the belt-tightening brought on by the British blockade.[9]

At a little past 0900, sailors began to prepare decorations for the captain's tour of the ship after dinner that evening. All of a sudden, voice tubes, buglers, and drummers sounded battle stations. A thousand pairs of feet started running in all their appointed directions, some stopping to see what was happening. Already, the ship's machine guns and 3.4-inch ordnance blasted away at two seaplanes approaching from the east three miles away. Through the din of fire, they heard the clanking steel rattle of the anchors coming up as the big ship struggled to get underway.

Having failed even to find the Zeppelin hangars, the raiders, two of seven launched, were speeding west to their rendezvous with Tyrwhitt's light forces.[10] Seconds later, two bombs exploded near the waterline of *Von der Tann* when the planes flew over. As the raiders exited a sky full of hot shell, they flew into the fire of a light cruiser also defending herself furiously while trying to raise more steam and pick up speed. In the ensuing alarm and confusion, the German ships collided at an oblique angle causing major damage to the light cruiser, but also fouling *Von der Tann*. The light cruiser crawled into dry dock, while *Von der Tann* tied up to a pier in Wilhelmshaven for repairs. She would receive more treatment in four weeks when the ship entered dry dock for her scheduled refitting.

■ ■ ■

Among German officers, sentiments about December 16, 1914, bordered on disgust over a tremendous opportunity missed.[11] One of Scheer's 2nd Squadron captains expressed this politely but pointedly in his after-battle report: "The apparent intent of the first change of course was to conceal the presence of the fleet. However, it was widely expected that the main body would make the kind of course corrections over the next hours to at least stay close to the planned point of rendezvous [with the Scouting Groups], even if this was made more difficult by the danger of submarines and loose-floating mines."[12] The last sentence seems to reflect other things Ingenohl's defenders were saying, but as other after-battle reports poured into fleet command, most still backed Hipper's complaint that the main fleet "did not remain in its supporting position, as required in the plan, until signaled by . . . [me] . . . that the [Yorkshire] mission was complete."[13]

Ingenohl's after-battle conference with his commanders on December 20 brought forth even harsher indictments. Scheer recalled,

> Great disappointment [reigned] on my flagship because the battle squadrons had been too far away to help the endangered battlecruisers and light forces against British battleships, but even deeper regrets that Germany had let victory in detail over the Royal Navy slip through their fingers. Our premature turning to east-southeast ruined for us the opportunity of engaging a portion of the enemy fleet according to the long prearranged plan, which had now been proven correct. The ties from the Kaiser binding the fleet commander explain why this clever plan, so full of promise, [but] short of being executed properly could achieve no result. . . . Missing a rare favorable opportunity like this one stuck in our memories. A second chance would probably never come.[14]

Tirpitz's reaction was the most vitriolic: "On December 16th Ingenohl had the fate of Germany in the palm of his hand. I boil with inward emotion whenever I think of it."[15] Those around Tirpitz believed he had it right—a widespread opinion lasting decades—for along with the opportunity missed by the army along the western frontiers four months earlier, this squandering of the chance to spring a devastating naval trap off Yorkshire, thereby weakening or perhaps ending the blockade of Germany, factored heavily into a formula for a lengthy war of attrition Germany had increasingly less chance to win.[16]

Ingenohl, who had the ultimate responsibility, saw things differently.[17] His fears of being outnumbered by enemy destroyers during either the predawn hours of the sixteenth or the following early night were, it is true, no less rational than the similar worries of Warrender and Jellicoe. Furthermore, substantial wireless traffic on December 15–16 pointed to the possibility that other British squadrons, perhaps the entire Royal Navy, had put out to sea. Finally, if he had reconnoitered with his torpedo boats, or fought a major engagement with them, he thought they might possibly have run too low on fuel. These fears were less rational (see chapter 3, note 38), however, and served to weaken the prudence of those concerns mentioned above—he should, that is, have sent his destroyers scouting. Stung by his officers' criticism, the C-in-C drew away from his commanders, for he believed that he had decided correctly and properly.[18] Ingenohl also knew that he possessed the manliness to make a different decision if an allegedly better opportunity presented itself. None of Ingenohl's explanations wriggled him free, however, from criticisms that cut to the quick over blown chances and scathing indictments about his real motivation and the stigma attached to this motive—namely, the sadder truth that he had ventured as far from the Bight as permitted by the Kaiser and felt he could go no farther. Consequently, although these accusations targeted mainly Ingenohl, they did nothing to improve the image of the emperor or the legitimacy of the monarchy.

Not everyone, however, blamed Ingenohl. Wilhelm von Lans of 1st Squadron nearest the encounter with the British destroyers had one of the more interesting reactions. Although admitting that his men were "happy as children" to be facing the English and "greatly disappointed" when "nothing came of it," he let up on his C-in-C. How could he, the one who maintained all along that just "fighting for fighting's sake" made no sense, blame him? As for the loss of civilian life in Yorkshire, moreover, he was "not so coarse and hard as to have no sympathy for the women and children." He could not understand, however, "why the English build fairly well armed fortifications near otherwise undefended towns. In the final analysis that [English] pack is so rude and mean that they don't deserve anything better. If only London would go up in flames."[19] Many German commanders simply glossed over the frightful loss of civilian life in their postwar writings, a morally guilty reaction;

but at the time, given the brutal conflict that the Great War had become by late 1914, they probably did not feel much differently on the surface than Lans in dismissing the matter by conveniently blaming the victims.

The higher-ups also disagreed over the "Hartlepool Raid," as they preferred to call it. Head of the Kaiser's Privy Naval Cabinet, Georg von Müller, paid a visit in Berlin to Hugo von Pohl, Chief of the Admiralty Staff, for just this reason on December 19.[20] The presence of the British 2nd Battle Squadron and other light forces at sea so close to both Hipper and Ingenohl, and at a proper moment to block German ships, had reactivated heated speculations: Were enemy submarines reporting German ship movements in the inner Bight? Were unfriendly fishing vessels colluding with the British Admiralty for the same purpose? Were British agents in Germany leaking information? Or Pohl's least favorite question, had German codes been broken?[21] Regardless of how the enemy's 2nd BS had positioned itself in such a clever place, Müller limited his queries to why German torpedo boats, and then the entire High Seas Fleet, had held back from alluring victories in detail, especially with "a calm sea" and "hazy weather" ideal for covering their approach. Pohl was not happy with this question, nor especially moved by his visitor's concerns that the missed opportunities had upset the Kaiser, still depressed since having a near breakdown upon hearing of Graf Spee's demise.[22] Just as familiar as his intruding interlocutor with the emperor's psychological frailties and foibles, the Chief of Naval Staff may well have merely shrugged and stared back assertively, for on the more germane points of discussion that really mattered this day—how to assess December 16—he had positioned himself squarely in defense of Ingenohl's argument that he could not have known whether Warrender's 2nd BS had sortied alone.[23]

The sands of naval politics in Germany could shift quickly, however, and soon enough Pohl's footing became less secure. A week later, after William and his imperial retinue had returned from Berlin to Charleville, the Kaiser's posh headquarters near the Western front, Pohl reported directly to his sovereign, swinging just a little toward Ingenohl's numerous critics. "I really moderated my judgment," he wrote his wife that evening, "and found the full agreement of His Majesty. But I had to issue a decree to the fleet, which caused me some pain."[24] In this pronouncement of December 23, William waxed surprisingly aggressive—no doubt coaxed by Müller, who constantly had to look over his shoulder at Tirpitz—specifically singling out the lack of initiative of Hipper's light forces at midday on the sixteenth, but also with broader strokes implicating Ingenohl's decisions throughout the day: "The effort to preserve the fleet, or separate parts of it, must under no circumstances be carried so far that favorable prospects of a success are not pursued because this pursuit may lead to losses." Such opportunities had to be "exploited to the fullest without regard for collateral matters."[25]

And then after another week Pohl received an even more jarring jolt, again from the Kaiser, ordering him on December 31 to ban Ingenohl from making any subsequent missions that destroyed private property "without any military benefit."[26] Throughout the autumn the Admiralty Staff Chief had opposed all sorties, believing (he thought) with the Kaiser that they could risk the fleet unnecessarily. He had then done the honorable (and also self-serving) thing and defended Ingenohl's caution against his harshest critics. But no one in the navy had criticized the operation's damage-to-civilians fallout until now, indirectly, when the imperial head man himself did so. No doubt one vein in the emperor's complicated psyche, probably the most representative one, was very sensitive to the "baby killer" and "murderer" indictments of his British cousins. Indeed, about a month before the Scarborough Raid he had admonished naval officers at dinner against waging "war against women and children."[27] His postbattle motives went beyond diplomatically minding British relations, however, for such sermonizing self-righteousness not only squared nicely with William's basically nonviolent nature, but also the need to bolster military authority slipping away from him. If this apparently deep-seated, meek side of him had somehow asserted itself in the planning stage and insisted on details from his admirals, it seems doubtful that he would have allowed the Yorkshire mission to go forward without insisting on more specifically traditional, civilized rules of engagement. It sometimes happens, however, that gentler, softer ones lack a full measure of resolve. In William's case, his resolute persona surfaced erratically and could then quickly disappear. Thus, when this more humanitarian sentiment reappeared, it was unfortunately a month too late. For all his efforts to appear as the head of the navy, its real chief, William was no hands-on, determined naval leader.

However, as the old year wound down, the emperor's treatment of Pohl and Ingenohl indicated to others that he actually leaned toward sea action promising more "military benefit." Speaking to William on the twenty-third, Tirpitz found him still "displeased that the torpedo boats hadn't attacked" a week earlier.[28] Over the next days, moreover, the Naval Secretary reacted with pleasant surprise to Müller's aggressive spirit—another sign that the Privy Counselor had finessed the decree of the twenty-third. Aware of the negative sentiments toward Ingenohl among naval officers, the influential adviser asserted that it "was naturally a big mistake [for the fleet] not to have been sweeping the North Sea to engage parts of the English fleet."[29]

He also convinced the Kaiser to have Pohl submit a full report after the New Year on the operational plans of the navy and the overall prosecution of the naval war against Britain. Insiders like Tirpitz knew they had to be wary of William's "peculiarity that he won't come to any resolve, or bear any responsibility," and beware, too, of Müller's chameleon-like, dissimulating qualities; but one could still be forgiven for thinking that the Kaiser seemed ready for more meaningful naval action. Indeed, word had filtered back to Tirpitz that William had "said to Müller several times, 'now the fleet must really do something.'"[30]

■ ■ ■

On "Second Christmas," December 26, Vice Admiral Reinhard Scheer, commanding 2nd Squadron in Cuxhaven, yielded command to Vice Admiral Felix Funke, heretofore commander of the state-of-the-art 3rd Squadron.[31] Scheer then boarded a torpedo boat for Wilhelmshaven to take over Funke's old command. Although Lans's following and other more timorous factions opposed Scheer, the new squadron chief of 3rd was nonetheless admired by many of his peers as one of the most operationally aggressive, confident battlers in the High Seas Fleet. He was fifty-one, a torpedo specialist, a close ally and associate of Tirpitz, and, like the fleet founder, a fervent believer, after overseas cruiser service, in Germany's imperial mission. "He is the man trusted all around because of his character, cleverness, and accomplishments," claimed Ingenohl's COS Eckermann. "He is energetic, thorough, has the backbone to do what he thinks is necessary, and is strong enough to assume responsibility." Others noted that his energy and intellect often manifested themselves in a penchant for thinking in unorthodox, out-of-the-box ways; consistent with this, in showing a tendency toward behaving instinctively and impulsively as a "man of the moment" (*Augenblicksmensch*); and oftentimes unleashing his characteristic acerbity and choler—whether warranted or not—on "pessimists and quibbling sticklers." His nickname was "Sic 'em" (*Bobschiess*) on account of his coarse tendency to verbally burrow in and root out colleagues whose doubting, skeptical natures or subpar performances angered him, just like his bobtailed fox terrier, whom he would sometimes rough-jokingly "sic" on friends' trouser cuffs. As this behavior shows, he could also be jovial and collegial, which, when mixed with his ingrained realism and normally calm self-possession, both traits reinforced by the need for rationality in ambitiously and opportunistically advancing his naval career, usually guided him away from impulsively choosing—or if rashly chosen, adhere to—extreme options. Scheer's was certainly a Janus-faced personality; therefore, one which combined conflicting impulses in only somewhat stable equilibrium, a psychological dynamic yet to be tested in the hyper-stress of combat command.[32]

Possessing these stellar credentials and strong personality traits, Scheer had fought against his father's opposition to joining the navy and risen above his bourgeois beginnings to attain high rank. And now he had been reassigned to command Funke's old squadron. Since the Yorkshire Raid, when 3rd Squadron contained five of the latest dreadnought battleships, it had received two more mighty vessels with a third expected on January 2, pulling High Seas Fleet battleships as close to a one-to-one ratio—seventeen to twenty-one (including two of Jellicoe's that had been refitted)—as during the entire war. The holiday season arrivals allowed Scheer to split the squadron into two divisions, the 5th and the 6th, each containing four modern imposing battleships. He chose SMS *Prinzregent Luitpold* as his flagship and spent the next few days getting oriented before reporting to Ingenohl.

Upon reporting to Wilhelmshaven, Scheer requested of Ingenohl time for a much-needed final shakedown of the new battleships in the safe confines of the Baltic. Long-range firing drills could not be conducted in the narrow river mouth, and the Bight, where peacetime drills had been held, was too dangerous in wartime. The same held true for the new ships' torpedo crews. To his surprise—presumably a pleasant one—the new chief of 3rd Squadron learned of a plan of Hipper's that the C-in-C wanted to execute before Scheer's ships could leave for the Baltic. Ingenohl, still smarting from his officers' censures, clearly believed he had something to prove.

Scheer, among the most disappointed after December 16, must have listened to the fleet commander with wide-eyed excitement.[33] Submarines had reported six big men-of-war off Grimsby on the Humber River, possibly Jellicoe's 2nd BS that had been at sea on the sixteenth, possibly exiting from there to the Dogger Bank, alerted in all probability by fishing trawlers in the service of the British Admiralty—German intelligence had no idea that Warrender had sortied from Scapa Flow. After a submarine scouted the area, returning around January 6, light cruisers would lay a seventy-five-mile-long minefield in the only channel between Grimsby and the Dogger Bank thus far free of mines,[34] and they would be sunk at depths that only the deep drafts of battleships could detonate. Simultaneously, Hipper's Scouting Groups would sweep the Dogger Bank of any suspicious fishing trawlers as well as destroyers and light cruisers that intelligence had alleged aided with early warning signals of approaching German ships. The mines and battlecruisers would decimate the British battle squadron when it again charged out to the Bank. Because further assistance was probably required, the entire High Seas Fleet would wait nearby. A similar operation—the original plan before big ships were reported off Grimsby—would follow later in January after the entrances to the Firth of Forth (Rosyth) and Cromarty/Invergordon had been mined, for intelligence had reported Beatty's battlecruisers and/or other heavy forces were likely at one or the other of these two bases.

Ingenohl, eager for redemption, had seized on these two operations—missions that corresponded with the bold signals he had gotten from Charleville (see earlier). As the last days of 1914 yielded to the first days of 1915, however, "one powerful storm after another followed with only little respite,"[35] recalled Scheer. It was then discovered that the Royal Navy had laid fresh minefields north and west of Helgoland, the same course the High Seas Fleet would take again on its way to the Dogger Bank. Mine sweepers began to clear these fields in early January, braving the continuing terrible weather, but the work went excruciatingly slowly as first one week passed, and then two.

By the time the light cruisers laid their mines southwest of the SWP on January 15, neither 1st SG nor the High Seas Fleet accompanied them. Ingenohl had placed the capital ships on alert to guard against another attempt that intelligence alleged the British would make to sink block ships. Even without this latest unfounded scare, however, it appeared doubtful whether battleship squadrons would sail to the Dogger Bank any time soon, for different, less favorable political winds blew from Charleville.

■ ■ ■

Thirty-five miles behind the German trench lines, near the train station of the French town of Charleville, lay an industrialist's well-appointed villa. William established his imperial headquarters there in the autumn of 1914, commandeering this exquisite residence from its refugee owner. He slept in; breakfasted at ten; chopped wood; took strolls in the nearby park; dined with his chiefs; played cards; monologued about art, architecture, and the need to decipher the Hittite language; toured the Sedan battlefield of 1870; and visited "the front," rear echelon Potemkin Villages carefully prepared by his generals to keep the top man happy. In contrast to the tactless and impolitic aloofness shown by William later in the war, at least during these visits he frequently spoke to the officers, troops, and wounded—a somewhat redeeming side to his problematic war leadership (also see chapter 8). Aside from his daily briefing, the generals kept army matters of great significance from him, and fittingly so, for he had weakly acquiesced to their push for war in 1914. Navy matters remained a slightly different story, however, for William, a man sinking in political quicksand, clung desperately to them, the only flimsy branches keeping him, the Supreme Warlord, from sinking into the oblivion of total military uselessness and irrelevance.

An insecure personality type since youth, a person characterized by low self-esteem and a sort of "inner emptiness" he carried into adulthood, the Kaiser had earlier compensated psychically with a papered-over, bombastic tendency toward exaggerated and poorly thought-through self-righteousness. Because of his inner deficiency and weak self-identity, however, William tended in reality merely to absorb the views of stronger, shrewder personalities. In army matters before the war, this subconscious emulating tendency had embroiled him in a series of outrageous contradictory stances as assertive military lobbyers finessed him back and forth in the interests of their service branches and divisions.[36] After war's outbreak, what remained of the Kaiser's need for bombast and swagger manifested itself strongly in his clutching to naval authority but not without more contradictoriness, as at moments he was drawn to the aggressive idea of invading England or to Tirpitz in wanting his fleet "to really do something" in North Sea battle against the British navy; while at other times championing lesser options—as all his own—like seeking a defeat-in-detail-style battle, at times strictly limited to the Bight, at times beyond it; or at yet other times claiming superior insight for the need of total inaction, as those counselors whose position this was in actuality smiled contentedly. Making matters even more adversatively helter-skelter, William's swaggering role of naval leader could also manifest itself in self-righteously resisting his admirals' indifference to civilian casualties in their prosecution of the naval war. But when it surfaced, was this more humane role merely a façade—like the others, not really a view of his own? Or was it rooted deeply inside the not-entirely-empty psychic core of the real William, a troubled soul, uncomfortable with violence, and worried about his unworthiness of redemption in the eyes of God (see chapter 8)?

As the long postmortem process on the Yorkshire Raid drew to a close in late December and early January, the various actors in Germany's hydra-headed naval establishment sought to influence their irresolute monarch. Pohl's staff, tasked with advising their chief, had high hopes of ending the cautious policies that had ruled since war's outbreak.[37] His chief of staff in Charleville, Captain Hans Zenker (captain of *Von der Tann* at Jutland) as well as the Acting Chief of Admiralty Staff in Berlin, Rear Admiral Paul Behncke (commander of 3rd Squadron at Jutland) both emphatic Tirpitzites, took consistently aggressive stances to what Pohl should argue before the emperor. Coastal raids should continue with the main fleet in much closer support than on December 16. Behncke even advocated engaging the entire Grand Fleet in a decisive battle.[38] Pohl struck this sentence from his own memorandum but, clearly getting caught up in the strong undertow of anger over recent squandered opportunities, accepted most of these ideas. The Kaiser "is much more cautious with the fleet than I," noted Pohl after the New Year, having convinced himself of this. "He is probably studying my position paper (*Denkschrift*) now. I'm anxious whether he agrees with me, or is still holding back."[39]

As the day of the emperor's decision approached, Tirpitz, the ultimate pressure politician, had spoken with Pohl and Müller as well as the Kaiser. The Naval Secretary began to sense a disaster in the making for his own efforts. William, "directly influenced by Müller," had a shield up "when I tackle and harangue him, which I never lose an opportunity of doing." The emperor refused to discuss the fleet "really doing something," rather he "simply evades me." Pohl had therefore made a big mistake by agreeing to submit his ideas in writing, a mere *Denkschrift*, rather than "acting on his own initiative." Given William's aversion to real administrative work, "holding discourses and leaving memoranda, where the Kaiser is concerned," just allowed "Müller and friends to take the decision into their hands." All of this became even clearer when Tirpitz did not get an invitation to the decisive meeting. "[Müller] only backs up the Kaiser's [penchant for] clinging to the servile Pohl. . . . To see my life's work turned to no account, as it is my conviction that it will be, is indeed dreadfully hard to bear."[40]

On January 9, the Kaiser received Pohl, Müller, Chancellor Theobald von Bethmann Hollweg, and the Commandant of Headquarters, Hans von Plessen, to hear Pohl's report on the conduct of the naval war and Bethmann's rejoinders. The admiral claimed he was not prepared, having submitted the written report days earlier and expecting only questions rather than having to make a formal oral presentation. However, that he came across with "more pathos than deftness," as Müller observed, more likely signaled that he did not have his heart in giving Ingenohl a freer hand to prosecute the war more aggressively. "The weapon that rests," he ventured, "rusts." Bethmann spoke next, deferring in a dissimulating way to the others. "It is a purely military matter, your majesty, whether or not the fleet takes the offensive more than it has." Bethmann's passivity reflected his alliance with Müller. "The correctness of the reasons made by the military, I, as the civilian head of your government, have to recognize." Probably with an appreciative nod to his respectful chancellor, and a glaring stare down of Pohl, William "spoke out against an energetic deployment of the fleet in the North Sea." Did he have to remind the Naval Staff Chief that the navy represented an important political asset should he ever have to negotiate with the English? Having already outmaneuvered Tirpitz as well as placed Pohl in a situation the man could not manage, Müller needed only to salvage something positive and seemingly aggressive from the meeting to keep himself in an ideal strategic position ensconced protectively between the emperor and Tirpitz's hot-headed minions. Surely all could agree that the High Seas Fleet should take a more aggressive approach, as long as the goal remained to strike only parts of the enemy fleet and avoid pitched battle with their superior concentrated forces. The Kaiser thought for only a moment, announcing that his decision would come the next day.[41]

On the morrow it became clear that William, normally high-strung but especially nervous and moody of late, had receded into his cautious shell. The directive to Ingenohl included the words Müller had suggested, but with the proviso that the Kaiser continue to approve all sorties beyond the Bight. Müller's victory seemed complete. The cautious Bethmann Hollweg, who wanted the fleet intact for possible war-ending negotiations and of late had conspired with Müller to bolster Germany's position in the court of international public opinion, got important concessions. U-boats would not attack merchant shipping, as Pohl wanted, lest neutral countries take offence, nor would Zeppelins bomb London lest more women and children die. As noted earlier, sanctioning humaneness of this sort bolstered the Kaiser's bid to safeguard his naval authority—in this instance against Pohl—and probably also reflected his inner nature.

Not surprisingly, the servile Pohl—unassertive thus far at least—came away pleased with the compromise, while Tirpitz did not. The "instrument of power created by the Kaiser," Tirpitz told William's brother, Prince Heinrich, "is definitely molding away in the china cabinet." Neither could say whether or not the emperor himself actually "steered the fate of the navy in this war." Tirpitz and the Prince rightly suspected the worst, of course, for those best at finessing usually got their way instead. On Pohl's staff, Zenker stayed consistently in Tirpitz's corner, scoffing that Ingenohl would now proceed as cautiously as he had on December 16. If the High Seas Fleet ever went out again, his order would be "to go back to the river mouths as quickly as possible while [the fleet was] still intact."[42] There can be no doubt that the hawkish Behncke agreed with fellow bird-of-prey Zenker.

In reality, Zenker had exaggerated Ingenohl's intentions, which corresponded somewhat with the prudent advice he continued to receive from 1st Squadron commander Wilhelm von Lans. Replying to Pohl on January 19, the C-in-C welcomed the decision giving him "greater freedom of action" while also appreciating that "an unfavorable outcome in battle would weigh very heavily in the scales." With better weather, the High Seas Fleet would be able to make—and should make—more frequent sorties to foil the Royal Navy in its goal of destroying the German fleet, but these missions should not target British shores. December 16 did not represent "a valid example" for seeking battle there again because the operation allegedly had taken the indispensable torpedo boats beyond their effective radius of action. Any damaged ships would never make it home from hostile waters, moreover, as predator destroyers and submarines sank these lamed vessels. It was therefore his "firm conviction that the decisive battle should be fought in our half of the North Sea and not on the enemy coast." In time, he predicted—probably with German knowledge of Beatty's aggressiveness in mind—"the enemy will have to come to us." And when the main fleets engaged, "we will have the possibility of bringing home our damaged ships and a chance, with our well trained torpedo boat flotillas, to heap the disadvantages of being pursued onto the enemy." Before that day came, however, there was "always hope" that mines and submarines would "bring the English down to size." And U-boats and mines did not exhaust these possibilities. He guaranteed that the main fleet itself would not "get rusty" before the day of the decisive battle.[43]

This response, sometimes seen as an indication that Ingenohl's initial willingness to take his entire fleet far out into the North Sea and his morale, so high two weeks before, had both been brought down to size,[44] shows, on the contrary, that the Kaiser's liege lord had not, in fact, lost the desire to win the war at sea. Although no aggressive sea commander like those who had this reputation—in December and January, Hipper and Scheer—Ingenohl was not yet a spent force. His worst critics complained about fleet inactivity, but this did no justice to a C-in-C who still wanted to prosecute Hipper's ambitious North Sea plans. Although not venturing as far as British coasts, the High Seas Fleet would enter the North Sea to support Hipper, guaranteeing thereby that it would not be "getting rusty."

◼ 5 ◼

MURPHY'S LAW

January 23, 1915, marked the second day in a row that the North Sea's violent weather of recent weeks had abated. Nevertheless, a strong easterly wind still penetrated the Firth of Forth, blowing hard from May Island at the entrance all along the twenty-mile channel to the Forth Bridge and the battlecruiser anchorage a few hundred yards behind it. Black puffs blew away from the chimneys of Queensferry on the south shore, joining the smoke and the pungent smell of burning coal from other towns on the way inland. A cold and sinister black sky shrouded the whole scene. Some of the officers and men sensed an air of foreboding on this Saturday afternoon, while others just felt the crush of boredom from life in harbor more than usual.

Lieutenant RNVR Filson Young, Beatty's War Staff communications and intelligence officer, belonged to the latter grouping. And even though he had more than once "plumbed the depths of boredom latent in two and a half hours on an Edinburgh afternoon," he woke up determined to go into town anyway on the closest thing one usually got in the cruiser squadron to a "leave." Young also resolved to take Beatty's hardworking, reclusive staff secretary, Captain Frank Spickernell, with him. "Come on now," he told the man firmly, "the novelty of seeing streets and houses and people in everyday clothes will cheer you up."

While the two half-day-trippers boarded a picket boat to Hawes Pier and walked to the local train station in Dalmeny,[1] an edgy Major Francis Harvey of the Royal Marines, his martial senses alerted by the Forth's gloomy skies, had to attend to routine matters. Accurate shooting facilitated by target practice remained one such necessity; but unlike the battleship squadrons at Scapa Flow, whose vastness afforded ample target shoots, the battlecruisers had to wait for much rarer opportunities at sea. So one concentrated on what one could control: rapidity of fire. Each of the four turret contingents on *Lion* competed to be the quickest to have shells loaded and ready to fire when battle stations sounded, and none were prouder or more competitive than Harvey's sixty marines of the midship Q-turret. Several times a week, accordingly, their apprehensive turret chief ordered a series of drills to keep the crew sharper than the Royal Navy contingents of the other turrets. On such occasions Harvey, sitting in the range-finder chair inside the "silent" control cabinet at the back of the gunhouse, stopwatch in hand, yelled into the speaking tube that carried his orders deep into the bowels of the warship for the drill to begin.

Fifty feet below, the leading hand of the magazine crew, carefully observing strict safety regulations, sent half of his twelve-man team into action to remove from magazine racks four tubular, brass "Clarkson" cases fitted with gas-release lids as a precaution against spontaneous combustion. Each case contained two one-quarter cordite charge bags with silk-encased gunpowder igniters inside. The men simulated tearing off protective disks to make the igniters explosion-ready and passed the charges out the open door to six mates in the adjacent handling room, who placed them in hoppers and then tipped the charges into powder hoist cages. Simultaneously, the leading hand of the shell room (underneath the charge room) mobilized his twelve-man crew, who muscled two monstrous 13.5-inch projectiles off racks and into shell hoists. As the shells and charges rose up separate trunk lines, antiflash doors slowly opened to let them pass and then closed behind them to block any flames from battle damage reaching the magazines.

High above in the working chamber, another ten-man crew loaded the bare charges into special cages consisting of two parts: a trough holding the projectile, and above the trough, a steel box with two compartments, each holding two quarter-charges. This cage then entered the gunhouse electronically and the time-consuming part of the process was over, for in a matter of eleven to twelve seconds, a gun crew hauled the first cage along a loading tray to the gun breech, a folding rammer rod was tripped and shot out, butted the tail of the shell, and propelled it into the breach, and then flicked back clear of the trough. Once the rammer was clear, one flap door of the upper box compartment opened, and two one-quarter charges dropped to the trough and were similarly rammed into the breach. Once the rammer flicked back again, the second door opened and the final two quarter-charges were pushed quickly into the gun, the rammer withdrew, and the cage dropped to the floor and was returned to the working chamber. While gun layers, gun trainers, sight setters, and the second turret captain stood by simulating their roles in a real battle, Gunnery Sergeant George Comley clapped the breach shut to simulate a salvo from the left gun. A second cage had been making its way up from the working chamber to the gunhouse to load the right gun in the exact same way. Finally, both five-man gun crews turned, saluted, and waited for Harvey to check his timepiece.

Harvey usually did not approve. Things had to move along quicker for him. Like the three navy crews, therefore, he had been experimenting with deactivating anti-flash doors and readying bare charges on the handling room and working chamber floors—anything to get guns ready to fire as quickly as humanly and mechanically possible. Others were doing these things already, and he had no intention of being slower than they were.[2]

Meanwhile, Young and Spikernell trained to the city and got off in a crowd of other naval officers. The day did not unfold according to the younger man's expectations. They window shopped on Princes Street, got haircuts and shaves, and put noses again up to store fronts, but nothing seemed to cheer up the secretary, who kept repeating, "I should get back." Finally, Young talked Spikernell into ascending to the top of Edinburgh Castle to take in the celebrated view of the Forth from the chilly, windy ramparts.

The admiral's indispensable administrator, unimpressed, continued to mope until noticing something down at the anchorage. "That's strange," he said. "There's an undue amount of smoke coming from our ships." He paused, and then began to get agitated. "There you have it, I knew this would happen! We have probably been ordered to sea, ciphers are pouring in, the admiral has probably come aboard, and here are you and I shivering on this God-forsaken rampart!"

Both men made it back to the ship on time. At a dark 1800 (6:00 p.m.), Beatty's five battlecruisers sailed under the Forth Bridge. He had divided his force into two battlecruiser squadrons: 1st BCS, consisting of *Lion*, *Tiger*, and *Princess Royal*, the three newest, biggest, and fastest, the latter having returned from her hunt for Graf Spee; and 2nd BCS under Rear Admiral Archibald Moore, sailing with the older *New Zealand* and *Indomitable*, the latter transferred in December from the Mediterranean. *Queen Mary* had gone into dry dock. Goodenough's four light cruisers accompanied the battlecruisers. The King Edward "Wobbly Eight" of 3rd BS followed at 2030, accompanied by three armored cruisers. Destination: the Dogger Bank.

■ ▦ ■

A day earlier, January 22, the first reasonably good weather day in northern waters since the New Year, Vice Admiral Franz Hipper caucused in his dayroom aboard SMS *Seydlitz* with his chief of staff, Commander Erich Raeder, and Captain Moritz von Egidy. The mood among Hipper's officers had been sullen since news of the Kaiser's cautious, meek orders to High Seas Fleet Commander Friedrich von Ingenohl had spread among them. They waited, anxiously anticipating better news, for the arrival of Ingenohl's staff chief, Paul Eckermann, who would report on his meeting with the C-in-C. Eckermann and Hipper had proposed another mission only a little less ambitious than Hipper's original plans of late December (see chapter 4). Now, without mining either off Grimsby or Cromarty/Firth of Forth as in those schemes, they again asked to use the battlecruisers and light forces to sweep the Dogger Bank with the main fleet in close support. Suspicious fishing trawlers spying for the enemy would be dealt with harshly and the same meted out to any Royal Navy destroyers and light cruisers aiding this alleged espionage. If the Royal Navy sortied with battleships as it had on December 16, the High Seas Fleet would destroy them. Hipper and Eckermann strove for the thus-far elusive—and for the most aggressive German officers, barely acceptable solution—victory in detail.[3]

Eckermann made his report onboard *Seydlitz* early that afternoon. Ingenohl preferred not to leave the Scouting Groups unsupported by the main body; but with the flagship and Scheer's entire 3rd Squadron leaving for drilling in the Baltic, the moment for support was not propitious. Furthermore, as part of his new maintenance plan for the fleet, the C-in-C had ordered battleship *Helgoland* from 1st Squadron, battleships *Lothringen* and *Pommern* from 2nd Squadron, and *Von der Tann* from 1st SG into dry dock or for refitting. Without so many of his capital ships, the admiral chose to wait until early February when the whole fleet could sail, and then proceed with the plan to mine Rosyth and Cromarty with all squadrons in support. Eckermann added that any expedition of this sort needed the Kaiser's permission, and Pohl, much to the anger and disgust of his staffers (Behncke and Zenker), could not be counted on for approval. Despite this unwelcome news, Hipper said he still wanted to clear the Dogger Bank with just the Scouting Groups. Would Eckermann try again to convince Ingenohl? Significantly, Hipper and most higher ups opposed the belief of Raeder and a fellow-traveling minority that broken codes, not fishing trawlers, explained the enemy's uncanny fleet movements, a view that had not yet resonated in the tin ears of the majority (see chapter 2, note 23, and chapter 4, note 21).

Ingenohl had begun to come around before Eckermann met with him again later that afternoon. It still rankled the chief that Pohl had accused him of letting the fleet "rest and rust," so the current proposal appealed because it meant some action with little apparent risk. Indeed, intelligence had reported Beatty's battlecruisers shifted to Scapa Flow and Jellicoe's dreadnoughts dispersed to Rosyth and Sheerness (Thames). That reportedly the whole Grand Fleet had been out sweeping three days ago, and now likely coaled, provisioned, and made repairs after steaming about in nasty weather, further strengthened the possibility that Hipper would not encounter heavy enemy forces. And the improved weather, as Eckermann had pointed out earlier, supported this proposed mission. Thus, when Eckermann entered Ingenohl's day suite, he learned that the chief now agreed to this more limited outing. He asked, however, for Hipper to come see him.

Eckermann departed to write the wirelesses for the next morning. In addition to Hipper's orders, he drafted several more in different codes to the lightships, the naval air station, and the submarine command. The U-boats needed to know when ships went beyond the Bight lest friendly fire mistakes endanger the twenty-seven German vessels identified in the orders: *Seydlitz*, *Moltke*, *Derfflinger*, and *Blücher*; light cruisers *Graudenz*, *Rostock*, *Stralsund*, and *Kolberg*; and nineteen torpedo boat destroyers.

Late the next morning (January 23), a communications officer surprised Hipper and Raeder, angry over Ingenohl's wait-until-the-moment-is-right cautiousness and Pohl's submissive genuflecting before the Kaiser. The man presented a wireless from SMS *Deutschland*, a predreadnought battleship in the Jade serving as Ingenohl's communications center and temporary flagship while *Friedrich der Grosse* exercised with Scheer in the Baltic. The wire read: "1st and 2nd Scouting Groups, Senior Officer of torpedo boats, and two flotillas chosen by Senior Officer of Scouting Vessels to reconnoiter the Dogger Bank. Proceed to sea this evening, return after dark the following evening." Hipper and Raeder struggled to conceal their surprise—they were pleasantly shocked—at being ordered out. It being late when Eckermann left Ingenohl the day before, he had not reported back to Hipper.

While the ships in this operation started preparations, Hipper called on his fleet chief. Ingenohl remained worried that the British, having somehow decrypted Germany's complicated codes and ciphers, would surprise Hipper with superior forces. While the Scouting Chief doubted this, he agreed to take a precaution against getting cut off from Wilhelmshaven and destroyed. By calculating speed to the edge of the Dogger Bank so as to arrive there at first light, spotters could signal any approaching enemy battleship squadrons. If so, 1st and 2nd SGs would return to base, easily outrunning the slower dreadnoughts. Further diminishing the chances of a disaster, intelligence had reported Beatty far away at Scapa Flow. After discussing everything, Ingenohl allowed Hipper to sail.

After returning, Hipper called on Raeder to check on the progress of their preparations. Despite the inactivity of recent weeks, coal burned for heating, power, and maintaining steam at several hours notice had to be replaced. Provisions had to be loaded. The men had to bathe and stow away all flammable material from their quarters and mess areas. Finally, to replace ships' crews attritted by sailors in sick bay, the brig, absent without leave—all three problems were getting worse—or drawn away to the crews of the new battleships, Hipper ordered a temporary draft of several hundred sailors from *Von der Tann* before she went into dry dock. The largest group from this draft, 174 men, went to *Blücher*, which, besides the other problems, had also suffered casualties off Hartlepool. This upscale armored cruiser had better speed than *Gneisenau* and *Scharnhorst*, four more 8.2-inch guns (twelve not eight), and upgraded barrels for excellent battlecruiser-like range—quite a bit better range, in fact, than Graf Spee's two sunken ships.

At 1745 (5:45 p.m.), the German expedition got underway. *Blücher*, along with her new shipmates, trailed the three battlecruisers into the minefield channel and headed out into the Bight. Shortly after they had cleared the channel, Hipper's squadrons turned hard to port, sailing just off the German coast to avoid mines laid recently by the British near Helgoland. At 2100, now northeast of Borkum, Hipper ordered Captain Egidy two points to starboard, steady on northwest, at 13 knots. And then he went below to rest.

Ten hours later (6:00 a.m. British time, January 24), with the first dim glow of dawn low on the eastern horizon expected soon, the light cruisers and torpedo boats took up station a few miles ahead in a twelve-mile arced screen. Hipper had come back up to the bridge of *Seydlitz*. The course and speed of 1st and 2nd SGs put them an hour later, near the 55th Parallel where it crosses the eastern side of the central Dogger Bank (see map 1.1).

■ ■ ■

A day earlier (January 23), shortly after 0930 (9:30 a.m.), the constellation of radio operators orbiting Room 40 of the Old Admiralty Building intercepted all the wirelesses Eckermann sent from SMS *Deutschland*, and then telegraphed everything to London. Once translation by the Germanists and vetting by the naval and code experts had determined these decrypts to be significant, first Captain Reginald Hall of NID, and then Fisher's Chief of War Staff, Sir Henry Oliver, and finally the grey eminence of the War Group, Sir Arthur Wilson, came into the loop. The early warning process had taken a mere two hours—without any help required from the "backup system" of fishing trawlers that were, in fact, helping the Admiralty.

Meanwhile, Churchill had been conferring with Fisher, sick in bed in his residence next door, Archway House. Jellicoe's worries over Beatty's transfer to Rosyth had somehow become an issue for the War Council, the influential subcommittee of the cabinet that dealt with critical wartime decisions—so much so that the Council's chair, Prime Minister Herbert Asquith, wanted the C-in-C to attend an upcoming meeting. This eventuality would not only embarrass the Admiralty—if he went, Jellicoe would be going over the heads of Churchill and Fisher—but also possibly reverse the First Lord's December decision (a wise one, he thought) to shift Britain's battlecruisers to Rosyth. "If they go [back] to Cromarty," Churchill had written Fisher three days earlier, "they will be quite out of reach for any action to protect the coasts of England."[4] Even though Fisher "hated" Rosyth, he agreed to back Churchill. Fisher also agreed that Jellicoe needed to be with his ships in Scapa Flow, not in faraway London. Rumors and rumblings from this controversy, probably with help from disinformational plants by Reginald ("Blinker") Hall in NID, had confused an outmatched German intelligence and Ingenohl about British redeployments: to them, Beatty seemed to be moving north where Jellicoe wanted him (chapter 5, note 27, and chapter 6, note 11).

This pressing business attended to successfully, Churchill left Fisher's bedroom. "It was nearly noon," he recalled, "when I regained my room in the Admiralty. I had hardly sat down when the door opened quickly and in marched Sir Arthur Wilson unannounced. He looked at me intently, and there was a glow in his eye." Behind him came Oliver with charts and compasses. "Winston, these fellows are coming out again," said Wilson, full of ginger. "When?" asked Churchill. "Tonight. We have just got time to get Beatty there."

Without hesitation, Churchill ordered Commodore Reginald Tyrwhitt's destroyers and light cruisers in Harwich to get up steam. They were "wanted tonight." Shortly thereafter, at 1225, Beatty got word to "get ready to sail at once with all battlecruisers and light cruisers and sea-going destroyers. Further orders follow." (Spikernell and Young had seen the billowing funnel smoke of these preparations in the Forth.) Next, they told Jellicoe to ready the Grand Fleet to sail from Scapa Flow and Cromarty "after dark this evening."[5]

After the orders went out, the three Admiralty conferees spread a North Sea chart on the War Room table. While Oliver drew semicircles with a compass to indicate the likely course, range, and advance of enemy ships, and the same for British ships, Wilson explained what seemed to be afoot. Four German battlecruisers, four to six light cruisers, and upwards of twenty-two destroyers would set sail this evening to scout on Dogger Bank, but a raid upon the British coast was to be expected. British agents in Germany had been reporting feverish activity at Kiel and Wilhelmshaven and also in the Bight. "Perhaps the High Seas Fleet itself will follow the battlecruisers once they report the Dogger Bank clear."

Wilson waited for Oliver to finish his compass circles, and then continued. Only Beatty and Tyrwhitt could reach a rendezvous east of (and behind) Hipper's scouting forces, cutting him off from his base. The Grand Fleet from Scapa Flow and Cromarty, supported by the King Edwards from Rosyth, could guard further north if needed there, but they could not reach further south in time. If Hipper advanced at 17–18 knots, he would be well inside the Bank at dawn.

The old sailor hesitated again, calculating speeds and distances in his head, finally concluding that Beatty and Tyrwhitt should join forces at dawn about fifteen miles south of the 55th Parallel where it crosses the eastern edge of the Dogger Bank. Having instantly given it more thought, he pointed to another rendezvous thirty miles farther east and well off the Bank. Oliver and Churchill did not agree, recalling how "thick" weather the month before had allowed German squadrons to escape. Wilson relented and chose the first rendezvous spot an hour below the 55th.

Oliver nodded deferentially and left to send telegrams to Harwich, Rosyth, and Scapa Flow. He thought the venerable "A. W." had erred, however, and therefore preferred a rendezvous thirty miles north of Wilson's, about an hour's sailing northwest of the 55th Parallel edge of the Bank, which he believed would be easier for British ships to reach in time. "I knew it was hopeless to argue [with Wilson] and we had no time to spare," Oliver wrote later. "So I agreed, he went away, and I telegraphed *my own* rendezvous to Beatty and Tyrwhitt."[6]

The War Group, minus Fisher, assumed Hipper would make a good 17 knots through the night. Oliver, too, believed his own rendezvous coordinates would place British interceptors at least a few miles southeast of Hipper. But what if the enemy did not sail at 17–18 knots? And what would happen to Beatty, *sans* Jellicoe, if "the High Seas Fleet itself will follow the battlecruisers," as Wilson had speculated? Had too much been wagered on quickly formulated and—witness Oliver's undermining of Wilson—conflicting opinions?

Throughout the afternoon and evening before turning in, Churchill, Wilson, Oliver, and Fisher, the latter having in the meantime agreed to their plans, went about their business, but "we shared our secret with none," wrote Churchill after the war. "In December we had hardly credited our sources of information. All was uncertain. It had even seemed probable that nothing would occur. Now with that experience wrought into one's being, only one thought could reign—battle at dawn! Battle for the first time in history between mighty super-dreadnought ships!" The next morning "Fisher, Wilson, Oliver, and I were all in the War Room when daylight began to grow out of doors."[7]

■ ■ ■

As daybreak beckoned, HMS *Lion* led her battlecruiser line southeastward with Commodore Goodenough's four state-of-the-art "Town-class" light cruisers in line ahead just off the port beam. The crews had maintained their normal nighttime watches with an "air of suppressed excitement," recalled communications specialist Filson Young. "For some curious reason we were confident on this occasion, in a way we had never been before, that we should meet the enemy on the morrow."[8]

Young joined Beatty and Flag-Captain Ernle Chatfield on the bridge at 0630. They could see the first glimmers of light in the east, "but it was still dark night about us." At 0710, with "daylight beginning to spread" and all battlecruisers and light cruisers approaching Oliver's coordinates "more or less in a bunch," Tyrwhitt's advance guard of light cruiser *Arethusa* and seven of Britain's latest "M-class" destroyers had already reached the rendezvous an hour inside the Dogger Bank. Because the arrival of the first group from Harwich seemed to indicate, in keeping with the Admiralty's assumptions, that there would be no enemy forces that far south, Beatty began to reverse course in anticipation of finding the enemy somewhere to the north, further inside the Bank. He ordered Goodenough's cruisers "to spread for lookout duties at extreme signaling distance in a line of bearing NE-by-N from the flagship." Beatty then ordered Chatfield to issue "action stations."[9]

The rest of Tyrwhitt's force—light cruisers *Aurora*, *Undaunted*, and twenty-eight slightly older destroyers—trailed his advance guard by fifteen miles. They had just reached the edge of the Bank right on the 55th at 0705 when *Aurora* sighted a light cruiser and several destroyers four miles to starboard. The unidentified ship answered *Aurora*'s recognition signal with a broadside at 0715, hitting her target three times with 4.1-inch shells. Fire was immediately returned, smashing into the bridge of light cruiser *Kolberg* on the left wing of Hipper's screen. *Seydlitz* sailed four miles farther east.[10] The Battle of Dogger Bank had commenced.[11]

On the bridge of *Lion*, Chatfield saw gun flashes in the southeastern distance and asked the yeoman of signals what ship was on that bearing. "The *Undaunted*, Sir."[12] After further flashes and the delayed sounds of gunfire, *Aurora* signaled at 0719: "Am in action with the High Seas Fleet." The report found a mixed reaction on the flagship: amusement, for the gunfire cracks came obviously from low caliber ordnance; but also alarm, for the British had not anticipated engaging the entire German navy. Unperturbed himself by such thoughts, Beatty calmly turned his light cruisers around to the south and changed his course from north to east. At 0730 and 0732, Goodenough's signals clarified the situation somewhat: "Enemy in sight consisting of [destroyers, cruisers, and battlecruisers], steering [away] between SE and E."[13] Beatty now turned the battlecruisers southeast and gave chase, increasing speed from 18 to 22 knots.

In hindsight one can say with a probability bordering on certainty that the British, in steering toward Oliver's ill-chosen rendezvous, had already missed one good opportunity. If the Rosyth and Harwich units had joined forces at Wilson's rendezvous thirty miles farther south—a spot below the 55th Parallel that, contrary to Oliver's rapid calculations, Beatty's ships could easily have reached by 0700[14]— the German battlecruiser line would have been about twenty miles northeast of them (with *Kolberg* and her destroyers four-to-six miles closer) as "the daylight was beginning to spread." The German ships may have been difficult for lookouts to sight at this distance in the early dawn but not the massive clouds of dark coal smoke pouring out of a small forest of funnels and drifting southwest with the northeasterly wind. Nor would the weather have hampered observation. The new day as it unfolded "was so clear," Goodenough remembered, "that only the [curved] shape of the earth prevented one from seeing everything on it"[15]—visibility from the foretop, in other words, to seventeen miles. As he had already done in actuality, Beatty would immediately have turned north-northeast to close the enemy, cut off his retreat, and force a running north-northeastward battle. As it was, however, Beatty had to give chase southeastward to the Bight, where the possibility existed—at least in the Briton's mind—of German battleship reinforcements. Did Hipper lure him toward bigger ships?

Gambling that he could eliminate an inferior enemy before any German heavy support arrived, Beatty charged the horses ahead, come what may, after his fox. "The battlecruisers increased speed to 24 knots," wrote Young, "and five minutes later to 25." Now the "great battlecruiser engine room complements [were] on their mettle," recalled Chatfield. "No ordinary full-speed trial was wanted, but every boiler and steam pipe to be strained to their utmost." "Get us within range of the enemy," said Beatty to his engineer commander as 0800 approached. "Tell your stokers all depends on them."[16]

On the bridge of *Seydlitz*, meanwhile, Hipper had also heard the gunfire and ordered his battlecruisers to alter course toward the action. Presently, a communications officer approached Hipper, Captain Egidy, and Raeder, all peering through binoculars into the murky morning twilight. *Kolberg* had reported smoke clouds west-southwest; *Stralsund*, smoke clouds north-northwest, and behind those, range 2,700 meters,[17] what seemed to be eight large ships using call sign "U-A-F," the same signal radio operators had heard repeatedly on December 16.[18] Oblivious to the presence at sea five weeks earlier of not only Warrender's battleships, but Beatty's battlecruisers too—they had heard *his* call signs, not Warrender's—the command group assumed they confronted the British 2nd Battle Squadron, which seemed all the more likely since a month ago intelligence had reported enemy battleships at Grimsby on the Humber. "Squadron turn, steady on SE, 15 knots," ordered Hipper at 0730.

Hipper may well have cast an unpleasant glance at Raeder, who wisely opted to remain silent lest his chief "fly out of his skin." Both men knew that none of the fishing boats they had passed in the last several hours would have been able to get such a massive enemy force so close, for to reach the Dogger Bank from the Humber, the British required an advance warning of more than half a day. If they had sailed from Rosyth, where intelligence more recently said Jellicoe had placed battleship squadrons, the enemy would have needed even more advance warning of German intentions. Broken codes then? Raeder knew from experience it was not the time for "I told you so."

The "squadron turn" that Hipper ordered required the battlecruiser line to alter course briefly to the north to allow the light cruisers and destroyers in the van arc to cross the bow of *Seydlitz* and steam to the rear, which became the starboard-side van when the battlecruisers reversed course to the southeast. But this maneuver, together with the earlier turn toward *Kolberg*'s brief skirmish, enabled the fast-moving British battlecruisers to gain a good five miles on their quarry, which fled only thirteen miles away at 0750.

This did not worry Hipper, for he knew he could outrun or at least stay beyond the range of Warrender's dreadnoughts. The admiral increased speed to 18 knots. Still standing next to Raeder and Egidy as the minutes passed 0800, however, all three men continuing to study the metallic shapes inside the smoke clouds that were coming into better focus with every passing second, his attention was diverted to

Blücher opening fire on Tyrwhitt's M-class destroyers, which had raced forward on reconnaissance to within 10,000 yards of Hipper's armored cruiser, still last in line. At 0820, her stern 8.2-inch turret blasted a few salvos at the outgunned destroyers, which immediately veered back to the northwest. Hearing through the voice pipes the jubilant reaction of their new mates throughout the ship, the replacement men from *Von der Tann* joined the others in loud cheering,

As this action unfolded, Beatty stared ahead trying to determine what was happening. He brought down his binoculars at intervals to order Chatfield to pick up the pace—and improve the odds of this wager. "Speed 26 knots," he commanded at 0823; "speed 27 knots," he ordered at 0834; "speed 28 knots" followed at 0843. "Speed 29 knots," shouted Beatty finally at 0854. "Proceed at your utmost speed."[19] The flag-captain telegraphed the order to the engine room with a look of incredulity, for the last command exceeded the design speed of all the big ships.

Below in the engine rooms of the squadron's battlecruisers, the chief stokers walked to and fro, encouraging their men to ever more exertion. "Now and then," as one midshipman on Beatty's trailing ship, *Indomitable*, recalled, "the telegraph from the engine room would clang and the finger on the dial move round to the section marked 'MORE STEAM.' The chief would press the reply gong with an oath. 'What do the bastards think we are doing,' he would exclaim, 'come on boys, shake it up, get going,' and the sweating men would redouble their efforts, throw open the furnace doors, and shovel still more coal into the blazing inferno." Applauding these efforts shortly before 0900, Beatty signaled the older ship: "Well done, *Indomitable*'s stokers."[20] Despite the efforts and their admiral's praise, however, *Indomitable* and the other older battlecruiser, *New Zealand*, began to fall behind the newer *Princess Royal*, *Tiger*, and *Lion*.

Observing the M-class destroyers drawing so close to *Blücher*, Hipper ordered Egidy to increase speed to 21 knots. His spotters had counted seven light cruisers and twenty-six destroyers on his heels with those ominous smoke clouds far behind. "Intend to attack [nearest pursuers] in the inner German Bight," he radioed Ingenohl at 0848 (8:48 a.m.), his third report in forty minutes.

For some time after his armored cruiser scared off the destroyers, Hipper had continued to scrutinize the large coal clouds further north. At last, as the minutes drew closer to 0900, a startled look spread across his face, but he kept it under control. Did Raeder see tripod masts, battlecruiser masts, with Beatty reportedly at Scapa Flow? Indeed, he could see them—the enemy coming on with bones in his teeth, making 26 knots, maybe more. Based on the call signs they heard before, moreover, even stronger forces trailed, likely one or more battle squadrons.[21]

Hipper peered again through his binoculars and then ordered, "We're in a stern chase, all ahead full." Hipper was given more to thought and calculation this day than lengthy discussion with his subordinates, which likely meant quick reckonings: distance and time to the Bight, still another 120 nautical miles, more than five hours; battle with Beatty to commence soon; various rates of fire before armor-piercing shells ran out; German visibility obscured badly by the smoke of both sides. And he had to have considered the weaker *Blücher*'s position in line: her maximum range was as far as *Derfflinger*'s, next in line—her speed was equal too—and with the rapid advance of the British bringing all their guns soon within range of *Seydlitz* in front of the line, moving *Blücher* to that point would therefore prove unnecessarily disruptive, especially given this heavy cruiser's impressive qualities. These were the factors he most probably weighed and calculated in a few moments of outward calm, repeated cigarette drags the only thing betraying inward stress.[22] Shortly before 0900, Hipper finally turned to Raeder: "Have communications contact the Fleet Chief: Enemy battlecruiser squadron in sight."

At 0845, *Blücher* fired ranging shots at the lead ship (*Lion*), which she had also identified as a battlecruiser. The shots came again from the aft turret to the exhilaration of the entire crew. The captain swung the ship a few degrees to the right in order to allow the starboard-side wing turrets and fore A-turret to bear unobstructed to the northwest. The range exceeded by a few thousand yards *Blücher*'s maximum of 19,000, however, so the shells fell short, sending columns of sea water high into the air and mushrooming for a few seconds before crashing to the sea. Beatty also maneuvered slightly rightward to give all port-side guns a clear line of fire to the southeast, and then gave Major Harvey's Q-turret the honor of firing the first ranging shot. This shell, too, fell short, shooting a much taller column of water into the air.[23]

This first duel of the big ships that commenced shortly after 0900 between *Blücher* and *Lion* did not augur well for the smaller vessel. Unlike Vice Admiral Sir Frederick Doveton Sturdee at the Battle of the Falklands six weeks earlier, Beatty, long a proponent of maximizing the potential of dreadnoughts to fire from ranges unheard of a few years earlier, intended to begin firing at 20,000 yards and—throwing accuracy concerns to the wind—decide the battle at longer ranges more to his advantage. The British flagship's salvos from eight 13.5-inch guns, moreover, vastly outweighed the German armored cruiser's broadside of eight 8.2-inch shells—two of her wing turrets were on the disengaged port side and could not fire. After coming in range at 20,000 yards and shooting over the target with a second ranging shot from Harvey's crew, a shell from *Lion*'s first salvo hit *Blücher*'s forecastle deck between the anchors

(0909), inflicting major damage but not hindering fighting capacity. *Blücher* struck back as best she could, smashing into (but not piercing) the armored roof of *Lion*'s B-turret (0925), concussing the gun house, stunning the crew, and incapacitating the left gun for two hours.

Derfflinger, the next in line, opened fire on *Lion* too, scoring "a terrific blow" below the water level on the port side, which gave the ship "a shake"[24] and flooded two wing coal bunkers. Sailors in the water damage control party rushed to repair the breach with hammocks and mess stools. *Moltke* and *Seydlitz* soon joined the fray, also firing at Beatty's flagship. Determined "to break the enemy's [4-to-1] fire concentration," Beatty told signal officer Ralph Seymour to order all ships "to engage opposite numbers,"[25] *Lion* on *Seydlitz*, *Tiger* on *Moltke*, and *Princess Royal* on *Derfflinger*. When *Indomitable* came within range, she should concentrate with *New Zealand* against *Blücher*. Only minutes after shifting to a new target, *Lion* registered a hit on the quarterdeck of *Seydlitz* at 0925, causing damage but not hindering fighting ability.

Hipper received this early good news with no visible reaction. The battle would be a long one. He ordered another wireless sent to Wilhelmshaven at 0933: "Heading SE, 23 knots. Am in battle with the 1st Battlecruiser Squadron of the enemy to the NW. Am asking for [battleship] squadrons and [destroyer] flotillas." Masking his grim calculation process inscrutably behind a cloud of cigarette smoke, Hipper knew it would be early afternoon before any rendezvous took place with Ingenohl—if the C-in-C made haste.

■ ▉ ■

Hipper's first three signals to Ingenohl (0809, 0819, and 0848) alerting him to the likely presence of one squadron of state-of-the art British dreadnoughts came as a surprise.[26] Although Britain's 2nd BS, or one like it, had earlier been reported at Grimsby/Humber, recent intelligence placed Beatty's battlecruisers at Scapa Flow and Jellicoe's battleship squadrons in the Channel (Sheerness) and Firth of Forth (Rosyth), all of them coaling, provisioning, and making repairs after a fleet sweep on January 19—a false report, as it turned out, which smacked of the modus operandi of that master of disinformation, Director of NID Captain Reginald ("Blinker") Hall, who likely had also conspired successfully against Graf Spee before the latter's demise (see chapter 6, note 11).[27] Because Hipper's third signal indicated that he intended to avoid battle until luring the enemy back to the Bight, this gave Ingenohl time to assemble his available forces: five dreadnoughts of 1st Squadron, five predreadnoughts of 2nd Squadron, plus light cruisers and about forty dangerous destroyers. Squadrons and flotillas were building up steam beyond the Jade by 0930 (9:30 a.m. British time).

Why Ingenohl had not acted more prudently, interpreted intelligence reports with a grain of salt, and supported Hipper from the start with these ten available behemoths would baffle, anger, and mobilize naval opponents who were already targeting him after Scarborough (see chapter 7). This support would certainly have been a military gamble—would Jellicoe's Grand Fleet be there too?—but a safer wager than Beatty's as it might have transpired, especially if the Admiralty would fail to detect, as it had failed to notice in December, that heavy forces had sortied, not to mention that Hipper's destroyer numbers would soon triple. The daring *political* gamble this would have required, namely, of presenting the Kaiser a bold, semimutinous fait accompli, was not, however, forthcoming.

Hipper's fourth and fifth signals (0859 and 0933), containing the alarming news that he did not lead slower British battleships back to the Bight but rather Beatty's larger, faster squadrons 110 miles away, must have sent Ingenohl's heart into his boots—and heart-piercing stares Eckermann's way—for there would be no trap in the Bight, just a rendezvous with what, if anything, remained of Germany's Scouting Groups after a battle long over. All this would have happened on his watch, but against his *initial* better judgment. To the sixth signal—"Urgently need support" (0955)—Ingenohl replied (1003), "The main body and flotillas are coming as soon as possible." Seven minutes later, still building up steam, they put to sea. The admiral was no gambler, but he was also no coward. He now sailed to the rescue just as he might have done had Beatty overtaken *Roon* and fired a month earlier (see chapter 3).

■ ■ ■

In the meantime, the battle many miles off the Dogger Bank had intensified for both sides. For three-quarters of an hour, the British had registered only two hits, most of their shells having missed badly, making Beatty, perhaps as early as this, begin to question the wisdom of long-range fire landing a decisive knockout blow (see chapter 6). At 0943 (9:43 a.m.), however, a heavy shell from *Lion* hit the barbette armor in front of *Seydlitz*'s aft D-turret, destroying several empty rooms used by officers; but a red-hot fragment of the barbette penetrated "with fateful effect" into the working chamber where crewmen unloaded shells and bare powder charges from the trunk hoist coming up from the magazine handling room. The fire ignited powder charges and shot flames up into the gun house and down the trunk line to the handling room. The panicked crew below fled through a fire door to the lower level of the adjacent C-turret, the fire spreading with them. Within seconds the roaring inferno had incinerated the crews of both turrets as well as sailors in the nearby torpedo room, the water damage control room, and other stations. The rest of the squadron looked on in horror as a huge ball of flames rising as high as the masts engulfed the stern of the flagship. The only things they could see of C- and D-turrets were "the blackened, abruptly silenced barrels staring out."[28]

The flagship had lost half of its firepower and 165 men, which explains Hipper's 0955 wireless "urgently" requesting support. Only the alert action of an officer and two assistants, who made their way through passageways full of intense heat and gasses to the flooding valves and let six hundred gallons of seawater into the aft magazine (directly below the two handling rooms), saved the ship from a keel-splitting explosion and instant destruction. To the relieved hurrahs of the other ships' crews, A- and B-turrets continued to shoot frenzied salvos. Thinking the ship might go down any second, Captain Egidy had ordered rapid fire, but the battle would go on for *Seydlitz*.

Indeed *Seydlitz*, with help from *Moltke*, had been concentrating on the British flagship with frightening effect. This two-against-one duel resulted from an unfortunate interpretation of orders by *Tiger*, which fired at *Seydlitz* inaccurately, not *Moltke*, for many minutes. *Lion* paid the price as the range narrowed to about 15,000 yards. At 0945, she "came very near her end" when an 11-inch shell penetrated beneath the water line and into a trunk line leading down to a 4-inch magazine but broke apart without detonating. However, "the engineer's workshop was flooded; the water spread to the open switch-board compartment, short-circuited two of the dynamos, disabled the aft fire control and secondary armament circuits, and the ship began to take a list to port." Minutes later another heavy shell smashed the roof of A-turret, temporarily disabling one of its guns, and then (1018) two heavies crashed into *Lion*'s water line "so violently that we thought she had been torpedoed . . . and the ship seemed to be shaking herself to bits." These four shells—altogether seventeen would slam into *Lion* this day—caused massive flooding of more coal bunkers and adjacent compartments up to the main deck. Salt water also began to enter a ruptured pipe into the condensers, slowly contaminating the boilers and threatening to halt forward propulsion. Incredibly, although several men were wounded, none had yet been killed. With the ship's list worsening, however, and water columns from numerous "shorts" rising so close around *Lion* that they "drenched the coning tower and turret hoods like green seas," Beatty ordered zigzagging.[29]

Around 1005, with the running battle fifty-five miles southeast of its 0715 starting point—and about sixty miles from the edge of the Bight—the action turned to *Blücher*.[30] Goodenough's light cruisers had been steadily gaining on the port side of Hipper's trailing cruiser, pulling to within 9,300 yards, while the M-class destroyers approached on the starboard side like hounds in a fox hunt at a distance of only 8,300 yards. At this point Hipper ordered the portside guns of all four of his big ships "to distribute fire from the right," each German ship raining down fire on her corresponding British light cruiser in line. Simultaneously, *Blücher* let loose a starboard broadside against the destroyers. A few salvos sufficed to push the sea dogs away on both flanks.

As Hipper's line continued to race to the southeast around 1015, however, a 12-inch shell from *New Zealand* slammed through *Blücher*'s armor belt at the water line, causing her to ship water, reduce speed, and fall slowly behind the other German ships.[31] Another, near-mortal blow hit the doomed armored cruiser at 1030. Two projectiles pierced through several decks amidships and exploded on the munitions gangway that serviced all four twin wing turrets, igniting thirty-five to forty powder charges and quickly engulfing B- and C-turrets, "like *Seydlitz*, in one single sea of flames."[32] Noxious cordite fumes infiltrated the trunk lines, voice pipes, and ventilation shafts to midship D- and E-turrets, moreover, quickly incapacitating them. The explosion also jammed the ship's rudder and shut down one of the three engine rooms. *Blücher*'s speed dropped to 17 knots and she yawed badly out of line to the northeast. A third direct hit started another fire at 1037 that took out the forward "Anna-turret." Only aft "Frieda" turret and the secondary 5.9-inch casemate armament kept firing, but upwards of three hundred men, a quarter of the ship's company, lay dead.

Over the next twenty minutes (1030–51), *Lion* seemed to be heading toward a similar fate.[33] Enemy shells found their mark six more times, penetrating the thin armor plating and detonating, shooting metal splinters through bulkheads and pipes, flooding more compartments and stations, shutting down all electricity, increasing the list to ten degrees, and slowing down the racing ship, which was soon overtaken by *Tiger,* second in line and also burning amidships from a direct hit, one of seven to smash into her this day—shells that killed ten and wounded eleven. *Princess Royal* and *New Zealand* passed the injured flagship too, while *Indomitable* pulled even to port.

While Chatfield and Beatty directed the battle from the compass platform, crew members fought hard to steady their nerves. Lieutenant Francis Jones of the Royal Marines, Major Harvey's Number One, stood in his station at the starboard aft 4-inch battery. Because his guns took no part in the long-range duel, he remained a somewhat nervous spectator, especially after a shell exploded in the lobby of A-turret, cries and screams rang out, and then the officer commanding the plotting station below the turret yelled, "That either means Kingdom Come or ten days' leave!" It had been *the former* for two of the crew there (with ten others wounded). In Q-turret, Harvey tried to maintain his typical cool by wondering "what's happening outside of our shell" and holding tight onto the idea "that whoever else is coming to grief, oneself will be all right." Fighting unsuccessfully against second thoughts, however, especially after hearing that A's magazines were on fire, he was "under no delusion . . . that if a projectile does hit one's turret, it will in all probability come right in and send one to glory." Would all be "sent to glory" soon? Filson Young in the foretop also listened anxiously, "waiting amid that terrible din [of battle] for the last gorgeous explosion and the eternal silence that would follow it"—but it did not come.[34] Captain Chatfield had ordered A's four magazines flooded. It would shoot no more this day, but *Lion* did not explode.

As the minutes drew on to 1100 and beyond, the suffering British flagship fell victim to what has been called Murphy's Law: "what *can* go wrong, *will* go wrong"—the same seemingly fate-driven ineluctability of malady, misadventure, and misfortune that had plagued the German mission from its inception, and the British mission too since Oliver's ill-advised intervention forced Beatty into a stern chase. At 1059, Beatty, whose stressing over a possible German trap of some sort had no doubt increased after nearly four hours of being shelled while chasing, believed he saw a submarine periscope wake off the starboard bow. After considering the alleged danger for a moment—as it transpired, no U-boats were in the area—he ordered Flag-Lieutenant Ralph Seymour to hoist flags for "turn eight points to port together" (1102) (i.e., almost north).[35] Neither wireless nor searchlights were an option with no electricity. "Good heavens, Sir," said his startled flag-commander, the Hon. Reginald Plunkett, "surely you're not going to break off the engagement?" The admiral explained the ninety-degree turn to Plunkett, but with only two halyards intact after the intense German barrages, Seymour simply hoisted the required two flags for an eight-point turn, but not also for "submarine warning." Thus, the other ships remained as baffled as Plunkett had been by the strange order, which they executed unquestioningly a moment later when the flags were brought down (to initiate execution of the order). Now both battlecruiser squadrons veered away from Hipper to the north-northeast—a command had been given, after all, by the quickest rising star in the Royal Navy.

With *Lion* falling a few miles behind, the judgment of Beatty's second-in-command, 2nd BCS commander, Rear Admiral Archibald Moore in *New Zealand*, loomed greater in importance. Beatty decided to begin turning back from the north to bring his squadron closer to the escaping Hipper. To clarify this intention, Seymour put new flags up the halyards for "course N-E" and "attack the rear of the enemy." He had wanted the second flag to be: "engage the main body of the enemy"; but when checking his signal book, he found that none such existed. When the two flags were lowered at 1109, therefore, Moore, in awe of Beatty, assumed his superior wanted all four battlecruisers to concentrate on *Blücher*, which had yawed out of line bearing northeast. "But Beatty was hoist with his own petard," explains James Goldrick. "The image of near-infallibility which had been created, of the man who was always right, misled Moore in no mean fashion. [Beatty], Moore reasoned, must have some good purpose in mind. What was the enemy's rear? *Blücher*. What did *Blücher* bear? Northeast. What did the signal read? 'Attack the rear of the enemy bearing northeast.'" With Moore forming the advancing battlecruisers into line toward *Blücher*, and a frustrated Beatty looking on in exasperation, Plunkett cried out: "What we need now is Nelson's signal [at Trafalgar], 'Engage the enemy more closely.'" "Yes, certainly. Hoist it," yelled Beatty. But Seymour, having rechecked the signal book only to discover that it no longer contained the famous historical words from 1805, hoisted "keep nearer the enemy" instead, which did nothing to change Moore's mind as he bore down on *Blücher*. "The massacre," concludes Goldrick, "would soon begin."

■ ▪ ■

Twenty minutes earlier (1055), before Beatty turned radically away, with *Lion* listing and hauling a point to starboard for a burning *Tiger* to pass, Hipper had reached a decision that would have converted the lengthy stern chase into the kind of slugging match that Beatty still longed for despite the punishment his ships had received in recent minutes.[36] Hipper had displayed little emotion since the battle began, but with his armored cruiser already several miles behind and coming closer by the minute to a brutal execution by the entire enemy force, the realization of "the full tragedy of *Blücher*'s loss [allowed] his human sympathy to break through." "There had always been a close bond of friendship and confidence between him and his captains," recalled a member of his staff. "He was especially fond of Captain Erdmann, who was in command of *Blücher*. He was therefore strongly tempted to go to his friend's help. His tactical instinct warned him against this course . . . [but] in these fleeting moments Hipper the man got the better of Hipper the tactician." Hipper turned to Raeder and Egidy, seeming to want advice. Could they not save *Blücher* with a destroyer attack followed by a flanking move of the battlecruisers across their bows? Was not now the time to exploit and compound the damage to their leading ships? Raeder and Egidy looked at one another, but said nothing for the moment—was Hipper's mind really already made up? They turned back to their chief with visible distress stamped on their faces. The torpedo boats would be going on the cavalrymen's proverbial death ride, while his battlecruisers, although crossing the "T" of the enemy, would also be vulnerable to attack by over thirty destroyers. At 1058 Hipper drew his foregone conclusions: "Very well then, destroyers stand by to attack, squadron turn, S-SE." He had begun to turn around (southeast to south-southeast) and close the enemy.

At 1100 the destroyers began to turn about and pass through the battlecruiser line on a westerly course that would enable them to rake Beatty's line with torpedoes 3,000–4,000 yards off his port beams. Once Hipper noticed the British battle line inexplicably turning sharply north (1102), however, he called off the attack, for at an instant the torpedo boats had been robbed of their best angle of attack—the only redeeming side, however fluky, of Beatty's order. But he did not call off the battle-cruiser flanking move, ordering "squadron turn bearing SW" (1108) to accelerate his circling maneuver and close the range on the British battlecruisers 17,000 yards away.

Egidy could no longer hold his tongue. This attack was unwise. *Seydlitz* had shipped water massively aft and only a depleted number of 11-inch shells remained for the forward guns. The flagship was no longer battle worthy. Hipper gave his flag-captain a withering stare. Seeing this, Raeder stepped close to the chief's ear and screwed up his courage for one last daring appeal. Could it not be sentiment acting here? Two and a half ships against four? And the English battle squadron whose call sign they heard earlier could be nearby too. Hearing these words from his annoyingly intelligent Number One, Hipper knew he had to revoke his orders: "The decision to refrain he found extraordinarily difficult. His face clouded; an expression of injured pride, grief for his comrades who had to be abandoned, was to be read in his eyes. Then suddenly a sharp, jerky movement—a curt order with the accustomed assurance." To the relief of his immediate subordinates, he ordered "squadron turn, SE, 21 knots. Radio the fleet chief that *Blücher* has fallen out" (1115). Forty-five minutes would pass before he found the resolve to amend the phrase to: "*Blücher* lost."

■ ■ ■

Even this wording understated reality. When the German battlecruisers resumed their southeasterly retreat, *Blücher* repulsed Goodenough's light cruisers 16,000 yards away with 8.2-inch salvos—portside wing turret "D" had resumed fire, joining the valiant crew of F-turret. At 1120, however, Tyrwhitt's light cruiser *Arethusa* and four M-class destroyers pulled 5,000 yards astern, let loose broadsides and torpedoes, and scored five hits. The burning German target vessel fought back valiantly, disabling one of the destroyers, HMS *Meteor*, inflicting six casualties on her and others that turned away, but *Arethusa* kept charging and firing to within 2,500 yards, knocking out *Blücher*'s electricity. By 1130, Goodenough's four cruisers had edged back to 14,000 yards on the other side and joined in the execution, collectively blasting away with all of their thirty-two 6-inch guns that had clear firing arcs.

Almost simultaneously, *Tiger*, *Princess Royal*, *New Zealand*, and *Indomitable* opened fire a mere 8,000 yards behind *Blücher*, furiously bringing the full weight of their heavy shells down on the stricken enemy "in a kind of obsession." Broadside after broadside continued gratuitously for fifteen minutes. At this range, accuracy improved.

> *Blücher* was under fire from so many ships [recalled survivors] that it seemed there was one continuous explosion. The ship heeled over as the broadsides struck her, then righted herself, rocking like a cradle. The shells came thick and fast, dropping from the sky with a horrible droning hum. The electric plant was destroyed and below decks you could not see your hand before your nose. There was horror and confusion, mingled with gasping shouts and moans as the shells plunged through the decks, boring their way even to the stokehold. The coal in the bunkers was set on fire. In [an] engine room a shell licked up the oil and sprayed it around in flames of blue and green, scarring its victims. Men huddled together in dark compartments, but the shells sought them out, and there death had a rich harvest. The terrific air pressure resulting from explosions in a confined space roared through every opening and tore through every weak spot. Open doors banged shut and jammed and closed iron doors bend outward like tin plates, and through it all the bodies of men were whirled about like dead leaves in a winter blast to be battered to death against the iron walls. As one poor wretch was passing through a trap door a shell burst near him. He was exactly half way through. The trap door closed with a terrific snap.

This man, fleeing in near panic like all the others, was crushed instantly, joining about eight hundred of his shipmates who were killed inside the ship this day, some dying of even worse "horrors too fearful to recount."[37]

Captain Erdmann struck the colors and the ship sank at 1213 near the edge of the German Bight. Hundreds of wounded and unwounded seamen abandoned ship only to succumb in minutes to the icy North Sea before British ships could haul them out. Others, like Erdmann himself, died in captivity of pneumonia. Counting the losses on *Seydlitz* two hours earlier, over 1,100 German sailors had died. The "obsessive" blood revenge for the "Scarborough Raid" was complete.

· 6 ·

PRIDE COMETH

Shortly before dawn on the dark foggy morning of January 26, 1915, the last two ships that had fought off the Dogger Bank neared May Island at the entrance to the firth. *Lion*'s engines, contaminated with salt water, had been shut down and the flagship brought under tow by *Indomitable*, a tricky operation that snapped a few thick hawsers before getting it right. Throughout the day, the badly battered Fast Cat limped home, protected by a bodyguard of destroyers to prevent any lurking German submarines from finishing the considerable destruction Hipper's ships had begun on Sunday. At May Island, *Indomitable* yielded to a pack of tugs, which guided *Lion* beneath a bridge full of cheering patriots, none aware of how much Beatty's entire force may have owed its continued existence to Ingenohl's lack of dash.

Below on the compass platform of *Lion*, Major Francis Harvey, Lieutenant Francis Jones, Lieutenant RNVR Filson Young, and a passel of officers joined the rest of the crew in returning the raucous greeting with hurrahs and cap waving. Beatty, ever conscious of showmanship, had formed up the ship's band on the 4-inch–gun deck, and as his vessel drew closer to the bridge, the musicians belted out "Rule Britannia" and other strains of nationalistic music. "And so, amid mist and cheers, true symbols of our warfare, the *Lion* came home," Young recalled.[1]

Once the full squadron lay at anchor, preparations got underway for repairing *Lion* and transferring Beatty and most of his staff officers temporarily to *Tiger*. As this commenced, every officer in Beatty's command who had anything to do with the combat performance of the guns faced another pressing task: the challenge of analyzing firing data and distilling the offensive as well as defensive lessons of what was already being called the Battle of Dogger Bank.

It is a safe bet that these gunnery topics mixed with postbattle celebrations at a dinner in the gunroom on the twenty-eighth that the midshipmen hosted for Captain Chatfield, Admiral Beatty, and his staff. One of the midshipmen must have opened the festivities by giving the loyal toast to the sovereign, and then another risen to toast "the bloody war," traditional on Thursdays, while also welcoming Beatty, the guest of honor, for his squadrons' smashing victory, during which, remarkably enough, only fifteen had been killed and thirty-three wounded. Some of the assembled may well have continued to discuss "the only topic of conversation in the ship" since Sunday.[2] "The German gunfire was better than ours," wrote Young, "and they got sooner on to the target. His shooting [also] appeared to be painfully accurate, and indeed, towards the end of the action, when two and possibly three ships were concentrating on the Lion, she was very nearly smothered by their fire."

Like Young and other officers, Chatfield had ruminated about German gunfire too, but also about why more German ships had not been put out of action. "There seemed no doubt that our gunnery officers had not succeeded in hitting the enemy sufficiently; or if they had, then why had they not been put out of action like Lion and Blücher? Were our projectiles the cause? But all the experts had faith in them."[3] Although Young had not dodged the issue of accuracy, the flag captain quickly moved past the fact that "our gunnery officers had not succeeded in hitting the enemy sufficiently": "Rapidity of fire and 'short shots' are what we want. Whoever gets the biggest volume of fire that is hitting will gain the ascendancy and keep it as the other fellow can't see past the water spouts to reply. Range does not matter as modern shell will knock an enemy out at any range you can reach. Lion fired too slowly, hampered by all the orders and restrictions on the subject."[4] Regarding the effectiveness of shells "at any range you can reach," clearly the flag captain also "had faith in them" (i.e., British projectiles), for despite the inevitable shell declination and oblique impact of distant firing, they would still "knock an enemy out." The real problem, the main culprits evidently, were antiflash doors and fireproof cordite cases retarding fire, a point that Harvey and other turret captains certainly seconded.

This would soon be Beatty's position too, for, prone as he was to "go cold all over [thinking] that there isn't another chance in front of us,"[5] when next in battle he would make sure his ships fired faster than the enemy. As he would repeat later, falling back on Shakespeare, when that opportunity was finally summoned and successfully seized, "gentlemen of England" would "think themselves accursed they were not [there], and hold their manhood cheap while any speaks that fought with us on our Great Day."[6] The guest of honor and his staff were soon called away from this dinner, for the Admiralty had ordered the seaworthy battlecruisers out again to support Tyrwhitt's Harwich force in another probe of the North Sea.

■ ■ ■

As the weeks since the battle stretched into a month, and then two, the Admiralty insisted on explanations for the escape of three German battlecruisers, and, finding no adequate reasons, looked for heads to chop off. Already on the day of the gunroom banquet on *Lion*, Beatty had received an irate letter from First Sea Lord Jacky Fisher, condescendingly correcting him on the alleged U-boat sighting that had prompted him to order the entire squadron to turn radically away: "You are mistaken about the enemy's submarines—we know from [wireless intercepts] exactly where they were—hours off you." But another matter angered him more: "It is ABSOLUTELY INCOMPREHENSIBLE to me why [your second-in-command Rear Admiral Archibald] Moore discontinued the action at noon when the *Seydlitz* and *Derfflinger* [were] both heavily on fire and very badly damaged and they had to scuttle into dock. . . . WHAT POSSIBLE EXPLANATION IS THERE? What excuse have we to offer?" The Admiralty's wrath also fell on Captain Henry Pelly of *Tiger*, who, like Moore, did not continue the pursuit: "He was a long way ahead [of Moore], he ought to have gone on . . . like Nelson. . . . In war the first principle is to disobey orders. *Any fool can obey orders*."[7] As explained earlier (see chapter 4), Fisher was aware of the dilemma posed by the obedience-minded, discipline-before-initiative passivity of many older naval officers and was determined to rid the corps of "old women."

In his frequent postbattle correspondence with Jellicoe, Beatty, pointing fingers shamelessly at others, also criticized Pelly of *Tiger*, both for failing to fire correctly in sequence on *Moltke*, leaving that ship free of enemy fire to pummel *Lion*, as well as for "running amuck after *Lion* fell out and not attacking [the] enemy's rear. . . . He rode the *P[rincess] R[oyal]* right out and she had to put her helm right over to clear him. I think the shell that landed under [the] control tower upset them and knocked those in [the] conning tower out temporarily although he won't say so, but for a time *Tiger* was all over the shop." Even though he felt Pelly was "a little bit of the nervous excited type," and Moore "not of the right sort of temperament," and that they had both been given "a chance which most fellows would have given the eyes in their head for," Beatty still wanted no changes in personnel lest this "destroy confidence."[8]

The Admiralty ruled otherwise. While visiting Rosyth, Churchill "was in a disturbed frame of mind and wanted the blood of somebody." Fisher agreed, and, according to Beatty, "they settled on Moore."[9] As February turned to March, the former favorite of Fisher was packed off to an exile of sorts in the Canary Islands commanding an isolated antiquated cruiser squadron, a fate even worse than Arbuthnot's a month earlier (see chapter 4).

As personnel changes were being debated and resolved, the Admiralty also raised questions about the northerly bases of Britain's modern capital ships. Should Beatty remain at Rosyth? Churchill thought not, preferring to have the Grand Fleet there instead, with Beatty's ships moved again even further south to the Humber estuary, both changes to provide "strategic advantages that are too obvious to require enlarging upon." Always blunter, Fisher spelled it out in caps and underlining, telling Jellicoe that "at Scapa YOU WILL NEVER BE IN TIME! ALWAYS 150 miles too far off!" To the C-in-C's constant refrains against Rosyth, both for his ships as well as Beatty's, Fisher countered didactically that "we should not have had January 24 if Beatty had been at Cromarty." In the end, Jellicoe's worries, reinforced by Beatty's, about inadequate antimine and submarine defenses at both proposed new bases, as well as tidal concerns at the Humber—for six hours a day around low tide, as at Wilhelmshaven, capital ships would not be able to move in or out—resulted in both fleets staying where they were. As the First Lord and the First Sea Lord, Churchill and Fisher could muster a lot of power and pressure for their proposals, but common sense, reinforced by tradition and the prestige of the country's flag commanders, sometimes dictated that the two lords defer to the men on the bridge. Thus, in late March, Fisher still complained to Jellicoe that "the Humber . . . [is] the Real Strategic Center and [yet] you won't agree to Beatty going there! Such is life!"[10] Some hints or obscured details of these disagreements probably reached the ears of German agents, confusing them even more about the location of enemy squadrons.

While these differences reverberated, the Admiralty took different steps to shore up the east coast. *Queen Mary* (back from dry dock) and *Australia* (shifted from the Pacific) augmented the four remaining battlecruisers of Beatty's depleted command shortly after Dogger Bank. On March 3, 1915, *Invincible* joined them from her extensive refitting in Gibraltar after the Battle of the Falklands. Sailing under the Forth Bridge to her new anchorage, smoke pouring proudly from all funnels, most of her wartime complement of a thousand sailors and officers on deck, and her Royal Marine band blaring patriotically, she was arguably the most famous ship in the Royal Navy by this date in the Great War. Taking the lead three months earlier, *Invincible* had done the lion's share of the destruction to Graf Spee's two armored cruisers, thereby happily ending one of Winston Churchill's high seas nightmares. As a reward for his victory, Vice Admiral Sir Frederick Doveton Sturdee received a promotion to command the 4th BS at Scapa Flow, which included *Iron Duke*. His former ship now flew the ensign of Rear Admiral the Hon. Horace Hood.

Invincible's chief gunnery officer, Commander Hubert Dannreuther, could not get too caught up in the fame his ship had acquired since the Falklands battle. Stationed in the foretop during the touch-and-go early stages of the fight, he had cursed the poor visibility through the ship's own smoke blown downrange and lamented the slow, inaccurate fire from ranges well above 10,000 yards, which his gunners had not yet target-shot. His after-battle report also noted the "curious" fact that two German shells that had penetrated the battlecruisers' characteristically thin hull below the water line—one near the bow coal bunkers, the other against the magazine handling room wall of midship P-turret—had not detonated. Even more remarkable was the fact that the latter shell, if it had hit a few feet to the right, even without detonating, would have flooded the ship's steam plant and eliminated all power to the turrets. Dannreuther knew that *Invincible* was a lucky ship, for that particular dud could easily have sunk or incapacitated her. Had he known at the time about the convoluted espionage schemes of the Naval Intelligence Division (NID) before the battle, he would have considered *Invincible* an even luckier ship.[11]

The Admiralty assuaged the victor of Dogger Bank in yet other ways. Against Jellicoe's judgment, they restructured Beatty's command into a "Battle Cruiser Fleet" (BCF) and assembled it piecemeal as winter turned slowly to spring. The BCF consisted of three squadrons: the 1st BCS of *Tiger*, *Princess Royal*, *Queen Mary*, and *Lion* (back after repairs); the 2nd BCS of *New Zealand*, *Australia* (from the Pacific), and *Indefatigable* (back from the Dardanelles [see below]); and Hood's 3rd BCS of *Invincible*, *Inflexible* (back from the Dardanelles), and *Indomitable* (returned earlier from the Mediterranean). Joining his ten battlecruisers, the majority (six of ten) having come to him—or back to him—from faraway waters, Beatty had at his disposal thirteen light cruisers and sixteen destroyers of recent design. "God *is* helping the navy,"[12] gloated Fisher, taking issue with Jellicoe.

"I [am] a proud man to get ten [battlecruisers]," replied Beatty, "and think with them we ought with little notice to be able to put the stopper on raids if they attempt them again, which is doubtful." As for a big battle at sea, "I only wait for the day to come before it is too late."[13] With British divisions attacking in the Artois region of

France in March, and again in May, losing tens of thousands of men, he complained to Ethel: "I don't think, dear heart, you will ever realize the effect these terrible happenings have upon me. I feel so impotent, so incapable of doing anything for lack of opportunity, almost that we are not doing our share and bearing our portion of the burden laid upon the nation. We spend days doing nothing when so many are doing so much." The continued inactivity of the BCF induced by the post–Dogger Bank caution of the German High Seas Fleet (see chapter 7) "makes me feel sick at heart."[14]

■ ■ ■

Like Beatty, Jellicoe ground through his own full range of emotions, which he poured out occasionally in conversations with Flag Captain Robert Lawson, asserted frequently in written missives to Beatty and the Admiralty, and always turned over repeatedly in his never-resting, hypercritical, cautious mind. Elation over the victory at Dogger Bank, which caused him to congratulate Beatty, mixed with private thoughts that much more could have been achieved if *Lion* had not fallen out, and that Moore had been sadly ineffectual and would have to go. He got "bitchy-minded" at the Admiralty's air of superiority, however, as if sea commanders were all "duffers" and the Admiralty's "inner circle" of "amateur strategists" made none of its own "mistakes of immense importance." He would be "hanged," for example, if there was "enough water" at the Humber for the entire BCF, and he bristled at Churchill's, Wilson's, and Fisher's plans for ill-advised fleet actions, respectively, against Borkum, Helgoland, and the Baltic that would only have weakened the Grand Fleet for "the day" of North Sea battle against the High Seas Fleet. His disapproval scotched these proposals. On such critical issues it took more than an "air of superiority" for the Admiralty to prevail.[15]

Exacerbating a bad case of "the piles" that winter—which he blamed on the Admiralty's ignoring his squadron commanders' requests and forcing him to intervene "to get things done which ought to be done without my having to step in"—were worries about Beatty, who had taken chances at Dogger Bank, a hard-charging subordinate he sought to finesse. The overeager cavalier had gambled and won but might conceivably have been trapped there (see chapter 5). And next time?

I should imagine that the Germans will sooner or later try to entrap you by using their battlecruisers as a decoy. . . . They know that if they can get you in chase, the odds are that you will be 100 miles away from me, and they can under such conditions draw you well down to the Helgoland Bight without my being in effective support. . . . In that case the loss of [your battlecruisers] seems inevitable if you are drawn into the vicinity of the High Seas Fleet. . . . The Germans also probably know you and your qualities very well . . . and will try to take advantage of that quality of "not letting go when you have once got hold," which you possess, thank God.

Much fretting about the substandard accuracy of Beatty's gunners at Dogger Bank further irritated Jellicoe's hemorrhoid condition, which was not helped by a lot of distressing about the "very surprising and somewhat disquieting" report about damage done below the water line to *Lion* on January 24—the five- to six-inch portion of the upper armor belt had been repeatedly penetrated, nearly incapacitating the flagship. "But if they can hit hard under water we can apparently hit harder above water."[16]

This last statement was telling. Jellicoe's implication that British ordnance was not properly penetrating German underwater armor belts, and that they might have to content themselves with bludgeoning enemy superstructures, disclosed a concern on his part that had gnawed at him for years. As Royal Navy Controller in 1910, the engineering-oriented, control-conscious perfectionist had conducted a series of tests on an AP shell that performed well enough along a short-range, flat trajectory, but failed at the higher shell declination of ranges over 10,000 yards. Later tests (1917) showed that inadequate fuses, unstable explosive, and open-hearth steel of poor quality caused plunging shells to burst prematurely. Already suspecting these specific quality weaknesses in 1910, Jellicoe ordered the development of a superior shell "that would perforate armor at oblique impact and go on [into the interior of ships] in a state fit for bursting," but cost concerns and bureaucratic muddling led to "the matter [not being] sufficiently pressed."[17] That German fuses, though not perfect (see chapter 13, note 11), functioned better; that they used a more stable explosive; and that they made their steel shell heads from superior material would exacerbate the effects of British shell deficiencies at Jutland in 1916.

Underlying much of this "bureaucratic muddling" and further stymieing the remanufacture of a superior Royal Navy armor-piercing shell was the fact that even after Fisher's revolution, the Admiralty remained stacked with older line officers who were "certainly lacking [in] the apportionment of adequate weight to technical and scientific knowledge and expertise." This deficiency, an unfortunate sign for Great Britain, indicated that the armaments race among Europe's long-feuding peoples, a longstanding, deep-seated, deadly competition ineluctably driving forward the creation of bigger and more lethal weapons of land and sea warfare, had not adequately resonated among certain leading Royal Navy cadres, which remained complacent about these threatening developments. Ominously, however, Germany, the one European nation most frenetically playing catch-up in naval terms, did not have—and had every reason not to have—such overconfidence. Clearly less insouciant about these threats, Jellicoe worried that "muddling-through" would not be enough against the High Seas Fleet.[18]

While not in Jellicoe's cautious nature, which usually bordered on alarm, to forget or forgive the errors of omission of 1910—with his unusually "retentive memory," recalled Lawson's successor, Flag Captain Frederic Dreyer, "he remembered everything"[19]— further tests in 1914–15 confirming the likely defects of existing 13.5-inch and 15-inch AP shells must have made the painful memory of four years earlier rankle and fester, especially when the overweening Admiralty seemed blind to the results, claiming the shells "were effective at all ranges." While able to buckle and partially hole armor plate, spray splinters that injured personnel, and severely damage superstructures, thus probably creating havoc and confusion, deflating morale, and disrupting enemy command and control—hence Jellicoe's belief that "we can apparently hit harder above water"—these large AP shells nevertheless failed to burst far enough inside the ship. The unprecedented long-range firing at Dogger Bank was a welcome development, but this had probably hurt accuracy, exacerbated AP-shell deficiencies, and facilitated the escape of the German squadron. While all of this nagged at the C-in-C, munitions redesign and remanufacture would have to wait, for with shells short on the Western Front, British industry straining to catch up, and the constant, day-to-day threat of another sortie from Wilhelmshaven, the navy could not expect to replace every AP shell in its depots even if bureaucratic obstacles were overcome. In the meantime, Jellicoe kept his doubts to himself and signed off on the Admiralty's stubbornly exaggerated reports, probably so that fleet morale would not suffer.[20]

Gunnery officers on *Lion* had already raised their own vexing ordnance questions, however, in a series of "discussions and conferences held among experts in the various technical branches," remembered *Lion*'s communications officer, Filson Young.

> Every one of [these experts] had been brought up on the theory of the big gun, the first blow, etc. We had the biggest guns and we got the first blows, but none of the results that the gunnery expert of those days had been taught to believe as gospel had happened. . . . The idea that one blow from a 13.5 shell was going to do the business of any capital ship had to be abandoned. We had gone on hitting, and hitting, and hitting—and three out of four ships had got home. Why?

Leaving aside the fact that Beatty's poorly shooting batteries had not, in fact, "gone on hitting, and hitting, and hitting" except at the end, point blank against *Blücher*, none of these gunnery discussions Young mentions, which included "matters having regard to the steep angle of descent of projectiles at long ranges," filtered up very far into the Royal Navy. Because of this, the reigning belief that "one blow from a 13.5 shell was going to do the business of any capital ship" strengthened the desire of BCF higher-ups to care less about accuracy and simply fire more rapidly, for if just "one blow" landed squarely, it would surely "do the business." Chatfield, as noted earlier, was one of the leading advocates of increasing the rapidity of fire and wanted to focus on that, not shell worries: "We had not yet lost faith in our shell; it would not be correct to say that we had supreme confidence in them, but we had no evidence to weaken our natural and proper belief in the Admiralty's 'assurances' as to their efficiency."[21] Drills and rare firing practices took place as the months slipped by to spring and summer, continued Young, but "there was no development or modification of [range and gunnery] tactics; and the reliance was still on the fallacy that all was well with our material, and that we had more of it than the enemy."[22]

Indeed, most top braid in the Royal Navy establishment mirrored Chatfield and harbored no serious doubts about British shell—Jellicoe again being the exception at the summit. Churchill waxed positive, for instance, writing that "the immense power of the 13.5-inch gun . . . and the effect of heavy metal . . . is clearly decisive in the minds of the enemy . . . and they have no thought but flight." Fisher sounded the same refrain, boasting that the Germans "are in holy terror of the 13.5-inch guns. . . . The High Seas Fleet won't come out for a big job—they'll emerge and retire!" Along the lines of what Young wrote, moreover, Beatty observed that the Royal Navy seemed obsessed with the big gun—perhaps too much so, he thought, especially with its apparent long-range failings at Dogger Bank. Although incuriously and indifferently oblivious to the reasons for this—shell, propellant charges, gunnery, battle smoke?—he now leaned common-sense-like toward making more "decisive" big blows at 12,000–14,000 yards: closer seemed better—for now at least. It is also bewildering why he could dismiss German 11- and 12-inch projectiles that had badly bashed *Lion* as "not to be compared to our 13.5-inch."[23]

When combined with other issues like the danger of enemy torpedoes, the AP-shell problem contributes to an explanation of Jellicoe's prudent Fabian posture in the North Sea as 1915 unfolded. When war broke out, shell concerns had him planning (in good visibility) to deploy at 15,000 yards, open fire at medium range of 9,000–12,000 yards, and then close for rapid decisive fire at 6,000–8,000 yards, a distance where shells penetrated plate more effectively and gunners shot more accurately. Already by September, however, he had altered tactics radically in favor of deciding actions well beyond the 10,000-yard range of torpedoes—this concern had trumped the other. Battle orders now featured deployment at 18,000–20,000 yards, opening fire between 15,000 and 18,000 yards, not closing "in the *early* stages of the action . . . much inside 14,000 yards," and only reaching 10,000 yards "as the enemy's fire is overcome." While still tempted by the goal of rapid fire within 10,000 yards, which had been his prewar preference, Jellicoe's battle squadrons nevertheless drilled repeatedly for the longer-range alternative (i.e., 14,000–16,000 yards) throughout the fall and winter in the open waters of Scapa Flow and elsewhere. Shell quality problems, exacerbated by the lesser accuracy anticipated at long range—especially by the notoriously under-practicing and hence poor-shooting battlecruisers—underscored the obvious disadvantages of this tactic, but he nevertheless opted for the skillet of long-range fighting over the frying pan of inviting torpedo attacks by enemy destroyers at short-to-medium range.[24] An option infinitely superior to either one, however, would be simply not to initiate action at all unless the Admiralty signaled that the Germans threatened to cross the North Sea. Adopting a passive defensive strategy is what he decided to do, all the others and their desire for jousting in enemy lists be damned. Such caution, mixed with Beatty's open preference for action over inaction, prompted the ever-scheming, aggressive Churchill to want to replace Jellicoe with the Hotspur in Rosyth.[25]

■ ▮ ■

As explained earlier, Chatfield dismissed his doubts about British AP shell and shelved any thoughts he had about accurate gunnery, concluding that only one problem was left to solve, namely, that of British firing speed, which he realized trailed that of the Germans by a great deal. "The enemy can fire very quickly . . . if we had been bolder in firing [*Lion*] should have annihilated them alone." Accordingly, Beatty's right-hand man undertook to ignore "all the orders and restrictions" that "hampered" *Lion* and made her fire "too slowly."[26]

This dismantling process had started, in fact, well before the war. Magazine doors in British battleships prior to 1898 had been fitted with revolving, self-sealing, antiflash scuttles, a feature of black powder days that allowed crews to supply ammunition charges with doors shut, thus preventing explosions in the gun house from flashing downward to explode magazines. Later designs omitted these scuttles, substituting a working chamber under the gun house, acting as a firewall. And then during the

Battles of the Bight and the Dogger Bank, turret crews among Beatty's battlecruisers, the Royal Marines taking the lead, began to improvise ways to increase firing speed by removing cordite quarter-charges from their fireproof "Clarkson Cases" and lining them up in the narrow magazine passages and out through open doors to the handling room as well as stacking the naked charges in the working chamber above—the exact cause of the massive fire on *Seydlitz*. At least twenty-five full charges, and probably as many as forty, were made ready in this way for the guns above, triple to quintuple the number that a turret's self-opening-and-closing antiflash trunk hoist doors were designed to contain if fire flashed—the flimsy doors were *inadequately designed*, one must add, amounting thereby to an alarming breach in the firewall. Making matters even more precarious, some crews had also wire-locked these antiflash doors in the open position, or even removed them.[27]

It was only a short logical leap for Chatfield, no doubt after consulting his turret captains, to order the stacking of unsheathed charges all along the line and removing all antiflash doors along the trunk hoist. "Speed of fire became all important, with accuracy a long way second," observed Julian Thompson. "The Battle Cruiser Fleet, based at Rosyth, did not get the opportunity to practice as often as the Battle Fleet based at Scapa, and its gunnery accuracy was beginning to be the subject of criticism. Now here apparently was the answer, and one that appealed to the BCF's panache. . . . The key to success was getting the maximum number of rounds off in the shortest possible time."[28] Although Chatfield's position next to "glorious *Beatty Beatus*,"[29] as Fisher dubbed him, gave BCF's first captain great influence, it is unlikely that he petitioned for these changes to spread to other squadrons, for there was no formal mechanism for such transmissions in the Royal Navy. Rather, the logic of these "highly dangerous ways"[30] occurred to other captains too, and, perhaps after discussions with turret officers and other captains, they acted. A steady flow of shells into the gun house meant in theory that gun crews could fire almost as fast as the shells came into the loading trays. Chatfield had solved the "only problem" left to be solved after Dogger Bank.

■ ▓ ■

Chief Gunner Alexander Grant hustled from Dalmeny Station onto the footpath leading to Hawes Pier. He followed it to the crest and then relaxed on the way down, seeing that the ship's boat waited for him. On board and underway to his new billet, Grant admired the fine engineering of the Forth Bridge as they passed underneath it; but viewing this technical feat paled in comparison to the sight of battle-grey *Lion* with her tall masts, huge funnels, and big imposing guns. "Here is a ship that will let them have it good and hearty," thought the Scotsman. But this was no time for daydreams. A war raged and Captain Chatfield himself had sent for the new man.[31]

Grant was forty-three years old in June 1915. While he had spent time at sea, most notably with the Channel Fleet flagship HMS *King Edward VII*, the noblest of the "Wobbly Eight," his real calling was naval gunnery, most recently as gunner-in-charge of grounds at Whale Island, the navy's elite instructional institute in Portsmouth. Chatfield had served there too and come to respect Grant's talents and squared-away approach. If anything that affects a ship's firing were amiss, he would put it in order. The flag captain clearly wanted his new chief gunner to fix any broken pieces remaining in the process of *Lion*'s becoming the quickest-firing battlecruiser in the Royal Navy—indeed, in the North Sea.

Grant soon found one broken piece when he reported the next day to the ship's gunnery officer, Lieutenant Commander Gerald Longhurst. "It's not the cheeriest bit of news," said the GO, "but your predecessor was court-martialed yesterday. The magazines were in a sorry state, but all has been put right and you'll have no difficulty." Grant politely nodded and smiled, saying only, "Right, Sir," but thought otherwise. "After twenty years of sorting out messes, I'll just see for myself."

And sure enough, inspecting the four 50-charge magazines of one turret, the chief gunner found a huge mess. Grant was undoubtedly aware of the faulty testing of loaded shells performed by the Royal Navy's Ordnance Board (OB), a far too lenient process full of "proof-testing loopholes of almost criminal scale" that allowed manufacturers to pass along to the ships an unacceptable percentage of defective projectiles in each numbered lot of four hundred shells. Keeping in mind the poor fuses, unstable explosive, and brittle shell heads causing deficiencies in exploding AP shell, shoddily made, nonexploding duds would become another costly failing at Jutland, an irremediable problem that day unredeemed by even greater German dud issues (see chapter 13, note 11). Grant could do nothing about these problems, but the navy also tested the highly flammable charges that propelled shells to their targets by periodically landing samples from ships' magazines for proofing—propellant also more unstable and liable to burst into flame in turrets after enemy hits than its German counterpart.[32] If any charge consisting of four one-quarter silken bags of cordite with gunpowder "igniters" failed, the entire lot, all potential dud charges, would be removed and destroyed. For this system to work, bad charge lots had to be easily located in the magazines, which meant that each Clarkson Case (containing two quarter-charge bags) had to be properly numbered according to the specific lots of the bags inside. On this day, however, Grant found a complete jumble of bags and cases, the lot numbers on the latter not corresponding to the actual lots of the bags inside, a situation so fouled up beyond all recognition as to make any further testing an exercise in futility and guaranteeing a badly subpar performance of all ship's guns in battle. With Chatfield's smiling approval, Grant fixed the problem in four hours by removing all 1,600 Clarkson Cases from *Lion*'s four turrets and inserting properly numbered cases, two specific lots of 800 full charges for the whole ship, 100 rounds per barrel—an impressive feat.

Grant's next coup proved more difficult to accomplish. He quickly got wind of the circumvention of safety regulations on *Lion* that had begun after the outbreak of war and accelerated with Chatfield's blessing after Dogger Bank. Confronting the problem head on, he met with Longhurst to put things right again:

> Sir, present arrangements mean Davy Jones's locker for the whole crew. During battle only one magazine door, not all four, should be open; no more than one full charge per gun in the handling room and working chamber at a time; and charges to be taken out of their cases only as required. During any lull in the action the open magazine door should be closed and watertight clips put on. And on no account should the magazines be flooded except on receipt of an order from a responsible officer. Furthermore, the crews can't wear shoes or boots lest sparks ignite gunpowder that falls out of the bags and accumulates on the deck of the handling room.

"I'll have to consult with the turret captains, Grant, but they will not agree."

As expected, all four turret captains rejected the proposal, Royal Marine Major Harvey's objections the most vociferous. He had worked hard to increase the pace in his station and did not want the newcomer to undermine his efforts. On hearing this, Grant said, "Give me the magazine crews to train and test the time." Longhurst pointed out that the captain would have to agree.

And to his credit, Chatfield not only approved the test but attended too. Using the new system, Grant's retrained crew succeeded in repeatedly supplying shells and charges to the turret gun house every thirty seconds or so, both barrels fully loaded with the first set of charges and shells in a little over five minutes. All this was done without having to stack extra shells in the magazine corridor, handling room, or working chamber, keeping only one magazine door open, holding to a minimum the unsheathing of cases, and with the antiflash doors activated. The key to success was having each station along the way to the guns supply the next station every twenty to thirty seconds. While two full charges and shells were in the loading trays in the gun house, another set of two waited in the working chamber, two were coming up the trunk lines, and two were in position in magazine hoppers in the handling room ready to hoist. The guns could only load and fire so fast, so there was no need for unsheathing and stacking charges or disabling antiflash doors.

To the dismay of disapproving turret captains, Grant also wanted magazine and handling room crews to remove their boots, a practice more in line with Crimean War days. In order to drive home this point, Grant suggested a further test to Chatfield, who green-lit the idea. Gunpowder-igniter and cordite sweepings from the handling room floor outside the magazines were gathered up, taken to the main deck, and laid out in a trail. A lighted match, simulating a spark from the boot of a magazine crewman in a hurry, was put to the end of the trail—all the sweepings flashed into flame. Grant's victory seemed complete.

But it was not complete, for the safer, orthodox-regulation approach did not spread to the rest of the BCF, a sadly ominous fact considering what happened a year later. Although hard to explain, the reason what happened on *Lion* stayed on *Lion* probably resulted in part from the lack of a general staff at Beatty's level that could transmit research and experimental results from below to those above and beyond. As noted earlier, Filson Young would complain that important discussions and studies went nowhere, like one talking to oneself. The Royal Navy was an impressive institution but very hierarchical and set in its ways, and one time-honored tradition was that each captain tended to set the rules on his own ship. Chatfield eventually realized the nature of the problem, complaining after the war about the "lack of coordination of fleet gunnery . . . there was too much independence of method—a greater concentration of method, a greater standardization was now required."[33] It is also likely that Chatfield was simply not yet fully convinced that Grant's system worked better. Only battle could offer a real test, so in the meantime it was mum, wait, and see. Similarly, Grant's sorting out of the magazine lot mess probably also remained a boon for *Lion* alone—like many of the Royal Navy's shell and charge/propellant inferiorities, lot messes had difficult-to-specify-but-probably-very-bad results for the rest of the BCF in its rematch with Hipper (see chapter 10).

■ ■ ■

By the time these events transpired on *Lion*, Winston Churchill and Jacky Fisher had departed from the Admiralty. Their dramatic exodus from power centered on the increasingly turbulent relationship between the two. Since his return to office in late October, the salty seventy-three-year-old First Sea Lord of the Admiralty had cooperated well enough with the dynamic younger man, whom he considered a close friend, but Fisher was not accustomed to Churchill's long-winded memoranda and bubbling pot of operational ideas. Although Fisher had his own controversial proposals—running the Great Belt and assaulting the Baltic near Kiel would probably have presented the Germans, not the British, with a Christmas present—by late January he leaned toward the strategically more cautious Jellicoe and his skittish skepticism toward Churchill's grandiose projects, especially the First Lord's preoccupation with battleships running the Dardanelles, knocking Turkey out of the war, subsequently opening a supply route to Russia, and then raising up the neutral Balkan states for the allied war effort. By May, after the Dardanelles debacle and unsuccessful Gallipoli landings had cost the Royal Navy two predreadnoughts (*Ocean* and *Goliath*), one dreadnought battlecruiser (*Irresistible*), and severe damage to another (*Inflexible*), Fisher had reached the snapping point. Would one of the navy's newest super-dreadnoughts, *Queen Elizabeth*, which Churchill had detached from Jellicoe in March to spearhead the Dardanelles landings in late April, be next?[34]

And then on May 14, even though Churchill had yielded by ordering *Queen Elizabeth* home, Fisher blurted in War Council that he had never favored the Dardanelles operation. The First Lord of the Admiralty did not take the blunt betrayal of the First Sea Lord seriously enough at first, assuming he would charm "the old boy," in the meantime asserting proudly to Prime Minister Asquith that "someone has to take responsibility—I will do so provided that my decision is the one that rules."[35] But Churchill's fall came quickly, for Fisher resigned on May 15, perhaps already contemplating slipping back into his old post after Churchill was pushed out. Indeed, the Conservative Party, which recently had ended its loyal opposition and joined a coalition government with the Liberals, never liked the leadership at the Admiralty of Churchill, a former Conservative who had crossed to the Liberal side—to many an unforgivable political sin. So the Conservatives insisted that the First Lord could not stay. Asquith agreed on May 17. Churchill's four-year tenure ended when Asquith demoted him to a far less important cabinet post: the chancellorship of the Duchy of Lancaster.

But now Fisher badly overplayed his hand, arrogantly demanding on May 19 that he stay on as First Sea Lord of the Admiralty under six conditions, including not serving with Churchill, Sir Arthur Wilson, or cabinet member Arthur Balfour, and his having "complete professional charge of the war at sea, together with the absolute sole disposition of the fleet and the appointment of all officers of all ranks whatsoever, and absolutely untrammeled sole command of all the sea forces whatsoever." Furthermore, Churchill's successor "must be restricted solely to political policy and parliamentary procedure." Asquith would have none of it, accepting Fisher's earlier resignation on May 22 and appointing Second Sea Lord, Admiral Sir Henry Jackson, instead. The PM observed that Fisher, who awaited a reply to his ultimatum in Scotland, "ought to be shot for leaving his post." The new First Lord, Arthur Balfour, agreed, telling King George that "Fisher's mind is somewhat unhinged; otherwise his conduct is almost traitorous." The fallen father of the modern British fleet had bargained foolishly for nearly as much naval control as the Kaiser—more, in fact, when considering William's personal weaknesses.

Sir Henry Oliver remained as Chief of War Staff at the Admiralty. "Undoubtedly a tower of strength," he was unfortunately a proprietary personality type who overworked himself. The grey eminence, Sir Arthur Wilson, opted not to vie for Fisher's old post, but stayed on "like some prehistoric figure, loosely attached to the Admiralty's War Staff, receiving copies of Room 40 signals, [and] consulted on important subjects."[36] Oliver, Wilson, and Director of Operations, Captain Thomas Jackson, who together had lock-control of Room 40 intelligence, were clearly the gainers, for Churchill's and Fisher's successors, Arthur Balfour and Henry Jackson, would not preside as pompously as had their predecessors. Only time would tell whether these recent gainers would be able to manage British intelligence as somewhat passably as when the Admiralty caught Hipper off Dogger Bank.

Although he also emerged a gainer, freer now to choose his own rendezvous coordinates, Jellicoe was still under the Admiralty's orders when to sortie, cut off from Room 40 secrets, and having to content himself with somewhat more leverage over lesser Admiralty superiors whom he hoped to steer away from operations he deemed unwise—gains surely nullified, however, if he could not control Beatty.

▪ 7 ▪

GERMAN EYES NORTH

On Monday morning, January 25, 1915, a clear, cold, and typically windy day in Wilhelmshaven, the dock master ordered lock chamber number one filled. After the water rose above thirty feet, fully submerging the ship's freshly scraped and painted hull to the water line, SMS *Von der Tann* rose gradually from the huge wooden keel blocks on which she had rested for two days. Observing the finished process from his flying bridge, Captain Max Hahn ordered "reverse engines," and the nation's first battlecruiser pulled out into harbor inside the Jade River bar. She then tied up at dock for a lengthy refit.

Once the warship was secured with hawser lines, hundreds of sailors began assembling on deck for job details. The last forty-eight hours had been a clean break from the tedium and annoyances of life in the German navy, for news and scuttlebutt, truth and rumor had spread like a dam break throughout the ship: The Scouting Groups would sortie without *Von der Tann*, but scores of comrades would ship out with *Blücher*; Hipper was locked in battle; Ingenohl and the battleships had hurriedly steamed out of the roadstead; British ships were being sunk. Were nearly two hundred mates and friends on *Blücher* dead at sea? What had happened?

As the work details got orders from their overbearing division officers, attention was diverted suddenly to the north. *Derfflinger*, battered, holed three times, and showing other unmistakable signs of battle, was sailing over the bar. All on deck gave the valiant, seemingly victorious vessel three rousing, echoing cheers, which were magnified by the roars of welcome from other ships in harbor. Next to receive loud acclaim was *Seydlitz*, her burned out stern quarter riding very low in the water as she too headed toward the dry docks. Then came little *Kolberg*, her bridge in ruins from a head shot. And finally came *Moltke*—but where was *Blücher*?

The next day a throng of seamen, all relieved to have gotten their twenty-four-hour leaves, headed over to the dry docks to investigate.[1] From the seamen of *Derfflinger* and *Seydlitz* they heard the story of the five-hour battle, of firing from unprecedented ranges of 20,000 yards, of the sinking of a British battlecruiser—so a Zeppelin, not seeing *Lion* anymore, had reported; naval officers reported *Tiger* sunk, not *Lion*—of the near explosion of *Seydlitz*, and of the sad abandonment of *Blücher*. Sorrow mixed with pride, however, when hearing that the Zeppelin had seen *Blücher* blasting away in all directions until the end.

The visitors also got a tour of the damaged ships. They saw a gaping hole big enough to ride a plow horse through on the starboard side near the third turret of *Derfflinger* and another shell cavern near the aft funnel. Other jolting "short shots" had generated such concussive power that they smashed back twelve inches of tough nickel steel armor plating below the water line, causing the vessel to ship large amounts of water into one of her many self-contained compartments before damage control crews could staunch the hemorrhage. But all this paled in comparison with the near catastrophic destruction on *Seydlitz*. All the guests could conjure up images of the frightful havoc that modern naval artillery had wreaked on German ships at the Battle of the Bight in August and the Battle of the Falklands in December—and on British towns during the "Scarborough" Raid—but today's sights were real, not imagined, and right before their startled eyes. Worse still, they heard tales of the dead:

> One shipyard worker employed on *Seydlitz* told me [recalled a magazine handler from 1st Squadron] that the men were found in the positions they occupied when death struck them. The man at the communication tube had his hands on his mouth and the tube as though he wanted to say something. The man at the range finder was still looking at his dials. The master gunner sat in the turret seat. The most touching scene occurred in the gun room, where several men hung on the lock in an attempt to open it.

At the first touch, he continued, "they all crumbled to ashes." The inactivity of the fleet, the grind of chores and drills, paltry rations, infrequent furloughs, and the chafing under overweening, denigrating division officers had already cut into sailors' morale before the battle—but now this? Could German sailors trust German naval leadership?[2]

Only one consolation in all of this destruction comforted somewhat: the knowledge that it could have been—indeed, should have been—much worse. Sailors on
Derfflinger and *Seydlitz* told the visitors about British armor-piercing shells failing
to penetrate, indeed breaking to pieces against the main 12-inch armor belt when
descending from high angles at long range. This certainly paid tribute to German
ship design but even more so to some flaw in the enemy's "laughable" ordnance,
or so the officers said.[3] Even the 13.5-inch shell that struck *Seydlitz* outside D-turret
splintered against the thinner 9.1-inch barbette armor, destroying nearby rooms
but not penetrating and detonating properly inside the turret—a fiery piece of the
barbette itself did the dirty deed.

■ ■ ■

Franz Hipper, still upset by the utterly unacceptable outcome of January 24, looked
over the latest reports from his squadron captains, this set concerning technical
improvements made necessary by the Battle of Dogger Bank. Late January had turned
to early April, so the task of pondering their recommendations and completing the
paperwork he hated took place in the vice admiral's familiar day suite on *Seydlitz*, the
flagship having been repaired from the extensive damage inflicted during the running
fight. The commander of Germany's battlecruisers also needed time in dock for rest
and recuperation. Seven months of war, especially the crushing, staggering loss of
his modernized armored cruiser, one of his favorite captains, and over a thousand
sailors, had clearly taken a toll. Already before the sortie he had complained of being
"overburdened" and in pain from arthritis, bursitis, and sciatica—"physically and
psychologically at the end of his tether," as one of his captains, the insensitive Magnus
von Levetzow, captain of *Moltke*, reported to superiors—but by spring 1915, Hipper
was well on the way to the severe combat fatigue and "terrible pain and exhaustion"
that would finally place him on medical leave a year later.[4]

Hipper would never admit it, but his staff noticed a definite demoralization setting in as the weeks passed after their harrowing return. The tremendous speed of
the British battlecruisers "rankled within him," recalled one subaltern. Because his
ships had been caught uncomfortably off guard by the long-range fire of Beatty's
squadron, moreover, "a sort of envy had awakened in his soul," which gave rise
to doubts whether "German shipbuilding was after all superior." Also "weighing
seriously upon his mind" was the fact that the enemy had reached the edge of the
Dogger Bank in such great numbers, leaving only one conclusion to draw: they
had "quite obviously been waiting for him." But where had the British gotten their

information? Had British submarines reported his departure from Wilhelmshaven? Was the harbor riddled with enemy agents? Or were the vocal critics grouped around Raeder right about compromised codes?[5]

These doubts and worries factored heavily into Hipper's postbattle report. In stark contrast to German intelligence reports placing British battlecruiser squadrons far to the north at Scapa Flow—trusted so disastrously by High Seas Fleet C-in-C Friedrich von Ingenohl—the experience of January 24 showed "that the North Sea can in no way be considered [to have been] clear of the English fleet." Given the overall "superiority" of that fleet, Germany should attempt in future engagements to lure a portion of the enemy into a battleship- and submarine-aided trap in the Bight, the battlecruisers, *sans* weaker predreadnought vessels like *Blücher*, venturing no more than seventy miles from Helgoland before inviting chase back toward the main fleet—exactly what could have happened on January 24 if the High Seas Fleet had given timelier support. Any advance of the Scouting Groups and supporting battleships closer to the heavily defended (and apparently poorly reconnoitered) British coast would only present "easy booty" to the enemy and result in disaster.

Privately, he told all this to his chief. In fact, he bluntly—and surprisingly one-sidedly—blamed his defeat on Ingenohl's lack of help. The loyalty of the admiral's captains, he added even more stingingly, had been seriously undermined by the battle. "I have been very frank and honest with him," Hipper noted in his journal.[6] One has to wonder, however, whether the vice admiral's own eagerness to give battle, his brushing aside of Raeder's doubts, and the fact that he, too, had trusted intelligence reports also "rankled within him," deepening his postbattle depression. Clearly, Hipper needed to have been more openly "frank and honest" with himself.

Hipper's report put him in the unfamiliar company of 1st Squadron Chief Wilhelm von Lans, undoubtedly the least aggressive German naval commander. His memorandum, "Reflections on Our Maritime Situation," began to circulate throughout the upper ranks after the battle. The treatise downplayed the fleet's favorite strategy of winning victories in detail because to achieve this, it would have to reckon imprudently on British mistakes. Such a gamble could easily fail far out in the North Sea, where Germany's "inferior number of ships," allegedly also "inferior in design," could not break off engagement with "the manifoldly superior [British] fleet." Like Hipper, Lans was impressed with enemy numbers, speed, and proclivity for long-range firing, but added naval ordnance to the list, namely, the Royal Navy's 13.5- and 15-inch shells, which he claimed were "decidedly superior to our [11- and] 12-inch [shells] at great ranges." As he had said many times before, Lans favored mine- and submarine-aided traps in the Bight that could produce partial victories far closer to home. Finally, he warned against the advice of those impulsive advocates of attacking simply for the sake of attacking, who strove for a risky showdown battle that would ruinously devalue the fleet's worth in postwar diplomatic equations.[7]

As Hipper's report showed, Lans was not alone in his reluctance to charge at British windmills, but this cautious sentiment now extended far beyond Lans and Hipper, in fact into nearly every corner of the German naval officer corps. The widespread notion that it appeared better to do nothing was especially evident, but especially saddening, to those officers who opposed this viewpoint. Thus Adolph von Trotha, the cerebral, circumspect captain of battleship SMS *Kaiser*, whose considered opinion on naval matters Tirpitz and many others at the top valued, pointed to the Kaiser's meek directives, the disappointment of December 16, and the tragedy of January 24 as factors "suppressing the drive to attack—the fleet has become more cautious." Tirpitz, too, mourned the "evaporation of the splendid spirit that prevailed in August," replaced by the sagging confidence of "a host of those who vote for remaining inactive." Albert Hopman, one of Tirpitz's loyal, aggressive aides, also bemoaned the poor seafaring fighting spirit he observed now in the German navy, a deficiency that would prevent it from "doing anything against a fleet like England's." Raeder agreed, lamenting the fact that "Lans's well-known think-piece is unfortunately judged all too favorably throughout the fleet." None of the squadron commanders, not even Hipper, who was "not a leader," nor Scheer, whose seemingly endless shakedowns in the Baltic "satisfied his sense of combat duty," possessed the right "offensive-minded" stuff. He would not "waste any words" on the rest of the top brass. "We don't have any leaders, they are all mere peacetime admirals."[8] Raeder's critique probably reflected his frustration with those lackluster leaders like Lans who professed confidence in German codes but were cowed further into inaction by their seemingly self-serving belief in other, less likely causes like submarine scouts or enemy agents, rather than bucking up, issuing orders securely by courier, and sallying forth like real men. The British may have been right, therefore, in assuming that their victory at Dogger Bank would result in a relatively quiet spell in the North Sea.

In this mood of subdued caution and diminished optimism about "whether German shipbuilding was after all superior," Hipper read over the aforementioned reports. In February, the C-in-C had asked what changes should be made to ships' material after the bitter experience of January 24. Hipper digested the suggestions of his battlecruiser captains, whom he canvassed in March, and submitted his recommendations.[9] Given the firing from unheard of ranges, the thicker belt armor on

German capital ships offered no protection from shells plunging through weaker deck and barbette armor. Therefore, a series of auxiliary measures in and around the turrets was required. Hatches from magazines to adjacent turrets needed to be padlocked and cross-ventilation ducks removed to prevent the spread of flash fires; topside ventilation ducks installed to direct fires and dissipate explosions upward; and armored grates placed on top of smoke funnels to guard against aerial bombing—the next airplane might have better luck than the lone homebound raider of the Cuxhaven raid on First Christmas. In new ship construction, moreover, thicker armor should be added to decks, turrets, turret barbettes, and belt armor near magazines.

But a few improvements that had "dawned quickly on those who stared at the burnt-out after turrets of *Seydlitz*" got underway in February, well before all reports landed on Hipper's desk.[10] These included the equipping of shell and cordite hoists "with [heavily layered double-asbestos flap] doors which close automatically after the cages have passed,"[11] as well as strict regulations against unpacking cordite charges from their flameproof metal cases and stacking them in working chambers. Those charges that had been unpacked would now be less susceptible to flash, furthermore, because the Germans encased the main portion of the charge and its black powder igniter in a brass cartridge while double-bagging the smaller portion of the charge in silk with no igniter. Obviously—and understandably—the German High Seas Fleet drew different conclusions from the Battle of Dogger Bank than the Royal Navy: while the latter loosened or abandoned safety regulations adopted earlier, the former atoned for previous laxity and introduced new rules based on a recent searing experience. Acting on another lesson learned from January 24, the Germans also increased the range of their big guns a few thousand yards by cutting away armor from the turret embrasures and elevating barrels from 13.5 to 16 degrees on battleships, and from 13.5 to 20 degrees on battlecruisers.[12]

■ ■ ■

These alterations spawned mixed emotions in Tirpitz, for any change at all represented an implied harsh critique of his prewar designs, and this made him bristle; but deep down he knew that improvements also meant a greater, not a lesser, chance of victory. When it came to Lans's circular, however, the former sentiment prevailed. He castigated the tract as nothing short of "poison for the spirit of the fleet" with its "incredible, entirely nonsensical, contaminating underestimation of our combative power and overestimation of the enemy's." Tirpitz had good reason to be angered about his detractors' "underestimation of our combative power," for he had built

German capital ships of sturdy stuff—they had thicker armor than British ships, from one to six inches more in the main belts, which was made of the highest quality: hard-to-penetrate Krupp nickel-cemented steel. He also backed up armor belts with cleverly placed coal bunkers, interior torpedo bulkheads, antimine double bottoms, and fifteen to eighteen watertight compartments, making his "honeycombed" vessels as close to unsinkable and impregnable as one could attain—a reason, perhaps, why turret rules, lax in retrospect, seemed adequate before Dogger Bank. Righteously incensed, therefore, the father of the German navy whipped his supporters into action to purge the navy of Lans's "ruinous" timidity.[13]

Their rebuttals during late winter and spring 1915 hotly disputed the assumption of a near inevitable defeat at sea. Besides the indisputable fact of good German ship construction, they had another ace in the hole, for they could convincingly dispute Lans's claims about the superiority of British gunnery and ordnance, pointing instead to "the superiority of German armor-piercing shells, which even the Fleet C-in-C has confirmed," said Rear Admiral Carl Schaumann, second-in-command to 3rd Squadron Chief Scheer. In fact, since Dogger Bank, it was common knowledge on the German side—from able seamen all the way up to the fleet commander—that this was the weak side of Lans' piece, for British ordnance had badly underperformed. "Our 12-inch gun performs just as well as the English 13.5-inch, in fact it is even better," exclaimed another Tirpitz man. "Our shooting, gauged by the number of hits and *their effect*, even at the longest range, was superior to the English." Yet another advocate of action confidently sounded this refrain: "A conclusion to take from the course of the January 24th battle is: (1) that our artillery shot better, and (2) that it had a *better effect*." Indeed, in the high-caliber duel of battlecruisers against one another—*Seydlitz, Moltke*, and *Derfflinger* versus *Lion, Tiger*, and *Princess Royal*—the former scored twenty-two hits; the latter, six.[14]

The aggressors added other arguments to the mix. Both times the entire German fleet had gone out—December 16 and January 24—the main body had failed to capitalize on golden opportunities for victory in detail: on the "Hartlepool" Raid because Ingenohl turned back prematurely; at Dogger Bank because he came out too late. Schaumann waxed especially assertive about going far out to seize victory after the British committed large naval forces that spring to the battle against Turkey underway at the Dardanelles Straits and Gallipoli Peninsula.[15] Further strengthening the case for action while the British drew away their ships, Schaumann pointed to the allegedly inherent advantage bequeathed to North Sea attackers: "It lies in the nature of offensives that they create uncertainty and force enemies into sudden purposeless decisions and mistakes, not to mention that the long open expanse of the English coast and the geographic contours of the North Sea theater make it unlikely the enemy in all his numbers will be able to block an attacking German fleet, for it, not the enemy, determines the time and place of the engagement."[16] Germany's superior gunnery and ordnance "in addition to everything else, must lead to the desired success of the operations we have proposed." The Hotspurs, of course, had chosen to ignore Lans when he wrote that the fleet "is especially restricted in its freedom of movement because English submarines and agents can easily observe our activities." Most of them had also swept aside the deep skepticism of officers like Raeder concerning the insecurity of German naval codes, even though his arguments merely favored a safer, more secure path to victory at sea.[17] Knowing that being "more cautious" could sometimes be the right way to attack, Adolf von Trotha of battleship *Kaiser* may well have been one of the skeptics alongside Raeder.

■ ■ ■

These widely differing points of view on operational issues narrowed almost to nothing when it came to Ingenohl's future as C-in-C. Opinions varied on who should replace him, but opposing factions united in wanting Ingenohl sacked, generating so much ire against him that only a little of this vitriol touched Hipper—Levetzow of *Moltke* intrigued against his 1st SG chief, and Raeder, too, said less than kind things, rumblings that would crescendo, but not until 1916. The most damning statement against Ingenohl, a very representative one, came from Captain Zenker, Pohl's staff chief in Admiralty Staff (and later captain of *Von der Tann*), who condemned the "lack of foresight and prudence" that shone through the chief's defensive after-battle report. The misplaced belief that British battlecruisers had been coaling at Scapa Flow could not excuse his "astonishing and regrettable" lack of back up for Hipper. It was certainly no "remarkable coincidence,"[18] as Ingenohl claimed, that other elements of the huge Royal Navy would be on guard duty far off their coast—even if the battlecruisers had been at Scapa—especially after the shock to Great Britain of the Scarborough-Whitby-Hartlepool Raid, which also demonstrated that nation's uncanny foreknowledge of German movements in the North Sea.

Also reading Ingenohl's report with raised eyebrows, Privy Naval Cabinet Chief Georg von Müller, who heretofore had resisted removing the fleet chief, came "with heavy heart" to the same conclusion. To his surprise, however, the task of convincing the Kaiser to dump Ingenohl proved very easy. The monarch showed "not a trace of human sympathy" for one of his favorite appointees, a coldness that took Müller aback even though he knew William so well. The damage after December 16 to his already tarnished reputation in Britain probably still rankled with the moody emperor so that he desired dissociation from Ingenohl. When it came to the next topic, the successor C-in-C, the cabinet chief ran through a list of unacceptable admirals before recommending Admiralty Staff Chief Hugo von Pohl, whose prudently cautious views thus far in the war had been compatible with those of his indecisive sovereign—at least the Kaiser's "prudently cautious views" since early January—that William accepted immediately. Whether Müller mentioned Reinhard Scheer's name among the unwanted is not known, but the wily adviser, ever mindful of the need to parry Tirpitz, seems to have been the one who undermined the Naval Secretary's machinations to promote the chief of 3rd Squadron, a ploy backed by Ingenohl's COS Eckermann and Tirpitz's loyal aide Albert Hopman. However, when Müller suggested Tirpitz—no doubt with a dose of dissimulating disingenuousness—as Pohl's replacement as head of the Admiralty Staff, the Kaiser "roundly refused," and then ranted against "nervous types" like the Naval Secretary who were completely "unsuitable" for service in his fleet. Clearly, William, a nervous type himself, had grown very tired of Tirpitz's intrigues and insistence on naval action that the head of state and navy believed—with the skillful finessing help of Müller and Bethmann Hollweg—to be politically, diplomatically, and militarily imprudent.[19]

Showing an impressive, seemingly genuine sympathy and concern for the human consequences of January 24, the sometimes insensitive Kaiser visited Wilhelmshaven. He observed the damage to *Seydlitz* and *Derfflinger* in dry dock and called on the wounded in military hospital. In the automobile drive to the infirmary with Tirpitz and Müller, the latter tried to wriggle an approval from Tirpitz on Pohl's appointment. "I had no other option. Among the admirals who came under consideration, he was the most suitable. I had to take him." "It's too bad that I was not asked," replied the navy founder and backer of Scheer. "I could have given you a better option."[20]

Hearing Tirpitz's remarks was too much for the emperor, who probably knew that his Naval Secretary had wanted Scheer. Arriving back at the imperial train for "second breakfast"—a common practice among well-to-do Germans before the blockade limited it to the super-rich—he seated himself between Tirpitz and his new fleet commander, Pohl, ignoring the former by turning with choice words to the latter: "I always said that our armor plate was too thin. *Blücher* was a totally miserable ship. Already in 1904 I wrote a memorandum which pointed out that we had use for only the very biggest cruisers. Much of the time Tirpitz had no idea, and regularly offended me."[21] Tirpitz must have rolled his eyes at the Kaiser's insulting—and ridiculous—assertion that he had anticipated Britain's battlecruiser revolution ahead of all his admirals and councilors. Müller undoubtedly enjoyed hearing Tirpitz put down so rudely until, shortly before the royal train departed for the Eastern front, the Kaiser turned to his loyal privy councilor: "What do you want here?" "To place myself at Your Majesty's disposal." "You call it 'at my disposal' when you always treat me so badly?"[22]

Müller's diary offers no direct explanation for why the emperor turned on him so abruptly but hints strongly at developments in the submarine war. Although Pohl had remained fairly consistent since August about not risking the surface fleet, he had waxed aggressive about using submarines against British (and other enemy) commerce, including this strategy in his recommendations to William in early January (see chapter 4). The Kaiser, however, favored the advice of Chancellor Bethmann Hollweg, who worried about repercussions among neutral nations like the United States if Germany sank their merchant ships by mistake. Bethmann finally gave in to Pohl in late January when the Admiralty Staff Chief agreed to give all nations a two-week warning before enforcing submarine warfare against enemy shipping in a declared war zone around Britain. Without warning, Pohl then plopped down the decree for the emperor's signature when William was aboard a steam shuttle to the dry docks at Wilhelmshaven. Outmaneuvered, and not consulted, Müller resented this "surprise attack" on the Kaiser, but His Highness seems to have blamed his privy cabinet chief for not shielding him.[23]

In early May, however, Pohl's maneuver put Germany on course to one of the worst atrocities of the war with the sinking of the British passenger liner *Lusitania*. Passing south of Ireland off the Old Head of Kinsale with no Royal Navy escort—very likely another scheme of NID Chief Reginald Hall, although this one failed to trigger American entry to the war against Germany[24]—she was hit with one torpedo from *U-20*. The ship sank in eighteen minutes, killing 1,201 people, including 94 children, many of them babies, and 128 American citizens. An irate British public shook fists at Germany over a crime that, incredulously, was much worse than the Scarborough-Whitby-Hartlepool Raid.

After another British liner, *Arabic*, went down in the same spot three months later, killing forty-four passengers and crew (and another three U.S. citizens), William and Bethmann ordered the submarine corps to abide by international law that required search, seizure, and abandonment of ships by crew and passengers before sinking. Rather than submit to a procedure they considered dangerous to U-boat crews—Britain had armed many merchant ships and issued orders to ram—sub commanders refused to wage commerce warfare under these restrictions, but Germany had again averted war with the United States. Nearly three hundred allied merchant ships had been sunk, but these losses did not seriously disrupt a British economy that drew four thousand ships to its harbors every month. The diplomatic crisis had claimed Pohl's replacement in the Admiralty Staff, Admiral Gustav Bachmann, whom William sacked for wanting to continue the sinkings. Tirpitz submitted his resignation, but the Kaiser, although tempted by what he saw as an unacceptable act of desertion, refused to accept it—another sign in 1915 of his struggle to guard more assertively his naval authority (see below). Nevertheless, mutinous rumblings, impossible not to hear or ignore, sounded.

■ ■ ■

Long before the subs were recalled, Pohl had faced the question of using the surface fleet to produce naval victories, end the blockade, and help win the war. Raising his flag on *Friedrich der Grosse* in early February, he immediately noticed the "subdued mood" among high-ranking officers who did not hide their feeling of allegedly technical inferiority to the British in torpedo boats, light cruisers, and capital ship armament, "sins" he and many others blamed on Tirpitz. Even Scheer seemed to have lost his desire for action, the circumspect side of his Janus-face in full view (see chapter 4). "Only when one actually has gotten an instrument in hand to do work with," wrote Pohl, "does he notice what difficulties there are in using it." These circumstances, reinforced by two of Hipper's ships in dry dock, Scheer's 3rd Squadron still exercising in the Baltic, and bad winter weather, quickly altered the more aggressive state of mind Pohl believed—not without a degree of self-flattering self-deception—he had adopted a month earlier. To his wife he poured out feelings about wanting so much to aid the war effort with the ships he now commanded, but only when the right moment appeared. "I must wait for an opportunity, but when and where is one offered me? It weighs heavy on my conscience having to work with inadequate means."[25]

By March, Pohl had *Seydlitz* and *Derfflinger* back from repairs and Sheer's eight dreadnoughts back from the Baltic. He also knew, as Schaumann noted, about the comparative advantages of German AP shells. Furthermore, he presided over ongoing safety and long-range firing renovations; plus Scheer, the fleet commander *manqué*, waxed cautiously more assertive (see chapter 7, notes 19 and 25, and chapter 8, note 8). All this increased Pohl's desire for action, which grew even more by the need he felt as early as this—a desire which burned hotter as the year unfolded—to upstage Tirpitz's "party of the opposition," which he had to assume included Scheer.[26] But Pohl also seems to have become genuinely more aggressive, lending credence to the old saying that "the office makes the man."

> They did not place me here [he wrote his wife again] to stay in harbor. Person-
> ally, I feel an inner pressure to do more. . . . . They had trust in me to make the
> best and the possible out of this difficult situation. I will show them that they
> were not mistaken. I will win when it comes to battle. . . . My staff and squadron
> chiefs are much more against this than I. It is really remarkable: I always have
> to struggle, earlier against the sorties wanted by Tirpitz, now against excessive
> caution. . . . I really want to go frightfully far out to sea to just once engage the
> enemy more closely. My fingers itch to go out, but I must wait, wait.

It was significant that he did not limit his newfound courage to spousal correspondence behind closed doors, but pressed Müller in mid-March 1915 to have the Kaiser
strengthen his January directive by giving the fleet chief a genuinely free hand. "It is a
contradiction to allow the fleet to make sorties, but with the proviso that for political
reasons, which I thoroughly understand, it must remain fully intact. Every sortie,
even if it extends only seventy miles from Helgoland, can lead to the full deployment
of the [High Seas] Fleet, for after the battle on January 24th, no one can expect me
to send the [Scouting Groups] out alone and not come to their aid with ships of the
line if they are in distress." To his chief of staff, Captain William Michaelis, Pohl
also expressed his burning desire "to do something" and "finally have that success."
For his part, Michaelis made it clear—obviously from discussions with Pohl—that
any move by the fleet into the Bight could produce something as inconsequential
as minor losses from mines and submarines, or, on the other hand, develop from
the mere sighting of "smoke clouds" into "the big battle"[27] as destroyers and light
cruisers sucked both main fleets into fiery conflagration.

However, in challenging the emperor's cautious operational decisions of January (see
chapter 4), the Admiralty Staff soon encountered a William who had been wrestling
subconsciously since then, and not without a measure of success, to further fortify the
flimsy façade framing his malleably fragile inner being. Pohl summarized his position
in a memorandum to the Kaiser on March 23. Weather permitting, and assuming the
entire fleet were available for action, for instance to support mining operations beyond
the Bight, he wanted to go out. Such circumstances could lead to clashes with either
a part or the whole of the enemy fleet. Battle could happen "automatically," in fact,
"because reconnaissance is too weak to report the position of the English fleet in a
timely [enough] manner [to break off]." If scouting forces on both sides engaged and

"the enemy accepts battle, our main fleet will back the battlecruisers in the attack. It follows from experience, as well as the spirit inherent in Your Majesty's [well]-trained fleet, that in such instances we accept battle even against a more powerful foe. And then at least the hope exists that the harm done is not one-sided."

When Müller laid Pohl's report before his sovereign, however, an angry William, his bombastic persona clutching the naval reins, the last area of real imperial control left to him, smashed his fist onto the table, shouting, "I don't want to see any more memoranda—I have ordered the fleet to stay in, and that's that!"[28] The nervous recipient of this outburst could at least be consoled that the brunt of it was aimed at someone else. The Kaiser dispatched one of his sons, Prince Adalbert, to Wilhelmshaven, who gave Pohl this bad news on March 30, a day after he had taken the entire fleet ninety miles beyond Helgoland past the edge of the Bight—his first uneventful sortie.

The deft Müller had at least gotten the emperor to agree to hear counterarguments from Admiralty Staff Chief Gustav Bachmann, another Tirpitz ally, whom the Kaiser sacked later in September. The confrontation went back and forth for some time, Bachmann pushing for Pohl to have a free hand; William insisting that "I have no intention of again placing my costly fleet at risk" in a "sea full of danger" teeming with "mines and enemy periscopes"; Bachman countering that Pohl had just gone out safely; the Kaiser then blurting "but I have ordered that the fleet make no more sorties!"; to which Bachman replied firmly that Prince Adalbert had told him of such an order, "but I found that impossible because an order like this would never have been issued without going through me." William then gave Bachmann a "moments-long entirely indescribable look and face that made me think 'you'll either be flying out of here undignified in a second or else you've gotten the upper hand.'" As Bachmann braced himself, the Kaiser's angry glare turned into "a sort of smile," his psychic meekness forced to the surface by the stronger Bachmann, and he said, "Well, if the North Sea is really not so dangerous the fleet can move out again, but of course taking precautions!"

And so a compromise was agreed upon. The C-in-C would have the freedom to sortie without prior imperial permission as long as he reconnoitered adequately and followed long-standing operational goals, namely, to avoid putting the fleet in jeopardy of being destroyed by superior British forces. Pohl would have to "break off" from such an "unfavorable" engagement. This is what Ingenohl thought he had done in December; but would Pohl do so, especially having stated his belief that fleets at sea, absent adequate intelligence and omniscient reconnaissance, could be drawn "automatically" into a major clash?[29]

Pohl's second sortie in force took place on April 17–18. His staff had patched together various reports from German agents and neutral steamship captains that pointed to intense British warship activity in the North Sea over the previous week—indeed, the Grand Fleet had been out. Reaching the conclusion that the enemy intended to maintain some sort of a siege on the Bight, Pohl sent two German light cruisers to lay a minefield about ninety miles south of the SWP. Pohl's fleet came out during the night to protect the returning light cruisers, destroy any enemy ships on siege patrol, and, if encountering heavier opposition they may have provoked into coming out, "accept battle even against a more powerful foe," thereby quashing "the enemy's claim that he alone controlled the North Sea [because] the German fleet was bottled up."

The Admiralty in London having been alerted by Room 40, Fisher warned Jellicoe, "VON POHL HAS SOMETHING ON! That is quite certain!" The British fleet went out again into its northerly defensive positions, but no clash occurred. "We really thought the battle would be joined today!" Fisher wrote again on the seventeenth. "Everything pointed to it. . . . They had arranged not to return till dawn of the 19th or night of the 19th, and suddenly a very urgent and immediate order was given [today] for the whole fleet to return home." Because it seems highly doubtful that either Pohl or Bachmann would have issued (or wanted) such an order, historians are left to ponder the possibility that either the Kaiser had changed his mind, as he would do again, admittedly feebly, that autumn, or some other interference came from higher-ups. Had William perhaps been finessed by others like Bethmann Hollweg and Müller, the man of many faces, to keep his "fleet in being" for postwar diplomatic leverage? Only three weeks earlier, Bachmann, reconsidering what he had accomplished personally with the Kaiser, wrote to his disappointed representative in Berlin, the hawk Paul Behncke, that any chance for "more offensive action . . . lay outside the realm of the possible . . . [given] the sovereign's contrary mood and opinion."[30]

Regardless, the cheeky C-in-C put out again on April 21–22, this time pushing much farther, 120 miles northwest of Helgoland, only an hour or so from the spot near the 55th Parallel Hipper had reached on January 24. Three Zeppelins up hundreds of feet peered ahead of the battlecruisers deep into the snowy, rain-and-hail-soaked Dogger Bank. Ready to spring, a mere ten miles behind Hipper, steamed the High Seas Fleet. Altogether, Pohl had ninety-seven war craft at sea.[31]

Although the wet, blustery weather obstructed visibility, an animated spirit swept through his massive steel armada. "Perhaps this time something will happen," thought a seaman on SMS *Helgoland* to himself. "And why not? If we went as far out as last time, maybe we would run across the English. Up ahead the [light cruiser] bait [in our trap] was calling back and forth on the wireless. Hopefully the English would intercept their messages and come out to find us. And then it will begin: crashes and thunder, splintering masts and a boiling sea."[32]

Nearby in SMS *Kaiser* of 3rd Squadron, her captain, Adolph von Trotha, one of Tirpitz's staunchest advocates (see chapter 8), strained to see anything, but also sensed through the mucky weather the proximity of battle action. In contrast to Pohl's first sortie, which Trotha mocked as a useless "walk in the park with no military purpose," the fleet chief's next two operations impressed him with their "wish and will for action," filling him with "more hope and joy as I look into the future."[33] Just as doubters like Lans worried, however, Trotha thought deeply enough to know that the "wish and will for action" could have its tragic side, the more or less so depending on the quality of German leadership.

Although neither man knew it, the British indeed listened this day—and the previous day too. Once again, Room 40 had alerted the recoaled squadrons at Rosyth and Scapa Flow, which had again put to sea a few hours before Hipper and Pohl.[34] And once again loved ones had said prayers for their men, who departed again into always dangerous possibilities. To the men of the Royal Navy themselves, however, the aggressive state of mind psychologically necessary when heading into that perilous unknown made them stoic. As Lieutenant Filson Young of *Lion* put it, he expected "circumstances at sea that could promise to be more than usually exciting." But this time, too, nothing happened—the two fleets did not collide. The letdown was universally palpable. "We had come back to harbor with that slight sense of anti-climax that always follows an uneventful stunt in the North Sea," lamented Young. "Another time of tension and strenuous expectation has not been fulfilled."[35] On the German side, this somewhat irrational sense of disappointment resonated with common seamen, captains like Trotha, and even the fleet commander himself. "Unfortunately, we saw nothing of the enemy, he has crept into hiding," Pohl wrote to his wife. "Too bad, for I really wanted to run a few of his ships aground."[36]

Like his seamen and officers, Pohl did not know that a larger fleet patrolled two hundred miles to the northeast, but the denigrating words in his letter reflected a clear awareness that "hiding" lay in British interests, while offering battle on German terms did not. Because Room 40 had not divined exact German intentions, the Admiralty, gambling that the Channel-Yarmouth area was not the aim of the enemy operation, had ordered Jellicoe and Beatty to take up defensive stations north and east of the Dogger Bank, locations about one hundred miles west of the opening to the Skagerrak channel between Norway and Denmark (see map 1.1)—after the gutting of the Cabal in May, Jellicoe would determine coordinates. Beatty's BCF represented the "advanced force" some sixty miles below Jellicoe, "far enough to the southward to deal with a direct attack across the breadth of the North Sea," while Jellicoe's Grand Fleet lay "far enough back to prevent the enemy evading it to crush the 10th Cruiser Squadron,"[37] whose forty armed merchant cruisers based at Liverpool, Glasgow, and other ports up to Scapa Flow manned the northern sea lanes of the blockade barring goods of all nations from reaching Germany. From their guarding positions, Beatty and Jellicoe could also block the Germans from seizing or mining the Skagerrak and depriving Britain of the remaining trade with Scandinavia. Maintaining the blockade and defending trade routes lay in Britain's interests, therefore, while looking for battle south of the Dogger Bank—and attempting against operational realities to guard Britain's entire North Sea coastline—did not.

■ ■ ■

In May, Pohl twice repeated his strategy of daring the British to foolishly forget their interests and cross into waters closer to Germany. The outcome of these sorties was again "too bad," for Jellicoe and Beatty came out, to be sure, but both times avoided the baited south.[38] As spring expired in June, therefore, Pohl drew the only conclusion he could that would lead to battle under favorable circumstances, the scenario he now so genuinely desired. He would threaten the commercial sea lanes west of the Skagerrak with Hipper's forces, while the High Seas Fleet itself lay in support only thirty miles south at Little Fisher Bank.

Pohl wanted to schedule the operation for late July or early August 1915 when all capital ships (with the exception of dry-docked battlecruiser *Derfflinger*) would be available for action. After the second April sortie, the C-in-C had seen scouting reports from U-boats belatedly informing him of the northeasterly position of the Grand Fleet that day. Intelligence gathered by the enemy, which he believed came from submarines, merchant ships, and embedded agents, "meant with great probability," Pohl wrote in his battle log, that the plans of the High Seas Fleet "must reach England with surprising speed," guaranteeing that "the enemy is always more or less exactly informed of our intentions."[39] By rushing north, therefore, "the Fleet Chief knew very well that in doing this he had to seriously consider the possibility of engaging not only isolated enemy forces," wrote Otto Groos, navigation officer in *Von der Tann*, "but also being drawn into battle with the entire English fleet."[40]

In early August, however, this bold and promising operation had to be canceled because Prince Heinrich, commanding Germany's obsolete Baltic Fleet, insisted on

Hipper's battlecruisers and 1st Squadron supporting an action against the Russians at Riga. The Kaiser's brother, determined to prove army critics wrong who scoffed at the navy's paltry contribution to the war effort, got the ships over Pohl's objections.[41] The rest of the High Seas Fleet had to idle in port even though the army itself had not placed great worth on naval help during its quest to overrun the long Russian Front stretching from the Baltic to Galicia. The prince's failed Riga operation was called off after two weeks in August, as well as the army's more successful offensive on the Eastern Front at summer's end, without, however, knocking Russia out of the war.

Pohl now returned his gaze to the Skagerrak, a plan that offered promise for the navy, not the army, to win the war. This would also represent a great personal victory for the C-in-C, not only by slaying the English Dragon, but also by "beating to death [Tirpitz's] party of the opposition,"[42] which had resumed a blistering critique of Pohl's alleged unwillingness to engage the Royal Navy.[43] In working out the operational plan early that autumn, Michaelis returned aggressively to an idea tested in prewar games and maneuvers, a strategy that Pohl had proposed repeatedly in May and June, namely, that his ships return via the Danish Belts to Kiel. Because this would have violated Danish neutrality, Bachmann of the Admiralty Staff could not gain approval for the earlier requests.[44]

The notion of running the Belts had grown even more controversial and widely discussed as a result of a remarkable trilogy of strategic think-pieces circulating in the German navy as summer turned to fall. Penned by the chief of staff of 1st Squadron, Lieutenant Commander Wolfgang Wegener, they doubted the likelihood of luring the British into the Bight, but also opposed the pet preferences of Tirpitz's satraps for rashly pushing across the Dogger Bank into unpredictable and unfavorable circumstances. Instead, Wegener substituted the much bolder idea of seizing the Skagerrak-Kattegat channels and the Belts, even to the point of flaunting international law, militarily occupying Denmark, and using Danish Skagen and the Faeroe Islands as naval bases. He wrote,

> It is evident that once we seize the Skagerrak, [English] trade and England's exercise of sea control will become so insignificant there that . . . the English might be prompted to [react]. . . . [Moreover], the Skagerrak, resting along the same latitude as Scotland, forms the gate to the Atlantic. England must feel extremely threatened militarily by the possibility that we could break her North Sea barrier and open the way to the Atlantic from [the Skagerrak]. . . . She will immediately recognize this position as our springboard to the Faeroe Islands. This broader, strategic importance of the Skagerrak position accords it such

value as to give the English sufficient inducement to do battle, even should
[control of] the sea lane alone not appear sufficiently important. . . . [To repeat,
preying upon the Skagerrak-Tyne sea lane] should not be judged according to
its absolute effectiveness as trade warfare, but as a means to lure English naval
forces closer to us—without running the risk of [perchance] having to engage
in a decisive battle . . . [further west in enemy waters].

Wegener realized that establishing a base on the Faeroe Islands and expanding
further into the Atlantic to the Azores and Cape Verde could very well be tasks for
the so-called Second Punic War frequently mentioned that year in German naval
circles, but "no one knows today what political surprises this war may still bring."
Even during the First Punic War, therefore, latter day Romans must look beyond
the North Sea. "The German fleet exists; we must help it into the saddle; it will know
how to ride."[45]

The Wegener treatises form the backdrop to Pohl's Skagerrak mission. Not surprisingly, Pohl, Michaelis, Fleet Operations Chief Hans Seebohm, and Wegener's
1st Squadron commander Vice Admiral Ehrhard Schmidt evaluated the trilogy
positively, as did Hipper and many of his staff who had liked the idea before the war.
Pohl consistently stressed the need to use the Belts whatever the Danish reaction,
while leaving aside Wegener's more far-reaching designs on the Faeroe Islands and
Cape Verde, which stood outside this operation. And once again the Admiralty Staff,
headed now by a sympathetic Admiral Henning von Holtzendorff, who had replaced
Bachmann after the submarine controversy in September, could not gain approval
for the fleet to return via the Belts to Kiel. Both the Foreign Office, which worried
about the reaction of other neutral nations, and the Army General Staff, which had
no extra troops to invade Denmark, had overridden him.[46]

Despite these imposed constraints, Hipper steamed north at 1900 (7:00 p.m.)
on October 23, Pohl following at 2200, altogether ninety-three warships at sea. Five
Zeppelin scouts rose to reconnoiter at 0200 on the twenty-fourth when the trailing
main fleet had reached thirty miles south of Horns Reef (see map 1.1). At this point
the fleet changed course to the northwest, intending to alter again to the north a
few hours later. The operation called for Hipper's battlecruisers to reach Little Fisher
Bank in early afternoon, the battle squadrons positioned thirty miles farther south.

The well-briefed officers knew that a clash at sea loomed as a distinct possibility.
German intelligence reported correctly that Beatty and the Harwich Force of destroyers and light cruisers had patrolled off the Skagerrak three days earlier and guessed
that they, or other squadrons, might return soon to guard the busy Tyne-Skagerrak

sea lane—"guessing" stood in such stark contrast, of course, to Room 40's superior assembling of operational hints and facts. While opinions remained sharply divided about Pohl's deep-down desire for battle, on this day most of the officers waxed "very exultant" that a great day of reckoning had come. Thus it came to many of them like "a blow to the head"[47] when the chief called off the mission shortly after first light.

The airships had returned to their hangars due to a boisterous southeasterly wind, depriving Pohl of his best reconnaissance. Moreover, during the night Holtzendorff had relayed Prince Heinrich's demand for the immediate detachment of two of Pohl's five destroyer flotillas, which deprived the capital ships of adequate protection from enemy submarines and destroyers. The resulting order, counter order, and disorder shed more light on the sad influence of German royals on the Great War at sea. Something similar may have restrained Pohl's initiative on April 17.[48]

However rational his decision to go back, Pohl had irreparably exacerbated his officer-relations dilemma by seeming to return to Wilhelmshaven prematurely with no trophies. His critics now took full advantage, lambasting his alleged over-anxiousness, lack of bold martial qualities, and unwillingness to push further out in the North Sea to punish the enemy, even excoriating his support for Wegener, whom Levetzow accused of defensive-minded cowardice for substituting attention on the Skagerrak for the allegedly superior strategy of taking the war directly to Britain's shores.[49]

A report to Privy Naval Cabinet Chief Müller by one of Pohl's destroyer flotilla commanders, Karl von Restorff, nicely illustrated the C-in-C's increasingly no-win dilemma. Many of the chief's opponents believed that the Kaiser had given him a completely free hand but that the coward simply would not use it. Restorff, who himself believed, incorrectly, that Pohl had been fully fettered—in fact he was free to go out without permission, but, once at sea, not to risk the most dangerous actions—wanted the Kaiser to come to Wilhelmshaven and state publicly that Pohl did not have a free hand, and in this way "take some of the odium away from the [C-in-C] for unnecessarily holding the fleet back in the river mouths."[50] As explained above, Pohl had not gone back to base because of shackling rules of engagement, but would the problematic Kaiser perceive the need to help his fleet commander and improve morale by visiting the naval base?

Restorff's proposal came in the aftermath of another episode that reflected the same confused state of affairs in the German navy.[51] Before and after Pohl's Skagerrak mission, Prince Adalbert asked his royal father whether Pohl had authority to undertake risky operations such as October 24 that appeared to serve only the personal vanity of the Fleet Chief. Although not exactly on the mark by disapproving of Pohl's newfound aggressiveness, Adalbert actually shot closer to the mark than most of the critics. William answered indignantly that Pohl must ask beforehand for permission. Hearing about this, Privy Naval Counselor Müller, wearing another hat for the occasion, lamented that "the Kaiser himself does not know anymore exactly what orders he has given the fleet."[52] So the privy counselor asked Holtzendorff to maneuver William back to his March decision. This done, the Kaiser agreed to travel to Wilhelmshaven and personally clarify the nature of Pohl's autonomy, which, given the hostile mood of the "party of the opposition" described by Restorff, would not have helped Pohl. His Highness kept postponing what he deemed his own publicly embarrassing loss of naval authority, however, and the wily Müller held back, so the controversy continued to fester at Pohl's expense. His no-win position now seemed irredeemable, in fact, for the ongoing row completely overshadowed a fact which might have helped him: namely, that on October 24 the British had not been at sea.

By early 1916, the controversy over Pohl's performance had grown even worse. On January 6, he sat through a severe two-hour critique of his leadership by the talented but fiery, sharp-tongued Captain Magnus von Levetzow of *Moltke*. The sixty-year-old C-in-C had gotten wind of the forty-five-year-old's views and summoned him for a face-to-face.[53] Pohl tried hard to convince the junior commander of the unfairness of such negativity, citing accommodations he had received, boasting of many instances of past personal bravery, pointing to the recent sorties he had in fact made; but arguing, on the other hand, that the dangers of mines and submarines as well as political difficulties with the Kaiser warranted caution. Someday history would render a positive verdict. Levetzow remained firm, however, claiming that the officer corps had no faith in their chief and that all prewar preparations had been for naught. Here the captain had crossed the line: he did not speak for the entire officer corps, many of whom remained wary of confronting the Royal Navy, but only for the "opposition party." Realizing too late the wisdom of the old saying that "explaining is losing," the C-in-C now lost all patience, asserting that it would go hard on those who disagreed with their chief but themselves lacked the ability to lead officers and men. Pohl had essentially thrown the younger man's criticisms back in his face.

The mounting criticism of his leadership and character took a toll on the chief's health, which had never been robust. Seeing Pohl once before the war, for instance, Jellicoe thought, he "does not look very healthy, always white and transparent-looking."[54] But the rigors and tremendous emotional weight of command, coupled with the added stress of the nasty, demonizing fight with the Hotspurs, seems to have exacerbated or perhaps even unleashed a hyper-stress-induced liver cancer. By late 1915, it had grown hard for him to carry on due to fatigue, waning appetite, and weight loss, but he "stuck through it without letting it become noticeable." Three days after the confrontation with Levetzow—and many contemporaries believed because of that meeting—Pohl's condition took a drastic turn for the worse. He "collapsed catastrophically"[55] and was transferred from his flagship to the infirmary. The incurable disease claimed him six weeks later.

Even after Pohl had passed, his opponents did not soften their judgment of him. Years later, his own flag lieutenant, Ernst von Weizsäcker, believed that his former chief had accomplished nothing except "to transform the fighting spirit of the fleet into apathy." One of Hipper's staffers, Hugo von Waldeyer-Hartz, recalled that Pohl "soothed his conscience with the assurance that he was at any rate doing something, [but] he never so much as contemplated the idea of seizing the initiative in the North Sea at any cost." Moritz von Egidy, captain of *Seydlitz*, hardened the tongue-in-cheek wish of Paul Eckermann—Ingenohl's COS had quipped that Pohl ought to be chloroformed (see chapter 2)—by praising Levetzow for pushing the man over the edge: "Oh this Pohl, this vain fop! Magnus, that you have freed us from this tramp; this is a deed worthy of recognition only by the *Pour le Mérite*."[56]

But perhaps Raeder, an officer never shy with his private criticisms, should have the last word. He disagreed that Pohl "sought in principle to avoid battle," believing that he had "expressly striven for it," but only "under circumstances he considered favorable." If the two fleets had met, moreover, Pohl "would certainly have led the German fleet with tactical excellence."[57] Naval history in Pohl's case, as in all controversial historical cases, will likely remain a debate without end. If Raeder was right, however, and Pohl had "expressly striven for [battle]," then was it not perhaps—along with other factors discussed earlier—the cancer, its presence felt subconsciously by him before the end-game symptoms surfaced in late 1915, a malignancy which spawned an underlying anxious awareness that death stood at the doorstep, a sickly kind of "inner pressure to do more" that drove him toward combat that year determined to prove the Hotspurs wrong, win at sea, or at least acquit himself well before time ran out?

▪ 8 ▪

GIVE ME COMBAT

A passel of destroyers and mine trawlers patrolled the Moray Firth off Cromarty, their smoke clouds swirling upward into a grey November sky. The black billowing gases overwhelmed the bleak autumn firmament until one was indistinguishable from the other, and then blew out to sea with a rude westerly wind. For two days the flotillas worked the long, wide firth, searching the turgid waterscape for their metallic catch, eager to proclaim the area free of U-boats and mines. Only then could BCF's flagship and 1st BCS safely set sail.

With destroyers and light cruisers guarding the perimeter of the coordinates chosen for this battle-shoot exercise, one by one the imposing battlecruisers, following regulations, fired a succession of single salvos, adjusting the range after each one, until the shell-splash water columns of these salvos had been spotted both short of ("a short") and beyond ("an over") the towed canvas target. Once this "bracket" of singly spotted splashes had straddled the target in this deliberate fashion, each ship in turn belched forth her full fiery fury in "rapid fire," every turret crew anxious to obliterate targets and demonstrate that months of competitive turret simulations in Rosyth had proven the old maxim that practice makes perfect. Indeed, although gunners had difficulty hitting the mark from long range—their "shooting was rotten,"[1] said some of the younger officers—the rate of fire after bracketing showed marked improvement over Dogger Bank nine months earlier.

Assessing the results in a letter to Beatty, Jellicoe assumed his correspondent "must have been very disappointed" at the battle practice results. "I fear the rapidity [of fire] ideas were carried to excess." Beatty, now vice admiral, admitted "terrible disappointment," but predicted that the C-in-C would not "be let down by the gunnery of the battlecruisers when our day comes." But Beatty would not be diverted from his main focus of the lesson from the day's shoot: "I feel very strongly on the subject [of rapidity of fire] and think we should endeavor to quicken up our firing [even more]—the Germans certainly *do* fire 5 to our own 2, which would be the very deuce if we were unlucky." Jellicoe stayed his ground—all tension, for now, remaining beneath the surface: "I am all for rapidity of fire, but my only fear is that ships may break into rapid fire *too soon*, as I think *Queen Mary* did. It's all right, even [when] not hitting, *if short*, but no use *if over*." Beatty, however, would not be deterred. Rather than use the next practice shoot either to improve accuracy at long range or to execute *Lion*'s Captain Chatfield's pet idea of affecting a "concentration" of two-against-one rapid fire "to crush the [enemy] van"—achieving "decisive results on a few ships," he had proposed unsuccessfully earlier that year, "was better than to inflict slight damage on all"—the BCF chief preferred to develop a yet "greater rapidity" so "we could pulverize [the enemy] *early*—as I said before, 'concentration' is a luxury, whereas rapidity is the life and death matter." Although he had said after Dogger Bank that "the percentage of hits is too small" at longer range, he seemed inexplicably more willing now, as he had been before the war, to gamble on winning "early"—the "one blow" theory with its indifference to good gunnery and ignorance of Germany's sturdy ships—was apparently alive and well with Beatty (see chapter 6).

A BCF practice shoot off the Orkneys and Shetlands in early December did not impress Jellicoe either, for he ordered his own battleships to practice-shoot one week before Christmas 1915 using methods that corresponded more to prewar battle orders. "I made *Iron Duke* fire 3/4 charges at 7,500 [yards] (equivalent to about 10,000 [yards] at full charges) so as to see by actual *hits* that we are not living in a fool's paradise by firing so much . . . at long ranges." The results, he added, were "satisfactory." This battle practice aimed to keep sharp at medium range gunners who had been practicing for a year at long range. Thus Jellicoe, despite torpedo dangers, remained clearly tempted by all the AP-shell–effectiveness and gunnery-accuracy advantages of firing from shorter ranges. He also knew that shifting North Sea mists suddenly clouding visibility could compel having to hit from these distances.[2]

Other issues besides the need for more accurate firing in the BCF created tension between the two naval chiefs. The 5th Battle Squadron, five *Queen Elizabeth*–class super-dreadnoughts, had drawn nigh on operational, which would give Jellicoe a twenty-nine to seventeen battleship advantage over the High Seas Fleet. Beatty, however, had repeated his push for stationing them in Rosyth. Jellicoe already worried that dubbing the battlecruiser force a "fleet" in 1915 had given Beatty a false sense of strength, one that would warp worse with the *Queen Elizabeth*s in his possession. Giving further encouragement to rash acts, Beatty believed the supers could steam at 25 knots, when 23.5 was their top speed. Thus 5th BS would not help the battlecruisers but only hamper them with its lack of speed. Jellicoe continued to be stressed over the nightmare scenario, therefore, that Britain could lose control of the seas if Germany succeeded in isolating and destroying his fast battlecruisers as well as his most powerful battle squadron—something akin to the potentially dreamy German scenario botched by Ingenohl in December 1914.[3]

While trying to keep his own house under control, moreover, the C-in-C had to convince his superiors in the Admiralty to avoid equally rash acts. First Sea Lord Sir Henry Jackson, for instance, wanted to entice "the Hun" out from Helgoland, asking, "Have you any ideas for it? I wish I had." First Lord Arthur Balfour had also written with operational ideas that Jellicoe opposed: "Have you, by the way, given much thought to a possible naval offensive against Germany in the Baltic or elsewhere?" That Jackson and Balfour chose to wield far less force than Churchill and Fisher had done made it easier to deflect these ill-advised schemes.

> As to a possible naval offensive in the Baltic, or elsewhere, [matters which are] continually absorbing my attention, I have long arrived at the conclusion that it would be suicidal to divide our main fleet with a view to sending ships into the Baltic. . . . No other naval offensive appears to me practicable [moreover] unless and until our objective, the High Seas Fleet, gives us the opportunity . . . and until the High Seas Fleet emerges from its defences I regret to say that I do not see that any offensive against it is possible.

The Royal Navy must wait until the enemy provided a favorable opportunity, which did not mean seeking combat near Helgoland and their submarine, destroyer, and Zeppelin bases. "Patience is a virtue, and we must practice it."[4] And for now at least, a patient Jellicoe prevailed.

■ ■ ■

As Admiral Hugo von Pohl lay on his deathbed in January 1916, Vice Admiral Reinhard Scheer became acting fleet chief and then commander in his own right two weeks later. The new C-in-C acceded to his position with little of the drama and controversy that had surrounded the sacking of Ingenohl and appointment of

Pohl a year earlier. All seemed to know that Scheer would take over. This did not mean, however, that the navy's badly factionalized circumstances had changed, or that Scheer was some sort of a white-smoke compromise candidate bridging the divisions, for insiders, aware of his tactical posturing for the past year, knew that he leaned toward the more aggressive Tirpitzites. His accession smacked, in fact, of an unresisted, portentous "hostile takeover" by the "opposition party," an acquisition so baked into naval expectations for what most assumed had become necessary to win the Great War before time turned against the Fatherland that Privy Naval Cabinet Chief Georg von Müller, the man who had likely blocked Scheer a year earlier (see chapter 7, note 19), did not attempt the same now, which certainly helped keep the Kaiser momentarily out of the equation.

The new C-in-C chose Adolf von Trotha, captain of battleship *Kaiser* and one of the most determined leaders of the opposition, as chief of staff. As chief of operations, Scheer selected Magnus von Levetzow, the man who confronted Pohl two days before his collapse, an "action-friendly" officer who, like Trotha, "stood up for his opinion."[5] The two appointees mirrored the new chief's genuine desire for action. While undoubtedly Scheer was not conscious of this fact in making these appointments, moreover, it is nonetheless true that the two new staffers also perfectly mirrored and reinforced dominant albeit conflicting sides of Scheer's personality (see chapter 4): Trotha, "the soberly contemplative" one, the "adviser who calmly, carefully, and cleverly considered all circumstances"; and Levetzow, "just as clever, but also the reckless advocate of a spirited offense," the one imbued with "a pervading and unconditional urge to push forward."[6] It would be fair to say that the "action-friendly" Scheer could just as easily be swayed by the advice of the one as by the other, or sometimes simply go his own way, but usually preferring to end up on rational ground.

He frowned, however, on operational squabbles that merely undermined morale without benefitting the German cause. Although remarking to Pohl in March 1915 that he saw much worth in the aggressive proposals of 3rd Squadron Staff Chief Carl Schaumann, for instance, Scheer told his subordinate to keep quiet about them lest he undermine the C-in-C at a difficult time.[7] There was more to it than helping Pohl in all probability, for Scheer, passed over by the Kaiser for the top position in February 1915, knew he and his staff had to leave Hotspur roles to others until he could be sure of the emperor's support. With such motives in mind shortly after his promotion, Scheer took Levetzow to the flagship of 1st Squadron, SMS *Ostfriesland*, for a talk with Vice Admiral Ehrhard Schmidt and his squadron staff chief, Lieutenant Commander

Wolfgang Wegener. Ostensibly, the meeting served the purpose of muzzling Wegener for his controversial (albeit action-friendly) trilogy of think-pieces the previous summer (see chapter 7) as well as to chastise Schmidt for favoring these operations. And who better to bring along than Levetzow, the main critic of Wegener's "truly malefic" emphasis on the Skagerrak, an operation proposed by a man of "ruinously sober calculation" who could never appreciate the advantageous "imponderables" inherent in an instinctively bold advance into British-controlled waters. Years later Levetzow still thought it had been exactly this punitive purpose that brought them aboard *Ostfriesland*. But Sheer's clever goal in silencing Wegener went much farther, for in quieting the one he would also be silencing Levetzow himself, the "hothead," the "go-getter," thereby eliminating the need for rebuttals and quashing a feud that hurt morale at a time when solidarity was imperative, and the right moment arrived to neutralize William.[8]

That Trotha did not attend the meeting is curious, but probably explained by the fact that he agreed with the young lieutenant commander. A dyed-in-the-wool imperialist and colonialist whose enthusiasm for forging Germany into a genuine world power never waned, Trotha had served two years in the East Asiatic Squadron (1899–1901) and a year with Graf Spee on the staff of Fleet Commander Prince Heinrich (1908–9), both advocates of building German naval strength in the world, not just the North Sea. Indeed, in the winter and spring of 1913–14 Trotha, now captain of *Kaiser*, led a flotilla of German warships to South America, a flag-showing expedition also meant to garner momentum for the strategy of permanently stationing more German squadrons abroad to force the British to deploy more of their navy overseas to hunt them down. Interestingly, this expedition raised false hopes in Graf Spee's homeward-bound squadron several months later that another such expedition was bringing battlecruiser reinforcements—hopes exploited by "Blinker" Hall (see chapter 6, note 11). Trotha seems to have convinced even Tirpitz to support this kind of idea in January 1915 after the debacle at Dogger Bank. Although an imperialist himself, Tirpitz never backed Wegener, a man too critical of the Navy Secretary's accomplishments; but Trotha, without rocking boats, could carefully do so, for he also yearned for global naval might.[9]

Significantly, Scheer, like Trotha an avid imperialist, also saw much worth in Wegener's proposals. While dealing with the sidebar personnel issues these treatises had provoked, the new C-in-C incorporated Wegener's Skagerrak ideas into a multifaceted naval action plan against Britain designed "through constant, systematic pressure on the enemy" to force him out of "his current wait-and-see position" and

compel him "to push forward certain strike forces" that could be cut off and eliminated "[without] seeking battle against the concentrated English fleet." If it came to
such a full-throttled battle, however, like his unjustly pilloried predecessor, Pohl, who
would have "accepted battle even against a more powerful foe" in the confident hope
that "the harm done is not one-sided" (see chapter 7), Scheer, his "action-friendly"
countenance glaringly evident, held iron dice in his hand and prepared to roll them.
He was too impressed with the sturdy construction of German capital ships and the
"splendid effectiveness" of German high-velocity naval guns, and aware, conversely,
of the deficiencies of British AP shells, to regard "a chance encounter of the two fleets
[as] a disaster [from] which we could only withdraw with much luck and a little skill."
Scheer's postwar assertions have the ring of truth, for the more cautious strategy of
defeating the British in detail—which, to be sure, possessed its own confident side,
namely, of crushing the British fleet, even if it were still larger, in a second, more
decisive battle—had always smacked more of mollifying the usually docile Kaiser
(and those advisers and officers who agreed with this strategy) than of mirroring the
inclinations of those around Tirpitz (see chapter 2), many of whom under the right
tactical conditions wanted to risk more in this initial battle (like the man Scheer
placed atop his old squadron, the elite 3rd, Rear Admiral Paul Behncke, who had
been pressing to confront the entire Royal Navy [see chapter 4]).

The new provocative, combative approach called for more Zeppelin strikes on
British cities, naval shelling of shore areas, mining of coastal waters, unrestricted
U-boat attacks on merchant trade, as well as surface naval threats to North Sea–
Scandinavian sea lanes. These combined naval and naval air operations would be
coordinated with one another and frequently supported by sorties of the main battle
fleet "as far as coastal Holland, the Dogger Bank, and the Skagerrak." The latter area
seemed especially well-suited for "a provocation" of enemy forces. "As a further
operation in connection with this [combined-arms scheme], or [perhaps just] as a
separate operation, comes the idea of a sortie to the Skagerrak and Kattegat with
our light forces supported by the battlecruisers and the main fleet to molest the
[Scandinavian] export trade to England . . . the return march [to our base taking
all squadrons, if necessary,] through the Small Danish Belts." To guard against the
Royal Navy surprising Germany with a clever strike of its own, moreover, Scheer also
proposed more extensive defensive mining and nighttime destroyer patrolling of the
outer Bight. Finally, to ensure that the entire navy, especially the doubting defeatists,
those "pessimists and quibbling sticklers" (see chapter 4), supported and internalized
his strategy and would know how to act quickly when orders came, the C-in-C held

informational meetings with all squadron and division commanders as well as the Admiralty Staff in Berlin, including its chief, Admiral Henning von Holtzendorff, who approved the new concepts and consulted his army counterpart, Erich von Falkenhayn. The Army Chief of Staff was preparing his famous attack against the French fortress zone of Verdun, set to begin in February, and eagerly backed the idea of placing additional pressure on Britain with the navy. For the first time in the war, the German army and navy somewhat coordinated their actions. The army and navy chiefs knew that the longer the war dragged on inconclusively the more the blockade lengthened the odds against Germany. An ugly war would now get uglier.[10]

This left one final step. On February 23, 1916, the third day of Falkenhayn's attack, Scheer brought his case before the Kaiser, who had finally come to Wilhelmshaven. The new fleet commander would be asking, however, for more. At war's outbreak the army had made it clear that its chief of staff controlled army operations, keeping the sovereign informed out of formality and politeness. Throughout 1914 and 1915, the navy chiefs did not exercise the same degree of military decision-making free-dom—limitations that had ruined Ingenohl's career and lamed Pohl as a leader and a man. Scheer asked not only for imperial approval of his bolder, riskier, combined-naval-arms approach, but also that the Kaiser state publicly that his C-in-C had the freedom to execute it. Knowing since late October what it meant for him to go to Wilhelmshaven to clarify before the naval officer corps the fleet commander's author-ity (see chapter 7), William had delayed the trip repeatedly, claiming at one point that it would be "too strenuous," until eventually even the mention of going made him nervous and excitable. Having seen the Scheer-imperative writing on the wall, Müller finally prevailed by stressing the trip's military necessity, thereby accelerating the trend to isolate the monarch in the military decision-making shadows.

Once in Wilhelmshaven, the Kaiser, more subdued than when making his more typically blustering "unforced"[11] remarks, stuck to Müller's script, itself evidently colored by Scheer's confidence concerning the fleet's readiness for a major battle going beyond defeat-in-detail if need be: "The newly named fleet chief, in whom I place great hopes, presented to me this morning all of his intentions and plans, which I approve of, let me make that clear, in every way. Indeed, I believe that these plans are well suited to produce success. Whether it will come to a decisive battle to the finish, dear God only knows, but I, your Kaiser, know for a fact that if it comes to this the fleet will stand up to it like men."[12] That the emperor had avoided saying that "the war must be waged this way or that," Scheer wrote a friend, or that "the fleet is being ordered to do this mission or that,"[13] lifted the huge weight of being micromanaged off his shoulders: "This declaration was of great worth to me, as thereby, before all the assembled officers, I was invested with an authority that gave me freedom of action to the very extent that I myself had defined, intentions . . . [that] were thoroughly understood in this circle, as I had discussed in detail the program of operations and had handed it in writing to those whom it concerned." It would not be the first time (witness his bowing to army imperatives in declaring war in August 1914) or the last (witness the rise of army chiefs Paul von Hindenburg and Erich Ludendorff later in 1916) that William's "insecurity" and "inner emptiness" (see chapter 4) had him yielding to stronger personalities in uniform. And with Scheer "invested with an authority" that Ingenohl and Pohl had lacked—namely, an imperial sanction of "freedom of action"—*Der Tag*, the "Great Day" of decisive battle for which his faction had clamored, drew nigh.[14]

It is noteworthy, furthermore, that William made no objections to the aerial bombing of British cities, especially after he had forbidden Pohl from striking London in January 1915. Although the emperor's negative traits exceeded his positive ones, it can still be said of him that he lasted much longer into the war than most of his generals and admirals without discarding many of the prewar assumptions about the correctness of sparing civilians the horrors of war. His was a wobbling, unstable stance righted and supported, to be sure, by diplomacy-sensitive Chancellor Bethmann Hollweg and his sometimes-ally, Privy Naval Counselor Müller; but William's basic nonviolent nature also reinforced it (see chapter 4) as did his personal-political need to uphold royal authority, somewhat like clinging as long as he could to the naval reins in general. At a dinner with naval officers in November 1914, for example, the emperor had declared, "Gentlemen, always remember that our sword must remain pure. We are not fighting a war against women and children. We want to fight a decent war, whatever the others do." In alluding this evening to the indecency of the British blockade, of course, the Kaiser had suppressed any knowledge of his army starving the Belgians and seemed unaware of the impending potential scandal of Scarborough, Whitby, and Hartlepool. Nevertheless, his initial pleasure with the December Yorkshire Raid rather quickly gave way to displeasure with Ingenohl for straying from military targets, and then, consistent with this in January, he refused Pohl's and Tirpitz's requests for air attacks on London. The German navy Zeppelin raiders of early 1915 had orders to avoid civilian centers, although innocent victims still fell, as at Yarmouth on January 19–20, 1915, the first air raid on Britain, when two died. Even after French airplanes bombed Karlsruhe in June, killing twenty-nine parents and children in a circus tent, William resisted pressure to retaliate for over a month before finally relenting in late July. Five attacks of entire squadrons of eight or nine Zeppelins followed in rapid succession over London and the midlands, killing and wounding over six hundred people—a brutal overreaction. By September 1915, after more Germans had been bombed in Saarbrücken and Freiburg, the Kaiser no longer wanted to hear about the inhumanity and diplomatic disadvantages of aerial attacks against British towns, blurting that "every means is just when a people fights for its existence"; but he eventually yielded to Bethmann Hollweg, and probably to his own instincts as well, by ordering a temporary halt. They feared that otherwise "the world will unite against us as advocates of naked brutality."[15] But now with Scheer commanding in 1916, the aerial assaults would resume.

William had still not altered his position on resuming unlimited submarine warfare, however, when Scheer made his presentation on February 23, 1916. The emperor's statement to the officers had carefully skirted the issue, but in the automobile with his new fleet commander beforehand, he demonstrated a touch of his humanitarian side when asked by Scheer about the U-boat issue: "If I were a submarine captain, I would never torpedo a ship knowing women and children were on board." This feeling was reinforced by the entire gamut of diplomatic considerations brought into clear focus by the sinking of the *Lusitania* and *Arabic* in 1915, namely, the need to avoid war with the United States. Still, the head of state remained badly torn, pleading with Müller, "It is terrible to think of sinking innocent passengers. After all, I bear responsibility before God for how we wage the war. On the other hand I have to ask myself: can I, against the views of my military advisers, accept the responsibility for prolonging the war on humanitarian grounds, thereby sacrificing the lives of so many more brave ordinary soldiers? I must make the most difficult decision of my life."[16]

In the end, William accepted a compromise finessed by Bethmann and Müller that outlined how only armed merchant ships of enemy countries, clearly identified as armed by the U-boat, could be sunk without warning, which assuaged no one in the pro-submarine camp and led finally to the dramatic and politically explosive resignation of Müller's nemesis Tirpitz. The Kaiser and his chancellor began to consider jettisoning even this approach, however, when a German submarine mistook a cross-Channel ferry, the *Sussex*, for a troop transport and nearly sank it on March 24, again killing civilians, including Americans, prompting a severe protestation from the United States. Four weeks later Scheer heard that he would have to conduct his campaigns, already well underway, under search-and-seizure prescriptions of international law, the same order that had prompted the U-boats to pull back from commerce warfare in September 1915 because of the danger of being attacked while surfacing to make these seizures (see chapter 7). With U-boat warfare, in other words, the Kaiser had managed somewhat to restrict the "freedom of action" he had given Scheer.

As noted, the German navy had already begun its aerial offensives. A Zeppelin squadron raided the British midlands (Hull, Sheffield, Manchester, and Liverpool)— the first such attack since September—causing damage to factories and iron works and killing almost two hundred civilian personnel and wounding many more (February 1). A task force of twenty-five destroyers swept into the Dogger Bank, escorted home by Hipper's heavier forces after sinking only one mine sweeper (February 10). The entire fleet sortied along the Dutch coast, moreover, the battlecruisers turning north toward Harwich to prey upon naval forces that might react to an attack of two Zeppelins near Grimsby on the Humber, which had damaged a light cruiser (March 5). None of these operations provoked the British sufficiently, however, to affect the kind of defeat of the Royal Navy that Scheer wanted.

■ ■ ■

By the first days of spring 1916, the officers of Beatty's BCF had settled into a routine much less hectic and strenuous than the early months of the war at Cromarty. To be sure, they kept steam constantly at four hours notice, which facilitated timely responses to the Admiralty's orders to put to sea, and sorties for rare target practice and tactical exercises also took place; but unless a ship were in dry dock, which meant some leave time, most days in Rosyth bordered on the tedious with the normal routine of chow, chores, drills, daily exercise, band practice, and morning and afternoon watches. For the ratings, occasional outings to Queensferry or Rosyth occurred that sometimes resulted in brawls when too much pent-up steam got released.[17] Officers went off to nearby Edinburgh much more frequently for meals, meetings with wives and mistresses, and general merry making—a luxury their counterparts in Scapa Flow did not have.[18] Because these half-day trips improved morale but could hamper quickly putting to sea, Beatty had established a telephone warning exchange between *Lion* and all the spots in Edinburgh and environs where naval officers relaxed. Operators on the receiving side had standing orders to find the nearest officer and instruct him to gather up all comrades in sight without alarming civilians, and then return to Rosyth.[19] So it was that on Thursday, March 23, phones rang all over town: the BCF was off on another "stunt down to the dear old Bight."

The Admiralty had approved the plan of Commodore Tyrwhitt to bomb German Zeppelin stations on the coast of Schleswig in order to destroy at least some of Germany's silver monsters before they destroyed more lives and property in Britain.

Room 40 had detected something in the works on the German side, interpreted the intercepts as evidence of another airship squadron assault, and decided to hit before being hit. Tyrwhitt would leave Harwich on March 24 and proceed toward Sylt Island (see map 1.1) with five light cruisers, eighteen destroyers, and HMS *Vindex*, a Channel steamer converted to a seaplane carrier. Beatty's entire BCF left Rosyth the same day—hence the recall of all naval officers on the twenty-third. His entire fleet of ten battlecruisers, well escorted by light cruisers and destroyer flotillas, had orders to wait in support off Horns Reef, for the Germans often sent out the fleet, or portions of it, in such situations.

On the morning of Saturday, March 25, Scheer sat in his work suite with Trotha and Levetzow finalizing preparations for the next provocation of the Royal Navy.[20] The 2nd Squadron of predreadnoughts, two battleships of 3rd Squadron, Hipper's 1st Scouting Group, and numerous light cruisers and destroyers arrived a squadron at a time from the Baltic via the Kaiser Wilhelm Canal. Once assembled, the fleet would approach full strength—*Von der Tann* was refitting, but a new battlecruiser, SMS *Lützow*, had finished her trials and joined Hipper. Once fueled and provisioned after sunset on Sunday, the main body would push north to the vicinity of Little Fisher Bank by the twenty-seventh while Hipper, who had preceded the battle squadrons by several hours, disrupted the sea lane into the Skagerrak. All would then sweep to the southwest that night into the Dogger Bank, flanked by minefields on the eastern and western edges of the Bank. As this unfolded, one of Germany's large new U-70 series mine-laying submarines would infest the Firth of Forth, while attack submarines waited off other harbors—exactly where the enemy stationed all dreadnoughts, the Germans still did not know. Zeppelins would provide aerial reconnaissance. Ultimately, if the sortie proved uneventful, all squadrons would return via Terschelling to their bases. The ambitious operational goal: to win some sort of combined-naval–arms victory by decimating the enemy with mines and U-boats and perhaps also winning a significant sea battle near the Skagerrak or Dogger Bank. With the French desperately holding on at Verdun, loss of sea control by Britain could dash the allied cause downward, cascading into crisis and catastrophe.

Shortly after 1030 (10:30 a.m.), a communications officer entered the suite and alerted the fleet's new brain trust to an airplane raid on Vamdrup, in north central Schleswig; a destroyer attack on List, on the northern tip of Sylt Island; and a destroyer sighting near Borkum, on the Frisian Islands near the mouth of the Ems River leading to Emden naval base. Behind the destroyers near List, apparently somewhere between Sylt and Horns Reef, British airplane carriers had evidently launched planes against coastal airship hangars at Hoyer and Tondern, a revenge raid for recent Zeppelin attacks, but the enemy's planes seemed to have strayed off course into parts of Schleswig of no military value (i.e., Vamdrup).

What to do? One answer to Scheer's question, perhaps that of the combative Levetzow, opined that if heavy enemy forces waited in support around Horns Reef, then they must be attacked. The other point of view, probably that of the more cautious Trotha, warned that heavy forces may lie behind the destroyer near Borkum screening a larger force. If so, a German counterattack to the north risked being cut off from base if enemy squadrons swept in from behind this lone destroyer. Scheer considered this advice and decided to await further developments.

While they returned to work, two airplanes took off from Helgoland and flew north ahead of a storm front moving in behind them. Fifty miles out, the scouts sighted what they reported—incorrectly, so typical to this early age of maritime aerial reconnaissance—as four *Lion*-class battlecruisers and six destroyers west-northwest of Sylt. This much more alarming news reached the hard-working German admirals around 1315. The enemy had preempted Germany's Skagerrak operation, prompting Scheer to improvise a new plan that he radioed to all squadrons at 1345, a more cautious mix of defense and offense that evidently leaned more toward Trotha than Levetzow. Ehrhard (with seven dreadnoughts in 1st Squadron) and Hipper (with four battlecruisers in 1st SG) would move out of Wilhelmshaven once they had steam up to provide support for destroyers and light cruisers already heading north; the mightier 3rd Squadron, eight battleships strong, would stay in the roadstead at short notice: it could either support destroyer flotillas reconnoitering to the west, or push north if needed. The night-fighting-by-searchlight-capable light forces ahead of Ehrhard and Hipper had orders to maintain contact with the enemy until nightfall and then engage his heavy forces with all additional destroyer flotillas Scheer could muster. The 2nd Squadron stood ready to exit the Kiel Canal after midnight, guaranteeing that Scheer would have nearly the entire German navy if the nighttime attacks failed and a surface battle took place at dawn.

Tyrwhitt's plan went awry from the start. His five planes failed miserably, two turning back due to weather and three eventually falling into German hands—and no hangars were hit. One of his destroyers, the *Medusa*, collided with another vessel trying to elude German planes counterattacking near Sylt and had to be brought in tow, thereby delaying the withdrawal of all British naval forces anxiously ordered by the Admiralty. Tyrwhitt refused to abandon *Medusa*, however, instead towing her many miles west—the alleged battlecruiser sighting by German planes—and

Beatty refused to abandon Tyrwhitt, steaming south on his own initiative at full speed from Horns Reef in the late afternoon to shield Tyrwhitt from the German squadrons Room 40 competently reported moving north.

At dusk, Tyrwhitt and Beatty commenced their withdrawal on separate headings, the former to the northwest and the latter to the north. The commodore finally let *Medusa* loose to her fate at 1840, ninety miles slightly northwest of Sylt. But at 2315, now forty miles northwest of Horns Reef, the commodore's force stumbled upon some of the German torpedo boats Scheer had sent north, resulting in the ramming and sinking of Germany's *G-194*, all ninety hands lost in the increasingly stormy sea. In the commotion, however, two of Tyrwhitt's light cruisers collided; and another ship, HMS *Undaunted*, came in tow. What could have gone wrong had again gone wrong.

Caucusing on the compass platform of *Lion*, which sailed now well to the north of Horns Reef, Beatty and his staff discussed what to do if they also encountered German destroyers beyond the edge of the outer Bight. The daring vice admiral did not allow the discussion to continue for long: "If I continue [on our present] course," he objected to his chief of staff, Captain Rudolf Bentinck, "I shall probably run into more of their destroyers in the dark, and lay myself open to night attack, but if I go back into the Helgoland Bight I will be in a good position to intercept them on their return in the morning. If I meet Hipper and his battlecruisers, I can deal with them. If their battle fleet is also out in support, I can retire on the Grand Fleet."[21]

Beatty intended to risk a maneuver designed not to salvage a rapidly deteriorating situation but rather to wrest from it another impressive victory over the German navy. At 0100, a jittery Admiralty ordered Jellicoe's Grand Fleet, nearly five hundred miles away, to head out in support, and then surprisingly allowed Beatty to turn back (at 0430), thereby incredulously nudging one of Jellicoe's worst-feared scenarios closer to realization. While Tyrwhitt's destroyers headed homeward out of the storm, three of his light cruisers steamed east to reinforce Beatty on his way toward the evacuated *Medusa*. He gambled that Hipper headed there too, and that this time, unlike the disappointment of Dogger Bank, his enemy would not escape.

Meanwhile, the heavy units of the German fleet moved north again. During the stormy evening, Hipper anchored his battlecruisers in the relatively still waters of Schmal Deep; but at 0100, with Jellicoe's main force exiting Scapa Flow 550 miles away, they pulled up torpedo nets and weighed anchor. Hipper rendezvoused with nearby torpedo boat flotillas twenty-five miles off Lister Deep at 0430, and then all went for the *Medusa*, reportedly stranded fifty miles farther west-northwest. At this point (4:30 a.m.), 3rd Squadron approached Sylt, two to three hours behind Hipper; 1st

Squadron, which had returned to base but now steamed north again, neared Amrun Bank with Scheer and *Friedrich der Grosse*; and 2nd Squadron passed Helgoland.

With Beatty's powerful BCF rushing directly toward a battle rematch with Hipper a few hours later—and Jellicoe unable to enter the outer Bight until after midnight—the storm, now a gale, prevented what might otherwise have become known as the Second Battle of the Bight. Already by 0500, Hipper's destroyer torpedo tubes were flooded and useless, and his light cruiser casemate guns were unable to fire—he sent them all home. By 0700, the storm had inundated even the middle-caliber casemate guns of the battlecruisers, making fighting any kind of action impossible unless he turned southwest directly into the storm, but away from Beatty. Hipper called off the battlecruisers at 0800, inducing an unhappy Scheer to cancel the operation.

Beatty continued steaming toward *Medusa*'s last known location, and then further "toward the enemy coast," approaching Amrun Bank at noon—with Jellicoe still well north of Dogger Bank many hours away. Beatty stayed there until 1400 "covering the northern approaches to the German bases . . . vainly hoping to bring the enemy to action . . . but to his great disappointment sighting nothing." The author of these observations, his junior navigation officer and later biographer, William Chalmers, also praised Beatty's dauntless charge across the teeth of the storm. "In vivid contrast, the German forces had been timid in their movements. Hipper . . . did not advance . . . because, according to their account, the weather was too bad for destroyers. . . . It is worthy of comment here that Beatty, on no occasion throughout the whole war, ever allowed either gales or fog to prevent him from carrying out his avowed intention."[22]

It takes little imagination for historians to sense that far different sentiments rushed through the mind of the British C-in-C as he steamed at 20 knots to rescue the BCF, which raced toward the High Seas Fleet. Jellicoe both admired and distrusted Beatty's aggressiveness and had warned him not to be drawn into a trap that would eliminate the impressive battlecruiser wing of the Royal Navy, without which the Grand Fleet would fight at a distinct disadvantage. If engaging superior numbers, would Beatty, his confidence buoyed by ten battlecruisers, fall back on Jellicoe's battle squadrons as he had said? Would he have a chance to do so if Hipper lured him back toward the advancing German 3rd Squadron and poor visibility obscured the arrival of these eight superior vessels with another seven dreadnoughts in 1st Squadron closing too? Moreover, even if Beatty managed to pull away, would German destroyer flotillas, menacing enemy piranhas known to be out past the edge of the Bight, bite off his retreat? Would the fate of the BCF be further sealed by poor gunnery and defective shells? The Admiralty's afternoon wireless reporting Beatty and Tyrwhitt finally retiring across the North Sea must have come as a tremendous relief to Britain's anxious commander, although he may still have silently cursed the failure of the Admiralty to give him adequate time to deploy.

■ ■ ■

Once back safely inside the Jade, Hipper summoned Raeder for what turned out to be an unusually odd conversation. When his chief of staff entered, Germany's battlecruiser commander struggled slowly, and obviously painfully, to his feet. At a time like this, the subordinate knew that silence came highly recommended.

"I have called you here to tell you that I will be asking for a short medical leave to deal with my back. And that brings me to the question of an interim leader of the reconnaissance squadrons. Do you think Boedicker is up to the task?" "Yes, of course Sir." Hipper paused a long while, staring worriedly into an empty corner of the room. Finally, he continued, "You know I'm very fond of music, I mean good and refined music—I'm particularly fond of Richard Wagner, especially *Lohengrin*! Our band, eh, is at the top of its form just now!" "Indeed it is, Sir! We will take the greatest care to see that it remains so. . . ." "I certainly hope so," Hipper interrupted, "for music is perhaps the best form of relaxation I get on board. What's worrying me is that there might be a change for the worse during my absence." He went silent again.

Raeder was worried. Both he and Levetzow had suspected for some time that Hipper was not holding up well under the strain of wartime, but this scene was bizarre. What should Raeder say? Should he say anything? He mustered the courage: "Sir, why should there be a change?" Hipper hopped up from his chair, wincing, and hobbled around the room, blurting out, "My second-in-command knows nothing about music. His taste runs to nothing but Prussian marches, treacly waltzes, and bits of *Fledermaus*. I'm sure he'll end up by mucking up my whole band, I tell you!" A proud Bavarian, Hipper was clearly a devotee of the militant *Zukunftsmusik* emanating from Wagnerian Bayreuth. Raeder knew for sure to be silent now, but suddenly Hipper's whole mood changed. "But I'll soon get them right again," he barked and then burst out laughing. "After all, I've had to show them how myself when the fiddles were going off!"[23]

A few days before this strange conversation, Sheer granted his vice admiral's request for medical leave based on "terrible pain and exhaustion" (March 27). In early April, however, the C-in-C, having no doubt heard an earful from Levetzow, and perhaps from Raeder too, and still rankled about Hipper turning back on March 26, advised Admiral Holtzendorff to sack him, for he "no longer possesses the qualities of robustness and elasticity which the assignment . . . demands . . . [and that] the end of leave will not affect a complete restoration of his abilities." Although Hipper had other things working against him in even higher places—a Bavarian commoner and "black comrade" of the "torpedo crowd"—Scheer had put off the aristocratic Holtzendorff, who thought "Sic 'em" was too harshly living up to his nickname (see chapter 4).[24] Hipper returned to his new flagship, the *Lützow*, on May 13, 1916, with a bad back but psychologically ready for action.

■ ■ ■

As evidenced by an interesting postmission correspondence, Jellicoe also continued to have questions about his immediate subordinate, Beatty, but went about his personnel problem-solving differently.[25] Beatty explained that he had been pushing hard to reach the wreck of Tyrwhitt's destroyer on March 26, where he also anticipated spotting Hipper's battlecruisers, an expectation he figured correctly in retrospect "[because the enemy] came close to where [*Medusa*] had been. I made *certain* we should have met them until I heard they had returned [to base], and was looking forward to drawing their 3rd Squadron, which presumably was in support, towards you." But the fact that his BCF came away empty handed, "bad as it was, showed us something more hopeful for the future, that they can under the new regime [of Scheer] be drawn [out]; that is something to think about. . . . I submit that the moment is opportune for sweeping operations on a large scale strongly supported, not only as a [defensive] precautionary measure [to guard the northern sea lane] but as a possible device for drawing him out." Beatty believed such action would have to occur south of the 56th Parallel, which ran seventy miles below the Fisher Banks into Lower Jutland, due to Scheer's alleged reluctance to commit himself north of it.

This type of thinking made Jellicoe cringe; but rather than state so openly, he characteristically sought to finesse the impetuous junior man by shifting the stigma of such combat-eager ideas to the Admiralty, the bugaboo of all fleet naval officers: "There is a feeling at the Admiralty which I think may lead to their trying to persuade me into what is called a 'more active policy.' I notice signs of it, and it shows itself in the air raids, heavily supported. I am being pressed to plan another, the idea being that it will bring the German fleet out. But the difficulty is this." He went on to explain that air raids would provoke battle in the Bight so far away from Britain that fuel shortages, especially for voracious fuel-burning destroyers, became a major disadvantage further aggravated by the threat of mines, menacing enemy destroyers, and the proximity of their submarine, airplane, and airship bases. "We must wait until they give us a chance in a favorable position. Patience is the virtue we must exercise. I am still trying to devise a means of drawing them further out, but I am bound to say I don't think air raids will do it. What do you think?"

Without a doubt, Jellicoe did not genuinely want to prod the High Seas Fleet to battle, for the virtuous patience he mentioned dictated playing a defensive waiting game. He succeeded brilliantly in moving BCF's commander closer to this position, first by Beatty admitting that "your arguments re the fuel question are unanswerable and measure the situation absolutely. We cannot amble about the North Sea for two or three days and at the end be in a condition in which we can produce the whole force to fight to the finish the most decisive battle of the war; [for the Admiralty] to think it possible is simply too foolish and tends toward losing the battle before we begin."

This realization seemed to move Beatty away from his desire to force "the great battle we are all waiting for" on the enemy by encroaching provocatively on his zone, which he himself had done on March 25–26, for this approach now appeared futile to him: "If the force they push out [to meet us again] is large, i.e. battlecruisers supported by battle squadrons (one or two), it would go no farther than is necessary to reconnoiter and expose the full strength of the force that we had in support. And as soon as they had made clear what constituted our force they would act accordingly. If we were greatly inferior they might be tempted to prosecute their investigation and attack further afield, otherwise they will withdraw." And he also agreed with Jellicoe's belief that "we must wait until they give us a chance in a favorable position." "My contention is that when the Great Day comes it will be when the enemy takes the initiative . . . [but] I think we can be quite sure that it will not be north of Latitude 56. What I am disturbed at is your remark that 'there is a feeling at the Admiralty, etc. to persuade me into a more active policy—and being pressed to plan another [air raid].' This is truly deplorable."

If it were true, however, that Scheer would not come north of the 56th Parallel, and Beatty agreed that fuel concerns and Scheer's alleged inclination merely to "reconnoiter" and then "withdraw" argued against provoking a decisive battle in the Bight with a sweep or air raid, both constituting "truly deplorable" pressure by the Admiralty, then a decisive battle could only occur, Beatty seemed to be saying, in very limited circumstances—for instance, if the Germans, anticipating British squadrons out in anger after another Zeppelin raid, "initiated" a sortie just north of Horns Reef, spotted the BCF, attacked "further afield," and then Jellicoe surprised and trapped them, all from the start with Room 40's aid. It is important to add that in such a scenario the Admiralty needed to share enough of its intelligence with Jellicoe so that he deployed his battle squadrons far enough south of the 56th—and close enough to Beatty—to spring the trap.

While the British discussed future operations, Scheer had resumed his strategy of prodding the British to action, this time with more air raids. He took advantage of better flying weather, but he also mourned a series of disappointments that seemingly only a major victory could absolve: the Kaiser's disappointing decision of mid-March to dilute unrestricted U-boat warfare; the frustration of Hipper allowing the BCF to escape the Bight unscathed on March 26; and the inability of Falkenhayn to break through at Verdun after six alarming weeks of mounting losses. The German navy launched its seventh, eighth, and ninth Zeppelin squadron assaults (April 1, 2, and 5), which hit London and other sites as far north as Edinburgh, where fourteen died and scores were badly wounded.[26] The aerial offensive inflicted frightful casualties, the worst coming with a direct hit on a munitions ship in the Thames River docks that snuffed out four hundred lives. "The Zepp raids are pure revenge," Jellicoe wrote to Beatty.[27] The ugly war had gotten uglier, but Jellicoe, as yet not pressed by First Lord of the Admiralty Balfour and First Sea Lord Jackson to do so, would not charge headlong into the Bight.

■ ■ ■

Having failed to provoke Jellicoe with three successive air raids in early April, Scheer sent the whole surface fleet to sea three weeks later, accompanied by another squadron of Zeppelins. The airships had orders to overfly East Anglia and attack while London slept during the night of April 24–25, accompanied by another morally dubious pre-dawn bombardment of the Norfolk coast at Lowestoft and Yarmouth by Rear Admiral Frederick Boedicker's battlecruisers. Scheer's battleship squadrons trailed the Scouting Groups by four hours in the hopes of trapping British forces vindictively retaliating against the Norfolk bombardments. Thus, the whole operation smacked badly of Germany's provocative intentions for the infamous Scarborough-Whitby-Hartlepool Raid in 1914 (see chapter 3).

With the battleships at sea around 1500 on the twenty-fourth, Wilhelmshaven wireless operators had orders to use Scheer's harbor call sign, "DK," while he maintained radio silence underway. Realizing like Pohl that knowledge of German operations "must reach England with surprising speed" (see chapter 7)—but seeming to doubt either enemy subs, merchant steamers, embedded agents, or code breaking as credible leak sources—Scheer narrowed the focus to British direction-finding technology (see chapter 1). Because these devices could approximate the sending location of signals, he hoped his DK ruse would deceive the enemy into thinking German battleships remained at base.

Room 40 managed to alert the fleet, but too late to intercept the enemy. The code breakers knew from intercepts that Scheer had plans of some sort. Their insight gained some clarity during the course of Easter Sunday, April 24, when Irish nationalists rose in Dublin: Did Scheer want to embolden the rebels? Not until early evening, however, could Room 40 report "HSF underway"; and only at 2014 that the High Seas Fleet included all German capital ships—although they could not say what, exactly, Scheer intended. *Seydlitz* had hit a mine north of the German coast, necessitating messages between the advance guard and main fleet, among them Scheer's ordering Boedicker to continue the advance with the rest of 1st and 2nd SG to the British coast. Only now did Beatty and Jellicoe receive orders to rush south.

The sortie proved disappointing for both sides. Weather conditions prevented any of the Zeppelins from reaching London, although they inflicted some damage on Cambridge, Lincoln, Norwich, and other sites. Further disappointing the Germans, eleven sailors died on *Seydlitz*, and the ship needed a month in dry dock. On the British side, Tyrwhitt's Harwich Force engaged Boedicker's screen, suffering damage to two cruisers but failing to draw him into battle long enough for Beatty to arrive. Hipper's replacement had opted for prudence over valor and bolted for home, much to the mounting frustration of Scheer, who saw another opportunity for victory over Tyrwhitt, and perhaps Beatty too, slip away, for Jellicoe trailed the BCF by 165 miles. First a battle-fatigued Hipper had turned back on March 26, and now Boedicker too—alleged failures that inflamed Scheer's resentment of a supposedly unaggressive attitude in 1st and 2nd SGs, a searing, embittering, swelling animosity exaggerated by two years of "opposition party" feuding against those perceived as unmanly. The Lowestoft Raid paid only one dividend for either side: in its postmortem, Room 40 apparently began the process of figuring out the DK ruse.[28]

The raid had significant repercussions in Britain. The naval bombardment of Lowestoft had wrecked two hundred houses, killing or wounding twenty-four people. The Zeppelins also caused damage and several casualties in other towns. Because press and politicians demanded better protection, Balfour had to act, which meant Jellicoe had to yield. "Another raid on the coast of Norfolk," wrote Balfour openly to the mayors of Lowestoft and Yarmouth on May 10, "will henceforth [be] far more perilous to the aggressors than it has been in the past, and if our enemy be wise is therefore less likely."[29] His public hint that part of the fleet would be redeployed to the south took concrete form behind closed doors at a conference with Jellicoe and Beatty in Rosyth on May 12. HMS *Dreadnought* would shift south to Sheerness on the Thames, joined from Rosyth by the predreadnought "Wobbly Eights" and armored cruisers of 3rd CS. The Admiralty also prevailed over Jellicoe with plans for eventually moving the Grand Fleet to Rosyth after enhancing antimine and submarine defenses.

On May 4 Jellicoe had no choice but to bend to the Admiralty again and support an air raid on Schleswig. This time, however, hitting the Zeppelin berths took secondary priority to the Admiralty's main object of provoking Scheer to battle in the Bight. Reflecting his recent correspondence with Beatty, he had advised the lords on April 12 not to use a first-light raid to entice Scheer into coming out, for this might result in a fleet action near Horns Reef around 1700 or later, leaving little light for battle and serious fuel shortages, especially for the destroyers, that would grow disastrously worse if the two sides reengaged in the morning. After the fleet arrived in the south on the morning of a raid, he reckoned that "we cannot afford to wait more than a few hours—probably twelve hours is the outside limit." On May 4, therefore, having lingered below the 56th Parallel for six hours with no BCF sighting of the enemy—the air strike had again failed badly—he ordered all ships home at 1400. "No purpose would be served," he reported afterward, "by our forces returning to the vicinity of Horns Reef at daylight on May 5th. In view of the possibility of a movement on the part of the enemy on the night of the 4th–5th . . . I deemed it advisable to replenish [fuel] as quickly as possible."[30] Although Jellicoe did not know it, during the night Boedicker had indeed preceded Scheer toward Horns Reef, his battlecruisers set to arrive there at first light on the fifth, so Jellicoe appears to have avoided a naval altercation he deemed destined to descend into debacle due to fuel-deprived destroyers.

As was his nature, Beatty saw things differently, blasting away at the Admiralty to Jellicoe on May 7 in an oblique attack on his C-in-C, whom he must have suspected had really given the retreat order:

> Everything promised well towards fulfilling our final objective at daylight the next day. I had husbanded my destroyers' fuel and they were well able to have had a good period of full speed the next day and get home at 15 knots if required. You can understand my disappointment when we were ordered to return to base. Why cannot the Admiralty leave the situation to those on the

spot? . . . If we had been in the vicinity of Horns Reef at dawn we should have had a glorious time. To miss opportunities which are so few and far between is maddening.

Beatty poured out even stronger feelings to his wife that same day: "We have returned disappointed beyond measure. These constant and continual disappointments are wearing to a degree. There were great possibilities, *but*—there is always a but—they were not made use of, and the opportunity passes away never to return again. It really is heart-breaking. For the life of me I do not know what to do to bring about the desired result. But something must be done; we simply cannot go on missing chances like this."[31] Jellicoe had nicely finessed his mercurial cavalryman in early April, but the days of doing so had passed. Shortly after writing these letters, Beatty received an old friend of the family and its unofficial chaplain, Albert Baillie, who met with "a large number of senior officers of the [BCF]," almost all of whom "expressed anxiety because they said that, great sailor as he was, Jellicoe had, as he grew older, become over-cautious—and they were all terrified lest David's fleet should catch the German fleet and that then Jellicoe would not come up in time."[32]

Finally, the C-in-C managed a compromise with the Admiralty in resolving the issue of where to station 5th BS, five of the newest super-dreadnoughts. With Beatty's 3rd BCS (*Invincible*, *Inflexible*, and *Indomitable*) scheduled to begin ten days of sorely needed target practice at Scapa Flow in late May, 5th BS would shift south to temporarily reinforce the six remaining battlecruisers of the BCF—*Australia* had gone into dry dock. Under the command of Rear Admiral Hugh Evan-Thomas, the newcomers sailed under the Forth Bridge to their anchorages shortly before noon on May 22, 1916.

■ 9 ■

TO THE FISHER BANKS THITHER SAIL

Vice Admiral Horace Hood stood on the flying bridge of HMS *Invincible* as his 3rd BCS entered Scapa Flow on the morning of May 23, 1916. *Inflexible* and *Indomitable* sailed astern. At the Battle of the Falklands, his flagship and her "chummy ship," *Inflexible*, had earned the great distinction of destroying Graf Spee's East Asiatic Squadron, a strange victory if there ever was one (see chapter 6, note 11). For ten days if trouble arose, Britain's prototype class (1908–9) of battlecruisers would now form the spearhead of Jellicoe's van. Trailing them by a few miles, up front in any fleet action, would be eight armored cruisers of 1st and 2nd CSs—the 1st sailing from Cromarty—the most modern heavy cruisers of the prebattlecruiser era, including squadron flagships *Defence* (1st) and *Minotaur* (2nd), which had participated in the hunt for Graf Spee.

That which would follow these eleven capital ships of the van into battle, most of it spread resplendently throughout the Flow as Hood's ships paraded into harbor, could not fail to instill a deep sense of awe and pride in Hood, for anchored on scores of square miles of tossing sea water rested two squadrons of sixteen dreadnought battleships, the 1st and 4th, which, when united with 2nd BS steaming out of Cromarty (with 1st CS), would raise the total of steel monsters to twenty-four. Thus, with the heavy cruisers and Hood's reinforcements, the Grand Fleet boasted altogether thirty-five capital ships, the largest assemblage of naval power in the world. Moreover, even without *Australia* and *Queen Elizabeth*, both in dry dock, Beatty's BCF and Evan-Thomas's 5th BS raised the total to forty-five, about 50 percent

138

above the maximum number of capital ships Jellicoe and Beatty could sortie with in December 1914. The last stage of the prewar naval race with Germany, which had seen a virtual explosion of new ship construction in Britain, had paid handsome dividends by 1916, returns augmented by shifting capital ships from the Pacific, the South Atlantic and Caribbean (after the Falklands), and the Mediterranean to home waters. Clearly, the quantitative odds on that long-awaited "Great Day" of sea combat had grown worse for Germany over the preceding eighteen months—and in retrospect, the magnitude of the Fatherland's missed or unseized opportunities of late 1914 and early 1915 loomed large.

Not long after dropping anchor, Hood would undoubtedly have been received on *Iron Duke* by Jellicoe; his chief of staff, Vice Admiral Sir Charles Madden; and the Grand Fleet's top gunnery specialist, Flag Captain Frederic Dreyer, to review the battlecruisers' target-shoot schedule as well as the C-in-C's latest plan for enticing the High Seas Fleet to battle. It is doubtful that Jellicoe had his heart in this operation any more than that of May 4 (see chapter 8), so as the explanation proceeded, it probably became clear that the genesis of the upcoming sortie scheduled for June 2 lay less with Jellicoe himself than with First Lord of the Admiralty Arthur Balfour and the pressure of public and political opinion, incensed after the Zeppelin and Lowestoft raids, to continue to press the navy into a "more active policy."[1] Beatty, too, was pressing hard for battle, critical that "we have lost sight of the old principle that 'the navy's frontier is the enemy's coastline' . . . [and that from] the relaxation of this principle has developed a policy of defense instead of offence . . . [a policy of holding back] instead of going for [the enemy] directly he shows himself outside his minefields."[2]

Britain's semiofficial naval historian of the Great War, Julian Corbett, explains Jellicoe's scheme (see map 1.1):

Two squadrons of light cruisers were to proceed to [Skagen], which they were to reach by dawn on June 2nd. Thence they would sweep right down the Kattegat as far as the Great Belt and the Sound, while a battle squadron would push into the Skagerrak in support. Such bait, it was hoped, could scarcely fail to draw a strong enemy force from the Bight. Possibly, as had happened before, they would not come far enough north to ensure an action, but at least they might be lured into a trap. To this end three . . . submarines were to be in position from June 1st to 3rd . . . southwards of Horns Reef . . . [with more mines laid to their south, while] east of the Dogger Bank would be two . . . [more submarines].

Finally, somewhere north of the mined area the battle fleet and [BCF] would be cruising, ready to move south and attack directly they heard any strong forces of the enemy were out.

Corbett believed this plan "went beyond anything [Jellicoe himself] had yet hazarded,"[3] but this glosses over the characteristically cautious side of an operation that clearly aimed more for a mine/submarine trap than a full fleet engagement. At least, however, it had pulled very close to the "limited circumstances" for full battle that Beatty's letters of early April had identified (see chapter 8).

Whether cautious or hazardous, the plan assumed that after the BCF took up its position ahead of the Grand Fleet "somewhere north of the mined area" (i.e., south of Horns Reef), Hood's battlecruisers would trade places again with Evan-Thomas' battleships. This moment, no doubt, could not come soon enough for Hood. "I think this is a great mistake," he had told his officers when hearing of the temporary transfer south of 5th BS. "If David has these ships with him, nothing will stop him from taking on the whole German fleet if he gets the chance."[4] While he may have been one of those BCF senior officers who worried about Jellicoe "coming up in time" to help Beatty, he seemed less critical of Jellicoe's alleged "over-cautiousness" and more concerned with the BCF chief's impetuosity. As for Jellicoe, once he had the 5th back, he too would breathe easier. "The stronger I make [Beatty]," he had written two months earlier, "the greater is the temptation for him to get involved in an independent action."[5]

As the last days of May passed, Hood's squadron engaged in intense gunnery drills that markedly improved the accuracy of his battlecruisers. After almost a week of this grueling training, Hood gave most of his squadron a day off. Unlike their former home, Scapa Flow offered none of the pleasures of "officers' country" in Edinburgh or the pub-crawling distractions of Rosyth and Queensferry town. But the Grand Fleet had laid out football fields on one of the islands inside the vast watery base, and it is a safe assumption that a match was held there between the best players from the home and visiting ships.[6]

■ ■ ■

Jellicoe and Beatty knew one another well, but neither had ever met Scheer, and while they both underestimated the German's audacity, which had grown over his four months in command, Jellicoe erred instinctively less here than Beatty. Illustrating the point, for the morning of May 5 Scheer had ordered Boedicker's four battlecruisers and light forces—*Seydlitz* remained in dry dock—to take up position south of Horns

Reef and if encountering superior enemy forces, pull back toward Amrun Bank where he waited with twelve modern battleships and eight predreadnoughts. Beatty and the seven battlecruisers he sailed with, anticipating a "glorious" morning, would have fought a running battle with Boedicker before sighting Scheer moving north. Not at all risk-averse, the German C-in-C lacked five dreadnoughts from his strong 3rd Squadron, but there is no need to see a "death wish"[7] in Scheer, whose bet this day may not have proven recklessly costly, for Jellicoe, if he had unwisely ignored fuel shortages and hovered north of Horns Reef, might not have been able to save a southward-charging Beatty from ruin by Boedicker and Scheer before they quit while ahead and withdrew. It seems better, therefore, to lean toward historians who describe Scheer as one "with whom boldness was never allowed to pass the limits of sane prudence."[8] Even this description disappoints slightly, however, because "Sic 'em" had two sides: one counseling circumspection, the other ready for risks and rude rejection of "pessimists and quibbling sticklers," and this side, while not insanely suicidal, was nevertheless implicitly and inherently *im*prudent. Perhaps, in other words, he would not be prone in action to quit while ahead and withdraw.

Indeed, he had good reason to want to risk more. Tremendous pressure weighed on the German navy to take action as the weeks passed in the spring of 1916. The army's losses at Verdun had exceeded 100,000 with no victory in sight. The British and French assembled a force astride the Somme River in preparation for a massive attack of their own, while Russia, despite suffering "a sea of tears immeasurable" in 1915, still persevered, tying down huge numbers of German and Austro-Hungarian soldiers. On Central European home fronts, moreover, the allied blockade had pushed civilian populations further down the merciless path of gradual starvation that would eventually kill more than 700,000 in Germany alone. Understandably, therefore, many Germans, afflicted by the distemper of these discontented times, turned angry eyes on the navy, demanding that U-boats produce a victorious end to this war of attrition, but these cries grew hysterically angrier in late April when the Kaiser and Bethmann Hollweg yielded to American pressure and abided by international law (see chapter 8).

Scheer, long an advocate of submerged subs sinking armed enemy commerce without warning, fought the decision for a week, and then engaged in a protest of sorts by withdrawing all submarines from the sea lanes in the first days of May rather than submit U-boat crews to the danger of operating on the surface. The C-in-C and other naval commanders were stung by their nation's surrender to Washington, especially Admiralty Staff Chief Holtzendorff's "incomprehensible" support for this decision. "If the U-boats were not used," wrote Trotha, "the navy will bear [the responsibility for] the loss of the war before the nation and be dead for the future."[9] But if not the U-boats, insisted many outraged patriots, then certainly the surface fleet had to venture forth. And even if that effort failed, wrote hawkish naval publicist Curt von Maltzahn, "and large parts of our [navy . . . end up] at the bottom of the sea, our fleet would [at least] have accomplished more than it does by lying well preserved in our ports." Such criticism of naval inaction equated in the eyes of its leaders to an unbearable charge of cowardice and, as Trotha had written, the postwar political evisceration of the navy. "For these reasons alone," bemoaned a now combat-ready Hipper on May 27, "I wish that we may soon be able to do battle."[10] For Scheer and Trotha, not to mention the hard charging Levetzow, the wish burned even hotter, emotions that could easily affect decision-making in battle.

The first step toward this long-desired battle came very easy for Scheer. Since the first five months of the war when German submarines sank five British warships, including HMS *Formidable*, a predreadnought battleship, he had favored using U-boats as auxiliaries of the High Seas Fleet.[11] Now, with these vessels freed up from commerce warfare, he would do so. A provocative plan drawn up when the U-boats went home called for Hipper's forces to bombard Sunderland, a few miles south of Newcastle (see Map 1.1). Special mine-laying subs, *U-75*, *U-72*, and *U-74*, would infest the waters off Scapa, Cromarty, and the Firth of Forth, respectively, with dangerous underwater explosives, while the bulk of the thirteen available attack U-boats for this operation patrolled the coastline ready to report and interdict enemy fleet movements. Zeppelins would aid this especially vital reconnaissance, for the exact location of all British squadrons remained a matter "speculated upon"[12] by Scheer and his advisers. The German C-in-C assumed that another punishment of the British coast could not fail to draw out the Royal Navy, especially after Balfour's assurance of May 10 that the navy stood ready to protect homeland shores, apparently even those shores further south. Before Jellicoe's Grand Fleet could help, he hoped to decimate Beatty with mines and torpedoes, lure his surviving ships into a tempting chase of Hipper, and crush him with the 1st and 3rd Squadrons—2nd would stay home—sailing northwest from their ambush lair near the SWP or from there to the southwest if Beatty came out of the Humber from Grimsby or up from Harwich-Yarmouth. The High Seas Fleet's cruel *navalis modus operandi* of the Great War—provoke and then entrap—was never more evident.

A series of delays, however, kept pushing back the date of the Sunderland attack. When several of 3rd Squadron's dreadnoughts developed condenser problems, Scheer postponed the operation's commencement from May 17 to May 23. Prolongation of the repairs to battlecruiser *Seydlitz*, which had hit a mine during the Lowestoft Raid, added another six days of delay, but persistent easterly and northerly winds continued to jeopardize the lift off of the Zeppelins and Practical Scheer refused to move into the potential shark pack of British coastal waters without their far-seeing eyes. With the U-boats already in place off British shores since May 17–18, and their fuel able to last only until the first days of June, he began to consider scrubbing Sunderland and substituting a Skagerrak operation similar to the one preempted in late March by a British raid on Zeppelin hangars (see chapter 8).

On May 27 Scheer sent Trotha to SMS *Lützow*, the new flagship of Scouting Groups' Commander Franz Hipper, to run these new plans by the leaders of 1st SG. "Many warships have been sighted recently," he informed them, between the north of Britain and Skagen. If Sunderland got canceled, 1st and 2nd SG would conduct cruiser warfare in the western Skagerrak, making their presence known with wireless messages. Reports indicated that "the enemy [has accepted] the [intended] challenge of the April operation against Lowestoft." Desirous now of "returning fire," they began making "repeated forays of considerable *portions* of the fleet into the northern North Sea." Scheer "wanted to exploit" this new situation. Hipper's wirelesses would lure these "considerable portions" of the Royal Navy to him while the main battle fleet waited in close support. Together they would spring the trap on enemy squadrons and "give them a little tickle." But what should happen if the high winds of late kept grounding the Zeppelins? Levetzow pushed hard to go regardless, even though he saw the Skagerrak mission as a weak alternative to Sunderland. He just wanted action, whatever it was, arguing that the Danish coast guards against surprises on the right flank, while U-boats could provide early warning on the left, but that if they could not, destroyers would.[13]

Evidently, Jellicoe's foray into the Bight on May 4 and Balfour's open letter of May 10 to the mayors of Lowestoft and Yarmouth (see chapter 8) had combined with German "reports" tapping, it would seem, into the anger and eagerness for "returning fire" of those around Beatty to inspire the alternative Skagerrak operation. To their visitor, Trotha, Hipper and Raeder gave their support. Wanting battle after returning from medical leave, Hipper liked this plan much better than Sunderland, in fact, having questioned the ability of thirteen to sixteen U-boats to spot and do damage to an enemy whose exact location along such an extensive coastline remained in doubt—"how to do it," he had observed, "therein lies the rub."[14] However, Raeder's views about Germany's compromised intelligence cover, which Hipper probably accepted by now, must have tempered their enthusiasm.

On the night of May 28–29, Scheer put the fleet on a "state of special readiness," meaning orders to sea were imminent. But which orders? At 1048 on May 30, he ordered all squadrons to assemble in their roadsteads by evening and build up steam. After receiving another negative weather report at 1500 indicating no possibility of airship participation for the next two days, he immediately decided to substitute the Skagerrak for the Sunderland mission. At 1640 the coded wire went out: "31.Gg.2490," which set the operation in motion for the early hours of May 31. One minute later, Rear Admiral Franz Mauve, who had lobbied Scheer to let the admiral's old command join the mission, got the word he had for weeks waited anxiously to receive: "2nd Squadron participates from the start, takes up position [in the rear] astern 1st Squadron."[15] Although clearly aware that "in all probability" he could be taking Mauve's obsolete vessels into "an unequal fight to which the enemy would bring only his best [ship types]," in other words that there were obvious "military reasons" not to do so, Scheer still positioned 2nd Squadron's six available predreadnoughts in his battle formation behind his sixteen newer, faster battleships. He admitted later that the "persuasive advocacy"[16] of Mauve as well as his own association with the 2nd as its former commander influenced the decision.

His choice, however, need not be interpreted negatively. Jellicoe, for example, brought 1st and 2nd CSs into the fray, eight predreadnought armored cruisers. Similarly, Scheer brought 2nd Squadron, whose time had also passed, but why exaggerate this as a "seriously incompetent and easily avoidable . . . 'death wish' mistake"?[17] He had spoken with Mauve at length in Wilhelmshaven earlier in May about the kind of battle he anticipated and 2nd's role in it "under the widest variety of circumstances." Presumably, Mauve heard that the chief planned to trap inferior enemy forces between Hipper and his own dreadnoughts. In such an engagement Mauve could either help or more likely serve as a rear guard. In the event of an unanticipated running escape battle against superior forces like what happened at Dogger Bank, the 2nd would be repositioned to the front, eventually joined by Hipper, as all squadrons turned simultaneously, leaving the outnumbered (but confident) 3rd and 1st in the rear to deal with enemy dreadnoughts even these faster German battleships could not outrun. The worst case scenario in this pursuit battle would posit the front of his line being cut off from base by the fast BCF, but with scores of 11- and 12-inch guns, Mauve and Hipper could inflict serious harm on Britain's thinly armored battlecruisers and stand a fair chance of blasting a path home, especially with some of Germany's torpedo boat flotillas spearheading the retreat to scatter capital ships vulnerable to torpedoes. For the 2nd Squadron and 1st SG to perform this vanguard retreat mission, they had to be close to full strength, enjoy adequate visibility, have tolerable gunnery circumstances, or better still, gunnery advantage—that is, to fire at targets silhouetted against the sun. Such were the scenarios probably included in their discussion of the "widest variety of circumstances."

In order to increase the odds of trapping inferior forces rather than being trapped by superior, Scheer planned to employ the "DK" ruse again. All messages to Scheer would go to a guard ship in an entrance channel to the Jade Roadstead using the C-in-C's harbor call sign "DK." This vessel would acknowledge wirelesses and broadcast them to the fleet, while Scheer and his main body listened at sea but neither acknowledged nor replied. By maintaining strict radio silence away from base, Scheer hoped to deceive the British into thinking that German battlecruisers (under orders to maintain radio silence but then break it once well past Little Fisher Bank) sailed alone while he monitored the operation with the bulk of the High Seas Fleet in Wilhelmshaven. For this to work, Britain's coastal "Direction Finding (D-F) Stations" would have to position "DK" there and not at sea. Remarkably, although a minority of officers' objections had rumbled for eighteen months, a majority of German fleet command still believed that coded messages of recent days had disclosed nothing to the enemy.

Hipper's five battlecruisers, five light cruisers, and thirty torpedo boat destroyers left the Jade Roadstead at 0200 (0100 British time) on May 31. The main fleet's sixteen battleships, six predreadnoughts, six light cruisers, and thirty-two destroyers weighed anchor in Wilhelmshaven and Cuxhaven at 0330 (0230 British time), the three battle squadrons uniting south of Helgoland at 0400 (0300 British time). Hipper had orders to sail past Little Fisher Bank and show himself near the southern tip of Norway shortly before nightfall "in the expectation," recalled Scheer, "that the enemy would receive news of the arrival of our cruisers in those waters."[18] Addressing his crew at sea on May 31, Captain Kameke of SMS *Helgoland* (1st Squadron) waxed much blunter about how this trap would work: "Our bait, the light cruisers, will draw the stupid fools out to sea with their wireless messages."[19] The terminus for the trailing main fleet lay fifty miles south of the Norwegian coast in the entrance to the Skagerrak. At some point on June 1, depending on when "the stupid fools" had taken Hipper's "bait," but most likely that afternoon, Scheer hoped to have a big catch trapped in the fishing nets of 110 German ships.

■ ■ ■

The operatives in Room 40's eavesdropping machine had heard much of this by May 30 and passed it all to their superiors in the Admiralty. The first indications that something stirred on the other side came already in mid-May when a decoded wireless hinted that the Germans intended to deploy U-boats with the fleet. When simultaneously no enemy submarines appeared to be stalking the sea lanes any longer, the Admiralty intensified antisub patrols off the coastline.

And then toward the end of May, wave after wave of clues began to flood into Room 40. In the night of May 28–29 they read Scheer's "state of special readiness" order. The next afternoon they decrypted German submarine command asking U-27 at sea how far it could penetrate the Firth of Forth. Other German wirelesses spoke of minesweeping activity from Amrun Bank to Horns Reef, the German exit route up the Danish coast. Next, late on the morning of May 30, arrived Scheer's order for *all squadrons* to assemble in their roadsteads by evening. Minutes later came a wireless alerting all U-boats to expect German forces at sea on May 31 and June 1—as Room 40 interpreted this signal. Others referred opaquely to established fleet procedures for supporting returning Zeppelins. Finally, in late afternoon the "31.Gg.2490" alert was intercepted, untangled and translated to mean, "On 31 May Most Secret [*Ganz-geheim*] 2490." Other missives at about the same time alerted the fortress commandant in Wilhelmshaven to expect a sortie between 0200 and 0430; made it clear that *all three battle squadrons* would go out; that ships would not carry prize crews, a clear sign that naval action, not commerce warfare, was anticipated; and that the German C-in-C was "taking over control of wireless transmissions," which tipped off Room 40 to the DK ruse likely being in play (see chapter 8, note 28).[20]

Sir Henry Oliver, First Sea Lord of the Admiralty Henry Jackson's Chief of War Staff, along with his colleague Sir Arthur Wilson, had long been Room 40's actual overlords, for unlike the Churchill-Fisher era, Jackson and First Lord Arthur Balfour did not play a hands-on role in naval decision-making. After discussing the most important decrypts with Wilson and Director of the Operations Division (DOD) Thomas Jackson, Oliver telegrammed Jellicoe: "There are indications that German fleet are to be in outer roads by [2000] tonight and may go to sea early tomorrow— object may be to have them ready to support returning Zeppelins." At 1728, Jellicoe was ordered to "raise steam." He immediately canceled his June 2 operation—no doubt gladly (see earlier)—ordered steam raised, and so ordered Beatty at 1740. At 1755 Oliver informed Jellicoe that the "Germans intend some operation commencing tomorrow morning and leave via eastern route and Horns Reef L[ight] V[essel]. Operation appears to extend over 31st May and 1st June." At sea he should steam "eastward . . . ready for eventualities." An offensive plan had yielded to another defensive sortie against German squadrons probably hovering near Horns Reef to meet their Zeppelins and engage enemy naval forces that may have been provoked to retaliate.[21]

With these sparse, somewhat confusing morsels of information, Britain's squadrons prepared to go out. Since the fall of 1914, problematic seeds had been planted that undermined the optimal transmission of decrypted information from the cryptanalysts to where it was needed most: with the sea commanders. Involved with Britain's intelligence mechanism since 1914, Oliver and Wilson appreciated the advantages it gave to the Royal Navy; but as officers atop a hierarchical chain of command, they, not the decoders and translators, interpreted importance and passed along anything deemed relevant to naval commanders without any further contact with Room 40. Any suggestion to the contrary from below, claimed Room 40 operatives, "would have been resented." A similar attitude, influenced mightily by the Admiralty's "absolute obsession" with keeping its intelligence system secret, applied to Jellicoe and Beatty, who received information, as the saying goes, "on a need to know basis," which only added to the acrimony between the Admiralty and naval commanders—after all, the land line to these bases was kept quite secure enough for details. However, DOD Thomas Jackson exacerbated the flaws in this system, it was said, by not only guarding the workings of his division and its cooperation with Oliver and Wilson from any interference from Room 40 subordinates, whom he regarded, allegedly, as a mere "party of very clever fellows who could decipher signals," but also by exhibiting a downright denigrating attitude toward their services. Once, during an interruption in the flow of decrypts caused by the Germans slightly altering their code books, Jackson is said to have remarked, "Thank God, I shan't have any more of that dammed stuff."[22] As they sailed into the night, therefore, Jellicoe and Beatty remained in the dark about the relevant information lying unread by them in the steady, red-metal flow Room 40 sent up the haughty chain of command. To Grand Fleet and BCF commanders already skeptical that the Germans would ever—under any circumstances—cross in strength far north of the 56th Parallel, doing so just to meet returning Zeppelins was hard to imagine. This sortie, like so many before it, looked like it would be uneventful business as usual.

The BCF pulled up torpedo nets and weighed anchors as the minutes ticked away to 2300, two hours before Hipper. As *Lion* passed under the Forth Bridge, Major Francis Harvey, in command of the Royal Marine gunners on *Lion*, stood conversing with Chief Gunner Alexander Grant. When they got around to the topic on everyone's lips, "Zepp" raids on Edinburgh, the Forth Bridge, or Rosyth, and a sort of preemptive strike against Germans expecting the British to come out in retaliation, Grant did most of the talking. His conversant kept largely silent and apprehensive, saying only, and very superstitiously: "We have left our [Royal Marine pet] cat behind. I don't like it,"[23] which Grant found only a little strange at the time.

Shortly after midnight, "the long black shapes" of Beatty's fleet, each ship steering only on "the dimmed stern light of the ship ahead," passed May Island, "ebon shadows in a world of shades," and entered the North Sea as "night, and the mystery of darkness, enfolded them."[24] The BCF would reach Great Fisher Bank by 1400—his terminus lay twenty-five miles east of it—while the C-in-C's three battle squadrons of two divisions each, led into the "mystery of darkness" by Hood's 3rd BCS and 1st and 2nd CSs steered toward coordinates sixty-nine miles slightly northwest of BCF's terminus. From these two spots the two wings of the Grand Fleet would converge, Beatty to the northwest, Jellicoe to the southeast, and then sweep together toward Horns Reef and ready themselves for "eventualities."

British dispositions for May 31, 1916, did not differ greatly from the defensive guarding positions the two British admirals had taken up on numerous occasions since early 1915 "as the prospect[s] of a fleet action [had grown] ever more remote," observed Julian Corbett (see chapter 7). Beatty lay "far enough to the southward" to intercept a raid on the British coast if it targeted the Firth of Forth, the Tyne, or the Humber; Jellicoe lay "far enough back" to prevent the enemy from raising the northern blockade; and both were in a good position to protect the Tyne-Skagerrak sea lane. "The disposition which Admiral Jellicoe now adopted had, after long consideration, become the approved normal whenever there were indications that the Germans were contemplating some large operation with an unknown objective." With no evidence in Jellicoe's hands that "a fleet action" was any less "remote" than earlier instances, Britain's squadrons "steamed for their rendezvous with nothing to encourage them to believe that what had set them in motion was anything more than one of the many alarms which had so often ended in disappointment."[25]

A question is imploringly begged here, however, when one considers the hypothetical historical alternative of an Admiralty more inclined to share with fleet commanders (over secure land lines) the wealth of intelligence Room 40 had gathered in May 1916. Whenever Jellicoe believed contact with the enemy was likely, as he did during offensive forays toward the Bight that spring, he stationed the main battle fleet about thirty-five to forty miles behind the BCF. Better informed by the Admiralty, which suspected strongly that the Germans intended to continue north of Horns Reef, and thus acting with more urgency, would he not have made certain to get closer to the coordinates he chose for Beatty's two o'clock terminus, a locale the Germans could easily reach by that time?[26] As it was, if battle with the High Seas Fleet suddenly became likely this day near the Fisher Banks, a sixty-nine mile gap between the two wings of the fleet would perhaps jeopardize the BCF and almost certainly exacerbate already existing tensions within British naval command. Beatty's preference for aggressive operations, which he had expressed in no uncertain terms, clashed with Jellicoe's defensive strategy of staying back, risking little, minimizing losses, and preserving Britain's upper hand in the naval war. In his polite, gentlemanly way, Jellicoe had also clearly expressed his preferences—and worries. After spreading the main fleet and BCF over such vast spaces of the upper North Sea, would the battleship squadrons be able to support the battlecruisers if the latter charged south with their captain of horse? Within the BCF, many of Beatty's commanders had their different concerns. If they assertively challenged the enemy, would the cautious C-in-C be there to help them do it? There were some, to be sure, who tended to agree with Jellicoe, fearing to rush in where Beatty wanted to go, but most did not, thereby castigating the C-in-C through worries of their own that essentially mocked his.[27]

■ ■ ■

Having heard advice from the top staff, C-in-C Reinhard Scheer pondered his options before lying down in the chart room below the bridge of his flagship. Almost 0700, he needed more sleep. His armada stretched out for many miles in the mine-swept channel west of Amrun Bank with Hipper ahead off the Lister Deep and about to enter the open sea (see map 1.1). Most of his officers basked in the early morning sunlight, enjoying a buoyant "pleasure cruise" mood with little expectation of seeing any enemy forces; but since Scheer's main body had passed Helgoland, his staff had presented three curious reports received in the fleet's guard ship and wireless hub in the Jade. The first came from *U-32*, stationed about eighty miles east-northeast of the Firth of Forth, reporting "two large warships, two cruisers, and several destroyers on a southerly course." The second came from the radio station and cryptanalysis center at Neumünster, reading: "two large warships or formations (*Verbände*) with destroyers left Scapa Flow." The third came from *U-66*, stationed a hundred miles east of Invergordon, reporting "eight large enemy warships in sight, light cruisers, destroyers on a northerly course." Sixteen submarines in British waters surely stood a good chance of detecting whether the Royal Navy steamed his way, but these reports of "fleet units of varying strengths" heading "in opposite directions," recalled Scheer, seemed to have "no connection whatsoever to our mission," and if anything, likely "enhance[d] the possibility that our plan to engage isolated units of the enemy could succeed." Indeed, as word of the reports spread, his officers got a little more serious in hopes of "feeding on small groups of Englanders." As for Scheer, with no reason to be anxious about "Most Secret" Mission 2490, he prepared to turn in with nothing more pressing on his mind than ordering his flag lieutenant to deal with "a trifle, namely, a rattling sliding door in the quarterdeck of [*Friedrich der Grosse*] so that it would not disturb his sleep as it had all night."[28]

In reality, of course, these were radio snapshots of the actual movement of two of the three main British naval forces leaving Rosyth and Invergordon for the Fisher Banks. That there were not more—and better, more accurate—snapshots is the best measure of the failure of this part of Scheer's operational plan. The reports of *U-32* and *U-66* did not convey the true easterly course of these squadrons because the U-boat captains sighted ships that zigzagged in waters likely infested with enemy submarines. With more recent experience sinking merchant ships, but less schooled in the complex procedure of reporting zigzagging ships' actual headings, both officers' reports essentially relayed misinformation.

Even more potentially insightful to Scheer—and never explained by historians—was the report from Neumünster. Most likely, given the cryptanalysts' description of "two warships or [warship] formations with destroyers," they had pulled off the airwaves an ill-advised coded wireless to Jellicoe from Vice Admiral Sir Martyn Jerram, commanding 2nd BS, as it passed from Cromarty/Moray Firth into the North Sea: "2nd Battle Squadron [radioed Jerram], 1st Cruiser Squadron, [light cruiser] *Boadicea*, [destroyer flotilla leader] *Kempenfelt* accompanied by nine destroyers, sailed." That Neumünster assumed these ships had left Scapa, not Cromarty/Invergordon, and could therefore not link the wire to *U-66*'s Moray Firth sighting of "eight large enemy warships," "light cruisers," and "destroyers," indicates that German cryptanalysts, woefully behind the expertise of Room 40, had only poorly and partially decrypted the wireless, and further that the German navy continued to wallow in the dark concerning the exact location of British "formations."[29] A more accurate and complete decrypt (along with a more accurate report of the formation's easterly bearing from *U-66*) would almost certainly have alerted Scheer to the fact that the Grand Fleet sailed his way, and that Flag Commander Behncke of 3rd Squadron would get his big battle wish, for Jerram had essentially told Jellicoe he would be joining him.

Another ill-advised British message that would have better informed Scheer—and would surely have pitted, like Jerram's wireless, practical and impetuous elements in the C-in-C's psyche against one another—went completely unnoticed by the Germans.

Sir John Fisher: Founder and inspirer of the
modernized royal navy. *Library of Congress*

The 12-inch guns of HMS *Dreadnought*: The first all–big-gun battleship (1906), but
soon outdated. *Library of Congress*

Sir Winston Churchill: The buck stopped with Churchill, but
Royal Navy opposition could stymie him. *Library of Congress*

Sir John Jellicoe: Great Britain's phlegmatic
master and commander worried incessantly
about many things. *Library of Congress*

Jellicoe's flagship HMS *Iron Duke*: Jellicoe was the only person in Britain capable of losing the war in a single afternoon. *U.S. Naval Institute photo archive*

Erich Raeder (*right*) and Franz Hipper (*center*): Hipper was a good-natured leader who occasionally "flew out of his skin." *U.S. Naval Institute photo archive*

Kaiser Wilhelm II: Crestfallen after news of Graf Spee's demise. *Library of Congress*

Alfred von Tirpitz: Roll the iron dice and come what may. *Library of Congress*

SMS *Von der Tann*: Germany's first battlecruiser. *Library of Congress*

Sir David Beatty: He liked the fast-paced hunt, the rough ride, and the hard charge. *U.S. Naval Institute photo archive*

SMS *Seydlitz*: The shells of Hipper's flagship missed the batteries and pierced factories, homes, and churches, killing scores of civilians. *Library of Congress*

Reinhard Scheer: A Janus-faced personality combining conflicting impulses. *Library of Congress*

SMS *Blücher*: The fast, upgraded armored cruiser featured four 8.2-inch wing turrets (B and D visible here). *Library of Congress*

Battle of Dogger Bank: A huge ball of flames rising as high as the masts engulfed the stern of SMS *Seydlitz*. *U.S. Naval Institute photo archive*

HMS *Tiger*: Beatty lambastes her captain for "running amuck after *Lion* fell out."
U.S. Naval Institute photo archive

The BCF takes shape in 1915: Hood's 3rd BCS returns from a sweep led by a blockade patroller, armored cruiser HMS *Drake*. *Library of Congress*

Prince Adalbert: In criticizing the C-in-C's aggressiveness, he shot closer to the mark than most of Pohl's enemies. *Library of Congress*

SMS *Moltke*: Her captain (Levetzow) "stands up for his opinion" in eviscerating Pohl. *Library of Congress*

SMS *Ostfriesland*: Scheer's visit there sought to impose officer corps solidarity before neutralizing the Kaiser. *Library of Congress*

Battle of Jutland at 1548: SMS *Seydlitz* fires on HMS *Queen Mary*. *U.S. Naval Institute photo archive*

Battle of Jutland at 1558: The British "did not shoot famously." *U.S. Naval Institute photo archive*

Battle of Jutland at 1600: HMS *Lion*'s midship Q-turret is hit. *U.S. Naval Institute photo archive*

Battle of Jutland at 1626: HMS *Queen Mary* explodes. She trailed *Princess Royal*. Under heavy fire, *Lion* had veered away and out of view to starboard. *U.S. Naval Institute photo archive*

Battle of Jutland at 1640: British painting depicting the 1st BCS's initial sighting of the High Seas Fleet stretching to infinity to the south. *Library of Congress*

Battle of Jutland at 1855: View from Jellicoe's 4th BS passing the remains of HMS *Invincible*. *U.S. Naval Institute photo archive*

The Illustrated London News, June 12, 1916: The capital honors fallen heroes Sir Horace Hood, Sir Robert Arbuthnot, and Captain Cecil Prowse, captain of HMS *Queen Mary*. *Library of Congress*

British cartoon print "So this is *Der Tag*": Sarcastic depiction of German sailors' mutinous turn against their officers in 1917. *Library of Congress*

With the fleet out of Scapa Flow, Jellicoe's staff sent the Admiralty the coordinates for the rendezvous terminuses of his own and Beatty's commands, a *wireless* that should have been more securely *telegraphed* much earlier: "Battle Fleet is proceeding to Lat. 57.45' N Long 4.15' E, Battle Cruiser Fleet to Lat. 56.40' N 5.0' E, both by 2 p.m. G[reenwich] M[ean] T[ime] tomorrow 31st." "Even if sent by low-power radio," wrote Holloway Frost, professor at Annapolis in the 1920s, "the message might have been picked up by a nearby submarine and forwarded to . . . Neumünster."[30] German cryptanalysts did not intercept the transmission, however, which must have been strong enough to reach London. Nor, luckily for Jellicoe, did the two submarines in the area, *U-43* and *U-44*. Antisubmarine patrols had forced them to dive below periscope depth well before Jellicoe's squadrons left, and consequently neither saw nor heard anything. The Admiralty's antisubmarine directive of mid-May had earned a second dividend this day—the first, due to zigzagging, had confused U-boat bearing observations. As explained presently, the sea lords soon earned additional dividends against *U-27* and *U-74*—a reaping of handsome early returns that would fade over the rest of the battle, however, as the Admiralty incurred only the steep costs of missed opportunities.

Flukes and fatalities factored further into the faults and failures of Scheer's submarine mission.[31] The totality of what went wrong off the Firth of Forth amounted, in fact, to a fiasco. Even before the operation started (May 25), *U-27* got tangled up in antisubmarine nets in the outer firth. The damaged vessel managed to extricate itself from its ambush site and get home but left those exit channels danger free. On the twenty-seventh, moreover, antisub trawlers that had been on alert since midmonth sank minelayer *U-74* before it could compromise the Forth. Finally, of the six attack subs scattered widely about these same coastal waters, five had not stationed themselves fortunately enough to be within sight of Beatty's exit lane— "how to do it," said Hipper about the U-boat operation, "therein lies the rub." Their unfortunate positioning resulted mainly from the fact that only two, *U-70* and *U-32*, had received the message from submarine command substituting the Skagerrak for the Sunderland mission. Consequently, most were spread from north to south along the coast to be able to sight and sink ships hurrying out of Rosyth and other northern bases to the vicinity of Sunderland. Of the two, only one, *U-32*, saw anything; but as noted earlier, it reported the ships' headings misleadingly. It managed to fire two torpedoes, which missed, but then its periscope jammed. Beatty got away scot-free.

Jerram's 2nd BS out of Invergordon had also gotten safely to sea. By surviving, *U-72* fared better that *U-74*, but an oil leak sent her homeward before laying mines in the Moray Firth. Nor did Jerram suffer any casualties from attack U-boats. One, the *U-47*, had also failed to receive the wireless scrubbing the Sunderland mission, so it waited too far south in anticipation of British ships rushing to Sunderland. The other, *U-66*, sighted eight battleships at 300 yards but was forced by antisub forces to dive before firing; and when rising again to periscope depth a while later, it was out of range. And he too misreported the enemy's heading.

Only *U-75* succeeded in mining its targeted waters off the southwestern sounds of Scapa Flow—orders that also fit the Sunderland not the Skagerrak mission: Jellicoe's fleet left via two eastern exits. Once at sea, moreover, Jellicoe and Hood were not threatened by either *U-43* or *U-44*, which as explained earlier had been forced under and thus lacked radio capabilities. Like most of the U-boats to the south of them and *U-75* to the north, therefore, they did not know about the cancelation of the Sunderland mission. If they had gotten that message, both probably would have shifted east to wait with more visibility at dawn for enemy squadrons.

■ ▪ ■

Circa 0800, the bridge of SMS *Lützow* buzzed with activity. Lookouts peered through binoculars for submarine periscopes, signalmen sent and received searchlight messages from the destroyers and light cruisers, midshipmen brought the latest wirelesses from the Jade, and a passel of officers advised the captain on fuel consumption, weather, navigation, and the ongoing difficulties the Zeppelins experienced getting aloft. Raeder, many of the chief's staff, and Hipper himself stood to the side. He had just ordered the leader of 2nd SG several miles ahead to deploy his five light cruisers and nineteen torpedo boats into an eight-mile, northwest-to-northeast arcing screen. Horns Reef lay twenty miles to the northeast.[32]

When circumstances allowed some free discussion, Hipper's entourage speculated with him about the prospects of seeing action this day or the next; and for the most part the same consensus reigned here as in the fleet flagship: this sortie would not result in *Der Tag* of major battle the navy had anxiously awaited for two years. The chief saw things differently. "By the afternoon we'll be at it hammer and tongs with the blue jackets," he had said. "There will be heavy losses of human life when we really get down to grips with them." There was nothing, however, that could be done to stop it. "Events are remorselessly driving to a decision." But he consoled himself with a shrug of fatalism not uncommon in military men. "It's all in God's hands."[33]

Most of the staff found these remarks astounding, indeed dumbfounding, because Hipper had never showed "the slightest inclination for the supernatural" or for "[playing] the role of soothsayer."[34] So why was he so braced for action? For one thing, he had read the same three wirelesses that Scheer had received about British fleet movements earlier that morning, so he knew that enemy ships sailed near the Firth of Forth, Cromarty, and apparently Scapa Flow (i.e., according to Neumünster). His remarks show that he believed the British knew that he sailed too, and that they would not be learning anything new when he "baited" their D-F Stations that afternoon.[35]

Indeed, Hipper's belief that combat would occur "by the afternoon" warrants further explanation. It seems highly likely that after the Battle of Dogger Bank Hipper had swung over to Raeder's belief (see chapter 2, note 23) that the British did not just position German ships at sea with D-F Stations but also deciphered and read German wirelesses. Before departing the Jade, he had probably heard his chief of staff expound at length on the probability—one he thought bordered on certainty—of the enemy pulling up anchors in perfect synchronization with the German C-in-C's orders so as to be far enough at sea on May 31 to block the German fleet. Hipper's fatalism that morning therefore contained a streak of realistic pessimism: the German fleet just might need God's help.[36]

At noon, as Hipper's forces crossed the 56th Parallel seventy miles below Little Fisher Bank, with Scheer trailing him by three hours, another curious message arrived from Neumünster. It included the early morning report on wind, barometric pressure, and weather sent out from the Firth of Forth, noting that "we generally observe these kinds of reportings only when the fleet formation (*Flottenverband*) is at sea."[37] While rainy and overcast at Rosyth, expectations on the German side cleared up somewhat with this wireless, for it now appeared likely that the entire BCF had gone out. Scheer does not mention this report in his memoirs, but, while omission can be telling, no evidence exists that he had become even a little fidgety given earlier news of "eight large warships" near Cromarty (*U-66*'s report), perhaps "two formations" leaving Scapa Flow (Neumünster's first report), and now maybe the whole BCF at sea—on the contrary, his demeanor stayed quite calm. Instead, it seems more likely that he waxed even more optimistic now that his "plan to engage isolated units of the enemy" looked even more promising. At any rate, this was no time in the world's Great War for panic: the course of the German High Seas Fleet would remain the same. And if this meant an unlikely albeit risky collision with Jellicoe, just as Pohl had before him, Scheer did not regard this as an unmitigated disaster scenario. He trusted his men and his material too much for such defeatist thinking.[38] As for Hipper's thoughts, he undoubtedly reacted more apprehensively to the weather report, for it surely reinforced his anxious expectation that blood would be spilled—and soon.

■ ▣ ■

Developments occurred on the British side, meanwhile, that detracted from their obvious advantages—developments that border on the incredible in the opinion of some historians. One occurrence relates to the Admiralty's decision to hold back Commodore Reginald Tyrwhitt's Harwich Force, which they did not deploy on May 30 or 31 despite an earlier assurance given Jellicoe that its necessary light cruisers and destroyers—five and eighteen, respectively, at this time—would always sortie to reinforce him. Tyrwhitt's group was "straining at their leash"[39] when the northern squadrons readied for sea on the thirtieth, but his first set of orders were to sail at dawn on the thirty-first, but then altered to merely keeping steam at one hour's notice until further word. At 0450 on the thirty-first, Tyrwhitt sent an urgent telegram to the Admiralty reminding them that he had no further orders; but he was properly (but curtly) told to stay at one hour's notice. Furious, and unwilling to wait longer, he put out at 1710 without orders—and was immediately and angrily ordered back to Harwich.

First Lord of the Admiralty Arthur Balfour and First Sea Lord Henry Jackson, who had either forgotten or never known about the promise to Jellicoe, left the detailed decision-making this day in the hands of Jackson's Chief of War Staff Sir Henry Oliver, whose main preoccupation in the southern theater, seconded emphatically by DOD Thomas Jackson, remained the constant expectation, as Oliver recalled, of "the Huns [making] some attempt to block the Channel ports and destroy our line of communications with the army in France, such as rushing the Dover Straits with pre-dreadnought type of ships"—an entirely legitimate concern. Until the Admiralty had evidence that the German navy had not set in motion a second simultaneous strike against the Dover Straits, they felt the need to guard against the German 2nd Squadron and destroyers based in occupied Belgium by reinforcing HMS *Dreadnought*, the predreadnought "Wobbly Eights," and the armored cruisers of 3rd CS in the Thames with Tyrwhitt's entire Harwich Force.[40] Although Room 40 had ample evidence already on May 30 that Rear Admiral Franz Mauve's 2nd Squadron would sail north with 1st and 3rd Squadrons and all High Seas Fleet destroyers—in other words, that neither the Admiralty's preoccupation with a predreadnought threat to the southern theater, nor a reinforcement of Germany's torpedo boat flotilla in Belgium was warranted—and that therefore Britain's Dover Patrol with two older flotillas could parry any threat from across the Channel, these subordinate intelligence analysts "were not asked to give their opinion on such matters,"[41] writes an incredulous Patrick Beesly. Room 40 analysts claimed to have sent their unsolicited information to Oliver on the afternoon of the thirty-first, but he did not notice it until much later that evening because, according to his counterclaim, it had not actually been sent until then.

One leading historian of the Royal Navy, Andrew Gordon, is more supportive of the Admiralty's Channel preoccupation than Beesly, but he believes that shortly before Tyrwhitt bolted, the argument for holding him back lost rationality, for his proper station became now the edge of the Bight between Terschelling and Borkum, and he should have been allowed to proceed there. Annapolis naval historian Holloway Frost argues similarly. If Tyrwhitt had assumed the Terschelling–Borkum station on the thirtieth, he could have blocked, delayed, or harried any attempt from Germany to run the Channel, or, as Gordon adds, guard this southern mine-free channel back to the German main bases, the only alternative exit/entrance channel to the Helgoland/Amrun Bank routes off the Danish coast.[42] Oliver and Jackson should not have reserved Tyrwhitt for the Thames, therefore, but rather have concentrated his light forces—with thirteen capital ships in Sheerness ready to steam his way—in this southern channel off Holland, a station where they might, hypothetically, have played a role (see chapter 11).

Even more mind-bogglingly perplexing is the DOD's infamous visit to Room 40 shortly before noon on May 31. Two versions have emerged. Since the previous evening, according to the first telling, Jackson had seen many decrypts of German signals using the call sign "DK." Unclear what these reports referenced, he made only his second visit to the underlings in Room 40—the first, months earlier, had been to complain that he had cut his hand on one of the red metal boxes—to ask where the network of coastal D-F Stations positioned this call sign. With outward deference and inward dislike, one of the operatives simply told him that "DK" was sending from Wilhelmshaven, whereupon "the insufferable Jackson, without further ado and without asking for an explanation or comment, turned on his heel and left the room," according to historian Patrick Beesly, who had the story from Room 40 sources. The historical revision of recent years disputes the veracity of the first version by questioning the accuracy and motives of top Room 40 operative William Clarke, pointing out inconsistencies and inaccuracies in his writing that undermine his credibility, even suggesting that he and others may have contributed themselves to the debacle to follow by failing to decipher a key DK-ruse–related wireless in a timely fashion, and therefore later pointed fingers of blame elsewhere. As argued earlier (see chapter 8, note 28), the truth, as often transpires, may lie closer to the middle. Room 40 probably had its suspicions after the Lowestoft Raid (of five weeks earlier) about the DK ruse, but not knowing for certain, and after previous unpleasant experiences with Jackson, opted not to express them, which afterward they blamed on Jackson to deflect from their own duty shortcomings.[43]

After Jackson's brief exchange in Room 40—which gave ominous military meaning to the old Vaudevillian lines, "Why didn't you tell me?! . . . You didn't ask!"—he relayed the information to the overworked Oliver, who, asking no questions and getting no answers (Arthur Wilson's role is uncertain, but whatever it was, it changed nothing) sent the following dispatch to Jellicoe and Beatty, received at 1241: "No definite news enemy. They made preparations for sailing early this morning Wednesday. It was thought fleet had sailed but direction signal placed flagship Jade at 11:10 GMT. Apparently they have been unable to carry out air reconnaissance which has delayed them."[44]

At 1241, Beatty zigzagged at 19 knots toward his first destination slightly behind schedule—he approached Great Fisher Bank thirty miles from his terminus for 1400. Jellicoe had proceeded out of Scapa Flow at 14–15 knots to inspect suspicious merchant ships and also to conserve destroyer fuel for any fleet action, however unlikely that seemed. He sailed further away from (and slower toward) the point of turning southeast for a rendezvous with 5th BS and the BCF.[45] His delays, in other words, had pushed back the moment when he could close the gap with Beatty. The C-in-C had even less reason now to anticipate battle, however, for enemy formations, if they had managed to get out at all, would not be sighted beyond the 56th Parallel this afternoon, assuming it was actually their uncharacteristic and therefore seemingly unlikely goal.

Jellicoe therefore continued to steam at the same pace. The Grand Fleet's three battle squadrons—Jerram's 2nd BS from Cromarty had joined the 1st and 4th—deployed abreast in a twenty-five-mile wide sweeping formation, six division columns of four battleships each. Although this force included ten older dreadnoughts, fourteen were state-of-the-art (or close to it), boasting an awesome array of larger caliber (13.5–15-inch) guns than Germany's first line (11–12-inch). Forty destroyers and ten light cruisers guarded around an even broader perimeter, scanning the sea for U-boats known to be away from their bases. Ten miles ahead of these light forces sailed the advanced screen of eight armored cruisers with eight destroyers. With two light cruisers and four destroyers, Hood's 3rd BCS scouted farther out, racing twenty miles ahead of the armored cruisers; so far out, in fact, that Jellicoe had to rein in his horses and back them up ten miles to their proper station.

At 1355, Jellicoe asked his staff to determine the rate "at which battleships could supply fuel to the destroyers at sea," for he expected "to remain at sea awaiting events owing to the Admiralty message indicating that the [German fleet] was still in harbor."[46] The chances that May 31 would be "the Great Day"—or even June 1 for that matter—seemed to be fading fast.

Circa 1400, Beatty's four battleships, six battlecruisers, fourteen light cruisers, twenty-seven destroyers, and a seaplane carrier lay perhaps eighty-seven miles south-southeast of Jellicoe's armada—an alarming warping of the C-in-C's already cautious plan, which assumed for this time point a sixty-nine-mile separation.[47] Sailing with no sense of urgency well east of Great Fisher Bank and no enemy in sight, the "rather bored" vice admiral made his turn to the northwest at 1415. Beatty wanted action but did not seriously expect any when he left Rosyth, and certainly not after the Admiralty's 1241 wireless. Not anticipating needing firepower up-front in battle, therefore, he had moved 5th BS's super-dreadnoughts (*Barham*, *Valiant*, *Warspite*, and *Malaya*) five to six miles *behind* 1st BCS in order "to ease their resumption of their customary station in the van of the [main] battle-fleet."[48] Accordingly, once Beatty's forces turned north, Evan-Thomas sailed five miles *ahead* of *Lion*'s port bow in position—he assumed based on dead reckonings—to lead the BCF northwest to close with the Grand Fleet. By arriving first in about ninety minutes, he could easily swap places with Hood (out in front of Jellicoe). After changing course, 2nd BCS (*New Zealand* and *Indefatigable*) steamed three miles in front of Beatty's starboard bow. Thus, his capital ship squadrons steamed in a "V" configuration with 3rd and 2nd Light Cruiser Squadrons (LCSs), respectively, below 1st BCS (*Lion*, *Princess Royal*, *Queen Mary*, and *Tiger*) and the low point of the "V," a formation that the day's unanticipated action would soon break up—and hurl into historical controversy.

Only 1st LCS did not execute the turn. These four light cruisers had led the eastward procession by ten miles when squadron flagship *Galatea* sighted a fish steamer fifteen miles east-southeast of her. She turned to inspect the situation and blinked back westward with signal lamp at 1410: "Two-funneled ship has stopped steamer bearing E-SE, 8 miles, am closing." At 1420 she hoisted the signal flag for "enemy in sight" and blinked again westward: "Urgent. Two cruisers, probably hostile, in sight bearing E-SE, course unknown."[49]

Galatea's signal reached Beatty's hands a few minutes later. "Visualizing the situation in a flash," remembered a navigation officer on *Lion*'s bridge, the chief assumed these two enemy light cruisers formed part of Hipper's battlecruiser van. At 1425, therefore, Beatty "acted immediately" by ordering his destroyer flotillas to begin shifting their antisubmarine screen south-southeast (i.e., toward Horns Reef). At 1432 all other ships, having closed the gap with Jellicoe nearer to 70–72 miles, received the same signal to turn south-southeast. He intended to cut the enemy off from his base. The Admiralty's 1241 telegram had come into clearer focus for the BCF's impulsive leader. Evidently through delays or bungling, the enemy's main force "was not at sea as far as Beatty knew."[50] Although no one could completely dismiss nagging suspicions that it simply could not be true, apparently German naval command had once again left its battlecruisers unsupported far out at sea. Heavily invested emotionally in the policy of "going for the enemy directly he shows himself outside his minefields," Beatty ventured forth, confident he would gain redemption for the incomplete victory purchased inexpensively at Dogger Bank.

At 1428 *Galatea* opened fire on two large German destroyers (identified incorrectly minutes earlier as light cruisers). They had stopped a Danish steamer for inspection. While the BCF's battlecruisers were turning at 1432, *Elbing*, a newer light cruiser anchoring the western wing of the German screen, returned fire at *Galatea* and hurried southwest to help the destroyers. One of *Elbing*'s 5.9-inch shells hit the base of *Galatea*'s bridge at 1437 and pierced below decks. "Luckily for us it did not explode," recalled an engine room artificer. "As it was right over the 4-inch magazine chamber, I don't need to state here what would have happened." The German dud problem likely stemmed from poorly designed fuse threads. Thus, from the start of this long-awaited day, shell deficiencies played an important role—just as they had earlier in the war.[51]

What Beatty's countrymen dubbed "The Battle of Jutland"—and Hipper's "The Battle of the Skagerrak"—had begun.

■ 10 ■

CAVEAT EMPTOR

The Battlecruiser Duel

When Beatty's squadrons turned north at 1415, fifty miles slightly northeast of them, the bridge of *Lützow* was again a busy place.[1] Each one of the twenty-odd officers and sailors there concentrated on his appointed task. Far ahead, visible only as spots of smoke, sailed the torpedo boats of Rear Admiral Friedrich Boedicker's 2nd SG; several miles closer to the flagship, his light cruisers fanned out in a wide screening formation; and then came the five battlecruisers in line ahead guarded by more destroyers. Behind them by fifty miles, having dropped progressively further behind, cruised Scheer's main body. May 31 broke as a warm, variably cloudy, late spring day with a light northwesterly breeze; but visibility, so typical of the North Sea, varied from seventeen miles, about as far as the eye could see, to merely a mile or two as haze swept up seemingly out of nowhere. Ships' smoke obscured visibility even more.

As Hipper's units pushed further and further north, they saw many clusters of boats drawn to the plentiful fishing bounty of these waters—the German flotilla sailed a few miles northwest of Little Fisher Bank. Each sighting prompted torpedo boats from either the advance guard or the antisubmarine screen disposed abeam the battlecruisers to break away at top speed to investigate these commercial craft. The escorts had to prevent possible enemy agents from disclosing the Scouting Groups' location before the appointed time for exposing their position a few hours later. A little past 1400, *Elbing* detached torpedo boats *B-109* and *B-110* from the port wing of the screen to investigate one of these suspicious vessels far to the west.

As Hipper sailed on twenty-five minutes later (1428), the delayed cracks of *Galatea's* first shots at the German destroyers alerted *Lützow's* busy bridge party to something amiss to the southwest.[2] Hipper and Raeder stepped onto the portside flying bridge and peered back fourteen miles through binoculars at the fire-red smoke of *Elbing's* return fire, followed seconds later by the loud booms of shellfire. As they stood there, couriers delivered three important wires in rapid succession. From *Elbing*: "Enemy main body of twenty-four to twenty-six ships of the line," but gave no location. From *B-109*: "Scattered enemy forces in Square 164," twelve miles south of *Galatea*, some thirty miles due southwest of Hipper. And then another from *Elbing*: "Enemy battlecruisers in sight NW."[3] Did this mean a strong battleship force to the southwest, and the BCF to the northwest, all threatening to cut him off if he continued north? Hipper ordered 1st SG to swing southwest toward Square 164, and then a moment later almost to due south. Light cruiser *Frankfurt*, flagship of Boedicker's 2nd SG, also turned hard to port and signaled the entire advance screen to follow.

The chief's "hammer and tongs" remark now seemed like a premonition—and the likely glance Raeder shot at his chain-smoking chief reflected this realization. If indeed Jellicoe sailed behind them, the Scouting Groups would need help from Scheer. *Lützow* broke radio silence to *Friedrich der Grosse* at 1435: "Several smoke clouds of enemy forces in sight Square 164."[4] But five minutes later the situation changed radically with a scaled-back signal from *Elbing* reporting the *only* enemy forces toward the northwestern horizon. With danger lurking apparently to the northwest, Hipper's entire force swung back around in that direction. What, if anything, *Elbing* had seen remains a mystery, for at 1440 the accelerating British battlecruisers cleared for action over the west-southwest horizon about thirty miles *beyond* what lookouts could see, heading south-southeast to trap their old battle adversaries. Similarly, *B-109's* sighting of smoke clouds in Square 164, which contained no British warships, must have been either an anxious mistake or smoke from fishing vessels.

Hipper's rapid changes of course interrupted many a mess deck discussion. Whereas one minute most seamen still doubted that the day of the big action had arrived, a moment later the voice pipes suddenly vibrated with the urgent call of "clear ship for action!" Drums and bugles repeated the order, which reverberated throughout ships with the sound of thumping feet running to stations. The first looks of shocked surprise quickly turned to excited glances back and forth, hardy handshakes, and *"macht's gut"* words of encouragement. In a flash, as years of deteriorating morale and sagging patriotism (see chapter 7) mutated into that strange mixture of eager anticipation undergirded with anxious tension that combat veterans know so well, men rushed off to prepare ships for battle: closing hatches; securing gun stations and turrets; readying materials for medical, fire, and shell damage emergencies; wetting all surfaces that could burn; and hurrying through many other parts of a prudent routine they had executed only once for major sea action—at Dogger Bank.

As they did these things, the battlecruiser line turned hard to port twice, accelerating to the south-southwest, and then altered a few times to starboard and a northwest bearing. Testing all component parts, barrels moved up and down, anxious bulls flipping massive heads before the charge. Ships' bows sent the same menacing messages, steel hoofs raising up and stomping down into the waves, shooting megaquantities of shiny white foaming seawater over quarterdecks, dousing bridges and all souls on them,[5] men who were keenly aware that "the spirits of the mighty dead, whose names our ships bear, are gathering together in the heavens above our heads right now, watching to see if the coming battle shall be worthy of them!"[6]

■ ■ ■

After ordering his destroyer flotillas to redeploy, *Lion* hoisted pendants seven minutes later for his capital ships to "turn in succession to starboard, course S-SE," quickly lowered the flags (i.e., to execute the turn), and sped up to 22 knots. The radical change of course and acceleration with engines whining higher, and then moments later the blaring sound of "clear ship for action" at 1438, jerked many a British sailor out of inactivity, some taking "doss downs" atop sunlit turret tops, others attending to routine matters, and sped them into the same well-drilled motions as their German counterparts.[7] Andrew Gordon wrote,

> By now in every ship under Beatty's command patrols were going through the ship systematically wetting the decks, laying tables and stools flat, lighting action-candles, and closing steel doors with all eight clips instead of the usual two. Medical parties were at sick bays and casualty distribution centers, laying out their surgical implements and medical bags, their stretchers, dressings, morphia and syringes. Fire-and-repair parties were sorting their splinter mats, boxes of sand, softwood wedges, mallets, shoring-up timbers, spare electrical gear, etc. On the upper deck, swivel-mounted fittings and guard-rail stanchions in the way of gunnery arcs were struck flat; hoses were faked out, turned half-on and left running [to dampen fires]; extra chain stoppers were fitted to the cables to prevent the anchors being let go by action-damage. The glass windscreens on the bridge were unshipped and stowed.[8]

Evan-Thomas's sailors were clearing their ships for action too, but they had not swung south-southeast as promptly as the battlecruisers. Consequently, 5th BS, which had been five miles ahead of Beatty's port bow before the turn, now sailed an ominous and problematic ten miles astern. The delayed execution meant that the super-dreadnoughts could not help when Beatty and Hipper opened fire eighty minutes later, an unfortunate development, especially for the BCF's older, weaker, now-unguarded 2nd BCS (*New Zealand* and *Indefatigable*).

Explaining what had happened takes historians into another controversial episode of the Battle of Jutland/Skagerrak.[9] Smoke and distance partially obscuring *Lion*'s signal flags, the bridge party in Evan-Thomas's flagship, *Barham*, assumed the signal meant Beatty wanted to resume zigzagging, which had been anticipated on the trek to unite with Jellicoe, so 5th BS turned a point to port (i.e., to west-northwest) rather than swinging around hard to starboard and following the others. Beatty's signal officer, Flag Lieutenant Ralph Seymour, did not immediately notice this, and *Tiger*, last in line, did not repeat the command because after the turn north she had no longer sailed closest to *Barham*—but now did again. After eight minutes, either *Lion* or *Tiger*—versions differ—finally repeated the signal. But none of this entirely forgives Evan-Thomas for not executing the south-southeast turn (despite the urgings of his flag captain) because he did not believe he had a clear order to do so. His by-the-book decision—Andrew Gordon prefers to say his "doubt and dither"—reflected service under Jellicoe and the admiral's proprietary top-down tactical manual (see chapter 4), as well as his inexperience sailing with the BCF, whose chief customarily "maneuvered his fleet like a huntsman with a pack of hounds."[10]

Beatty receives more criticism. Although he had incorporated into BCF battle orders awareness of these personal traits as well as the duty of all ships in the BCF to closely follow the flagship's moves, and may even have passed these written procedures along to Evan-Thomas shortly before they sortied, he had not taken the time to speak with the new man, however, even though he had campaigned hard to get 5th BS. Nor did he slow down in order for Evan-Thomas to catch up, probably overestimating 5th BS's speed (see chapter 8). Besides, even if 5th BS continued to lag, Beatty seemed sportingly confident that his battlecruisers could strike Hipper down all by themselves. Beatty's biographer Stephen Roskill writes,

> I am convinced that Beatty regarded Hipper as his particular quarry, and on [May 31] he was determined that this time he would "bag the lot"—as he considered his force should have done at Dogger Bank. A clue to Beatty's

possible feelings on this matter is provided by a remark made by his intimate friend Walter Cowan of the *Princess Royal* . . . [who recalled] that during the approach to the battle he had at first feared that the "damned 5th Battle Squadron is going to take the bread out of our mouths."

Roskill believes it "reasonable to extend Cowan's thinking to the [vice] admiral," which is all the more insightful to Beatty's jousting mindset this day when one remembers that rumors posited (falsely) the German 1st SG sailing with a new battlecruiser, the *Hindenburg*, fitted allegedly (again, false) with 15-inch guns.

After *Galatea's* brief gun battle with *Elbing* and German destroyers, she led the rest of 1st LCS around and away to the northwest.[11] Rushing to the sound of the action, 3rd LCS followed 1st, cutting across the battlecruisers' bows as the BCF executed its radical turn. Both light cruiser squadrons intended to draw the enemy northwest toward Jellicoe and enable Beatty's and Evan-Thomas's capital ships to move far enough south and east to get behind the Germans and cut them off (see map 10.1). These were classic and instinctive tactics for light cruisers. By 1452, the south-southeast course of the BCF and 2nd LCS had taken them eight miles farther in that direction.

Shortly before 1500, Hipper, having narrowed the distance to Beatty with his first turns to the southwest and south, made his sixth recent course correction and now sailed northwest, thirty miles slightly northeast of the BCF. The signals from *Elbing* reporting "twenty-four to twenty-six ships of the line" having been determined to be false, his screen flagship, light cruiser *Frankfurt*, further clarified the situation by reporting *only* enemy light cruisers now in sight—neither battleships, therefore, nor battlecruisers. With less cause for alarm, Hipper decided to stay the northwest course and reconnoiter what sailed behind these light cruisers. The first alarming reports had certainly stirred his competitive juices and braced everyone on the bridge for an imminent fight to the finish, but no one there saw the chief shaken, as one historian reads into Hipper's "sweeping course changes." Rather, he "led his division in a tactical sense with a positively remarkable self-reliance—his unruffled calm communicated itself to his staff and all those on the bridge of the flagship."[12] This outward calm no doubt sheathed an inner resolve, however, to have revenge—and earn redemption—for Dogger Bank.

Beatty received reports from *Galatea*, meanwhile, that confirmed his initial sense of his enemy consisting of much more than a few torpedo boats and light cruisers. At 1439 she signaled *Lion*: "Have sighted large amount of smoke as though from a fleet"; and at 1451: "Smoke seems to be seven vessels besides destroyers and cruisers.

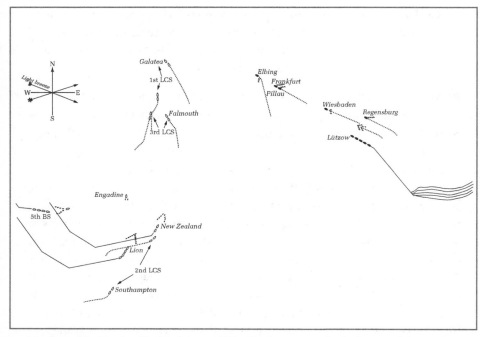

MAP 10.1. The Battle of Jutland at 1515: "The black monsters looked powerful, massive, even at this great distance."

They have turned north." Now Beatty—also not shaken in the least—swung his squadrons around toward the enemy with "sweeping" course changes of his own: from south-southeast to southeast (1452); from southeast to east (1501); and east to northeast (1513). By this time, 2nd BCS, in the lead several thousand yards off *Lion*'s starboard bow, sailed about nineteen miles southwest of Hipper.[13] Several minutes later, *New Zealand* reported "five enemy ships on starboard bow."

The German ships sighted the British too around 1515. In his station atop *Derfflinger*, directly astern *Lützow*, First Gunnery Officer Georg von Hase had waited long for this moment, dreaming of "battle and victory." During twelve years of gunnery practice, he "had learned all about it. It was a sport I understood. Once I had fixed the target with the periscope and once the first salvo had crashed from the guns, nothing could disturb me. It is true I did not yet know how I should get on in the dense hail of enemy fire. But that did not worry me. I should find that out all in good time." But as he peered southwest through a Zeiss stereoscopic range finder, greatly magnifying enemy vessels and seeming to lessen distance to them, a "marked hush" descended over all those in this perch. "The horizon ahead of us grew clear of smoke. . . . Suddenly my periscope revealed some big ships. Black monsters. Six tall, broad-beamed giants steaming in two columns. They were still a long way off, but they showed up clearly on the horizon, and even at this great distance they looked powerful, massive." The shocked awe of what they saw lasted "only a minute or so," however, and then nervous "humor broke out again."[14]

If at this point the British ships had turned again to the north, their heading would have closed the distance to Evan-Thomas—and not only have brought all of Beatty's command to within fifty miles of Jellicoe by 1600,[15] but also increased the distance to Scheer in the south. Anticipating a risky running battle to the north away from where Scheer could support him[16]—obviously still wishing "that we may soon be able to do battle"—Hipper, still heading northwest at 1529, ordered distribution of fire from the right; that is, *Lützow* to target *New Zealand*, *Derfflinger* firing at *Indefatigable*, and so on down the line. The chief then stared down his staff chief, blurting in a dialect not all his aides could understand: "Raeder, I'll eat my broomstick if that's not Beatty again!"[17]

But Beatty, still determined "to keep between the German ships and their base" to the south, did not lead the Germans to Jellicoe or close the gap with 5th BS but rather "immediately turned [back to] east" instead.[18] Beatty wanted Hipper for himself. At 1536 (3:36 p.m.) he ordered 2nd BCS to follow him by cutting back drastically hard to starboard and falling in astern 1st BCS—altogether some very problematic maneuvering.

With the distance falling to about fifteen miles, Hase continued to study his foe. "I could now recognize them as the six most modern enemy battlecruisers. . . . It was a stimulating, majestic spectacle as the dark-grey giants approached like fate itself. The six ships, which had at first been proceeding in two columns, formed line ahead. Like a herd of prehistoric monsters they closed on one another with slow movements, specter-like, irresistible."

While Hase made these observations and readied his crews to strike down enemy "giants" and "monsters," Hipper ordered: "Wire the main body, heavy enemy forces in sight." And then, with Beatty making his complicated maneuver only twelve miles away, the German reversed course (1535) by turning in succession to the southeast. Having completed this shift, Flag Captain Viktor Harder grabbed a nearby officer and shouted, his "scintillating eyes" only inches from the junior man's face: "Happy now midshipman? Are you happy? Another five minutes and we're in battle!"[19] Raeder and the staff suppressed smiles in the seriousness of the moment, but Hipper nodded confidently and all-knowingly, for he had told them so that morning.

Even though his battlecruisers were still completing a complicated maneuver and forming into eastern line ahead, when Beatty saw Hipper's turnabout he ordered his battlecruisers to turn again to the east-southeast and speed up to 25 knots. He remained determined not to let his "quarry" escape, foil the BCF's moment of "bagging the lot," and claim a redeeming bargain. Hipper countered by altering course from southeast to south-southeast and close the enemy. Thus the "Run to the South" got underway. It was now 1545 and opposing forces sailed nine-and-a-half miles apart—about 16,500 yards.

On the compass platform above the bridge of *Lion*, Flag Captain Ernle Chatfield had been waiting impatiently—but, like Beatty and Cowan, confidently—to open fire. "We had sunk *Blücher* and badly damaged *Seydlitz* and others at Dogger Bank . . . [so] why should we not now sink some more of our old opponents?" However, as the range descended rapidly toward medium range, and the trailing battlecruisers arced at high speed and barely controllable centrifugal force to keep up with 1st BCS, the chief—busy below on the bridge dictating an "urgent" wireless to Jellicoe, reporting "enemy battlecruisers, five in number, bearing NE"—may have been too distracted to notice the descending range; or perhaps the haze made the Germans look further away than they were (see below); or did Beatty revert to preferring medium range based on the ineffective long-range firing at Dogger Bank (see chapter 6)? Finally, at 1548, Chatfield "could wait no longer [to tell Chief Gunnery Officer] Longhurst to open fire." Just then, with distribution of fire from the left, *Lützow* opened fire on *Lion* at 14,900 yards. Some thirty seconds later, when *Lion*'s turret captains obeyed Longhurst's order to fire, "Seymour hoisted the '5' flag (engage the enemy) and off went the double salvos" from the rest of the BCF when he hauled it down.[20]

■ ■ ■

Ninety minutes earlier on the bridge of *Iron Duke*, Jellicoe and his staff learned about *Galatea*'s sighting of hostile light forces. The news did nothing to disrupt the routine southeasterly cruise of Britain's main battle fleet. While any enemy sighting certainly caused Jellicoe to consider making changes, the C-in-C continued at 14–15 knots to conserve fuel, boilers cut back, in contrast to careening off like Beatty's initial reaction. Ten minutes later (around 1430–35), however, a dispatch from one of his battleships reported heavy wireless traffic along wavelengths used by the High Seas Fleet. These were undoubtedly Hipper's destroyers and light cruisers, for neither German flagship had yet broken radio silence. Jellicoe, however, did not know this. Accordingly, he made his first cautious response by ordering all ships to begin raising steam for 20 knots. Over the next fifteen minutes as *Galatea* reported a "large amount of smoke as though from a fleet," and then "seven vessels besides destroyers and cruisers," Jellicoe stopped zigzagging and tightened his columns into battle order. With speed at 18 knots, the C-in-C urged: "raise steam for full speed with all dispatch" (1457); and moments later: "assume complete readiness for action in every respect."[21] Simultaneously (1500), he altered course from southeast to south-southeast. Speed reached 19 knots at 1518. As late as this, however, the Admiralty's midday report that German heavy forces remained in the Jade still colored Jellicoe's expectations, for he ordered Hood's 3rd BCS to speed off toward the mouth of the Skagerrak, three hours to the east, anticipating that these overmatched German light forces would attempt to evade the BCF by escaping home through these waters.

At 1526, minutes after the battlecruisers sighted one another, Jellicoe sailed 71 miles north-northwest of Beatty, about the same distance as when Beatty darted to south-southeast at 1432. While for half an hour a taut Jellicoe did not know whether the gap had narrowed, when he learned that firing had started—Beatty radioed this information and his position at 1555—these hopes had faded, for the BCF still sailed sixty-six to sixty-seven miles away and had increased pace to 23 knots.[22] Based on Hipper's reported southwesterly, and then later southerly, heading, would Beatty attempt at even higher speed to cut off the enemy to the south, widening the separation to seventy miles and beyond? Knowing his BCF commander well, and no doubt worried again about a German-laid trap—did Hipper retire on Scheer's High Seas Fleet, its powerful squadrons not tied down in the Jade after all?—the understandably suspicious Jellicoe must have fumed inside his calm exterior at the prospect of his naval juggernaut dropping further back, for not until 1559 could he finally order 20 knots.

At 1605, therefore, sensing a disaster in the making, Jellicoe ordered 3rd BCS to "proceed immediately to support BCF,"[23] one of the most important orders of the entire day. From his present station fifty miles north of Beatty's last-reported position west of Little Fisher Bank, Hood, having already turned away from the Skagerrak toward the reported battle action in the south, increased speed to 25 knots. By cutting corners to south-southeast, he hoped to close Beatty, reportedly hastening southeast.

In the boiler and engine rooms of 3rd BCS, scores of stokers increased speed too, their toil pushing more sweat out onto their already grimy, shirtless torsos. Oddly enough, however, the speed up did not prompt the typical litany of cursing against the allegedly lucky, gin-guzzling, officer softies topside, a chorus most of them usually joined gleefully. Rather, much like the reaction below decks on the German side, mates put their backs into it for king and country, Jellicoe, and Beatty, the man they knew from the voice pipes they rushed to help. The Sausages, the Krauts, the Huns, the Jerries, the Scarborough Murderers, the Zepp Raid Killers—the criminal racial foes of their island people—would get their comeuppance.

■ ▇ ■

Beatty had written Jellicoe earlier that the "Germans certainly *do* fire 5 to our 2," and that this could "be the very deuce if we were unlucky."[24] But on May 31 the misfortune that befell the BCF in the early minutes of battle had less to do with the devil—among other factors discussed later—than the nearly uncontrollable approach of Beatty's battlecruisers before firing began. While "their formation at this instant will never be exactly known," wrote Holloway Frost, it seems likely that while *Lion* and *Princess Royal*, the first two ships in the line, turned southeast with all guns bearing, the other four—or many of them—were in the process of fanning out to port (i.e., northeast) in order to follow their leader on a northwest line of bearing Beatty had ordered, thereby blocking all except the fore turrets from firing. Smoke from the battlecruisers, and from destroyers swinging in front of the battlecruisers, further obscured visibility. Compounding these problems, the frenetic maneuvering of the BCF after 1530 made it impossible for normal range-finding, especially for 2nd BCS, which had radically reversed course to fall in behind 1st BCS, and then fanned out to port, creating "conditions of heel, vibration and rapidly changing bearings that made ranging impossible."[25] Consequently, *Queen Mary*, *Tiger*, *New Zealand*, and *Indefatigable* could not begin fire with forward guns until 1551–54.

In the quarter hour before first salvos, Hipper disposed his forces more calmly. Earlier (1524), in preparation for the running battle he expected to the northwest, he had slowed his line from 25 knots to 18, which reduced vibrations for his range finders. This slower speed also facilitated the course reversal to the southeast he made at 1535 after spotting Beatty's easterly turn. Hase and the other gunnery chiefs got timely orders at 1539 to prepare for fire distribution from the left and calculate their ranging as the distance to the enemy narrowed. At 1542 the battlecruisers tightened their formation to 500 meters between ships. And then at 1545 Hipper decreed a "battle turn" to the south-southeast. To avoid having to play catch up, the last ship, *Von der Tann*, turned first; then *Moltke*; then *Seydlitz*; then *Derfflinger*; then *Lützow*. Practiced to precise perfection in countless prewar maneuvers, this *Gefechtswendung* brought all forty-four 11- and 12-inch guns to bear with side armor at an oblique angle to the likely direction of British fire, thus lessening the chance of shell penetration.[26] In addition, the breeze blew the smoke of the German ships away to the east, while the British smoke presented fewer difficulties for the impressive Zeiss fire-control mechanisms. The late-afternoon sun also provided excellent silhouettes for German gunners of what could be seen through the smoke. In short, Hipper had put himself into excellent position to exploit firing on Beatty during the Briton's last-minute maneuvers—to be caught while maneuvering was the least desirable scenario.

But visibility, "misty in patches," varied by miles from minute to minute, which threw off the calculations of the range finders, even the more sophisticated German devices. "It was one of those typical North Sea summer days with a thin white mist varying in intensity and having too much humidity for the sun to break up." This deceptive, optically illusionary haze misdirected the first salvos on both sides well over the mark. The spotty, "slow and uncertain" British "bracket" firing (see chapter 8) overshot some 2,000 yards, putting light cruiser *Regensburg* sailing far off *Lützow*'s port beam in more danger than the flagship. German shells fell "over" by 1,750 yards, prompting a surprised Hase to order "down 400 [meters]," then "down 400" again, and finally "down 800" before his ranging salvos, fired nearly simultaneously at different distances by the more efficient "ladder" system, began to straddle *Princess Royal*.[27] After a few minutes, as the BCF turrets that were able to fire missed badly—the BCF took "an endless time in getting on [target]"—German shells began to splash all around Beatty's line, throwing up "huge columns of water, higher than the funnels. . . . Some of these gigantic splashes curled over and deluged us with water." The British "believed they were literally sailing through a forest of fountains." The watery woods they traversed further obscured vision for BCF fire control—gunnery that to begin with was far from tops in the Royal Navy.

By 1551–52 hours, with the range falling under 13,000 yards, Hipper's 5.9-inch gun crews opened fire too, letting loose two salvos for every one of the big guns. Every seven seconds now his ships fired a shell, creating "an ear-splitting, stupefying din." By 1607, *Lützow* had hit *Lion* at least six times—some sources put the figure as high as ten.[28] "Shells were all over the place and splinters by thousands were flying all over the whole ship and the air was full of them—it was a wonder the officers and men on the bridge weren't hit," recalled a midshipman there. One serious hit hampered communications all day by destroying the main wireless antenna. Another two (1552) were more troubling, piercing the port 4-inch gun casemate and wreaking havoc among the artillerymen of Y-battery opposite Royal Marine Captain Francis Jones' crews.[29] From disengaged X-battery, the startled marine crossed over to inspect the damage and supervise the movement to sick bay of the maimed, the burned, and those gassed by the noxious fumes emitted by shell detonations.

Derfflinger also did harm to *Princess Royal*. Like *Lion*, she took two or three early hits, and then three or four more circa 1600. One pierced the side armor and exploded in a coal bunker, while others hit the forward funnel, both forward turrets, and below the bridge destroying electric power to range-finding and fire-control gear. Another came into the lower deck flats where 4-inch gunners had taken refuge. "The shells are dropping all around us, Sir!" said one able seaman to the officer in charge there.

"All right," he replied, "get your respirator, there may be gas shells." Then, all of a sudden, we got an armor-piercing liquid fire shell in the flat. Everything went red hot. I fell to the deck. After a while I heard people moaning. Everything was in darkness. No lights. I came to and put my hands to my head and thought, "I'm not dead, my head's still on!" Then I was picked up by the First Aid men. . . . When I got to the sick bay there seemed to be about 150 dead and wounded, worse than me, I thought, so I walked away and went to the mess deck. An hour later I blacked out.

Queen Mary presumably suffered in like measure, while 1st BCS's last in line, *Tiger*, also took eight or nine quick shots, including two that put Q- and X-turrets out of action for a time. As casualties mounted, distribution stations "[were] packed with dead and dying men," recalled the ship's chaplain. Some "were brought in sometimes with hands and feet hanging off," others were gassed or burnt, so many that as "fresh cases were brought in one had some difficulty in avoiding stepping on the others."[30]

Potentially worse, the third or fourth hit on *Lion* (1600) nearly killed all hands when a high-explosive shell penetrated the armored roof of Q-turret, detonated above the left gun, blew the front roof plate over four hundred feet into the air, and sent a column of yellowy-orange cordite smoke high up out of the gun house and down the trunk lines to the handling room. The explosion meant instant death for both five-man gun crews and several others near the gun house breeches. As the smoke cleared, the blackened sergeant of marines, George Comley, rushed to help Harvey, who was badly burned, concussed, bleeding profusely, his legs fractured.

The dying marine major must have cried out for assistance, pointing to the voice pipe. Once lifted into position by Comley, Harvey yelled down with as much volume as he could muster, "Close magazine doors, Q-turret out of action!" That done, he gasped his last orders to help two severely wounded crewmen and report damage to the bridge. Then he blacked out.[31]

Comley, the only man in the gunhouse relatively unscathed, laid Harvey down and then ordered the men below in the working chamber to help the two badly wounded men down to the handling room, up the ladder to the mess deck, and on to the sick bay. Seeing that the rest of the turret crew were safely wearing their respirators, Comley made his way to the bridge, where the junior navigation officer, Lieutenant William Chalmers, saw him come up.

A bloodstained sergeant of marines appeared on the admiral's bridge. He was hatless, his clothes were burnt, and he seemed to be somewhat dazed: on seeing me he approached and asked if I were the captain. While directing him to the compass platform above my head, curiosity got the better of me, and I asked him what was the matter: in a tired voice he replied: "Q-turret has gone, Sir. All the [gun house] crew are killed, and we have flooded the magazines." I looked over the bridge. No further confirmation was necessary: the armored roof of Q-turret had been folded back like an open sardine tin, thick yellow smoke was rolling up in clouds from the gaping hole, and the guns were cocked up in the air awkwardly. It was evident that Q-turret would take no further part in the battle.

Comley, his face "black from fire, his hair singed," then reported up to Chatfield, who "briefly questioned him about the disaster and ordered him to be taken to the dressing station—he had done his duty faithfully."[32] Comley's boss and all save two from the gun house crew were gone, but much of the explosion had shot upward with the roof plate, and in flooding the one open magazine, the last action of Harvey's life, he had insured that Q-turret presented no further danger to *Lion*—an act that would save the ship again in an hour.

At the rear of the line, *Indefatigable*, left to fend for herself until 5th BS caught up, would not be so fortunate. She was probably the most adversely affected by Beatty's immediate prebattle fox chase orders that hindered ranging, such that for four minutes *Von der Tann* fired at her without any reply. While *Indefatigable*'s first shots from the fore turrets missed (1552), the German ship's gunnery officer, Commander Mahrholz, sent his shells closer and closer. And then at 1559, having fired eight or nine salvos, he yelled to his turret gunners: "*Gut schnell Wirkung!*"—and *Von der Tann*'s "rapid-fire for effect"[33] four-gun salvos began to fall alarmingly all around the British battlecruiser. At 1602 three shells pierced the stern and exploded lethally deep within it, destroying the steering gear and flooding aft compartments. Already sinking by the stern, thirty seconds later another salvo penetrated A-turret and in all likelihood ignited powder charges stacked in the working chamber, sending flames down the trunk line into open magazine doors, blowing the ship to pieces and killing the remainder of her thousand-man crew. A sailor in Evan-Thomas's squadron, still straining to get into the action, "thought for an instant that the last ship in [Beatty's] line had fired all her guns at once, as there was a much bigger flame, but the flame grew and grew till it was about three hundred feet high, and the whole ship was hidden in a dense cloud of yellow brown smoke." The lone survivor of the "terrific explosion," a signaler in the foretop, recalled that "the magazines went—I saw the guns go up in the air just like matchsticks—12-inch guns they were—bodies and everything."[34]

Indefatigable's dreadful demise appeared just as spectacular from 18,000 yards away on *Von der Tann*. Whether hearing the news broadcast through the ship's network of voice pipes, or viewing it from mastheads and slits in the armor, German patriots cheered wildly, although a sense of reverence and respect for fellow men of the sea quickly tempered the celebration. The same, after all, could happen at any second to them.

■ ■ ■

Once the BCF had all forty-four of its 12- and 13.5-inch guns bearing—2nd BCS did not follow 1st BCS to the southeast until 1554—ineffective fire compounded the adverse effects of earlier signaling errors to 5th BS, the difficulty of determining distance through the day's haze, and ranging problems during frequent course changes. The squadrons' prioritizing of rapid fire and nonchalant approach to Jellicoe's ideal of "actual hits" translated into a mere six scores in twenty-seven minutes by 1615 despite firing around eight hundred shells. In contrast, the German fire, even though just as fast as the British, was over four times more accurate—twenty-five or more hits by 1615. Their fall-of-shot "seldom landed very close to our ships," recalled Hipper blandly. "What astonished me," wrote Hase in a similar vein, "was that so far we had apparently not been hit once—only quite rarely did a shot stray near [*Derfflinger*]." A turret gunner on *Lützow* waxed even more bluntly: "enemy salvos fell either short or wide . . . the English did not shoot famously."[35] Because the main haze-related problem at this point caused British shots to sail far over the mark, many of these short shots may have been the product of defective propellant that had not been removed from Clarkson cases, the charge-lot mess Grant had discovered on *Lion* a year earlier (see chapter 6).

Compounding the fact that BCF gunners "did not shoot famously," German maneuvering exacerbated Britain's multiple AP-shell issues (see chapter 6). Indeed,

1st SG's four shifts of formation between echeloned battle turn and line ahead in the first twenty minutes presented British gunners with different angles at changing ranges, all far in excess of 10,000 yards, which put their ordnance at a distinct disadvantage. When descending from long range into German ships obliquely, the handful of BCF shells that hit and exploded tore into superstructures and inflicted "big thumps" and "terrific roars" on armor that made ships' "steel hulls tremble," but rarely penetrated. British shells "had broken to pieces"—they had "burst outside and had no effect locally," one of Hipper's officers recalled. "One small observation at the commencement of the action was surprising and reassuring at the same time," said another. "The general effect of the English hits . . . [was only that] they proved the weight of their large caliber: where they hit there was a mighty shock and a large hole. There, however, it stopped; the effect of the explosion was comparatively slight." The fire of the British battlecruisers, Hipper remembered in more charitable language, "did no serious damage to our [battlecruisers]"; but others rendered harsher, mocking judgments of British AP shells. Once it became clear to those aloft in German fire-control platforms that British ordnance had not improved since Dogger Bank, "we knowingly smiled at one another." Duds added to the smiles: every eighth British shell that hit metal this day did not explode.[36]

This was, however, the Royal Navy. After seven or eight minutes, as noted, Beatty's battlecruisers began to inflict damage. *Seydlitz* took two 13.5-inch shells from *Queen Mary* right before and after 1600, one piercing a 5.9-inch shield and killing a starboard casemate gun crew and sending splinters, smoke, and gas into a bunker and turbine compartment. The second hit evoked no smiles either, piercing the 9.2-inch barbette armor of C-turret, killing or wounding twenty crewmen, and putting the guns out of action; but unlike the same kind of hit at Dogger Bank, safety precautions introduced after that battle (see chapter 7) prevented the flash from reaching the magazine or threatening D-turret and the rest of the ship. *Lion* also hit her German counterpart, *Lützow*, four times: three 13.5-inchers bursting ineffectually on thicker armor, while a fourth crashed through the *unarmored* deck between A- and B-turrets, destroying the forward action dressing station and all medical personnel in it. Of the five shell hits *on armor* of all thicknesses, two burst close to properly inside (i.e., 40 percent bursting effectiveness), but all three on belt armor failed (0 percent).[37]

Shortly after the explosion of *Indefatigable*, moreover, Evan-Thomas's sharpshooting 5th BS had come within range of Hipper's rear guard. The huge dreadnoughts turned to starboard, joined the Run to the South, and launched 15-inch salvos, first driving away Boedicker's trailing 2nd SG, and then targeting *Von der Tann* and

Moltke. Soon the massive projectiles landed in tight straddles in rapid succession, erecting a forest of gargantuan water columns around the two ships, which "shivered and groaned from the explosion of shells falling all around [them] in the immediate vicinity of [their] hulls." Finally, one smashed into *Von der Tann*'s starboard-side aft (1609) and another into *Moltke*'s casemate (1616), eliminating a 5.9-inch gun and its crew and flashing down the hoist, but German safety precautions saved the *Moltke*. The two ships got slammed six more times between 1620 and 1630, losing forty-three men killed or wounded, the surprisingly low casualty rate explained by the "extremely slight explosive effect" of giant shells that "had broken apart on impact." Of these eight hits on armor, which caused great concussion and physical damage to be sure, only one (12.5 percent) had penetrated fully and burst inside—but on thinner casemate armor. It was "nothing but the poor quality of the British bursting charges," Hipper recalled, "that saved us from disaster."

Nevertheless, although casualties were slight, the episode left survivors badly shaken. The first shot on *Von der Tann* reverberated throughout the ship, converting it eerily into a giant "tuning fork" as the "vibration traveled from the stern to the bow and back." Magnifying this unnerving effect, the massive ship "oscillated backwards and forwards very violently" as other shots landed. "The bow and stern dipped in and out five or six times" as she shipped hundreds of tons of water and settled slightly deeper in the sea at a slight list. Seamen, knocked to the deck, stared at one another in cold terror. Were they only seconds away from the horrible fate of those men in *Indefatigable*, waiting as they had "amid that terrible din of battle for the last gorgeous explosion and the eternal silence that would follow it," as Filson Young described his emotions a year earlier at Dogger Bank? Like *Moltke*, *Von der Tann* did not sink, but only C-turret amidships remained able to fire.[38]

For over half an hour, the vice admiral had dictatorially directed the German side of the battle, tactically outdueling Beatty. Just before the firing started, as Raeder and the gunnery officer discussed fire distribution, Hipper waved them off, saying: "That is *my* business, no one need worry about it." Twenty minutes later, when his navigation officer exclaimed that *Indefatigable* had been sunk, the chief, remembering embarrassing false claims after Dogger Bank about sinking *Lion* or *Tiger*, rudely advised the man not to count his chickens. "It was only when he had seen for himself through the telescope that there were only five instead of six ships in the enemy's line that he felt real satisfaction. He rewarded Commander Prentzel for his piece of news with a grateful glance and lit a fresh cigar." Minutes later (1607), hearing his fire controller aloft report the distance to the British widening beyond 20,000 yards, he ordered "course SW, close the enemy more rapidly, reopen fire when back in range"; but shortly thereafter he focused his telescope on Evan-Thomas's punishment of his rear ships and barked: "Increase speed, 23 knots!" (1612). A few minutes later, his attention shifted back to Beatty: "He's turning, trying to close across our bows." Just then, with the range dipping below 15,000 yards again, two 13.5-inch battlecruiser shells broke up ineffectually against the flagship (1616) and Hipper ordered "commence fire!" And next, to confuse British gunners with yet another shift of formation: "Line ahead!" (1618).[39]

Indeed, neither Beatty nor Flag Captain Chatfield were at all nonplussed by the pummeling their ships had taken during the early firing, including the violent elimination of one of their six battlecruisers, for they knew that casualties would occur but that one had to press on in spite of high costs. While Chatfield undoubtedly regretted the explosion of their rear ship, he seems to have taken the tragedy coolly in stride. "The *Indefatigable* was a smaller and more weakly protected ship than those of the first division," he wrote later, "and was not a really serious tactical loss." More the cavalier romantic, Beatty thought men should welcome the honorable opportunity to die for king and country in a noble cause. "No one could have died a more glorious death,"[40] he would say of another instantaneous loss of a thousand men at sea this day. Obviously, both men remained eager to close the enemy in Nelsonian fashion and strike back at Hipper, especially with Evan-Thomas's reinforcements at hand—any earlier worries about 5th BS "taking the bread out of our mouths" had no doubt vanished.

At 1612, therefore, *Lion*, without signaling, turned sharply two points to port, followed shortly by another two points: the rest of the BCF knew from battle orders to follow their leader. Before the turns he sailed ten miles (20,000 yards) to the southwest of Hipper, six miles farther south of him, and speeding two knots faster. Three minutes later, British destroyers went onto the offensive (see below). British tactics in this "second phase" of the Run to the South strike one recent historian, John Brooks, as "impetuous" because Beatty had once again disrupted the station-keeping of his line, which pursued him to the southeast on what appeared to the last ship, *New Zealand*, to be "a snake-like course." The dash "cannot have helped their ranging and aiming," writes Brooks, difficulties exacerbated by the smoke of charging destroyers. Beatty had also put his command once again "within the Germans' effective range" and sacrificed "the [long-range] advantage of his heavier guns."[41]

Although he would surely have agreed with Brooks, post–World War I historian Holloway Frost detected a typical Beatty-like quality in his equestrian destroyer assault (see below). If torpedoes forced Hipper to turn away to the east, Beatty could "cut off the retirement of the Germans to the southward and envelop the southern flank [with the BCF], while the battleships [of 5th BS] were turning the northern flank, [a] double envelopment [designed to] force the enemy against the Danish coast." That Beatty had radioed his 13th Flotilla as early as 1555 that the "opportunity appears favorable for attacking" points to just such a premeditated tactic to achieve his goal, very consistent since *Galatea*'s signal nearly two hours earlier, of confidently cutting off and annihilating Hipper's force. But Frost added an important qualification: "If the [German] main body were not in the vicinity, [this] line of reasoning was excellent."[42] There is little reason to doubt that double envelopment and destruction of his foe is what Beatty was attempting, for, as argued presently, he continued to assume that Scheer lay at anchor in Wilhelmshaven.

Well before the British destroyers got close enough to launch their torpedoes, the battlecruisers locked horns again at ranges dipping below 15,000 yards. Their "artillery duel" quickly and deafeningly "reached an intensity that could scarcely be surpassed." As before, the British fired quickly and inaccurately. Hase remembered the "fabulous rapidity" of British guns, "but [their shots] were almost always over or short—only twice did the *Derfflinger* come under this infernal hail, and each time only one heavy shell hit her"; most of them, however, making distant "colossal splashes" and shooting up "poisonous yellow-green columns of water, giant fountains beside which the famous fountains of Versailles were mere children's toys." During this twenty-minute second phase of the battle, Beatty's five ships fired about six hundred shots and made only five more hits, a 1:120 ratio. *New Zealand* set a truly frenetic pace, firing about two hundred rounds and hitting nothing. Chatfield's postbattle report corroborated the negative impressions of the Germans: "Hits with heavy shell were seldom seen, especially with lyddite AP, which constituted the chief proportion of shell fired from battlecruisers." The "effect of our shell" also disappointed: only one hit of the five (i.e., 20 percent bursting effectiveness) smashed through a 5.9-inch shield and wiped out another starboard gun and crew on *Seydlitz*, but again antiflash features in the hoist prevented a devastating explosion.[43]

In contrast, the British line took seventeen to twenty additional hits from German guns firing just as fast. And while German shells had their own problems at Jutland—22–26 percent were duds—when their delayed-action fuses worked as designed, they burst far inside armor (of 5-inch thickness or more) at a rate of nearly four times the British.[44] Two of the first hits slammed into *Lion* amidships, inflicting many casualties along the mess deck where resting and wounded sailors had congregated. Engulfed in flame and smoke, she hauled out of line to starboard. *Princess Royal* and *Tiger* took four more apiece, both by now severely battered vessels that had accumulated scores of casualties, the latter ship listing.

Far worse, at 1626 *Queen Mary* suffered the same grisly fate as *Indefatigable*. Two early hits were followed by two salvos that landed squarely. "An explosion forward was followed by a much heavier explosion amidships, black debris of the ship flew into the air, and immediately afterwards the whole ship blew up with a terrific explosion—a gigantic cloud of smoke rose . . . 300 to 400 meters." She had been fighting back impressively to this point, but after *Lion* veered away, *Derfflinger* shifted from *Princess Royal*, now first in line, to *Queen Mary*—fire distribution from the left—while *Seydlitz* continued to fire at her too. As a gunner on *Tiger*, behind *Queen Mary*, observed,

> The German squadron had been poking about for range for some minutes without effect, when suddenly a most remarkable thing happened. Every shell that the Germans threw seemed suddenly to strike the battlecruiser at once. It was as if a whirlwind was smashing a forest down, and reminded me very much of the rending that is heard when a big vessel is launched and the stays are being smashed. . . . After a minute and a half, all that could be seen of the *Queen Mary* was her keel, and then that disappeared.[45]

It seems highly likely that careless handling of cordite charges had claimed a larger and more significant victim. Indeed, the loss of this grand ship and over 1,200 men stung Beatty like a shot rabbit. A young telegraphist coming up to the compass platform recalled being "almost pushed over the side by the Admiral Sir David Beatty as he stormed up and down, and I actually heard him angrily exclaim: 'What's the matter with our bloody ships today?!'"[46]

The battlecruiser duel quickly subsided after this sinking. Beatty had turned two points to starboard, while the rest of his rattled BCF swerved around the wreck of *Queen Mary*, narrowly missing it, and then struggled to turn right and regain station behind the smoke-engulfed flagship. For his part, Evan-Thomas continued to try to close Beatty, veering two points to starboard (i.e., to the southwest) to escape attacking German torpedo boats—there would be no double envelopment for now. On the eastern side of the action, Hipper, too, had gone east-southeast to avoid British destroyers (see map 10.2).[47]

Indeed, an action within the main naval action was underway in the no man's land between the battlecruisers. At 1620, having narrowly missed colliding with a light

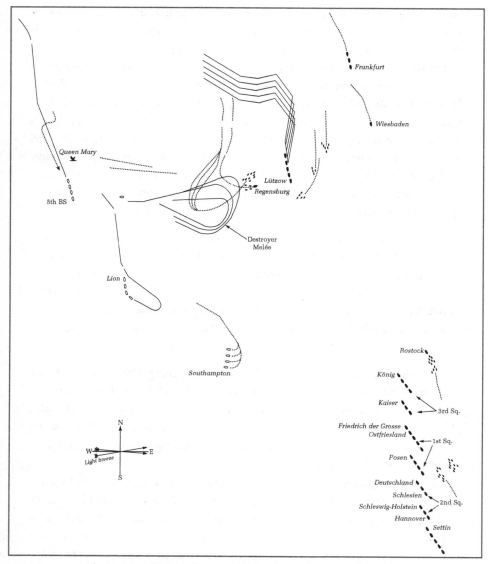

MAP 10.2. The Battle of Jutland at 1648: "Now hear this, now hear this, our main body is in sight!"

cruiser of 2nd LCS, and having struggled at 35 knots to get ahead of *Lion*, a force of fourteen British destroyers swung around the flagship from the disengaged side in disrupted, disorganized, but daring disarray. Two from the engaged side, whose smoke had been obstructing the view of Beatty's gunners, rushed out to join the others. All sixteen destroyers swung to the northeast and headed for the German line of advance, the most favorable position for a torpedo attack. In *Lützow*'s conning tower, Hipper's staff noticed this enemy move across his bows. Should not the German line be alerted to this threat? "I've seen everything, gentlemen, and will give the order when the signal is to be given!" A few minutes later, Hipper ordered his line to "slightly reduce speed" to enable his own destroyers to move out, and then at 1626, as *Queen Mary* blew to pieces, German torpedo boats heard the order, "9th Flotilla, go for them!"[48]

As the German light forces of nearly equal strength raced out to block the British charge, looking "sinister and menacing" with "gushing funnels, high bow waves and sterns tucked down in foaming wakes," what has been described variously as a "fierce dogfight," a "magnificent spectacle," "mayhem between the lines," a "glorious sort of disorganized melee," and "an epic combat, the nearest approach to those ancient single-handed combats of the Homeric heroes" took place. "It was a wild scene of groups of long low forms vomiting heavy trails of smoke and dashing hither and thither through the smother and splashes, and all in a rain of shell from the [battlecruisers'] secondary armament."[49] Above the clatter of small-caliber guns, the jousting destroyers fired at one another; in fact, their crews began to hear the "frightful howl" of bigger shells as the casemate gun crews of the battlecruisers joined the fray. On *Lion*, to counter the German casemate crews, Francis Jones deployed his marines from starboard X-battery to man the workable portside guns whose crews had died from earlier hits.

Circa 1640, the medieval tournament subsided as the flotillas on both sides turned for their own lines. In terms of casualties, two German vessels and one British were lost with hundreds killed or wounded. Of the many torpedoes fired at capital ships, all missed except one, which slammed into *Seydlitz*, violently jarring the ship; but Tirpitz's torpedo bulkheads just barely managed to keep out the sea. Tactically, the BCF came away a clear beneficiary of the destroyer action, for Hipper had been forced away and out of range, unable to exploit the devastating, morale-debilitating loss of *Queen Mary*. But Evan-Thomas had been forced away too. Otherwise, how long would 1st SG have managed to stave off "disaster" from somewhat defective shells that nevertheless crashed like massive boulders into her armored walls—and exploded horrifically above decks? "Splinters of shell were hurled screaming across the deck and through the superstructure," wrote one German lieutenant. "Huge flames blazed up, roaring from the bursting of giant shells, melting and charring everything that they touched."[50] Indeed, as Jellicoe had written a year earlier after Dogger Bank, it soothed somewhat that even if German shells can "hit hard under water," British shells can "hit harder above water" (see chapter 6).

Although Beatty headed almost due south by now (1630) seven and a half miles to the southwest of Hipper, who steered away to the east, the BCF chief's "will to win" remained strong and "permeated every man under his command," recalled junior navigation officer Chalmers. "The thought of retirement never entered anyone's head." As Captain Chatfield remembered it, "We had four good ships left. The enemy must be damaged, and [5th BS] was coming into action. We continued the pursuit." He also felt Beatty had shaken off the panging loss of *Queen Mary*. "Events in action rapidly pass out of the mind as new excitements occupy it."[51] With Hipper heading east, would the "new excitement" be a renewed attempt at double envelopment?

But exogenous events intervened to radically alter any such tactical possibilities. At 1633, HMS *Southampton*, the flagship of 2nd LCS sailing two and a half miles ahead of *Lion*, flashed with lamps to Beatty: "Battleships SE." Scheer's 3rd Squadron had come into view eleven miles away (see map 10.2). In slightly less than an hour, the Run to the South had brought Scheer almost forty miles closer to Hipper and the action.

■ ◼ ■

Circa 1415, the moment a "bored" Beatty made his first turn to the north to close Jellicoe, the German High Seas Fleet passed the 56th Parallel and entered that region where British admirals agreed Germany's prudent C-in-C would wisely and sanely fear to tread. Twenty minutes later, while Scheer took an afternoon constitutional on the quarterdeck, his flag lieutenant, Ernst von Weizsäcker, brought word of enemy battlecruisers in sight from light cruiser *Elbing*.[52] "Composed and almost without emotion," he then moved up to the conning tower, where Trotha and Levetzow, casting eager glances at their chief, relayed Hipper's report of several smoke clouds of enemy forces in sight. Scheer welcomed the news, for like his two top staffers he eagerly anticipated catching British capital ships at sea and destroying them. However, another wireless dashed this expectant mood around 1500. It came from light cruiser *Frankfurt*, Boedicker's flagship of 2nd SG, reporting that she had spotted only light cruisers earlier, not battlecruisers. The bearer of this bad news winced stoically at the leader's "irritated" reaction, the only outward symptom thus far of the conflict churning inside the chief.[53] Scheer's irritation indicated that the morning's wireless messages placing British units at sea, including the BCF, had whetted his appetite not only for destroying Beatty but also much more, reaping in the risky process redemption for December 16, 1914, and January 24, 1915. Like Tirpitz, not an end-all, be-all advocate of defeat in detail, Impetuous Scheer would not shy away from gambling for higher stakes (see chapter 8).

Although the chances of netting a big catch continued to look bleak fifteen minutes later when Hipper confirmed the light cruiser sighting, Practical Scheer took the same kind of tentative steps that Jellicoe, himself skeptical of impending action, ordered over 120 miles to the north: he increased speed from 14 to 15 knots and signaled "general quarters" (1510) with searchlight. His ships stayed line ahead, however, rather than shifting to the regulation "preparatory formation" of columns disposed abeam (like Jellicoe), a sign that he guessed battle would not occur, at least not soon. However, he also shifted SMS *Hannover*, leading the last division of 2nd Squadron, to the end of the line to lead a retreat if it became necessary, a not uncharacteristic move for a complex man whose circumspect side struggled with its scarier psychic nemesis to contain "boldness [within] the limits of sane prudence" (see chapter 9).[54]

But Scheer's spirits soon revived. After hearing of "heavy enemy forces in sight" (1530) and "six ships" strong (1535), the chief decreed "full speed ahead" (1540). Not long after learning that the battlecruisers had engaged (1554), he decreased the distance between squadrons and ships at 1610, but stayed line ahead. Presently his line altered course westward to envelop Beatty (1620), but then charged quickly back to the north (1621), come what may, after learning that Grand Fleet dreadnoughts—reportedly Jerram's 2nd BS, although actually Evan-Thomas' 5th BS—had joined the action. Even if Jellicoe himself sailed with Beatty, the German C-in-C seemed unperturbedly eager to present both with a rude surprise.

Meanwhile, these rapid changes of course complicated dead reckoning calculations, making it hard to know if Scheer's three heavy squadrons would miss the battle area entirely. "We could not predict exactly how we would fall upon the enemy battlecruisers," recalled his flag lieutenant. "Our deliberations were somewhat unruly. We leaned over the charts, unable to make up our minds. Indicative [of this confusion], suddenly helmsman Reding, a subaltern factotum on our staff, also began to give the fleet chief advice." The absence of any reports from the Scouting Groups describing the course of battle spawned further anxiety on the bridge, for no one there knew how serious a fight raged to the north. Were the battlecruisers persevering against ever worsening odds and engaging these newly arriving dreadnoughts? Or perhaps the opposite: "not biting down hard again" as at Lowestoft? Had they "perhaps even disengaged" again and "run for home"? Feelings ran high against the battlecruiser leadership because it seemed like the main fleet might "lose the chance of getting its roast."[55] Emotions morphed again, however, when Scheer's light cruiser *Rostock*, sailing far ahead, signaled with searchlight at 1628: "Firing observed N-NW-by-W, distant about four miles." The van of the High Seas Fleet could see the chaotic destroyer melee amidst the heavy shelling of bigger ships.

Emotions below decks differed from those on the bridge as Scheer raced north into the unknown. Excitement and anticipation spread rapidly through his three squadrons when he tightened up the line. One magazine handler on SMS *Helgoland* of 1st Squadron, the central squadron, had duty on the bridge as lookout.

> It was apparent that something was approaching. The signalmen ran all around and removed the canvas bridge-rail covering. The captain informed the lookouts that the enemy would be sighted in half an hour. Our battlecruisers had already engaged six large English ships. Gradually our speed rose to 19 knots. How beautiful it was to see our twenty-two primeval elephants charging forward to the sound of the guns! Quickly, quickly staunch ship, up ahead our brave cruisers are already fighting and bleeding. If you don't hurry they will sacrifice themselves. "There they are!" shouted the Adjutant. Sure enough, dim lighting could be seen through the haze off port. One, two, three, four, five, six, seven of them! "Bugler! Battle stations! Clear for action! Ta, ta, ta, ta." The men ran around like mad. In a minute and a half everyone was ready. "Lookouts down! Battle stations!" yelled the First Officer. Pretending not to hear, I continued to look feverishly through the binoculars. I noticed that the lead ship had a triple mast. "Get going," came a yell from the command tower. I yielded and made my way down the ladder to the munitions chamber of B-turret.

The greatly relieved officers and men on Hipper's ships could see and hear what was happening too. "When smoke clouds were sighted to the south," navigation officer Otto Groos of *Von der Tann* wrote later, "from every command tower [of the Scouting Groups] news that could scarcely have elicited greater jubilation on December 16th 1914 and January 24th 1915 passed through voice tubes to all action stations: 'Now hear this, now hear this: our main body in sight!'"[56]

As noted earlier, Beatty's 2nd LCS saw the German main body too—at first from eleven miles away, just a few battleships and a cruiser firing at two British destroyers that had also spotted the enemy and undertaken a rogue attack that sacrificed HMS *Nestor*. Soon the British cruisers sighted more enemy battleships, and then even more of them, a miles-long line of grey behemoths stretching to infinity toward the south "like some legendary creatures from the underworld caught in the broad light of day charging at ten yards a second." A few miles behind *Southampton*, *Lion*, the "lead ship with a triple mast," too far away to see, altered course a point to the southeast toward the alleged sighting.[57]

This news sparked a variety of reactions throughout the BCF. While 2nd LCS's chief Goodenough exclaimed "astonishment" at seeing the "highly surprising" arrival of the High Seas Fleet, 2nd BCS chief William Pakenham in *New Zealand* professed "no surprise" at all because after Dogger Bank "it had been constantly assumed that the German battlecruisers would never be found far from adequate support." With Chatfield, the Admiralty's misinformation reporting Scheer "still in the Jade River" raised more eyebrows: *Southampton*'s report "was therefore a surprise, yet not a great one, as it was a possibility Beatty had always had in mind."

It seems probable, however, that Beatty reacted more strongly than Chatfield implies. Historian Andrew Gordon feels the BCF chief was "momentarily spellbound" by the "Wagnerian drama of this moment. For nearly two years the High Seas Fleet had been the monster these officers had talked about, day after day and month after month; whose methods, qualities and tactics had been the subject of endless speculation, and whose downfall had been planned and rehearsed, [yet] not one of them, since the outbreak of war, had actually seen it." While Gordon's keen observation belongs in the mix, the situation must have been more complicated than mere Wagnerian drama, for it appears that Beatty also remained suspended in a state of suspicious skepticism given his assumption that Scheer would never cross the 56th Parallel (see chapter 8), not to mention the Admiralty's 1241 wireless putting him in the Jade, a bogus report that would spark angry postbattle comments (see chapter 13). For six or seven minutes, charging at fourteen yards a second, his flagship and trailing command hurried southeast for confirmation—"to see for himself," recalled Chalmers, who stood there. What he saw, observed Nicholas Jellicoe, "took [him] totally by surprise." Earlier in the day, Beatty had placed full credibility in reports from *Galatea* that confirmed his intuition, turning and speeding "immediately" eastward for an hour before seeing the enemy he knew would come into view. Now, although the prudent course bore north if he believed the observations of 2nd LCS's veteran commander, BCF's chief rushed incredulously further into harm's way. Only at 1640, having seen with his own eyes—and having finally realized the Admiralty's incredibly bungling disservice—did Beatty reverse course sixteen points to starboard and recall 2nd LCS. At 1648, finally, as the Queen Elizabeths approached from the north on his port quarter, he ordered them to make ready for the same radical turn in succession sixteen points to starboard.

Although Evan-Thomas, like Beatty before him, seems to have had his own problem believing that Scheer had appeared, the twenty-seven mile Run to the South had ended. Evidently, opinions about Beatty's over aggressiveness, his desire to "take on the whole German fleet if he gets the chance," views of himself he had stoked with bellicose talk of wanting action on the "Great Day," had been exaggerated. At Dogger Bank in 1915, as well as in the Bight in late March 1916 (see chapter 8), he aimed to destroy Hipper before the High Seas Fleet arrived. Today, clearly, he had tried to do the same until the moment he saw the High Seas Fleet. As Jellicoe knew only too well, however, Beatty's steeplechase mentality and penchant for gambling could very well lead to disaster. The question remained whether it would today, for before turning north he had raced southward for an hour, extending the distance from his C-in-C beyond 70 miles again in a costly solo quest to bag the lot.

Goodenough's four light cruisers of 2nd LCS continued on their southeasterly course toward the onrushing High Seas Fleet for several minutes after alerting Beatty (1633) that this formidable array steamed toward the BCF. As the range descended below 19,000 yards, however, the spearhead 3rd Squadron held its fire, unable to identify the approaching cruisers as friend or foe—had they sighted Boedicker, followed by Hipper, running away? Finally, *Southampton*'s executive officer, Commander Edward Rushton, perhaps witnessing the execution of *Nestor*, coolly advised Goodenough to send his detailed follow-up report: "If you're going to make that signal, you'd better make it now, Sir—you may never make another." The commodore made it at 1638, but just as coolly stayed the course to a range of only 12,000 yards until it became evident that 2nd LCS could not make a favorable torpedo attack. At 1645 he finally hauled down the recall flags Beatty had ordered at 1640. As his squadron pivoted hard to starboard, the distinctive four-funneled profile of British light cruisers triggered immediate fire from the leading German battleships. Seconds later, Goodenough's squadron sailed through the same forest of watery shell columns the battlecruisers had experienced earlier. It continued this way, but remarkably no shells hit the targeted cruisers as they dodged and zigzagged, steering away from where they guessed the next salvoes would fall. "Forty large shells fell within seventy-five yards of us within the hour," remembered one officer, "[but] we seemed to bear a charmed life."[58]

Whereas Goodenough had exhibited considerable initiative in ignoring Beatty's recall for five minutes in order to complete his scouting mission and perhaps launch torpedoes, thereby showing the kind of keen attention to tactical imperatives, regardless of orders, that Beatty demanded of his officers, Evan-Thomas, a product of Jellicoe's system, once again did not take independent action. The BCF Chief's flag officer, Lieutenant Commander Ralph Seymour, hoisted the signal for 5th BS to turn in succession sixteen points to starboard at 1648, but did not haul it down until 1654; consequently, Evan-Thomas hurtled at full speed toward the entire High Seas Fleet, closing from 25,000 yards to within 18,000 yards, only reversing course when *Lion* took down the flag. That it stayed aloft so long obviously meant another signaling breakdown on the flagship, perhaps understandable given that "all hell was breaking loose" as Scheer was sighted, Hipper reversed course to the north and came back into range, the destroyers recalled, *Queen Mary* survivors picked up, and 5th BS approaching—no less than six signals had been hoisted and hauled around this same time.[59] Andrew Gordon, for one, empathizes with Seymour while curtly dismissing the arguments of those who blame the much-maligned signaler, not Evan-Thomas, whose "punctilious" respect for "obedience to commands," admittedly "the very foundation of discipline," they defend. "But what if the delay in *Lion*'s executing the signal had been extended indefinitely," he asks, "with Scheer bearing down on the 5th BS at a combined closing speed of more than twenty yards a second? For how many more minutes does the 'obedience' school consider Evan-Thomas should have continued rushing headlong to oblivion? Common sense says that . . . when Beatty passed on his opposite course, an admiral worthy of 120,000 tons of capital ships should have maneuvered them of his own accord." While this observation should be weighed heavily given Evan-Thomas' disciplined obedient nature—and also his apparent knowledge of Beatty's standing battle orders to follow the chief—historians should also weigh circumstances as Evan-Thomas saw them. *Lion*'s signal at 1645, "HAVE SIGHTED ENEMY BATTLEFLEET BEARING SE," seemed as hard for Evan-Thomas to believe as *Southampton*'s had been for Beatty twelve minutes earlier. As far as 5th BS's commander knew, the heat of action at that moment still came from Hipper. Indeed, *Lützow* hit *Barham* at 1646. Evan-Thomas defended his action after the battle by stating that he did not see Scheer's main body until *Barham* "had steadied on her northerly course." Having not yet seen the High Seas Fleet for himself, Evan-Thomas had no imperative reason to preempt *Lion*'s hauling down the flag and turn earlier. If the alleged sighting were true and Scheer had actually arrived, would not Beatty, who could see the distance to these enemy squadrons, have the correct sense of exactly when to turn?

Only as *Barham* and her next astern, *Valiant,* steadied on their new course to the north (c. 1656–57) did it become painfully clear that the danger to 2nd LCS and the rear of the BCF was indeed a new one, coming not just from Hipper's 1st SG to the east but also from the elite battleships of Scheer's 3rd Squadron to the southeast, a peril that Evan-Thomas' ships now faced too. Indeed, *Warspite* and *Malaya*, the last two Queen Elizabeths to turn, took five hits from heavy shells as they pivoted, most shot by the new arrivals, while *Barham* herself absorbed four between 1658 and 1710. As for the BCF, with their greater speed and a course alteration to the northwest around 1700 (see below), "it was not long before the four English battlecruisers vanished from our view in mist and smoke," wrote Hase; but as they did, Hipper and Scheer concentrated their joint efforts on Evan-Thomas. During what came to be known as the Run to the North, they pummeled *Warspite* and *Malaya* an additional thirteen times. Casualties rose to 250 in the hotly targeted 5th BS, horrific wounds, hellish deaths, and much physical destruction that a timelier turn could have avoided—but ultimately, much of this charged to the Admiralty's dwindling account. None in 5th BS had sunk yet, however, or been crippled to the point of dropping behind and falling prey to the Germans.

Meanwhile, Beatty's turnabout and subsequent maneuvering to the northwest completed the tragedy in *Lion*'s Q-turret. The explanation requires back-tracking an hour to Chief Gunner Grant's inspection of the magazines and handling rooms of A- and B-turrets around 1548. After finishing up front, he climbed up to the mess deck, walked aft, and then down the hatch to the magazines of Harvey's midship command. Arriving there some fifteen minutes after the shell pierced the gun house (c. 1615), he found the shell and cordite crews "standing about in silence, in fact they all seemed stupefied."[60] Grant inquired what had happened, confirmed that the one open magazine had been flooded "some time" ago, ordered many of the men mulling about to a small first-aid flat halfway up the ladder to the mess deck, and then went further aft to X-turret to complete his tour. During a "lull in the firing" there—*Lion* checked fire at 1633 (just as 2nd LCS sighted Scheer)—he climbed up and out and slogged slowly back amidships through a debris-clogged mess deck covered with six inches of water. And then sometime around the top of the hour, a second huge explosion destroyed what was left of Q-turret and her crew.

What had happened? During the initial explosion, cordite charges had slipped backward from the damaged barrels of Q's guns and burst onto the floor in a smoldering state. While the two wounded men went to sick bay and working chamber crewmen descended to the handling room, the potential danger above went unnoticed. Grant later regretted not checking up top "as a subsequent disaster might, or might not, have been averted." According to Captain Chatfield, a "good deal of smoldering material" needed only "a draught of air to burst into flame," and that "air current was provided when the battlecruisers altered course 180 degrees to the northward" after sighting Scheer (1640–44). Chatfield's timing corresponds to one portion of Grant's memoir: "I did not stay very long [in X-turret], feeling rather uneasy about the flooded magazine of Q, and made to that place again. I had reached the hatchway leading to the flat above the magazine and by the providence of God had only one foot on the step of the Jacob's ladder, when suddenly there was a terrific roar, followed by flame and dense smoke." Apparently, the explosion occurred while *Lion* turned, but it probably came a little later. While Grant wrote in 1947, Royal Marine Private Willons, writing only three years after the event, remembered that "the Chief Gunner came along," descended the ladder to the handling room, "[and ordered] several of us to put out fires [up] on the mess deck. Just as he and I got clear [of the hatch] the ignition of the cordite occurred and the blast pushed us along." If Grant had the order of events reversed and had gone down again before the blast as Willons recalled, perhaps the second devastating blow came quite a few minutes after the northward turn.

As to the cause of the explosion, Grant mentions the possibility of a "strong draught of air being forced down igniting the cordite in the gun-loading cages," but he also considered a second possibility: German shells. In fact, the enemy hit *Lion* three times between 1659 and 1702, causing the BCF to veer "hard" to port (i.e., northwest), so these hits and/or the additional draught induced by this second turn away may have flashed fire down the loaded trunk line. The Germans saw the explosion at 1701, a good twenty-five minutes after Grant left X-turret, attributing the cause to their hits making "a still smoldering fire in the heavy gun turret hit earlier flare up more intensely and ignite further cartridges." Most of the remaining forty turret handlers packed in the handling room or first-aid flat were incinerated instantaneously. However, because (1) after Grant's reforms *Lion*'s turrets had fewer charges lying about, antiflash flaps had been reactivated, and, thanks to Harvey's heroic action, the one open magazine door had been closed, and fortunately it held; and (2) much of the blast dissipated through the open mess deck hatch and the exposed turret roof, *Lion* avoided the fate of *Indefatigable* and *Queen Mary*.

After coming to his senses and helping others put out mess deck fires, Willons reported to X-battery in the starboard topside casemate. The Royal Marine in charge there, Captain Francis Jones, had his hands full. A German shell had hit there too, igniting cordite at his 4-inch guns and starting a fire that he and his crews struggled to put out, for earlier hits to *Lion* had punctured the fire mains. Another shell had penetrated the mess deck sick bay below them, killed all there, and pushed smoke out through lower decks, prompting a worried Chatfield to order the magazines of X-turret flooded. All three of these hits and fires amidships and aft explain the radical course alterations of *Lion* and her consorts to the northwest. Circa 1715, after the BCF "vanished from view in mist and smoke," Willons went aft and told shocked mates about the two devastating explosions that had destroyed Q-turret and almost everybody in it. Jones sent Willons and a detachment back to remove Harvey's body, a "charred piece of humanity near where the voice pipe was,"[61] and the remains of his turret crew, bring them back to the marine barracks, and sew them into their hammocks for later burial at sea.

■ ▨ ■

As the battle of Scheer and Hipper against Evan-Thomas intensified in the half-hour after 1706, the German ships suffered too. Two of the leading battleships in 3rd Squadron, *Grosser Kürfurst* and *Markgraf*, as well as *Derfflinger* and *Lützow* in 1st SG, took hits on the belt armor, making "terrific crashes" that caused whole ships, even the conning towers, to "vibrate"; but the huge 15-inch projectiles of Britain's newest battle squadron failed to penetrate, "bursting amidships without seriously injuring the main armor deck." Other hits, however, destroyed both wireless rooms and a 5.9-inch casemate gun on Hipper's flagship, causing "severe casualties," while punishing *Seydlitz* mercilessly: two turrets were damaged, another lost to a cordite fire, and two portside casemate guns and their crews eliminated. Zigzagging, *Moltke* avoided the hail of shells.[62] *Von der Tann* did too, but her last working turret broke down, leaving Captain Zenker with a difficult decision: fall back to the Bight or keep firing with secondary armament to obstruct British gunners with short splashes and also prevent the enemy from shifting fire to the rest of 1st SG. He chose to trust in turret repairs rather than abandon his squadron.

As the bottom of the hour drew near, the Run to the North brought the British ships nearer to the latitude of the Fisher Banks they had left two hours earlier. Only the van of the 5th Division of the German 3rd Squadron, led by *König*, and the spearhead of 6th Division, led by *Kaiser*, could still reach the faster *Malaya* and *Warspite* at the rear of Evan-Thomas's line, and only with their forward turrets. *Friedrich der Grosse*, at the head of 1st Squadron, had fallen beyond 20,000 yards and out of effective range, while Beatty, as noted, had "vanished."

Now "the leaders of the fleet had the impression that the enemy was getting away." It takes little historical intuition to read between the lines of Scheer's memoir and imagine the scene on the bridge of *Friedrich der Grosse* while the British raced northwest. Eager anticipation of victory in detail certainly absorbed Trotha, always ready to consider aggressive action, but also cautiously mindful of Raeder's repeated warnings about broken codes and the need to be prudent when pushing up into the North Sea. And the operations chief stood there too, the ever anxiously overheated Levetzow, salivating over the prospect "of playing the role of the wolf in a flock of sheep," showering the normally calm but usually impatient fleet chief with urgent advice. Indeed Scheer, while managing to appear calm, nonetheless responded characteristically by "siccing" an order to Hipper: "*Verfolgung aufnehmen*," accompanied by "9R," the signal for "*Ran an den Feind!*" 1st SG had to "pick up the chase" and "have at the enemy" lest this bountiful "roast" escape the Fatherland's tables. Had Hipper's leave really brought back the hard charger of old, Scheer must have wondered, his earlier doubts resurfacing. Evidently there were good reasons why his closest colleagues called him *Bobschiess*.[63]

▪ 11 ▪

CLASH OF THE STEEL CASTLES

s Hipper's Scouting Groups slipped past the latitude of the Fisher Banks for the second time this day, visibility conditions had been changing.[1] At the time, they headed northwest to close the faster BCF according to Scheer's orders. Off *Lützow*'s port bow, where Beatty and Evan-Thomas sailed roughly 16,000 yards away, the blinding late afternoon sun shining through the haze made spotting nearly impossible for German gunners, but not for Evan-Thomas's 5th BS, which continued to lob heavy shells at 1st SG, whose battlecruisers now shipped more water. As the weather changed, the day's thin white mist thickened and mixed with funnel and cordite smoke, all clinging to the surface of the sea at times so densely that Hipper's ships were socked in; but then moments later, as the natural-cum-man-made fog seemed to lift, they exited into areas where visibility ranged from 2,000 yards on some bearings to 16,000 yards on others. Worse still, the wind shifted from northwesterly to westerly, and then again to southwesterly, blowing the foggy muck to the north and east and virtually blotting out visibility in these directions—a providentially unwelcome bad break, some would say later.

When Beatty's forces bent back to the northeast shortly after 1730, closed, and reengaged (1740) to lend support to 5th BS, Hipper, his flagship hit once by *Lion*, also turned away to the north-northeast (1744) to stay at medium range while he readied a massive torpedo boat counterattack from light forces that had been pulling up off his starboard quarter (see map 11.1). Glancing to the enshrouded north-northeast, Hipper did not like what he saw. He began to worry, in fact, that the evil-looking haze-bank there harbored a rude surprise. "Mark my words, Harder," he sooth-said to his flag captain, "there's something nasty brewing—it would be better not to get ourselves in too deep!" High up in the foretop, chief gunnery officer Günther Paschen also felt apprehensive as he failed "to get rid of the idea that trouble is brewing."[2]

On the bridge of *Lion*, uneasiness also reigned. 5th BS was under steady fire from Hipper and Scheer with six to nine salvos a minute splashing around the line or actually hitting. This meant that at any moment, unfortunate hits could disable the steering or reduce the speed of these super-dreadnoughts and inevitably render them stranded, pummeled, and unable to survive.[3] The earlier loss of two capital ships and ships' companies could morph into a disaster of war-changing magnitude.

Jellicoe's presence therefore seemed imperative, but where was he? Two hours earlier the C-in-C had broken radio silence and radioed his position as of 1515, which still lagged somewhat behind where plans said he would be by 1400, but with action imminent against a weaker opponent beaten once before, the seventy-one-mile gap to Jellicoe probably generated no concern. But then around 1720–23, well into the anxious Run to the North, another message from Jellicoe arrived listing his coordinates as of 1713—actually the 1700 position, but somehow in the signaling process the time of position had been omitted. The main battle fleet, which Beatty's squadrons *assumed* they had hurried directly toward for forty-five minutes while Jellicoe moved south with dispatch, still sailed *apparently* a good forty miles away to the north-northwest—the two wings of the fleet, closing at around thirty miles an hour, would *evidently* not meet for over an hour.[4] The unwelcome news, felt keenly on the bridge, may well have brought a sort of disrespectful smirk to the face of the vice admiral, and perhaps already now the seeds of an argument sowed in prebattle discussions among cavalier BCF officers began to sprout. Had it actually come to pass? Could Beatty simply not count on someone far too cautious for the good execution of his position?[5]

At 1725, therefore, Beatty, now resigned to reversing the fortunes of battle on his own, ordered the BCF to "prepare to renew the action." The welcome prospect of bagging the lot alone that his squadrons had felt hours earlier had mutated into a dire—although still not entirely unwelcome—necessity. However, although the sting still stung from what an hour earlier had been something akin to acute buyer's remorse, Beatty most certainly did not appear to be a "decisively beaten admiral."[6] Two minutes later, he redirected 3rd and 1st LCS to the northeast to close Hipper, cross his bows, and prepare to fire torpedoes. Shortly after 1730 he altered the battlecruisers "to N-NE," and at 1740 ordered them to "open fire and engage the enemy," and finally at 1747 told the light cruisers to "attack the enemy with torpedoes." The

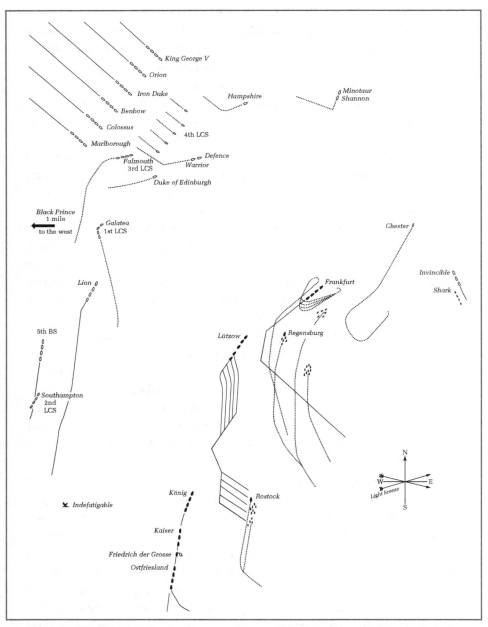

MAP 11.1. The Battle of Jutland at 1745: "It would be better not to get ourselves in too deep."

audacious starboard turns sent the BCF heading away from Jellicoe's presumed northwesterly position, which meant delaying further Jellicoe's arrival, and instead onto a different vector to cross Hipper's "T," hence the German's turn away at 1744. With 5th BS firing from the west, Beatty threatened to trap Hipper between at least two fires and perhaps three, for Beatty believed that Hood's 3rd BCS approached from the northeast—Hood had relayed his request for Beatty's position well before the BCF reengaged.[7] With these reinforcements coming within range in minutes, he stood a chance to beat Hipper quickly without facing further threat from the slower High Seas Fleet, thirteen miles behind and falling further back by the minute, before Jellicoe might finally arrive. To be sure, as he had done at Dogger Bank in January 1915 and the Bight in March 1916, Beatty gambled again, but with an ongoing threat to 5th BS he surely thought he had no good alternative.[8]

Britain's naval commander-in-chief, meanwhile, had grown increasingly uneasy himself by 1730. Although Jellicoe had known for almost an hour from *Southampton*'s wireless signals that fleet action seemed "imminent," as he reported to the Admiralty (1651), his sharp analytic mind lacked the input needed for proper decision-making in an impending battle that could decide the outcome of the Great War this very afternoon. For one thing, after eighteen hours at sea, with all the course changes and zigzagging, British ships sailed off their dead reckonings for determining positions, such that he could not know his own position exactly, let alone the location of the BCF, 5th BS, Hipper, and Scheer. The most frequent and detailed signaling had come from 2nd LCS on the southern point, but "even the *Southampton* was not exempt from [dead reckoning] errors" caused by the shaking and rattling of compasses by heavy shell fire. Further distressing to Jellicoe, *Lion* had sent only one garbled wireless after the turn north at 1645 reporting the enemy battle fleet "bearing SE."

Thus as Jellicoe steered south-southeast about an hour from where he assumed the fleet action would take place, he lacked the specific information required to deploy out of his six-columned cruising formation with the greatest tactical advantage. Would the enemy be to the southeast, south, or southwest? Should he deploy to port or starboard into his battle line to have the best chance of crossing the enemy's "T"? And how many ships would he face? *Lion*'s one report, sent over *Princess Royal* due to wireless room damage on the BCF flagship, was received on *Iron Duke* badly jumbled (i.e., incorrectly) as: "26–30 battleships, probably hostile, bearing S-SE." Did this mean Scheer had brought two predreadnought squadrons along? Would the older German battleships have more of a chance in this scrap with the late afternoon's low and worsening visibility reducing fighting ranges and speeds and compacting the battle space—or as Jellicoe put it, would the enemy have "not so great a discrepancy" when battle was joined?[9] Furthermore, would Scheer have more destroyers too? The British started the day with a fifteen-destroyer edge, but Jellicoe did not know this. And would this mass of worrisome wasps emerge on unanticipated bearings out of the soupy mists at dangerously close range to sting and stun him with their lethal torpedoes? Or if the Germans retired, would their light forces set a trap by sowing mines?

And where was Hood? Since reporting at 1615 that 3rd BCS steamed south-southeast at 25 knots to "support the BCF" as ordered, the rear admiral commanding had sent no further reports. Through intercepts, Hood's wireless operators had kept the men of his powerful flotilla informed, on the other hand, about the presence of the High Seas Fleet at sea and the "imminence" of fleet action, news which spread quickly throughout the squadron. "The ship almost literally seemed to shake with the cheering in some places as large numbers of voice pipes connect the various departments and stations," one of Hood's turret crewmen wrote later. Down the voice pipes "the cheers came booming from the boiler rooms, torpedo flats, turrets, gun positions, and everywhere in the ship as the infection spread."[10]

Although Jellicoe, Hood, and Beatty did not know it, circa 1730 3rd BCS, off dead reckoning calculations like everyone else, approached ten miles northwest of Little Fisher Bank and in fifteen minutes would overshoot the Run to the North raging fifteen to twenty miles to the southwest. Hood's right wing light cruiser, *Chester*, sailing six miles off his starboard beam, prevented this from happening at 1727, however, when she spotted "flashes breaking the mist" in the distant southwest, the only visible sign of 5th BS's ongoing slugfest with Hipper. But after another minute, one by one the destroyers and cruisers of Boedicker's 2nd SG exited phantom-like from the mist hiding them, turned to starboard, and at 1736 unleashed a punishing fire on *Chester* from 6,000 yards (see map 11.1). "Within five minutes she had three of her guns disabled: the majority of the guns' crews was lying dead or wounded, and with only her after gun in action she turned away northeastward at utmost speed, dodging the salvoes like a snipe."[11] However, the brief deadly engagement had alerted Hood, who turned his big cruisers hard north-northwest toward the sound of the guns (1740)—and into the Run to the North.

■ ■ ■

While Hood hurried with his heavy artillery to aid *Chester*, Hipper's telescope remained focused westward on his barely visible opponents, Beatty and Evan-Thomas.

The BCF's fire intensified in the first quarter hour of reengagement (1740–55), especially *Lion*'s, which let salvoes loose every thirty seconds, but "the shooting of the [British] battlecruisers" continued to be "bad," with Beatty's flagship scoring the only hit on the base of *Lützow*'s command tower. Visibility stayed far from ideal from the British vantage point, but despite this "the fire [of 5th BS] was considerably more accurate," with *Barham*'s and *Valiant*'s shots falling in tight patterns around the German battlecruisers. With the range narrowing rapidly, Hipper alternated between line ahead and echelon, and to further disrupt British ranging, he changed course from northwest to north-northeast (1744), to north-northwest (1747), and then to north (1750). Circa 1753–55, however, four prodigious battleship projectiles smashed into *Derfflinger* and *Seydlitz*. Descending obliquely from 16,500 yards, none of these shells penetrated, damaging superstructure or bludgeoning armor belt instead, but one of the hits on *Derfflinger* ripped away two 4-inch pieces of armor plate from the bow and flooded the forward torpedo compartment. The whole area had to be evacuated and shut off to contain flooding as the ship began to list. The cannonade also forced Hipper to alter course again to the east (1755) and command torpedo boats that had been concentrating near the van "to have at" the BCF (1758).[12] Thus Britain's not so "decisively beaten" vice admiral had succeeded in driving an already apprehensive Hipper "in too deep" to the east.

As explained earlier, moreover, an otherwise engaged 2nd SG could not attack a hard-charging Beatty. Circa 1753, while chasing *Chester* away to the northeast, Boedicker's light cruisers (*Frankfurt, Pillau, Elbing, Wiesbaden*) noticed short shots falling from the northwest a few thousand yards off their port beams. Was this more atrocious shooting off to port from Beatty missing Hipper badly, or some new adversary? The water columns rising from the surface shot up in the air less than 12–13.5- and 15-inch shells, so perhaps these shots came from another force, but which? Barely visible in the shaded background to the northwest, however, "were seen a mass of destroyers and light cruisers," so could this be Jellicoe's advance guard? And then suddenly they heard a roar in the east, the opposite direction, from a lone salvo of incoming heavier ordnance, and then another—perfectly aimed 12-inch "bracket" ranging shots from *Invincible* as it transpired—that hit *Pillau*, killing or wounding twenty-three and smashing lethally into the engine room of *Wiesbaden*, abruptly stopping her dead in the water. Several minutes later (1755), the moment Hipper's 1st SG headed east, Hood's 3rd BCS emerged "like something from the spirit world" from the murkiness further east, "dim, dark shapes in the mist and smoke," all three of Hood's Invincibles firing from 8,000 yards.[13]

Boedicker turned 2nd SG back hard right, dropped artificial smoke boxes, fired torpedoes, and retreated to Hipper, who, feeling his Scouting Groups were being trapped, fell back himself on Behncke's 3rd Squadron. Two of 2nd SG's destroyer flotillas (6th and 9th) covered this retreat (with help from the main fleet's 2nd) by charging toward Hood, by-the-book destroyer tactics when Germany's bigger ships retired. Hood's ships veered away, the desired result, but then at 1804 his 3rd BCS turned back to port (i.e., west), still attempting to find Beatty.

During the German destroyers' courageous assault, one of Hood's destroyer escorts, *Shark*, had gotten even harsher punishment than *Chester* a half hour earlier, eventually going down with eighty-six of ninety-two crewmen killed. Another destroyer, the *Onslow*, had dropped down from the BCF's engaged side to launch torpedoes and also got beaten back with several casualties. These victories did little to console the alarmed leader of 2nd SG, however, who joined his captains in firing off reports to Hipper and Scheer on what they thought they had seen to the east.

■ ■ ■

Meanwhile, as Hood inquired again at 1812 about *Lion*'s whereabouts, Beatty's forces had unexpectedly stumbled upon Jellicoe's. Over half an hour earlier (1733), 3rd LCS's flagship, *Falmouth*, running five miles ahead of *Lion*, sighted armored cruiser *Black Prince* six miles northwest on the far-right wing of Rear Admiral Robert Arbuthnot's 1st CS (*Defence, Warrior, Duke of Edinburgh, Black Prince*), sailing seven miles southwest of Jellicoe's rightwing 6th Division flagship, *Marlborough* (see map 11.1). If *Falmouth* had passed the sighting along to Beatty, *which she did not*, the vice admiral would have known that he sailed due south of *Marlborough*, not southeast of *Iron Duke* as faulty dead reckoning had indicated. Not until 1750, however, did the bridge party on *Lion* see *Black Prince* "on the port bow"—twenty-five minutes after Beatty veered right to reengage—and not until 1756, while continuing the north-northeast battle against Hipper, did they see "the leading battleships of the Grand Fleet bearing north 5 miles," ships his own uncommunicative van had spotted somewhat earlier and again failed to report. Beatty immediately altered course to east-northeast, and then at 1800 to east, placing him ahead of the starboard divisions (6th and 5th) of the main fleet. If Jellicoe deployed into battle line from *Marlborough*, Beatty would very soon spearhead this deployment.

A minute later, *Iron Duke*, having asked for and received the correct recognition signal from *Lion*, inquired by signal lamp: "Where is enemy's battle fleet?" Although Beatty would state in his postbattle dispatch that he saw three enemy battlecruisers followed by battleships of the *König* class, the reply on May 31 that "he had leading signalman Alec Tempest flash back to *Iron Duke*, after a delay of five minutes," writes an incredulous, disapproving Andrew Gordon, "merely said: 'Enemy battlecruisers bearing SE,' which was not what the C-in-C needed to know." Similarly, Holloway Frost found it "all the more remarkable" that the BCF chief "failed to mention the all-important battleships . . . in that Jellicoe had just inquired about them." Nigel Steel and Peter Hart use harsher words, describing the sparse, delayed reply as "shamefully opaque," even "criminal." One of *Lion*'s signal crew at the time, Edwin Downing, seeming to precede the judgment of these later historians, wrote what appears to be a thinly veiled criticism: "Somewhere around 6.00 p.m. . . . we got a message [from] the Commander in Chief in the *Iron Duke* asking in what direction and where was the enemy? I am not quoting what Beatty said on being given the message." Could it be that Beatty, still irked with the allegedly tardy pace of Jellicoe's advance, was not impressed—as others were in the hard-pressed 5th BS—with the timeliness of the main fleet's arrival? Downing's superior, Tempest, wrote afterward of the bad feeling on the bridge against the main battle squadrons because they "did not make their best speed during the approach to the battle." Jellicoe flashed another query at 1610 but, with every minute counting and crucial, continued to wait for a reply.[14]

Observers in Jellicoe's rightwing divisions also saw the BCF as it "suddenly burst through the mist" to the southwest and turned east. "They were a wonderful sight, these great ships, tearing down across us, their huge funnels silhouetted against a great bank of red cordite smoke lit up by sheets of flame as they fired salvo after salvo at the enemy whose flashes could be seen in the distance between the ships." The exhilaration of the moment broke down almost immediately, however, as scores of ships large and small crowded into a space of a few square miles that the Royal Navy would dub "Windy Corner." Accompanying Beatty's 3rd and 1st LCS came his 9th, 10th, and 13th Destroyer Flotillas, dodging, weaving, fighting for space, "everyone starboarding and porting to avoid collision" with Jellicoe's 4th LCS, 12th, 4th, and 11th Destroyers, and the bulk of Arbuthnot's 1st CS, all joined around 1800 by Beatty's four battlecruisers. The melee soon got "a bit thick this end" from 1st LCS's vantage point, while ahead in 13th Destroyers "it seemed like Piccadilly Circus with the policemen on strike and the motor buses pushing their way through all the smaller vehicles."[15] Indeed, cramming into the near chaos and confusion crowded eight huge capital ships of Jellicoe's 1st BS when, seriously contemplating deploying from squadron flagship *Marlborough*, the C-in-C turned his six columns from southeast to south (1802) "in order to bring the fleet into action at the earliest possible moment."[16]

And then, with little to go on, he had to decide what to do. In a classic, oft-quoted passage, Julian Corbett described the historical significance of the moment poignantly and without hyperbole:

> Many had been the critical situations which British admirals in the past had been called upon suddenly to solve, but never had there been one which demanded higher qualities of leadership, ripe judgment and quick decision, than that which confronted Admiral Jellicoe in this supreme moment of the naval war. There was not an instant to lose if deployment were to be made in time. The enemy, instead of being met ahead [where dead reckoning errors had placed him], were [somewhere] on [the] starboard side. He could only guess their course. Beyond a few miles everything was shrouded in mist; the little that could be seen was no more than a blurred picture, and with every tick of the clock the situation was developing with a rapidity of which his predecessors had never dreamt. At a speed higher than anything in their experience the two hostile fleets were rushing upon each other; battlecruisers, cruisers and destroyers were hurrying to their battle stations, and the vessels steaming across his front were shutting out all beyond in an impenetrable pall of funnel smoke. Above all was the roar of battle both ahead and to starboard, and in this blind distraction Admiral Jellicoe had to make the decision on which the fortunes of his country hung.

"With every tick of the clock," in fact, the "situation was developing" very ripe for exploitation—by Scheer. Circa 1810 his most powerful 3rd and 1st Squadrons bent gradually to the northeast behind Hipper, whose 1st and 2nd SG fell back to form Scheer's van after 2nd SG's clash to the northeast with—well, with what, Boedicker wondered, had he clashed? While Jellicoe pondered the pros and cons of deployment from the right and waited for Beatty to report, the first several enemy "overs" descended into Windy Corner, raising giant water columns among his three rightwing divisions (6th, 5th, and 4th). Visibility permitting, German battleships would shortly come into effective range of them.

■ ■ ■

Standing on the open bridge of *Friedrich der Grosse*, Scheer also pondered his options. For twenty minutes as clocks ticked past 1740, lookouts on the flagship saw gun flashes and heard the delayed cracks of low- and high-caliber ordnance coming out of the hazy muddle to the northeast some 30,000 yards off the starboard quarter.

These foretop sounds and sightings, which only confirmed the impression gleaned on the bridge, seemed to open a new dimension to the Run to the North, for the fight against Beatty and Evan-Thomas still raged equidistantly in the mist and smoke off the port bow.[17] Not confident from his inferior vantage point which course to take, Scheer turned this decision over to his new appointee, battle-eager Rear Admiral Paul Behncke in *König*, leading 3rd Squadron up ahead several miles behind Hipper. Next, the C-in-C ordered his squadrons to reduce speed to 15 knots and resume orderly station in line ahead. This order allowed Beatty and Evan-Thomas to pull further away, thereby reducing the likelihood of furthering the fight against them, but also tightened up the German line in readiness for shifting into divisional "preparatory" columns from which the fleet could deploy to its best tactical advantage.[18] The chief then stepped into the conning tower to confer with his staff (circa 1755–1805) about "how long the pursuit battle was to be continued given the onrushing time of day."[19]

While they talked, the encounter of 2nd SG with what their postwar accounts identified as Hood—the source of the distant gun flashes to northeast—took place. Some of the attacking German torpedo boat captains closest to the phantom attackers signaled Boedicker that they had spotted three or four British battleships of the *Iron Duke*, *Agincourt*, or *Malaya* classes. Was it Jellicoe, that far east of the German fleet? These officers assumed that at least a battle squadron, if not the entire Grand Fleet, perhaps "more than twenty enemy battleships," sailed behind the haze bank. Destroyers and light cruisers had earlier been reported to the northwest—if not Jellicoe's advance guard there, then more likely now his rear guard? Further back than their torpedo boats, light cruiser captains did not go so far, believing they could see only three battlecruisers or battleships. At 1800, therefore, Boedicker radioed Hipper and Scheer cautiously: "Am being fired on by enemy ships of the line," which he repeated at 1802, and again at 1810, along with these ships' position and northeast bearing.[20]

Toward the end of Scheer's businesslike deliberations with Trotha and Levetzow, the leadership troika received a handful of these alarming dispatches from 2nd SG, another from Hipper, as well as others reporting the disabling of *Wiesbaden*. They had been discussing the distinct probability that "the [enemy] ships we had encountered [thus far] would offer battle the next day" and the steps that "would also have to be taken to shake off the English light forces before darkness fell in order to avoid any loss to our main fleet from nocturnal torpedo boat attacks," in particular, whether or not the battlecruisers and the main fleet should "separate" in order to accomplish this task.[21]

But now suddenly a new situation arose. Afterward, Trotha recreated his version of the moment:

> Admiral Scheer calmly oversees the situation no differently than what we were accustomed to on many training exercises. It was his custom in such moments of hard decisions to focus on the whole [picture]. . . . The British battle line is obscured from full view; smoke and haze, also artificial smoke that was to have covered *Wiesbaden*, blocks an unhindered view. From a report of Admiral Hipper we could *suppose* that the head of the enemy line lay in the east, and from the reports of several torpedo boats the *perception* emerged that we *probably* stood opposite the entire English fleet, a superior force.[22]

Although no overwhelming evidence supports the following scenario, it seems that before learning of the new developments, Trotha had been in the process of convincing the chief to safeguard the fleet for the approaching night by dropping back into "preparatory" columns, main fleet and scouting forces together, and avoiding torpedo attacks in order "to engage the enemy in the morning with no depletion of strength"[23]—and now may have consistently and characteristically counseled caution. Like Hipper, perhaps, he felt anxious about "getting ourselves in too deep" and wary of Beatty's bold easterly turn toward what in Trotha's "perception" lay in the east, namely, as some destroyer captains sensed, "the entire English fleet, a superior force." Light cruiser captains, however, were not so sure of this.

But Trotha was not the only one giving advice. In fact, the discussion became "somewhat unruly and not coordinated by the chief of staff—everyone had the fleet chief's ear."[24] In all likelihood Levetzow, the hot-headed "go-getter," the one who wanted "the powerful German spear" to be allowed "to reach its target,"[25] fought hardest for "the fleet chief's ear," and he did not agree with Trotha. The Chief of Operations' urgings amid the suddenly altered circumstances probably explain why, as Trotha recalled, "attack—however strong the enemy may be—was the rallying cry."[26] Scheer's recollection asserted that there was "never a question of avoiding an encounter—the resolve to do battle with the enemy stood firm from the first."[27] But was this not actually one of those divisive times, as Trotha wrote years later, when "[Scheer] could not stand me"? Was it not now that the staff chief consoled himself somewhat with the thought that "a man like that . . . [who] showed his great gifts [at] Jutland . . . a very different person from me . . . must be allowed to drive his subordinates mad"?[28] Seemingly listening placidly to the optimistic hard-charger and snubbing the "pessimistic quibbling stickler," the chief turned two points to port at 1817 "so as to draw nearer to [Boedicker] and render assistance to the *Wiesbaden*."[29]

Now Behncke, the Hotspur leading 3rd Squadron's charge, followed Hipper blindly into the murk, leaving the triumvirate in the fleet flagship's conning tower to guess what lurked there. Given his comments above, Trotha probably worried that it was Jellicoe and the Grand Fleet. Levetzow, and Behncke too, probably did not care. Scheer likely did not expect the entire British array, but impetuously trusting what his sixteen battleships could deal with, forged ahead à la Levetzow and Behncke. If at this time Jellicoe deployed to starboard, however, the brashness of Scheer, Levetzow, and Behncke—"in and of itself understandable and obvious after such a long time of caution [in the war at sea]"[30]—would have enabled Hipper and Scheer in the short span of six to seven minutes from 1816 to 1823 to hurl hundreds of steel-tipped, trotyl-filled, delayed-fuse AP shells inside the concentrated field of fire into which Jellicoe's 5th and 6th Divisions poked forth silhouetted against the northwestern sun (see map 11.2). As the German squadrons overlapped the British and crossed their "T," this fiery advantage would not have been undercut much by the arrival of Beatty and Hood.

■ ▧ ■

Even before Jellicoe deployed, the British began to pay a stiff price for confronting the advancing German line. *Defence* and *Warrior,* armored cruisers of 1st CS commanded by Rear Admiral Sir Robert Arbuthnot, suffered first. His squadron, minus *Black Prince* off to the west, sailed five miles ahead of the battle columns when they observed the skirmish flashes of Boedicker's 2nd SG and Hood's *Chester. Defence* turned to port and fired a few 9.2-inch salvos circa 1750, which fell well short, their water columns puzzling the German light cruisers about what lay to the north. Arbuthnot, a hard disciplinarian, naval martinet, and close friend of Christopher Cradock, whose flotilla Graf Spee had decimated at Coronel in 1914, no doubt felt an urgent need to avenge the death of his comrade. He must also have wanted to redeem himself for underperforming *by not firing* during the Yorkshire Raid in 1914 (see chapter 3). With these thoughts in the back of his mind and determined to help *Chester,* to eliminate his enemy's outgunned scouting force, especially the stricken *Wiesbaden,* and to reconnoiter the rest, all which fell well within his battle orders as a cruiser commander, Arbuthnot charged wildly south at top speed, "firing incredibly fast" with everything he had, "one mass of flashes from end to end."[31] As he did so, *Lion* had assumed station steering southeast two miles ahead of HMS *Colossus,* flagship of the 5th Division, and *Benbow,* flagship of the 4th Division, the proper position to lead the main fleet into what Beatty and his staff probably assumed would soon be a deployment from these rightwing columns. *Defence* and *Warrior*

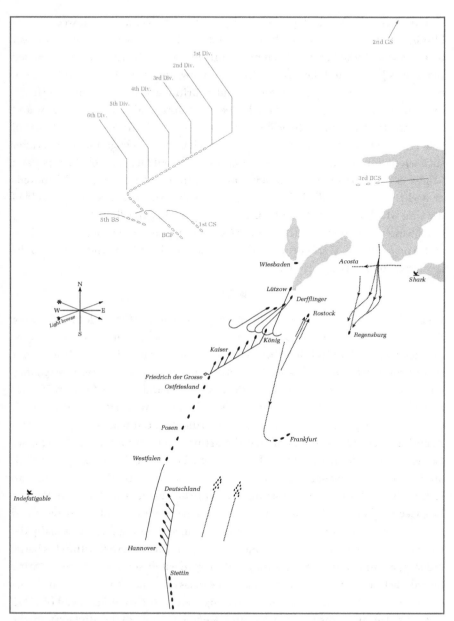

MAP 11.2. Hypothetical Rightwing Deployment by Jellicoe circa 1820: With every tick of the clock the situation might have developed very ripe for exploitation by Scheer.

cut in front of *Lion*, however, forcing Chatfield to jam the helm over violently hard to port at 1816 to avoid a crash.[32]

Arbuthnot either did not see or did not concern himself with what emerged from the haze in front of him: Hipper's battlecruisers, which had assumed station ahead of the German main fleet and reversed course to the north; and the battleships of Behncke's 3rd Squadron. As the range narrowed, nine dreadnoughts let loose a hail of projectiles from primary and secondary armament upon Arbuthnot's latter day Light Brigade. *Lützow*'s gunnery officer, Günther Paschen, wrote:

> And then something unexpected happened . . . [for] there appears in the field of the periscope a ship, improbably large and close. At first glance I recognize an old English armored cruiser, and give the necessary orders. My arm is clutched [to fire, but then I say]: "Don't fire, that is [light cruiser] *Rostock*." But I can see the [armored cruiser's] turrets fore and aft. "Four funnels. Bow left. Left 30. Range 7600 meters, Salvo." Five salvos rapidly follow, of which three straddled; then was repeated the now familiar sight of a ship blowing up, this time before the eyes of both fleets, for the English main fleet could see the *Defence* although we could not [yet] see them.[33]

Defence disappeared from view in a cloud of cordite smoke at 1820, all 903 officers and sailors dead. *Warrior* absorbed twenty-one hits, killing or wounding 107 men, but miraculously managed to crawl back away, eventually sinking, but her 800-plus survivors offloaded.

Evan-Thomas and 5th BS, meanwhile, had sailed into Windy Corner, which by about 1815 had become only a little less "thick." Assuming, like Beatty before him, that Jellicoe would deploy to starboard, *Barham* turned two points to the right in order to pull up on *Marlborough*'s starboard quarter, overtake her, and aid the main fleet's deployment ahead of 6th Division. Minutes later, the steering gear of the third ship, *Warspite*, damaged from an earlier hit, jammed. The ship began turning in a circle toward the Germans, closing to 12,000 yards before she circled away, and then, continuing to circle, back toward the enemy, the sea surrounding the battleship "red, lurid, and beastly [with] heavy firing all round and splashes everywhere." For some ten minutes this went on, the "wounded elephant"[34] hit twelve times and suffering the bulk of its forty-six casualties for the day before the problem got solved. *Warspite*, fortunate to have survived at all, strove to catch up and rejoin her squadron but, badly shot up, was sent home. In a matter of minutes, therefore, three capital ships had been forcibly removed from Jellicoe's line. A fourth would soon follow, this one, like *Defence*, blown to bits.

■ ■ ■

While the tragic drama of *Defence*, *Warrior*, and *Warspite* ran its course, Jellicoe deployed from columns into battle line. Already at 1806 (6:06 p.m.), after holding a southerly course for only four minutes, he altered back to southeast, and then at 1808 sent two of his destroyer flotillas to assume station ahead of *King George V* leading Jerram's leftwing 2nd BS. These appear to have been almost instinctive change-of-mind reactions to enemy shells falling into Windy Corner, the danger of a destroyer attack out of the mist, and the apparently rapid approach of enemy battleships. "There was no time to lose," he wrote later, "as there was evident danger of the starboard wing column of the battle fleet being engaged by the whole German battle fleet before deployment [of the other five columns] could be effected." Now he required only a few reliable scouting reports from Beatty and Evan-Thomas before completing the process of convincing himself that deployment from the right would be "suicidal." The former finally answered at 1814—a difficult-to-defend delay of thirteen minutes—and the latter a minute later.

Although still out of sight from *Iron Duke*, Scheer's battle fleet seemed to be a mere 12,000–14,000 yards south of *Marlborough*. Jellicoe recalled,

> If the German ships were as close as seemed probable, there was considerable danger of the [British 1st BS], and especially *Marlborough*'s [6th] Division, being severely handled by the concentrated fire of the High Seas Fleet before the remaining divisions could get into line to assist. Included in the [1st BS] were several of our older ships, with only indifferent [armor] protection as compared with the German ships, and an interval of at least four minutes would elapse between each division coming into line astern of the [6th] Division and a further interval before the guns could be directed on to the ship selected and their [deliberate "bracket"] fire become effective. . . . The German ["ladder"] gunnery was always good at the start, and their ships invariably found the range of a target with great rapidity, and it would have been very bad tactics to give them such an initial advantage.

With the possibility looming of having his "T" crossed from medium range and his battleships overwhelmed one division at a time (map 11.2), Flag Captain Dreyer remembered,

[Jellicoe] stepped quickly on to the platform round the compasses and looked in silence at the magnetic compass card for about twenty seconds. I watched his keen, brown, weather-beaten face with tremendous interest, wondering what he would do. With iron nerve he had pressed on through the mist with his twenty-four huge ships until the last possible moment. . . . I realized as I watched him that he was as cool and unmoved as ever. Then he looked up and broke the silence with the order in his crisp, clear-cut voice . . . "Hoist equal-speed pendant SE" . . . [Fleet signal officer A. R. W. Woods said]: "Would you make it a point to port, Sir, so that they will know it is [deployment] on the port-wing column?" . . . Jellicoe replied at once: "Very well, hoist equal-speed pendant SE-by-E" . . . Woods then called over the bridge rail to the signal boatswain: "Hoist equal-speed Charlie London" (CL denoting SE-by-E). . . . We had not yet sighted any German vessel from the *Iron Duke*.[35]

Flags for deployment into battle line from *King George V*'s leftwing column went flying up the halyards at 1814 and yanked down at 1815 (after Evan-Thomas replied). The ships began the precision maneuver (see map 11.3). The cautious British commander had deferred the opening moment of the battle in order to seek out his own "initial advantage."

Indeed, deployment from the starboard wing would have been a mistake, for this would have temporarily concentrated Scheer's strength against the weakest parts of the British line as they sailed south or southeast toward German squadrons that were bending and "overlapping"[36] to the northeast across Jellicoe's "T." What actually happened to *Defence*, *Warrior*, and *Warspite* circa 1815–20 might have been mere prologue to the fearsome pounding of perhaps half of the main fleet only minutes later. Britain's 4th, 5th, and 6th Divisions contained some powerful vessels, to be sure, but even *Marlborough*, *Revenge*, and *Benbow* with their 13.5- and 15-inch guns had one or two inches less armor protection than Scheer's best with none of the interior design features of German ships to maximize buoyancy under heavy fire (see chapter 7), not to mention the defects of British ordnance. The other battleships in these columns were mostly older dreadnoughts (laid down in 1906–9), protected by far less armor, firing 12-inch guns with lower muzzle velocity/armor-piercing capability, and all of them, like the newer British ships, without Tirpitz's "honeycomb" watertight compartments.[37] The fire effectiveness of these rightwing divisions would have been further reduced by an already battered—and now vulnerable again—5th BS interfering on their right with ranging, all masking Jellicoe's stronger 1st, 2nd, and 3rd Divisions, in the midst of deploying and unable to reply.

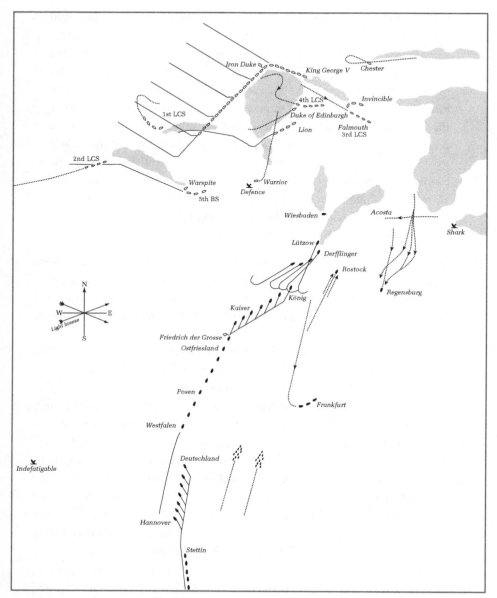

MAP 11.3. The Battle of Jutland at 1820: "The resolve to do battle with the enemy stood firm from the first."

■ ▇ ■

By 1819–20, with the demise of *Defence* and the pummeling of *Warspite* and *Warrior* providing a grim spectacle for their crews, the bulk of the Grand Fleet's battleships sailed northeast toward a southeasterly bend in their battle line leading to the guide ship, *King George V*, whose powerful 2nd BS had largely maintained its previous course. Jellicoe had to hold fire and order ships to reduce speed by four knots (1826) to allow the BCF, armored cruiser *Duke of Edinburgh*, and 3rd and 4th LCS to pass ahead toward the van. This maneuver extended the disruption of Windy Corner to the deploying main fleet as delays in transmitting the speed reduction order meant that some continued at 18 knots while others cut back to 14, causing several battleships to sheer out of line, overlap others, and cut back engines full to avoid collisions, but in the process masking the firing arcs of many ships moments before engagement. A thick curtain of smoke from the BCF and the others further complicated the prospects of opening fire accurately. The disruption balked Jellicoe from seizing his "initial advantage" and moving in for the kill, for, spotting enough of the silhouetted enemy to see he could cross Scheer's "T," he had ordered his squadrons to close by altering course from east-southeast to south-southeast (1829) but then immediately negatived the order to wait for Beatty and the others to get ahead. Although none of this smoky mayhem from other squadrons near the battle fleet aroused the externally imperturbable Jellicoe, not so Dreyer and others on the bridge: "How we cursed them at the time!"[38]

After avoiding colliding with the ill-fated armored cruisers, *Defence* and *Warrior*, Beatty's battlecruisers had resumed their own firing, however, with ranging salvos at Hipper's 1st SG from around 12,000 yards. To the Germans trying to fight back, Beatty's line "often became invisible in the slowly advancing mists mixed with the smoke from guns and funnels [blown from the southwest]." Consequently, Hipper's salvos went about 2,000 yards "over." Conversely, the German ships, silhouetted against the setting western sun, made much better targets. Hase, atop *Derfflinger*, wrote: "This will be difficult to understand for anyone who does not know the sea, but it is a fact that in this sort of weather the differences in visibility are very great in different directions. . . . In misty weather the ships with [the sun behind them and] their shady side towards the enemy are much easier to see than those [whose enveloping haze is front-] lit by the sun."

At 1819, after the BCF's range had descended to 8,500 yards or less, two 13.5-inch shells from *Lion* slammed into *Lützow*, one exploding at the base of the conning tower, the other penetrating the port casemate roof and exploding against the rear wall of B-turret—both shells, even at this short range, apparently breaking up without producing proper penetrating destructiveness. After hitting *Lützow*, Beatty's battlecruisers opened into ineffective, hitless rapid fire. British luck continued to be bad too, for, still shooting at armored cruiser *Warrior* trying to get away, two "overs" from *Markgraf* of Behncke's 3rd Squadron hit *Princess Royal* instead, one badly damaging X-turret, the other inflicting many casualties on the starboard-aft 4-inch gun crews.[39] However, Beatty had amassed more tactical points—critical ones—by forcing Hipper to turn further away, this time to the southeast (1820).

In the meantime, Hood's 3rd BCS had assumed the van-station ahead of *King George V.* Upon sighting the BCF and its smoke-belching fellow travelers barreling in front of Jellicoe's awkwardly deploying battle line, Hood allowed 3rd LCS to pass in front of him, circled around to starboard circa 1815, and took the lead (see maps 11.3 and 11.4).[40] Soon thereafter, spotting the enemy's "back-lit," silhouetted "shady sides" from their own cloud of mist and smoke, the "invisible" 3rd BCS added their fire to Beatty's (circa 1820–21) from around 8,000 yards, the distance rising quickly above 9,000 as 1st SG made its own hard southeasterly starboard turn. From the visibly impenetrable murk of the northeast, roaring like aerial freight trains out of this proverbial nowhere, 850-pound shells began to straddle and douse the leading German battlecruisers.

Adjusting the range from these closely bracketed "overs" and "shorts," Hood's gunners zeroed-in on their targets with a precision made markedly more perfect from practice. In seven or eight minutes, 1st SG absorbed eleven hits, four of which, coming from *Invincible* at shorter sub-10,000-yard range, penetrated *Lützow*'s forward torpedo rooms and leaked into adjacent compartments (36.4 percent bursting effectiveness), including the now useless magazines under A-turret. Down at the bow, Hipper's flagship slowed to 15 knots, and then to only 12, but would not sink. "Your fire is very good," exclaimed Hood through the voice pipe to Gunnery Commander Hubert Dannreuther in the foretop. "Keep at it as quickly as you can—every shot is telling."[41]

These were some of Hood's last words. At 1829, "the veil of mist in front of us split across like the curtain at a theater," wrote Hase. In his ship and *Lützow* too, with enemy shells "straddling us completely," the Germans' automaton-like gun-laying mechanism shifted into gear without a second's hesitation:

"Range 9000 [meters]!" roared seaman Haenel. "9000—salvos fire!" I ordered. And with feverish anxiety I waited for our splashes. "[Two] over. Two hits!" called out Lieutenant Commander von Stosch. I gave the order: "100 down.

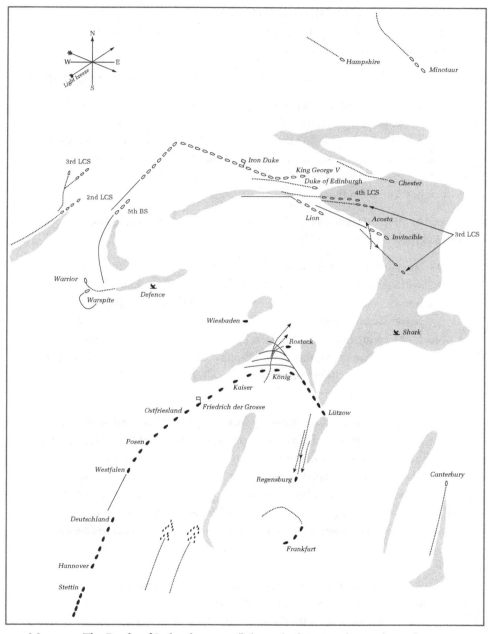

MAP 11.4. The Battle of Jutland at 1830: "The veil of mist in front of us split across like the curtain at a theater."

Good, rapid fire!" And thirty seconds after the first salvo the second left the guns. I observed two "short" splashes and two hits. Von Stosch called: "Hits!" Every twenty seconds [now] came the roar of another salvo.

In *Lützow*, Paschen also "felt delight at having one of these tormentors clearly in sight."

> Like lightning the orders are given. . . . I hear through the telephone everything said at the gunnery centers and look again at the enemy. "Over! 400 down. Salvo. A straddle! Salvo." As the sound of the fall-of-shot indicator squeaks, the red flame flashes up nicely and unmistakably from the water columns around the enemy. Signs of a hit like these make a very definite impression if one has seen them twice.

Several of these "red flame flashes" were also seen from *Indomitable*, but her flagship seemed indeed to be invincible, unconquerable.

> We observed two dull glows amidships. The appearance was that the armor was withstanding the impact of the shells. But a few moments later a great mushroom of smoke rose to the clouds. When it cleared our flagship was in two halves sticking out of the water in opposite directions and slowly sinking into it. We young *Indomitable* officers had particularly poignant feelings since the day before we sailed, the junior officers of *Invincible* had come aboard us and a merry and riotous time was had by all. Now every one of those was "asleep in the deep."

For the third time this day, an enemy shell had penetrated a British battlecruiser turret, exploded, ignited naked cordite charges, and flashed fire down into open magazines (1833). Only six of her ship's company of 1,032 survived, Dannreuther among them, having dropped miraculously safely to the sea with the falling mast. Viewing the disaster from *Inflexible*, one on-looking sailor remembered being "entirely unafraid until I saw *Invincible* in trouble—not because I was brave, but I was so inexperienced and naïve that it never struck me that we could be sunk."[42]

■ ■ ■

Invincible's sudden demise momentarily demoralized the British, especially after what had happened shortly before to *Defence*, *Warrior*, and *Warspite*. Understandably, this evoked opposite emotions on the German side. "Our enemy has blown up!" shouted Hase into his telephone. "And above the din of the battle a great cheer thundered through the ship and was transmitted to the fore-control by all the gunnery telephones and flashed from one gun position to another. I sent up a short, fervent prayer of thanks to the Almighty and shouted to my [subordinate]: 'Bravo, Haenel, jolly [good shooting]!'" But "the battle continued,"[43] he noted, and *Derfflinger's* guns quickly shifted their fire to *Inflexible*.

The battle would not continue, however, for the doomed *Wiesbaden*. As Jellicoe's trailing divisions prepared to open fire after Beatty and the other obstructers had passed—*King George V* and the 1st Division, however, remained blocked until well after 1830—they trained their guns on what they could see first: light cruiser SMS *Wiesbaden*. Flagship gunnery officer Geoffrey Blake wrote,

> Nobody dared to open fire before the *Iron Duke*. They all had a sort of sympathetic feeling that it was bad luck going on hammering a poor sinking ship. However, I asked Captain Dreyer if I might have permission to open fire. He said he would ask the [C-in-C] and after a bit of an argument [Jellicoe] gave permission. We then opened fire which I was very glad to do just to clear the bores, and the whole remainder of the Grand Fleet, as the *Wiesbaden* passed, opened fire too, and gave her an awful hammering.[44]

To be sure, she had already been badly damaged in earlier scraps with Hood and Arbuthnot. One of Beatty's destroyers, the *Onslow*, had also preyed on *Wiesbaden*, launching a torpedo "that shook the whole ship and jacked it up in the air." But now hundreds of massive projectiles fell around her in less than fifteen minutes, dousing sailors with sea water "so mixed with cordite gas that we turned yellow." Ten or twelve of these shells hit, devastatingly exploding and mangling even more metal and men. A tribute to German engineering, the ship took seven or eight hours before she sank, her sixteen watertight compartments keeping out the sea that long. However, only one man from the crew of nearly 600, Chief Stoker Hugo Zenne, lived to tell their tale.[45]

The slow annihilation of *Wiesbaden* and her crew, all save one, marked a dramatic tipping point in the already quite tragic, four-hour-long Battle of Jutland/Skagerrak. While Jellicoe's difficult deployment maneuver found most of his battleships unable to spot anything through smoke, mist, and friendly vessels blocking firing arcs, shortly before 1830 the van of Behncke's 3rd Squadron began to come blurredly into view for a portion of the British line. Once they could focus on better targets, "one by one [these] British battleships shifted their fire from the *Wiesbaden* to a more equal foe."[46] The first to fire at worthier opponents were *Marlborough* and *Hercules* (6th Division), *Iron Duke* (3rd Division), and most of 2nd Division (*Orion, Monarch, Conqueror*). By 1833, when *Invincible* met her end, about 150 payback projectiles were landing 11,000–12,000 yards to the south, concussing and ripping apart hundreds more fish, whose belly-up bodies littered the sea as far as the eye could see. Many of these shells shot massive water columns up around Behncke's flagship, *König*, and the third astern, *Markgraf*. *Orion* hit the latter once, causing deadly damage to two casemate gun positions. *Monarch* hit *König* once, but the crack gunners of *Iron Duke* scored seven hits on her. Although British shells failed to penetrate thick armor, others did considerable damage, holing the hull below the armor belt, inducing a 4-degree list and killing forty men. Another struck the top of the conning tower and deflected away, but concussed and wounded those inside, including Behncke, who, like Beatty two hours before, had been forced to realize that he should have been more careful with his wishes.[47]

Lützow and her consorts continued to have "a hot time of it," moreover, despite the fact that *Invincible* had sunk, the BCF had stopped firing at 1829, and the main British fleet could not see Hipper's squadron.[48] The credit again goes to the remainder of 3rd BCS, *Indomitable* and *Inflexible*, which had resumed rapid fire. "We now led the line for some time," remembered a Royal Marine turret officer on *Inflexible*. "I was glad to see that we got some hits on [*Derfflinger*]." Another salvo slammed into *Seydlitz*. A British midshipman on *Indomitable* recalled similarly that "I very soon forgot the disaster to *Invincible* in the excitement of seeing a steady series of red splashes along the enemy's long line which indicated that we were hitting with some regularity and effect."[49] Although the end of Hipper's "long line," *Moltke* and *Von der Tann*, were not, in fact, targeted, the cumulative fatigue of four hours of combat, the lightning cracks of enemy fire all around, and frightening talk through voice pipes of "thundering flashes" emitting from the fog like "fire from sinister eyes"[50] did nothing to raise the sagging spirits of their crews, already casting renewed doubt on the faith in German naval leadership so ephemerally rekindled that afternoon.

Sailors in Hipper's flagship felt these sentiments fervently too, but combat circumstances there spawned even direr emotions, for unlike *Moltke* and *Von der Tann*, *Lützow* was not spared the vengeful wrath of *Invincible*'s squadron sisters. Shells from both British battlecruisers rained down along with 6-inch salvoes from the advance guard of 3rd LCS (see map 11.4). "The leading ship, *Lützow*, was out of line and obviously hurt badly—shells were falling all around her while red flashes in every salvo and clouds of smoke made it quite clear that she was being hit repeatedly."[51] Both forward turrets had sustained damages and only three of fourteen 5.9-inch guns still fired. Even worse than the casualties mounting in these positions were those inflicted by shells that had fallen with "deadly accuracy" in sick bays between decks fore and aft where eighty wounded sailors along with doctors and their helpers lay dead "in a scene of gruesome destruction."[52] Still harder to accept for survivors, seventeen sailors got cut off in an inaccessible dynamo compartment beneath the flooded, ripped-open bow.

Hipper had no time to think about his earlier "hammer and tongs" remark as successive damage and casualty reports from all stations reached the bridge, but his premonition had certainly come tragically true. Accordingly, Captain Harder veered further away (from southeast to southwest) in order to escape what seemed like the enemy's impending *coup de grâce*. As the ship slowed to 5 knots, a courier brought word that Scheer had ordered the fleet to make a "starboard battle turn." As the trailing battlecruisers of 1st SG followed this command and steered westward away from their dangerously decelerating, stricken flagship circa 1837–38, "a kind of paralysis seemed to descend upon Hipper and his face expressed bitter disappointment—it was the first time that he had had nothing to say."[53]

Emboldened by these critical circumstances, Staff Chief Raeder screwed up the courage to approach his distraught boss. "Do you think the moment has come, Sir, to transfer your flag to another battlecruiser?"[54] Hipper finally had something to say. "I have given no thought to abandoning my flagship!" he snapped testily. From painful experience Raeder knew how to play this hand. He stood silent a long while as both he and Hipper stared at the rest of their command pulling ever further away from them. Finally, he offered renewed counsel, "We can't lead the squadron from *Lützow* anymore, Sir." "But I can't leave my flagship!" "We've been unable to signal by wireless for over an hour, Sir, and our speed isn't enough to keep up. We can't lead from here anymore!" "You make sense, Raeder, but this is my flagship!" "Sir, the squadron needs you!"

From these words Hipper "seemed to have [gotten] an electric shock," recalled an officer on the bridge. "In a flash he was the Hipper of old. 'You're right!' he said, and then turned, every inch the officer and leader of men, to take leave of the staff and seamen on the bridge of the *Lützow*. 'We'll come back! We won't forget you!'"

Harder now ordered G39 and her three destroyers, which *Rostock's* Torpedo Boat Leader (Commodore Michelsen, main battle fleet) had sent from the northwest to the rescue, to pull alongside and transport the vice admiral commanding to another vessel. Having said his upbeat farewells to those on the bridge, Hipper stepped up to the captain: "Scuttle her, Harder, once you believe the damage has become too great."

Exploiting what had been a lengthy lull in the enemy's fire, Hipper started down the side of the ship, adeptly—and impressively to those watching who knew about his sciatica—negotiating the descent on a violently bobbing and swaying rope ladder, from which he hopped onto the forecastle of G39. Raeder and the staff followed him down. As the smaller vessel pulled away through 1st Half-Flotilla's smoke screen—it was now passing 1900—Hipper "calmly and cooly" ordered the destroyer's captain to find 1st SG. It would take several hours, however, before he succeeded in transferring his flag.[55]

■ ■ ■

Over the half hour before 1830, Scheer stood with his staff inside the crowded conning tower of *Friedrich der Grosse*, struggling to stay aware of the battle situation, his awareness limited to what he could see, augmented somewhat by a stream of wirelesses from the fleet delayed a few minutes by the necessary process of sending, receiving, and couriering the most important of them. Exacerbating the anxiety of these moments, enemy "shorts" landed to port, their gargantuan, dead-fish littered waterspouts rising into the smog of battle and further obstructing the admiral's visibility as he peered through the narrow slits of this command citadel.[56]

What were his ships fighting out there? Adding to reports from 2nd SG of "being fired at by enemy ships of the line" (1800, 1802, 1810), another at 1825 relayed what had been alleged by British prisoners captured after the afternoon destroyer melee: at sea were "sixty big ships, including six battlecruisers and twenty of the latest ships of the line."[57] So, did he face twenty-six dreadnoughts? Scheer had roughly a hundred vessels, including five battlecruisers and sixteen modern battleships, *twenty-one* dreadnoughts in some ways of superior quality to the British, plus Mauve's potentially useful 2nd Squadron. To the best of his knowledge, moreover, only *Wiesbaden* had yet sustained serious damage, for no others had issued distress calls.

But what would they be fighting out there?[58] As far as Scheer surmised, reinforcing the BCF, reported earlier by Hipper as "*six* ships" strong, and the *four* battleships he could see sailing behind Beatty (i.e., 5th BS), were as many as "*twenty* ships of the line" that 2nd SG's destroyers thought they may have glimpsed. This accounting meant perhaps *thirty* dreadnoughts to confront, which corresponded roughly to the *twenty-six* of which British prisoners had boasted; but in recent minutes he had seen two great explosions of enemy ships and two others driven off. Frustrated by impaired visibility and the dizzyingly uncertain math, he darted outside to the unshielded bridge, his preferred perch. With no choice here, Trotha, Levetzow, and his flag lieutenant followed.

From his new vantage point, Scheer observed the gradual crescendo of British fire after 1830. As he did, the frustration of a previously blinded leader quickly morphed into alarm and barely suppressed anger at his van. "The entire arc stretching from north to east was suddenly a sea of [gun]fire," he wrote, recalling *what turned out to be* Jellicoe in the north; and Beatty, Hood, and the van of 3rd LCS in the east (see map 11.4). He could see "several hits and consequent explosions"[59] on Behncke's 3rd Squadron, but Hipper's battlecruisers had disappeared from view, obviously bending to southeast ahead of Behncke, who followed them. Such a tactic could mean that these squadrons merely shifted into a southerly running battle, an "unavoidable"[60] reaction to the approaching British. On the other hand, perhaps another cut and run by Hipper's forces?[61]

Scheer's irate suspicions were exacerbated by the troubling realization that the pivot point where the 3rd, 1st, and 2nd Squadrons would follow Hipper to the southeast lay dangerously exposed to the concentrated fire of what remained of the enemy's reinforcing dreadnoughts after those explosions. Scheer, going by the earlier reports from 2nd SG, placed these late-arriving squadrons—probably two of them?—several miles further southeast than the actual position of *King George V* leading Jellicoe's leftwing. Thus the enemy appeared to have enveloped Scheer's fleet, crossed his "T."[62] Just as bad, the German fleet, silhouetted by the setting sun, made decent targets for the British, who sailed behind a visibly impenetrable screen of cordite and funnel smoke curling around inside the spotty mist bank.

Visibility on the bridge remained far from ideal, but it took Scheer only a few minutes to "divine" the new reality for his command. "While the battle is progressing," he wrote years later to American historian Holloway Frost, "a leader cannot always obtain a really clear picture, especially at long range. He acts and feels according to his impressions."[63] Always wont to seethe when subordinate commanders seemed to be underperforming, *Bobschiess* turned to the nearest signals officer at 1836: *"An Alle: Gefechtskehrtwendung nach Steuerbord."* The man hurried down to the radio room to pass along this order for the entire fleet: "Starboard battle turn together." To cover this apparent retreat, the main fleet's Torpedo Boat Leader (Michelsen) on light cruiser *Rostock* ordered twelve destroyers of 3rd Flotilla to charge (1837). Unsure of Scheer's intentions, however, he quickly ordered them back (1839 or 1842) and waited for the situation to clarify, but in the process the Grand Fleet obliterated *V48* with ninety crewmen aboard.[64]

Trotha remembered it as "several tense moments" while they waited to see if the fleet could execute the turnabout.

> [Scheer had ordered] a maneuver, often made sharply in practice, but today's test comes amidst heavy enemy fire with signal halyards and radio antennae partially destroyed. With over a hundred ships and craft rushing intensely

forward into hard fighting comes a signal to turn about. One must [picture] a
radio room below decks, [a] crammed, overheated cell, with a life and death
struggle raging outside . . . and then suddenly an order arrives for the whole
fleet. In a few seconds [we need] certainty to prevail that the signal will be
properly understood and able to be executed. Several more seconds [follow]
of the highest tension! Then [we see] flags on all ships run up, flares being
shot—even during daylight—a veritable flourish of signal flags, and then as if
on a parade ground, without any hitches, helmsmen on ship after ship turn
about, a brilliant triumph of our peacetime maneuvers.[65]

First SG also turned with the High Seas Fleet circa 1837–38,[66] all but the now leaderless
Lützow, falling back to southwest. Scheer had reversed course to west to prevent
having his "T" crossed, a retreat maneuver recalled so exhilaratingly by Trotha that
extrication from impending disaster is no doubt what the wary COS wanted—and
expected—at the time.

With German ships heading westward by 1840, the British cannonade sounded
no more. This sudden battle silence, an eerie kind of hush, contrasted starkly with
the ear-splitting cracks and booms, the "infernal din of the big guns"[67] heard before.
An air of impending peril, amplified by smoke and fog that swirled tauntingly about,
disappeared, and then mockingly reappeared, intensified a sense felt by all, both
officers and men, that danger lurked in nearby waters. Gripped by the drama of the
moment like everyone else, the leadership troika on the exposed bridge of *Friedrich
der Grosse* turned its attention to the obvious pressing question before them—and
the entire German navy: "What now?"[68]

There was one side of Scheer, the ambitious side that the weight of command
responsibility always reinforced, which needed to hear first from his even-keeled
COS. But Germanic staff protocol alone would have made Practical Scheer turn to
his Number One. True to Trotha's phlegmatic nature, he had been silently agitating
over the best course of action during the preceding moments. Scheer had ordered
the battle turn, an escape maneuver carefully rehearsed before the war, so it was
only logical that Trotha would offer advice about the best means of completing this
retreat. Rationality dictated that the British would soon reappear out of the mist: the
fast, powerful *Queen Elizabeths* and the BCF from the north, apparently, while the
battleships he assumed had blunted Hipper's advance and punished 3rd Squadron
closed from the east—in Trotha's opinion, probably the entire Grand Fleet. This
foreboding scenario presaged a disadvantageous retreat like Dogger Bank with some

ships falling prey, except worse, for unlike 1915's debacle, Scheer could be unable to reach home. "For the night [we must] succeed in breaking the battle lines free from one another so that we do not let ourselves be cut off from our base, but rather that we stand ready to confront the enemy by first light at the entrance to the German Bight."[69]

Retreat was not welcome advice, not to Impetuous Scheer, who had made the turn to avoid having his "T" crossed, but apparently "with a view," it was said later, "to immediately resuming the engagement under more favorable tactical conditions"[70]—not, in other words, to facilitate withdrawing more than a hundred miles. It was much less welcome to his Number Two, the belligerent Levetzow. As for both of them, however, would not reason and rationality dictate that they must listen, that they must face the facts facing them?

As time drew on to 1845 and beyond, strangely enough, Trotha's inescapably dire scenario vanished just like the goings and comings of the smog. Soon enough the situation had morphed, in fact, into something that seemed quite different, for the British had simply not followed the German fleet and now threatened neither flank. *Moltke* confirmed this more welcome reality shortly after 1845: "enemy van bears E-to-S."[71] This sighting placed these mystery battleships' southeast-heading eight miles farther along this vector than their *actual* position, which seemed to indicate that now *the enemy rear* lay dangerously exposed, except the already hard-hit *Queen Elizabeth*s and BCF, which seemed to be perilously isolated north of the enemy's reinforcements.

Perhaps poor visibility lay behind the enemy's decision not to close. Or did British casualties explain this timidity, ventured Levetzow the Hotspur. Two spectacular capital ship explosions fifteen to thirty minutes earlier; other ships also badly damaged or sunk; plus whatever harm Hipper had inflicted during the afternoon—Scheer had no reports of this yet. All of this logic strengthened the aggressor's argument: "It is still too early in the day, the enemy cannot come to the realization, cannot be allowed to say that we retreated from the field before him—besides, *Wiesbaden* is back there. So reengage, push hard into the broad bend of enemy power! He should sense that we feel stronger, even up against his greater strength!" Levetzow, a consistent advocate of taking the offense in Nelsonian fashion, could point to the opportunity lying before them to cut the British in half with raking "Trafalgarian" fire, gain gunnery advantage away from the setting sun, and return victoriously to Germany.[72]

Scheer stood there, inscrutable, indecisive. He would say later that what happened next just happened. No complicated explanation based on war gaming, naval science, theoretical musings applied, nor advice just received.[73] Proceeding on "our westerly course" his attention was drawn to the battlecruisers, which had come back into view since the battle turn. That *Lützow*—as far as he knew, undamaged—and her destroyer escort pulled away from the rest further south may have especially caught his eye: "In our [westerly] disposition, suddenly our big cruisers, which according to our observation had been withdrawn, appeared to break free . . . on a southerly course with a tangle of torpedo boats. This view was reinforced by the impression that they sought to move out of the enemy's fire, therefore: [they were making a] retreat."[74] Scheer's prejudices and predilections swirled and swarmed and started to emerge agonizingly and dialectically from subconsciousness to take hold of him. Is the German position really so critical? Should he make another dishonorable retreat like his predecessors? Could he let the war at sea turn out like the dismal stalemate on land? Are not British squadrons hurt, their shells defective? Are not German ordnance and gunfire splendidly effective? Has the mettle of this strong fleet, all its good men and material, really been tested? For once should they not be tested at unfavorable but almost even odds? Did not a few hours of daylight remain to seize this opportunity to annihilate several British battle squadrons and achieve a long-desired victory in detail—but a really smashing one—over the Royal Navy?[75]

Tempted to go back, Scheer initiated the maneuver by ordering the proper preparatory maneuver shortly before 1848: "*An Alle: Divisions-Gefechtsschwenkung zwei Strich nach Steuerbord*." The signals officer descended to the radio room once again, and in a few minutes Scheer's battleships started a regulation two-point turn to starboard by division.

Not yet aware of the main fleet's maneuver from his vantage point to southeast on light cruiser *Regensburg*, 2nd SG's Torpedo Boat Leader (Commodore Heinrich) ordered "a ruthless mass attack by the [6th and 9th] Flotillas" (1852 and 1854). Sailing near the *Lützow*, which had "fallen out, unmaneuverable," the author of this attack against that portion of the enemy that had come briefly into view through the mist and smoke believed it would not only help the wounded battlecruiser—and Vice Admiral Hipper, who had not yet left his flagship—but also cover the rest of the fleet in its "critical moment" of retreat.[76]

As Scheer surveyed the execution of his order, all at once the mists parted and about 12,000 yards behind his line could be seen the valiant *Wiesbaden*, firing away with all guns she had left and launching torpedoes at her British tormentors. Temporarily with nothing else to target, they had once again concentrated on the doomed light cruiser, a pitiful sight that "emotionally moved" most on the bridge of *Friedrich der Grosse* to feel that they were "leaving *Wiesbaden* in the lurch," recalled Scheer's flag lieutenant a few days later. Scheer wrote more blandly in 1919 that "encouraged by this sight, we [had] to turn the line around and advance to her." His mind more at ease and resolved to gamble, shortly before 1855, the C-in-C pulled the nearest subordinate officer toward him to complete the maneuver: "*An Alle: Gefechtskehrtwendung nach Steuerbord*." A moment later, *Rostock*'s Torpedo Boat Leader (Michelsen), on his own initiative, sent *G-39*'s 1st Half-Flotilla to pick up Hipper (1855). And then at 1900, Scheer ordered Michelsen to offload the crew of *Wiesbaden*. These three orders had the combined effect of negativing 2nd SG's (i.e., Heinrich's) destroyer attack, which was also unneeded now that there was no retreat.[77]

With the maneuver underway, Scheer's COS tried unsuccessfully to suppress a look of exasperation. The C-in-C was "driving his subordinates mad" again. Only one faction of them, however, for the operations chief and his kin, in contrast, beamed in anticipation. And why not? Scheer's armada, "the powerful German spear," was steaming back to "reach its target"[78] and realize the long-frustrated dream of winning the war at sea and terminating the stalemate of the Great War.

■ ■ ■

From the bridges of Jellicoe's battleships, the trickster mists appeared suddenly to envelop the leading German squadrons. One minute passably silhouetted, the next not, the enemy had just vanished, the apparent beneficiary of some sinister black magic. "After what seemed a very short time there was a violent ringing of the 'cease fire' gongs bringing everything to a standstill," remembered a midshipman on 2nd Division's *Orion*. "We in the gunhouse wondered what it could be—had we sunk our opposite number in the enemy line or what? The lieutenant in charge of the turret put us out of suspense by reporting: 'Enemy obscured by mist.' Another low down trick on the part of the weather."[79] With nothing to see, Britain's disappointed gunners could no longer continue to hammer the front of the High Seas Fleet. An "ominous silence"[80] descended on the Fisher Banks.

Atop the compass platform of *Iron Duke*, Jellicoe also wondered what it could be. Was the enemy's course the same, but simply "obscured by mist"; in other words, would he soon reappear, his van bending as before to southeast? When, after a few minutes, Scheer did not come back into view, it became clear he had turned, but in what direction? West? Southwest? And then later southeast to the Bight? Assuming it would eventually have to be the latter, Jellicoe knew he must block that retreat, so at 1844 he ordered the fleet to turn from east-southeast to southeast. With the change completed, the C-in-C queried *Marlborough*, flagship of Vice Admiral Sir

Cecil Burney's 1st BS (5th–6th Divisions) at the rear of the line: "Can you see any enemy battleships?" (1855). Burney replied, "No."[81]

Over these fifteen to twenty minutes of uncertainty, a wise caution guided the British commander's decision not to plunge "fools-rush-in" style into a blind south-southwest or southwest pursuit.[82] While retreating, was the enemy preparing to unleash destroyers, letting his sizeable shark pack even the odds with torpedoes? Did he also intend to cover his withdrawal by sowing the waters with mines? Would lurking submarines assist these threatening endeavors? Despite these worries, although still blind, Jellicoe nonetheless altered course to the south separately by division at 1855 to potentially close the distance somewhat to a not-yet-visible Scheer. A moment later, alarmingly, Beatty's report of a "submarine in sight"[83] reached *Iron Duke*, but her course remained to the south.

In the immediate aftermath of this shift, three events must have twisted the stomach of the inwardly anxious British C-in-C. Shortly after 1855, *Iron Duke* passed the shocking wreck of *Invincible*—was it German or British? That she was friend not foe soon proved depressingly true, her demolished bow and stern pieces jutting upward, a destroyer picking up survivors. "It was assumed at the time that she had been sunk either by a mine or by a torpedo, and the latter appeared to be the more probable," Jellicoe recalled. Just a minute or two later Burney reported that his flagship had been "struck by a mine or torpedo, but not certain which." The body blow, most probably a torpedo from *Wiesbaden*, gave the vessel "a heavy heave and shook [her] up and down violently for a minute or two," causing considerable damage, a list, and reduction in speed to 17 knots, but *Marlborough* managed to keep position ahead of her squadron. And then *King George V* alerted *Iron Duke*: "There is a submarine ahead of you." A minute later, *Duke of Edinburgh* also saw one. The Germans had none, in fact, but this recent succession of reports sufficed to revive the commander's preoccupying pre- and-post-1914 concerns with the perils of sneaky submersibles, especially given that the Admiralty's intelligence division had informed him "the Germans had succeeded in producing a torpedo which left little or no track on the surface"—as it transpired, they had not. Only circa 1900 did some certainty intervene to calm nerves and gird crews for renewed action. Having seen from very long range the readvancing Germans through a momentary tunnel-like clearing in the mists, Beatty reported: "Enemy are to westward."[84]

2nd LCS had seen the Germans again too. Commodore William Goodenough's four light cruisers, sailing off the port quarter of 5th BS as it followed Burney's squadron to the southeast pivot of Jellicoe's battle line, turned south "to observe the enemy's rear, their course being in doubt." While underway at 1847, Goodenough spotted *Wiesbaden* and three minutes later 2nd LCS opened fire, supported by *Malaya* at the end of 5th BS. An officer on *Southampton* wrote,

> Having nothing particular at that moment on his hands, our commodore decided to run over towards [*Wiesbaden*] and work our wicked will on her. We could see several shells, in fact a very large number, burst on her. The six rear ships of the [westward-bearing] German line had, in my opinion, preserved an ominous silence whilst we advanced to batter their helpless brother. It was the calm before the storm, for when we were about 6,000 yards from the three-funneler [i.e., *Wiesbaden*] and 12,000 from the German battle line, the rear ships of the [westward heading] German line opened a very heavy fire on our squadron. We fled helter-skelter to the rear of our line, pursued by a perfect shower of 11-inch shells.

It is interesting that the young officer, Lieutenant Stephen King-Hall, seemed to think it inevitable that naval honor would probably induce a German reply to the not so merciful killing of "their helpless brother." It was, in fact, this lopsided engagement between 2nd LCS, *Malaya*, and *Wiesbaden* firing her few remaining guns that caught the attention of Scheer's "emotionally moved" bridge party and induced them to complete the battle turn. Circa 1900 Goodenough alerted Jellicoe: "Urgent. Priority. Enemy battlefleet steering E-SE. Enemy bears from me S-SW."[85] The Germans had turned (see map 11.5).

Also in sight, onrushing to the north-northeast about 7,500 yards away, steamed the source of another "perfect shower of 11-inch shells," *Derfflinger* and 1st SG. Hipper's acting replacement, Captain Johannes Hartog, guided his four badly battered battlecruisers, blazing away first with all secondary batteries still able to fire, and then all yet functioning big batteries too, toward the point where they would turn east and assume the vanguard of Scheer's battleship squadrons. "'Light cruisers on the port beam!' was reported," recalled Hartog's chief gunnery officer, Hase. "In order to spare the heavy guns for more important targets, I ordered Lieutenant-Commander Hausser to engage the light cruisers with the 5.9-inch guns. He opened fire at 7000 [meters]. Meanwhile I scanned the horizon. As there were no other ships in sight, I also opened fire with the heavy guns at one of the ships reported as light cruisers."

As the minutes ticked past the top of the hour, however, Hase made a startling observation: "The enemy ships were at the extreme limits of visibility [i.e., 10,000–11,000 meters]. Now they opened a lively fire, and I saw that the ship I had

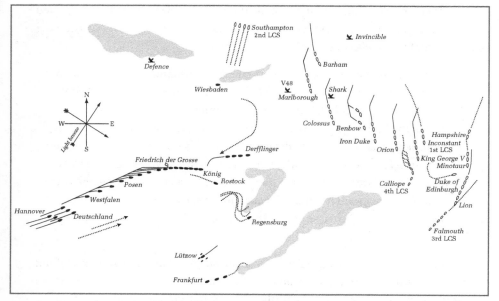

Map 11.5. The Battle of Jutland at 1912: *Bobschiess* turns back to attack.

selected as a target was firing full salvos from four double turrets. The light 'round
the enemy cleared for a moment and I saw distinctly that they were battleships of
the heaviest class with 15-inch guns! Fire was now flashing from them."[86] He had
probably spotted the heavily armed HMS *Revenge*, sailing in Burney's 6th Division.
At almost the same time (circa 1904–6), the German van came under fire from the
12-inch guns of *Agincourt*, also 6th Division, as well as those of *Neptune* and *St.
Vincent* at the rear of 5th Division.[87] Four battleships, half of Jellicoe's right wing
1st BS, had reengaged. Hartog turned east (1906) to bring available guns to bear on
these barely visible targets to his northeast.

The reports of Goodenough and Beatty indicated to the British C-in-C that his
entire fleet, visibility permitting, would soon have another opportunity to punish
enemy squadrons. To close the range, Jellicoe altered course three points starboard
to south-southwest at 1905, but then turned back to south at 1909 to avoid torpedoes
coming at 6th and 5th Divisions, probably from *Wiesbaden*, but also perhaps from
torpedo boats of the advancing 3rd Flotilla. A moment or so earlier, moreover, Jellicoe
told a signals officer to have Burney's 1st BS form astern of *Iron Duke*'s column (4th

BS) and *King George V* and 2nd BS to take station ahead.[88] The latter maneuver had become necessary to straighten a battle line that had been broken up into separate columns after the fleet headed south "by division" at 1855. Unfortunately, Jellicoe's correctional order to reform the line, given amidst the flurry of two course changes, did not get sent until 1912 and thus could not quickly overcome a significant problem whereby firing arcs to the southwest were partially "blanketed" by squadrons sailing immediately ahead. "The whole thing struck me as fearfully disorganized," remembered a turret midshipman on 3rd Division's *Royal Oak*. Thus 6th Division blocked *Barham* in the front of 5th BS, 5th Division hindered most of 4th Division, which in turn obstructed the end of 3rd Division, and so forth. Rapid course changes and blanketing, both exacerbated by the "fearfully handicapping"[89] murky weather, explain the fact that as time drew on to 1912 and ranges closed to under 10,000 yards for the British right, and well under 20,000 yards for the left, only *Valiant* (1910, 5th BS), *Marlborough* and *Hercules* (1912, 6th Division), and *Colossus* (1912, 5th Division), had reengaged with the others—from his right, only eight of Jellicoe's thirty-three dreadnoughts (including the BCF) had commenced firing. While Jellicoe's preference for centrally controlling his fleet (see chapter 4) functioned to fairly good effect in certain circumstances—his initial difficult deployment off the port column, for example—the "fearfully disorganized" situation shortly after 1900 shows that limits existed to what could be done from the top. But would decentralization have worked better?[90]

Nevertheless, even a cursory glance at the battle maps shows Jellicoe, despite these difficulties, moving closer to once again crossing the German "T" and placing his enemy in an extremely critical position. On the other hand, it should be easy to appreciate that from Scheer's blurred vantage point, "this was not the case." However suicidal it strikes some historians today, the objects of the battle turn appeared attainable as far as Scheer and Levetzow could see. Shortly after 1900, elements of the 3rd Torpedo Boat Flotilla passed between 3rd and 1st Squadron on their way toward the hapless *Wiesbaden*. When they came under British fire almost immediately, Scheer ordered light cruiser *Rostock* to reinforce the attempt (1905). Over the next seven or eight minutes, as eight ships of Jellicoe's right wing fired salvos that drove the destroyers back and also ranged ever closer to the advancing German battle line, these apparently squadron-strength gun flashes to the northeast probably confirmed the supposition that British fleet units might be vulnerably isolated there, capital ships that could be sunk as the main units of the German fleet—with destroyers held back[91]—maneuvered to exploit Trafalgar-style the presumed gap in the enemy line.

This was no time, therefore, to cast aside the "powerful German spear"; but at 1913, when Hartog suddenly turned *Derfflinger* and 1st SG onto a southeast course, and then moments later headed south (1915),[92] it struck the German C-in-C as if they retreated again. "His behavior created the impression with me," remembered Scheer, "that they seemed to be glad to be able to withdraw from the battle on a southerly course with high speed." Flag Lieutenant Weizsäcker complained similarly that "the battlecruisers did not at all execute the desired maneuver." Levetzow would not have it either, maintaining later that he abruptly recommended that the suspect battlecruisers make "a death ride" (*rücksichtslose- und Todeseinsatz*), and then repeated the words he had probably used thirty minutes earlier, "Fall upon the enemy, jolt him, and then punch on through" (*und dann die Schlacht durchschlagen*). Scheer complied: "*Grosse Kreuzer Gefechtswendung rein in den Feind! Ran!*" (1913). The battlecruisers were to "battle turn [right back] into the enemy," to "have at them" (i.e., not to withdraw "on a southerly course with high speed"). Knowing that Trotha disagreed—and perhaps seeing more disapproval on the face of his COS—Scheer turned to another staff member and said bluntly, "I don't care if they kick me out of the navy because of this!" This remark, one of only a few times this day that he had vouchsafed any outward emotion, exposed the fraught, fiery inner feelings that had been fighting since midafternoon against his forced facial flaccidness. The admiral knew that he had rolled the iron dice, gambling that he, not Trotha, would be right.[93]

On *Derfflinger* a minute or so later, a signalman brought this message to Hartog: "Close the enemy. The ships will fight to the death."[94] "Unfortunately," remembered Levetzow, "Scheer lessened (*abgeschwächt*) the deployment a short while later to a weaker (*mildere*) one." Indeed, at about 1914–15 the German C-in-C overturned his operations chief and ordered 1st SG instead "to operate against the enemy's van."[95] As he had not yet altered course back to the east, Hartog continued on his southerly bearing.

The somewhat inexplicable reason for Scheer's *volte face* has never been adequately explained—but often, however, incorrectly so.[96] It is quite possible, for one thing, that *Lützow's* report of her crippled condition, first wired to *Rostock* (1700) and then relayed to *Friedrich der Grosse—Rostock* had not alerted Scheer earlier (see chapter 11, note 55)—finally reached the admiral's hands. Hipper's flagship and her escort of destroyers, flanked by most of Boedicker's injured 2nd SG, could not be left behind. It is also probable that the first salvos from 3rd Division (*Iron Duke* at 1913) and 2nd Division (*Orion* and *Monarch* at 1914), all three sets of flashes more easterly than northeasterly, gave the skeptical Trotha an opportunity to gain back a measure of control over the "unruly" Number Two by repeating his belief that in all likelihood they were confronting "the entire English fleet, a superior force." His probable point would have been reinforced by the first direct hits (1913–14) on *Derfflinger* and *Seydlitz* of 1st SG and *König* and *Grosser Kurfürst* of 3rd Squadron from what were not just *eight*, but now *eleven* enemy dreadnoughts.[97] Levetzow may well have objected, pointing out again that by "holding course" they could place "the English fleet in a tactically highly unfavorable situation" by reversing the enemy's gunnery advantage for "dusk and nightfall" [*die einbrechende Nacht*], but Trotha and a quickly deteriorating battle position had revived Practical Scheer.[98]

Indeed, the battle situation for the Germans fell apart over the next few minutes to 1917 as more of the British battle line opened fire—and quite possibly came suddenly into better view. Thus a sailor on SMS *Posen*, far behind in the midst of 1st Squadron, made a shocking observation: "Suddenly we were practically surrounded. We were being fired at from every side. The entire British fleet had suddenly appeared. We were in a tight corner and I said to myself, 'You will be a lucky fellow if you get out of this!'"[99] Joining the cannonade, *Royal Oak* (1915, 3rd Division), *Lion*, *Tiger*, and *Princess Royal* (1915, BCF), *Benbow*, *Bellerophon*, *Temperaire* (1917, 4th Division), and *King George V* (1917, 1st Division) belched forth their fiery fury. *Nineteen* British dreadnoughts now found decent targets; but at 1920 it rose to *twenty-one*, at 1922 to *twenty-three*, and soon even more steel behemoths had entered this veritable turkey shoot.[100]

Indeed, making shooting easier for the enemy, the back-lit German line had also bunched up when the battleship squadrons, approaching too quickly from the west as 1st SG made the turn east (1906–9), had to reduce speed, a problem originating with *Derfflinger* stopping on the way north to the pivot to the east to free torpedo nets from her propellers.[101] Adding to the disorder, *G39* steamed at high speed into the middle of this "absolute sausage boiler" that the German fleet found itself in, hoping to pull alongside *Moltke* and deposit Hipper in a new flagship. With the Battle of Jutland/Skagerrak reaching a climax, however, with "sea and sky gone mad before the raging forces of humankind," the battlecruiser could not stop.[102]

Scheer and Levetzow had steered the fleet into "a regular death trap."[103] As a succession of massive projectiles slammed into German nickel steel, British secondary gunners cheered, for with the heavy guns carrying the fight, they were essentially spectators at a sporting event. "One was soon able to distinguish the difference between the flash from the German guns and the resulting explosion when one of the German ships was hit. I am sure we served out a lot of punishment at this particular time and it soon became like a football match. Every time there was a hit, a roar would go up from the lads, with a few appropriate adjectives for emphasis and everyone was very excited."[104] In this zero-sum game, of course, feelings were vastly different on the losing end. On *Von der Tann*, which absorbed one hit that killed four, all turrets had stopped firing long before the "death ride," therefore no answering big gun booms lifted the depressed mood of officers and men, convinced one and all that they would be "lucky fellows" if they got out of this. *Moltke* came away luckily completely unscathed, but not *Lützow*, limping away too slowly to the southwest, which took five hits and became even more of a slow-moving wreck. Worse, *Seydlitz* suffered six hits and *Derfflinger* no less than fourteen. Collectively, several hundred men died with scores more wounded, but *Derfflinger* clearly got the worst. Jellicoe's heaviest ordnance—15-inch shells shot from *Revenge* (6th Division) at a mere 9,000 yards—penetrated her two aft turrets (one even through thick turret roof armor, the other through thinner barbette plate) and burst inside. Fire prevention measures introduced after Dogger Bank saved the ship from the worst fate, but not 152 of 158 turret crewmen.[105]

But it could have been far worse. Of the twenty-six British shells that found their marks in Hartog's battlecruiser line within a horrifying few minutes, thirteen damaged decks and superstructures, nine deflected off steel without penetrating, and four burst inside, but only one, the hit on *Derfflinger*'s C-turret, through thick armor. Tellingly, 5th and 6th Divisions, firing from less than 10,000 yards, landed three of the four shells that successfully detonated inside ships—the fourth probably came from medium range too. Thus, Tirpitz's foresight in building stout ships and Pohl's antiflash precautions instituted after Dogger Bank, when combined with the Royal Navy's long-range–shell deficiencies, certainly helped German ships avoid the mass death at sea experienced by the BCF and 1st CS. Defective ordnance does not enter the equation, however, when gunners miss their targets—blasting away with gunnery advantage from 16,000–17,000 yards, the BCF scored no hits during this phase of the battle.[106]

The British also hit four of the first five ships in Behncke's 3rd Squadron: *König* once, *Markgraf* once, *Kaiser* twice, and *Grosser Kurfürst* seven times, altogether claiming sixteen lives and wounding another twenty-three. Back in 1st Squadron, *Helgoland* also absorbed a hit, probably from an "over." Of these twelve strikes, four tore into decks and superstructures, six exploded against armor without penetrating, and two managed to pass through thinner armor and burst inside but did not destroy the vessel.[107] The fraction of shells detonating inside armor—25 percent (two of eight)—was less than against the battlecruisers—30.7 percent (four of thirteen)—probably reflecting the fact that they were fired from thousands of yards farther away. Once again, therefore, the results could have been far worse—so much so that German officers and men remembered British ordnance as "laughable."[108]

But no one was laughing at the time. In contrast to the fairly decent, silhouetted targets in British crosshairs, German gunners saw only muzzle flashes in the mist unless a momentary clearing improved ranging. Consequently, only HMS *Colossus* suffered two or three hits causing minor damage and wounding a few sailors. Attempts to sight on enemy flashes and confront the Royal Navy proved impossible. The recoiling impact of one such effort from *Friedrich der Grosse*'s 12-inch turrets knocked Scheer to the deck of the bridge and ripped off his coat, an embarrassment included rather gratuitously by Trotha in his short memoir of the battle. Probably beginning to wonder, after his spearhead divisions had been hit thirty-seven times in just a few minutes, whether he would indeed get "kicked out of the navy"—unflattering remarks Trotha did not hesitate to tell others after the battle—Scheer ordered the fleet to turn around again at 1918 and head west: *"Gefechtskehrtwendung nach Steuerbord."* Three minutes later, he ordered torpedo boats forward to cover the retreat.[109]

Unfortunately, few of the remaining fifty-nine destroyers accompanying the German fleet—three had been lost—were in position to attack. "The reason for their absence from the van is not clear when we consider the desperate character of Scheer's deliberate thrust," wrote historian Holloway Frost, especially given that "he depended upon his destroyers for the accomplishment of his purpose."[110] But what purpose? If Scheer had intended to hit and retire as Frost and many historians allege, all six torpedo boat flotillas should have been ordered up near the van to fall upon the enemy and drive Jellicoe's battle squadrons away from the retreating High Seas Fleet, but Scheer and Levetzow had wanted to "punch on through" and accordingly kept their boats in protective flanking stations—fully twenty-three of them in the rear (5th and 7th Flotillas) with another thirteen boats far astern (2nd Flotilla), almost the identical destroyer dispositions as circa 1815–20 hours when the German fleet sailed blindly into battle against whatever had come to reinforce the BCF and 5th BS.[111] Rather than a mass assault capable of launching the flotillas' 224 remaining torpedoes, therefore, only thirteen "Black Hussar" torpedo boats ventured forth at 1915 on the repeated initiative of 2nd SG's Heinrich on *Regensburg*, six minutes *before* Scheer finally ordered an assault he had not anticipated making. Heinrich's destroyer assault twenty minutes earlier had been nullified by the battle turn.

In the event, the initial staggered assault of thirteen speeding craft, what was available from 6th and 9th Flotillas, proved enough to accomplish one main goal of any such assault: turning away the enemy. As the assailants emerged from 1st SG's smoke screen, they took in "a fantastic sight," seen by the German side largely for the first time: "Twenty-four English battleships stood there before us in bright light in a wide curve from north to southeast," *V28*'s captain wrote later, "and we gave the corresponding report that the entire English fleet had been sighted, as previously only individual ships and a single unit had partly come into sight."[112] Immediately, the primary, secondary, and tertiary ordnance of the entire Grand Fleet flung furious, ferocious fire at "the black-painted, narrow-waisted boats racing in towards us." One recalls here the frenetic fire of American warships against the similarly deadly threat of kamikazes in World War II. The bubble trails of twenty-two torpedoes sped toward targets, and then the raiders turned away to starboard, laid down more smoke, and went back. "I remember that German torpedo attack as the bravest and most exciting incident I saw at Jutland," recalled a petty officer on *Iron Duke*. "It was the kind of dashing naval action prominent in boyish dreams."[113]

All four battleship captains of 6th Division took spontaneous evasive action to avoid incoming missives, as did *Colossus* (5th), *Iron Duke* (4th), and *Thunderer* (2nd). Jellicoe evaded too, ordering all divisions four points to port at 1921, and then another two points away at 1925. "The turn-away received much criticism from the 'after the event' boys, although it undoubtedly saved several battleships and probably the *Iron Duke* from being torpedoed."[114] Indeed, the maneuver ensured that torpedoes would have farther to run before impact and, while slowing down at their maximum range, be easier to avoid. The British C-in-C opted against an alternative known to him, namely, turning back Hollywood-style into the torpedoes, for this would have meant moving back into the torpedoes' effective range when they still had good speed—especially dangerous if the bubble tracks could not be seen, as the Admiralty had incorrectly reported. "A turn towards," Jellicoe added, "would have led to great danger if the first attack had been followed up by a second and third, and no one could say that this would not be the case."[115] Surely enough, when a second wave (3rd Flotilla) exited the thickening smoke screen around 1930, the British battle fleet had pulled out of sight having suffered no losses, only British light forces in view advancing to meet the enemy threat. A third attack wave ten to fifteen minutes later (5th Flotilla) would also peer into seas devoid of the main capital ship prizes they sought (see map 11.6). Several torpedo boats had been damaged by the intense British storm of steel, suffering a score of casualties, but one, the *S35*, paid the ultimate price. Hit by a heavy shell amidships, she broke in two and sank with all hands. Amplifying the tragedy, the eighty-seven lost included German survivors picked up from the afternoon melee.[116]

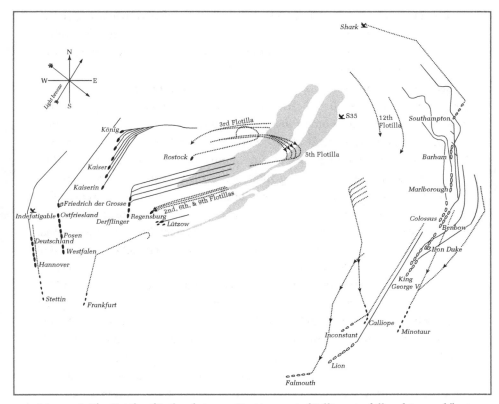

MAP 11.6. The Battle of Jutland at 1955: Beatty wanted Jellicoe to follow him and "cut off whole of enemy's battle fleet."

■ ■ ■

Scheer altered course from west to southwest at 1927, and then south eighteen minutes later. Jellicoe shifted from southeast to south at 1935, and then southwest at 1940, placing the opposing lead battleships, *King George V* and *Westfalen*, over fifteen miles apart on approximately the same latitude circa 1955, and on slightly converging courses. Beatty's BCF, however, had not turned away with the battle fleet: it kept sailing southwest (see map 11.6).[117] Thus his van, *Falmouth* and 3rd LCS, had closed to within ten miles to the southeast of light cruiser *Frankfurt* and 2nd SG.[118] Convinced that he had spotted the German battle fleet, Beatty reported this to Jellicoe twice

(1940 and 1945), and then (1947) relayed a coded message by searchlight over armored cruiser *Minotaur* (2nd CS), and thence by lamps to *King George V*, finally received in *Iron Duke*'s radio room at 1954: "Submit van of battleships follow battlecruisers. We can cut off whole of enemy's battle fleet."[119]

Beatty's "frustration" had come "to a boil"[120]—an emotion felt by everyone on his bridge. Twenty-five minutes earlier as *King George V* hauled out twice to port in compliance with Jellicoe's orders to avoid torpedoes (1921 and 1925), jaws dropped in collective disbelief among *Lion*'s top braid. "I shall not forget our agony of mind," Beatty recalled to historian Julian Corbett. Commander Reginald Plunkett, heading up the chief's staff, described being "horrified": "I felt instinctively that here was the sad climax of all our long discussions about [Jellicoe's preference for] defensive tactics. The Grand Fleet was . . . about to break off the action and probably lose the best chance it ever had of achieving decisive victory. I remember thinking then that I was witnessing a regrettable movement which I should remember to the end of my days . . . I feel little doubt that Beatty's views were similar to mine." As the BCF pulled away at 22 knots to the southwest, soon to lose sight of the slower-paced *King George V*, Plunkett decided to embolden his chief. "[After] seeing the van ships [of Vice Admiral Sir Martyn Jerram's 2nd BS] hauling off to port, I said to Beatty, 'Nelson would have signaled 'Follow me.' He at once replied, quite rightly, '[But] I cannot do that, I am not the C-in-C.' The . . . [7:47 p.m.] signal, 'Submit van battleships' . . . was then drafted and at once approved by Beatty."[121] There was more involved here, therefore, than Jellicoe's prudent tactics, for one has to ask why Jerram would need a "follow me" signal and not just have instinctively followed the "huntsman with a pack of hounds" while he still had a timely chance, if sailing at full speed, to remain in visual contact with the BCF? The answer redounds negatively on the C-in-C's tight-reined, controlling command system (see chapter 4), one that tended to stifle the kind of initiative needed at this moment. As it was, the lengthy drafting, sending, and relaying process of Beatty's fifteen-word message, followed by the signal being deciphered on *Iron Duke*, finally brought it to Jellicoe's attention at 2000, a good half hour after Beatty's staffers decided they needed to send one.

A few minutes earlier, having gotten Beatty's reported sighting of the German battle fleet (1959), Jellicoe at once shifted the Grand Fleet from southwest to west (2000) to close the enemy, and then shortly thereafter, having received Beatty's "submit van of battleships follow battlecruisers" request, and probably assuming Jerram had Beatty in sight, ordered 2nd BS to "follow our battlecruisers." Jerram, "another uncharismatic, tramline disciplinarian,"[122] could *not* see Beatty, however, nor did he immediately request the BCF's position and course, apparently thinking that heading west at 17 knots was what his C-in-C wanted, and that Jellicoe, presumably in possession of more information than he, must have known the best course to close Beatty. Thus *King George V* did not follow the BCF to the southwest; but at least the gap between *King George V* and *Westfalen* now closed much faster—by 2015 only a little over ten miles (20,000 yards) separated them, while *Derfflinger* and 1st SG (minus *Lützow*), overtaking their 1st Squadron to starboard, bore to the west only seven miles away. An hour and a quarter of dusky daylight remained.

At this time action resumed between light forces of the two fleets. Turning northwest to probe, light cruiser *Calliope* and 4th LCS (at the rear of Beatty's line), supported by 11th Destroyer Flotilla, sighted the German 5th Flotilla returning from its torpedo run and chased it several thousand yards westward until being driven back in turn by fire from *Kaiser* (3rd Squadron). *Calliope* absorbed five heavy hits, killing ten and wounding twenty-three. Simultaneously, Beatty's light cruiser van, which probed to the west in line abreast formation, charged at *Stettin* and the German 4th SG. 3rd LCS's bigger 6-inch guns quickly drove *Stettin* and 4th SG behind battleship *Hannover* and the "Five Minute Ships" of the advancing 2nd Squadron. Hearing the gunfire, *Lion* and her armored pride hurried west at 2017, and then back southwest (2025), their engines revving as if eager to reenter and end the rapidly reescalating high seas encounter.[123]

Simultaneously, BCF lookouts spotted the silhouettes of four German battlecruisers steaming south about 10,000 yards to the northwest pulling ahead to regain the lead off the port bow of *Westfalen*. Somewhat further west, predreadnought battleships in line ahead (2nd Squadron) also came into view. *Princess Royal* opened fire at 2018, *Lion* at 2019, and by 2044 Beatty's command had fired 55–60 salvos. Most of the BCF targeted Hartog's line, which had slowed to allow Hipper finally to board *Moltke*, thus making the likelihood of hits even greater—once again Hipper had to veer off. 1st SG returned fire as best they could, registering a few minor hits, and then turned away sharply to starboard, cutting off 1st Squadron, which also turned abruptly west to avoid collisions. *Derfflinger* got hit once; *Seydlitz* five times. While the BCF's shooting proved redeemably more accurate, *New Zealand* scoring its first three hits of the day, German armor again prevailed over insufficient British ordnance: five of the six hits caused damage and killed five sailors but failed to penetrate; the sixth destroyed a casemate position shielded by thin 5.9-inch armor—a 16.7 percent proper penetration ratio. Vice Admiral Mauve's 2nd Squadron also took two hits and splinters from a short shot detonating on the water. Details of one hit are lacking, but the other failed to fully penetrate thin 4.8-inch armor from 8,600 yards.

After scoring a few reputationally redeeming hits of their own (circa 2034–36 hours), the "Five Minute Ships" also turned abruptly away to starboard (i.e., west). Strangely, the BCF, which shortly after 2030 had turned hard (southwest to north-northwest) and charged Mauve's 2nd Squadron, did not follow. Battleship *Posen* (1st Squadron) had also opened fire (2028–35), which was supposedly enough for Beatty, who pulled back to the southwest (circa 2044), prudently retreating just as he had four hours earlier. "Enemy battleships [had been] sighted," he claimed in a preliminary report days later, "necessitating our hauling off to port." He had "wished to close the enemy van," recalled navigation officer Chalmers, "but in the low visibility he felt, quite rightly, that it would be unwise to press into close range of the enemy battle fleet without battleship support."[124] Begun circa 1720–25, mendacious BCF finger pointing was getting worse.

Beatty's "hauling off" may have been even more so the effect of a mysterious—but no doubt unnerving and threatening—buffeting that shook his squadrons. Indeed, one of the most peculiar happenings of the Battle of Jutland/Skagerrak had occurred toward the end of his assault on the head of the German line. At 2037, *Indomitable*, at the rear of the BCF, received a violent jolt that shook the ship as if it had been hit by a torpedo or struck a mine. The shock knocked her captain all the way off the compass platform and forced the big ship to haul briefly out of line, but strangely caused no serious physical damage. Over the minutes to 2044, the mysterious force rudely rocked *Inflexible* and *New Zealand*, and then *Tiger*, *Princess Royal*, and *Lion* in their turn. Although no historical consensus has emerged, it appears almost certain that the boiler of HMS *Nestor*, sunk in the afternoon destroyer melee, her grave only a mile and a half away, exploded, sending a powerful shock wave through the area south of the Fisher Banks, aided in its intensity by the shallow waters there, shaking the BCF—whose van, heading north-northwest, sailed somewhat farther away from *Nestor* than *Indomitable*—as the force spread to its terminus several miles away. Interestingly enough, seconds before *Lion* felt the shock wave (circa 2043–44 hours) she still barreled to north-northwest firing at a now silent enemy—*all* German fire had stopped seven-eight minutes earlier—and then the BCF, "to the wonderment of all [in the German van]," veered away to the southwest. Interestingly, in his final dispatch to the Admiralty, Beatty "did not repeat this [firing by enemy battleship] excuse for his turn away to SW."[125]

The BCF's abrupt departure had also lifted hearts slightly on Scheer's flagship, directly behind 1st and 2nd Squadrons. Those on the bridge of *Friedrich der Grosse* had been straining through the waning twilight to see what sort of action had broken out up at the head of the line. "The dickens with the sun," cursed the officers assembled there. All knew that darkness offered the "best guard" against being denied the safety of the Bight at dawn. Even though Beatty soon vanished, which had not seemed possible until, "inconceivably," it happened, the odds-makers remained pessimistic. "Our course to Horns Reef was too obvious," said one days later, and surely the British, drifting further to the south of them, "had cleverly blocked the homeward path."[126]

But Beatty's attack would be the last shooting between dreadnoughts during the final waning minutes of twilight. As the BCF kept watch a safe low-visibility distance 11,000 yards south of the German battle squadrons, which resumed their own southerly course around 2045, Beatty asked armored cruiser *Minotaur* for Jerram's position, learning from her (2055) that *King George V* had much earlier fallen back out of sight. Finally receiving a request from Jerram for the BCF's position six minutes later, he sent it, but by this time had given up all hope that friendly battleships would join him. That grating thought did nothing to reduce the temperature of the BCF chief below the boiling point.

Jellicoe continued sailing west, meanwhile, but then, hearing gunfire southwest of him, altered to west-southwest at 2021 and southwest at 2028, bringing *King George V* just five and a half miles (11,000 yards) slightly northeast of *Westfalen* and the German 1st Squadron by the top of the hour. Two light cruisers of the British 4th LCS to the west of Jerram's 2nd BS actually sighted the German battle fleet and launched torpedoes from 8,000 yards at 2100, and then ordered 11th Destroyer Flotilla to launch theirs, but Jerram, convinced that the targets were the BCF, not the Germans, negatived the attack. When the cruiser commander, Captain Ralph Crooke, insisted that these vessels were German, Jerram responded (2106), "If you are quite sure attack," but the flotilla leader pulled back out of the battleships' firing arcs instead because he "expected the fleet to open fire on [the enemy]."[127] Not yet in receipt of Beatty's position, however, and clearly still having his own doubts about what was targeted, Jerram did not open fire. Jellicoe had also altered the fleet's course from southwest to south (2101), which seemed to indicate that it was time to redispose forces for the night, not to reengage the enemy, which no one had ordered him to do.

Indeed, the British C-in-C had decided to break off and sail southward during the night, keeping the tactical edge by blocking Scheer from his bases and then reengaging him at first light. Unfortunately for Great Britain, Jellicoe once again did not possess enough good information from his scouts. He had reason to doubt Jerram's belief that the BCF bore due west of his 2nd BS, for the earlier sound of battle eleven or twelve miles away to the southwest was more convincing, and accordingly the Grand Fleet had been shifted in that direction at 2028.[128] But where was Scheer? Twice Beatty had reported (1940 and 1945) the enemy battle fleet west-northwest of him, ten to eleven miles away, steering southwest, but then nothing more came into *Iron Duke* during the battle with Hartog and Mauve forty-five minutes later—Beatty should have kept his C-in-C better informed. Left on his own, Jellicoe assumed the Germans sailed more to west than north: "I was misled by the firing of our battlecruisers ahead, which was at ships well to the northward of them, and not, as I was inclined to think, at ships to the westward."[129] And with only minutes of twilight remaining, turning farther west seemed imprudent. Andrew Gordon writes,

> Were the fog suddenly lifted and daylight miraculously restored, the enemy would be clearly seen, just over there, within easy range of 13.5- and 15-inch ordnance. But in the prevailing conditions, with lanes of visibility alternating erratically with almost total clamp-down, to carry on advancing would be like taking heavy cavalry into hostile terrain of woodlands and hedgerows; and the Grand Fleet was in no kind of predicament which could justify such recklessness. The predicament was all Scheer's. Jellicoe therefore eased around towards southwest and then south as dusk crept forward by the minute.[130]

The prudent British chief disfavored what would likely be a craps-throw, close-range confrontation at night, for the German fleet possessed better searchlights, better synchronizing technical "arrangements for the control of the searchlights and the gunfire at night,"[131] and better-trained crews for such a risky action.

And so the Battle of Jutland/Skagerrak, the "Great Day" so eagerly anticipated by many on both sides, slipped into the darkness of night—and entered the murkiness of counterfactual historical controversy. Professor Arthur J. Marder has asserted that the Admiralty's wireless to Jellicoe at 1248 (12:48 p.m. on May 31) delayed the C-in-C's progress toward the Fisher Banks, speculating that had he been told Scheer had left port, the Grand Fleet "would undoubtedly have steamed at high speed and arrived in the battle area somewhat earlier and so gained an hour or two of daylight." While attempts to diminish DOD Thomas Jackson's mistake and characterize the whole affair as myth are not entirely convincing (see chapter 8, note 28, and chapter 9, note 43), Marder's claim does not hold up, as shown convincingly by Andrew Gordon. Jellicoe's higher speed would have united him with Beatty farther south, but only—at most—eighteen minutes earlier. Counterfactual analysis therefore eliminates this possibility of gaining 60–120 minutes of daylight.[132] However, as argued earlier (see chapter 9, note 26), if the Admiralty had informed Jellicoe initially (i.e., on May 30) via secure land line of their belief in the probability of the entire High Seas Fleet putting threateningly to sea, he would not have stationed his squadrons sixty-nine miles behind Beatty—more likely it would have been thirty-five to forty miles back, thus bringing up his reinforcements about thirty to forty-five minutes earlier. This *ceteris paribus* scenario gains British forces, therefore, more valuable daylight.

What would have happened if the daylight battle had continued for nearly three-quarters of an hour? Clearly, this would have gone badly for the German fleet, which would have been pushed further to the west, further from Wilhelmshaven and Cuxhaven, and probably with the loss of some capital ships, especially among the already badly damaged 1st SG. German destroyer attacks would have again deflected Jellicoe, eventually providing Scheer with the cover of darkness, but probably making a return via Horns Reef and Helgoland next to impossible. Return in the morning via Terschelling-Borkum may also have been out of the question if Jellicoe had been there to block it, and would have been even more problematic if the Admiralty had decided to station the Harwich light forces as well as the armored cruisers, predreadnoughts, and HMS *Dreadnought* from Sheerness there too (see chapter 9). The day-long compounded errors of the Admiralty (plus others discussed in chapter 12) may well have squandered all chances of another Trafalgar.

▪ 12 ▪

NIGHT, MORNING, NOONTIDE

The short, four-hour night of May 31–June 1, the late spring norm in these northern climes,[1] produced its own share of debate about hypothetical alternatives. At 2106 Scheer instructed his naval air division to provide "urgently necessary"[2] early morning Zeppelin reconnaissance astride Horns Reef, 105 miles away. At 2110, the German C-in-C ordered his squadrons, which were then sailing southwestward far to the southwest of Little Fisher Bank, to steam at 16 knots south-southeast-by-one-quarter-east. His fleet shifted again to south-southeast-by-three-quarters-east at 2146. This course led straight for Horns Reef, and thence through a secure mine-free channel over Lister Deep, Amrun Bank, and Schmal Deep to Wilhelmshaven (see map 1.1). Never one to shy away from risk—witness his second battle turn toward the British at 1855—Scheer intended simply to blast his way to the reefs through whatever enemy forces tried to bar his way—or be destroyed trying. At acceptable cost to his desperate forces, he succeeded by 0324 on June 1 to begin entering the swept channel, leaving to posterity the difficult task of explaining how the British could have let this happen.

For most of the preceding day, Jellicoe had used his intellect and intuition to make a series of tactically correct decisions despite having been badly misled by the Admiralty and poorly informed about enemy dispositions by his scouting forces—and this did not change. Beatty reported at 2138 that the German fleet bore "N-by-W, steering W-SW." In his postbattle dispatch he added that this sighting "as near as could be judged was correct."[3] The weather and expiring twilight had tricked again, however, for although he still bore north-by-west several miles from the BCF, Scheer,

236

as noted earlier, had steered south-southeast-by-one-quarter-east since 2110 (see map 12.1). This last "sighting" gave Jellicoe the impression that his adversary sought to reach base by steering toward the Terschelling-Borkum channel along the Dutch coast. By continuing to sail south, British squadrons in their nighttime defensive formations could presumably remain slightly southeast of Scheer in good tactical position to maul or destroy him at dawn.

With the BCF sailing twelve miles to the southwest of him, Jellicoe placed 1st–5th Divisions in three close columns line abreast. 5th BS's three super-dreadnoughts sailed astern these five divisions with 2nd LCS well to starboard and northwest of Evan-Thomas' flagship, *Barham*. The 6th Division, with a damaged *Marlborough* struggling to maintain fleet speed of 17 knots, trailed 5th BS. The battleship van of this phalanx began to slip further to the south of the Germans during the first hour of darkness. As a precaution against his enemy attempting either to harry the Grand Fleet with destroyer attacks, or what seemed to the British C-in-C less likely, to escape to the east or southeast, Jellicoe amassed all his destroyer flotillas in five columns behind 5th BS and 6th Division, each stationed about a mile apart. If Horns Reef were indeed Scheer's destination, the destroyers would drive him back west for an early morning reckoning.

As time passed to 2230 hours and beyond, Jellicoe's destroyers wandered southward into the darkness and came abreast of the enemy.[4] As they did, Scheer's leftwing destroyer/light cruiser screen inevitably collided with the rightwing of Jellicoe's rear guard of destroyers and *Southampton*'s 2nd LCS. Over the next four hours to 0230, seven separate clashes pitted the entire force of outgunned and technically overmatched British light cruisers and destroyers against German vessels big and small, all better equipped for—and more adept at—nighttime fighting, their searchlights and guns coordinated in staccato succession, an impressive but deadly show of ear-splitting sound and blinding light. "In a moment," wrote Julian Corbett, "all was a roar of passing and exploding shell and a wild confusion of gun-flashes, dazzling searchlight beams and rapid changes of course. It was work in the old style at point blank range, with missing hardly possible on either side."[5]

A massed assault of British destroyers never occurred, but rather a series of surprise encounters as first the British 4th Flotilla, then the 11th, then 2nd LCS, and then the other flotilla columns were taken on in their turn and smashed by the German juggernaut as it escaped to the south-southeast across the sterns of Jellicoe's battle squadrons, which continued to drift ever further southward without engaging. Five destroyers went down, about 10 percent of the rear guard, as well as armored

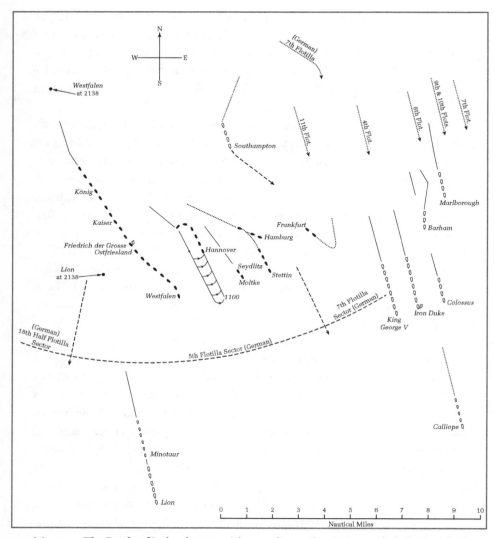

MAP 12.1. The Battle of Jutland at 2210: The weather and expiring twilight had tricked again, for Scheer sailed south-southeast, not west-southwest as in Beatty's 2138 report.

cruiser *Black Prince*, blown apart by the German 1st Squadron while attempting to rejoin 1st CS. Several other destroyers and 2nd LCS were also badly damaged—of altogether 1,531 British casualties, 1,401 died in action. While they took one enemy destroyer, three light cruisers, and the predreadnought battleship *Pommern* with them, inflicting 1,216 casualties, 1,200 of whom died, the men of the brave British rear guard could not stop Scheer from reaching the safe confines of the Bight. The *Lützow* had also been left behind, however, sunk by her own destroyer escort at 0145 after losing her pumping battle with the North Sea, which had reached as high as the bridge tower before friendly torpedo fire gave up the rest. Over a thousand crew survivors had been offloaded to four destroyers, and later to light cruiser *Regensburg*; but shortly before the destroyers' coup de grâce, Captain Harder had "assumed the heavy responsibility of informing the men [still trapped in the forward dynamo compartment] that they would soon die."[6]

Questions are imploringly begged here. Why did British destroyer flotillas fail to push Scheer back to the west? In addition to superior night fighting technique, their enemy enjoyed an element of surprise. In possession of British night recognition signals, which had been captured by the German 4th SG from a careless BCF wireless at 2132, the German ships identified their targets as hostile as soon as the British signaled, and then opened a hot fire on them. The battle-grey paint of the larger German ships also provided more camouflage effect at night (counterintuitively enough) than the black ships they targeted. Quite often startled and thrown onto the defensive, most British flotillas could not launch any coordinated torpedo attacks of their own. The deadly fire fighting "in the old style at close range" also explains why only one British destroyer, HMS *Faulknor* at 0156, reported sighting German battleships to Jellicoe, but the C-in-C never received the wire due to the "feeble" and "primitive" wireless sets in use in his destroyers that German operators easily jammed. Clearly, unlike Captain Stirling of *Faulknor*, most British officers were too busy fighting, or hampered by destroyed bridges, antennae, and radio rooms to report what they saw—these hypothetical wirelesses, of course, would also have been vulnerable to jamming—and signal flags had no use at night.

Harder to understand, why did the officers of 6th Division and 5th BS—trailing Jellicoe's three-columned battleship formation initially by two to three miles, and then later by five to six miles—make no reports? Indeed, they observed much of this, especially some of the hottest action between 2nd LCS and 4th SG (2215–45) and 4th Flotilla's battle with the German 1st Squadron (2330–0020). The question is not whether Jellicoe would have turned around to engage if he had known the facts, for he wanted no nighttime action, but rather that he would have altered course from south to southeast (i.e., toward Horns Reef) to prevent Scheer from escaping by morning, even though altering the course of his tightly formed, blacked-out squadrons would have been a very difficult maneuver—but still a likely one despite his long-standing objections to engaging the enemy south of Horns Reef (see chapter 8), worries that admittedly would have become more pronounced by the hour. The pyrotechnics behind 6th Division and 5th BS seemed, however, to be exactly what Jellicoe anticipated, namely, his flotillas shielding the fleet against enemy torpedo attacks. This explains the postbattle report of Vice Admiral Craig Waller, captain of 5th BS's flagship, *Barham*:

> It is certainly doubtful whether the various observations of enemy ships made by our battle fleet ought to have been reported to the C-in-C. I was on the bridge all night with [Rear Admiral Evan-Thomas], and we came to the conclusion that the situation was known to the C-in-C and that the attacks were according to plan. A stream of wireless reports from ships in company with the C-in-C seemed superfluous and uncalled for. The unnecessary use of wireless was severely discouraged as being likely to disclose our position to the enemy. The same reasoning probably influenced the *Marlborough*'s [6th] division.

While certainly illogical for the trailing divisions to make it easier for German destroyers to find their prey by beaming "severely discouraged" signals, the hesitation of these British officers to make reports points once again to the negative potential of "C-in-C-knows-best" battle orders to produce counterproductive results by undermining initiative. Although Jellicoe also interpreted the German star shells, searchlight beams, and gunfire to the north as signs of the attacks from Scheer's light forces that he expected, he did not wait long to break radio silence in asking 11th Flotilla at 2246: "Are you engaging enemy's destroyers?" They replied, "no," but that they opposed "enemy cruisers" (2250), shed little light on the situation. "I saw the actions which were taking place astern," recalled a gunnery officer on *Iron Duke*'s bridge "and we were all agreed that the indication was that fighting was going on between the Germans and our own flotillas and that [they] were engaged in protecting the stern of the battle fleet from the attack by German destroyers." Lost somehow in the darkness, however, lurked the potentially illuminating fact that this current action was north, while the BCF "sighting" of the German battle fleet at 2138 had placed it north-northwest. The course vector of the Germans headed roughly southeasterly (northwest to north), therefore, across Jellicoe's sterns.[7]

Jellicoe continued southward, but his conviction that Scheer maintained his southwest heading must have been undermined somewhat by a disturbing message from the Admiralty that reached the nearly exhausted admiral shortly after 2315. Sent a half hour earlier, it referenced a German order of 2114—two hours ago from Jellicoe's vantage point—to steer "S-SE-by-three-quarters-E, speed 16 knots." Although alarmed, the chief had reason to be skeptical. For one thing, the previous day's "news" from the naval lords that Scheer had not sailed sufficed for substantial discounting of information from the Admiralty. Adding to his doubts, an earlier wireless from London had reported Scheer's *rear* escaping eight miles southwest of the BCF circa 2100, but Beatty had reported at 2138 sighting Scheer's *van* still well within grasp ten or eleven miles away to "N-by-W, steering W-SW"—an 18–19-mile discrepancy. Jellicoe could not know that Beatty had inaccurately reported Scheer's actual course.

Soon the usually reliable light cruisers of 2nd LCS, which sailed several miles west of *Barham* and 5th BS, restored Jellicoe's conviction that he, not the Admiralty, knew Scheer's bearing. At 2330 he received *Birmingham*'s placing German cruisers and battlecruisers slightly northeast of her steering south. Moments later, with his sense of past time no doubt confusingly warping, he got *Southampton*'s delayed signal reporting close combat at 2215 with German cruisers west-southwest of her. "Which should I trust," Jellicoe asked rhetorically in his account of the battle, "reports from my own ships which had actually seen the enemy or a report from the Admiralty which gave information as to [enemy] movements at a time *over two hours earlier* than the *Birmingham*'s report?" Although the enemy sailed consistently to starboard of *Barham* as she went twenty miles farther south, taken together, however, the two cruiser reports indicated enemy bearings moving from west-southwest of 2nd LCS circa 2215—*Southampton*'s (see map 12.1)—to northeast of 2nd LCS at 2330—*Birmingham*'s. Was the enemy trying to cross Jellicoe's wake to the southeast? Probably "too tired to choose correctly" between the various signals, writes John Brooks, the C-in-C soon retired for a two-hour rest behind the bridge. Knowing what would have been the correct decision to choose often comes easier with hindsight, however, as Jellicoe himself would experience over the next three weeks.[8]

The Admiralty had it right after all, but they could have made Jellicoe a believer if they had passed along six German signals deciphered in Room 40 giving Scheer's course and/or position at points between 2243 and 0100 hours. Two additional German wirelesses dutifully sent to Jackson and Oliver—Scheer's 2106 request for morning airship reconnaissance off Horns Reef, and another from his light forces (2232) ordering all destroyers to assemble there at 0200—Room 40's haughty-albeit-tired superiors did not send to the C-in-C. There can be little doubt that June 1, 1916, would have exceeded the fame of the "Glorious First of June," Lord Howe's smashing of a French fleet in 1794, if these eight wirelesses, or only the last two relating specifically to Horns Reef, had been forwarded. But the Admiralty—exasperatingly enough—felt no urgency: Scheer's course for home had already been reported; and they knew, after all, that Jellicoe would not engage at night. Oliver, and probably Jackson too, retired for a rest, leaving their post tragically–comically in the hands of a duty officer who filed away Room 40's reports.[9]

At 0239, June 1, 1916, with dawn gaining in intensity before sunrise, Jellicoe ordered his squadrons and the BCF to turn back to the north. Visibility remained as poor as May 31, but it became clearer by the minute that Scheer had not headed for Terschelling-Borkum. A little after 0400, Jellicoe read a depressingly correct wireless from the Admiralty informing him that the German fleet had sailed an hour from Horns Reef at 0230, and thus by now was well into the secure channel thirty-five to forty miles east of Jellicoe. At 0404, Beatty, assuming the enemy still bore to the west, asked for permission to reconnoiter to the southwest. In reply he received "the crushing news"[10] that Scheer was well on the way to his Wilhelmshaven base.

■ ■ ■

Many more hours would pass, however, before German fleet command could feel good about their enemy's "crushing news." As it had been for many of the preceding hours, in fact, the situation continued to look bleak. Throughout the blind nighttime hours into Thursday June 1, Scheer's fleet had sailed south-southeast-by-three-quarters-east. "*Durchhalten*," hold course, was the admiral's refrain as he appeared from time to time on the bridge to receive reports. Like others there, he stared out into "the dark wall of night." At repeated intervals, fierce fights with enemy destroyers, light cruisers, and one old armored cruiser set ablaze the pitch blackness of those anxious minutes, too slowly passing. Surely, thought the admiral with no facial emotion vouchsafed, these attacks were but prelude to renewed battle with British battleships, for these enemy light forces would certainly report "our position, our course, and our speed" to Jellicoe. Ideal if they did not, but such good fortune bordered on the "incomprehensible."[11]

Joining the bridge watch, Scheer's flag lieutenant, Ernst von Weizsäcker, mulled over the operational assumptions and decisions made by the leadership prior to leaving port. Incoming casualty reports from squadrons had darkened his mood: light cruiser *Rostock* "unable to maneuver" (0009); light cruiser *Elbing* "helpless" (0030); battlecruiser *Lützow*, which had dropped back out of sight hours earlier, also "unable to maneuver" (0152); and battleship *Pommern* "annihilated" (0220). Nothing had been heard, moreover, from battleship *Nassau*, Germany's first dreadnought. Finally, Weizsäcker began to doubt whether "the whole day could be justified—[and] the others [I heard] hardly felt any different."[12]

Included among "the others," Scheer himself, who approached his flag lieutenant at first light (circa 0300), pointing out flatly that Saturday's invitation for General von Heeringen to dine on the flagship—and presumably hear about a great victory at sea—"no longer made sense—we'll want to cancel that." Indeed, how could the navy now claim to have helped win a war at sea stalemated by the army on land? Scheer's order strengthened Weizsäcker in the anxious feeling that Thursday's early morning fog offered "welcome protection," as had the night, against the unwelcome prospect of "a fight to the finish."[13]

The leader of Scouting Groups had also struggled through a harrowing night. After Beatty pulled away at 2044, Hipper finally managed to get on board *Moltke* and resume command. Although Scheer, anticipating action before first light, had ordered his battered 1st SG and weaker 2nd Squadron to the rear behind the battleship spearhead, wireless damage on *Moltke* blocked the order—so Hipper followed his instincts: "We must get [back] to the head of the line, that's our proper place!"

"Meanwhile darkness had been falling," wrote a staff member. "The gloomy mist continued to blanket the night. The ships were grey shadows flitting hither and thither. The very silence was full of mystery. Where was the head of the line?" No answer to this query came during much of the night. *Derfflinger* and *Von der Tann* had assembled aft as ordered, but *Seydlitz* and *Moltke* steamed somewhere ahead until losing contact with one another. Sailing on *Moltke* more southerly than Scheer, Hipper and his staff anxiously debated on two occasions whether to fire at ships of the line they spotted—Jerram's *King George V* and 2nd BS as it turned out (see map 12.1). Hipper had reached the head of *Jellicoe's* line—but no command to fire came from either side. Not until 0320, shortly after first light, could *Moltke* optically signal 1st Squadron that she had taken the point.

To his staff, Hipper joked, "I bet that one day the armchair experts at the Naval Academy will scratch their heads as to what we've all been thinking about, but I say we haven't done any thinking, we've been too busy trying to navigate!" His levity could not ease the stress level very much, however, for while they had managed to reach Scheer's rendezvous near Horns Reef, no one knew where the rest of 1st SG, including *Lützow*, sailed at that moment. And what he heard from earlier ships' reports sounded bleak (0255 hours): "*Derfflinger* and *Von der Tann* have only two heavy guns [each] clear for action; *Moltke* is shipping 1,000 tons of water; *Seydlitz* also badly damaged."[14]

Still uncertain, fifteen miles off Horns Reef, whether battle would soon recommence, Scheer reformed his "scattered and crippled ships,"[15] recalled one sailor, prior to entering the channel past Lister Deep and Amrun Bank. They escaped one division at a time, starting with 1st SG at 0324 hours, and then 2nd Squadron at 0335 (see map 1.1). Surrounded by light forces, 1st and 3rd Squadrons stood guard and waited with the last ounces of hope for *Lützow* and her escort of four torpedo boats. Moods sank to their lowest point at about 0400, however, when it was heard that the pride of 1st SG had been "detonated and left behind." At 0408 Scheer therefore ordered his two top battle squadrons to follow the others home, but even this unpalatable retreat did not prove uneventful when battleship *Ostfriesland* of 1st Squadron hit a mine (0525–0625 German time) laid only hours earlier by the British. The C-in-C immediately fired an emboldening signal at 0628 to the trailing 3rd Squadron: "*Durchhalten!*"[16]

An hour later, Scheer's battle-weary line stretched for miles off the long coast of Sylt Island leading to the Amrun Bank channel, which 1st SG and 2nd Squadron had already entered. At this point the flagship initiated what appeared to be the normal postbattle procedure of making damage and casualty reports to the rest of the fleet: "*Friedrich der Grosse* no damages." *Westfalen*'s reply, however, seems to have been an effort to establish a precedent for the battle squadrons of the High Seas Fleet after their first major engagement. Because 4th Division's flagship had received only a few hits killing two men, she proudly signaled instead that she had sunk five enemy destroyers during the night.

As the morning hours unfolded and further reports streamed in, the earlier impression of those around Weizsäcker, jaded by the anxiety of the previous evening's battle turns and blinding night actions, that *Der Tag* had been "no defeat, but also no victory, no real satisfaction," gradually morphed into the new consensus of satisfying tactical victory that would dominate official German thinking for decades. Even more enemy destroyers had been sunk or badly damaged during the night, which added favorably to the early evening's witnessed sinking of two unidentified capital ships (*Defence* and *Invincible*) and—they thought—a third (*Warspite*). *Moltke*'s long report proclaiming the afternoon sinking of *Indefatigable* and *Queen Mary*, unknowns for the High Seas Fleet's three battle squadrons until 1220 on June 1, bore witness to the battlecruisers' redeemingly blood-soaked badge, acquired while "bearing the brunt of the battle," not being borne in vain. Although Hipper's mood, affected by losing the third ship he had once commanded (see chapter 2), remained a "growling" one for a few days, this missive in particular helped turn officers' opinions around. The more upbeat mood swelled with further reports that the crews of *Lützow* and light cruisers *Elbing* and *Rostock* had been successfully offloaded; that *Nassau* had rejoined her squadron; that *Ostfriesland* did not sink after all; that even though *Seydlitz* shipped dangerous amounts of water, she could be pumped and saved; and especially elating: that the High Seas Fleet had captured several score British POWs.

Thus, although most officers would "not deny that they were extraordinarily fortunate, and that if the action had been prosecuted with energy on the British side, and if the 'Nelson touch' had been in evidence, things might have gone very badly for Germany," they were nevertheless more and more convinced that they had good reason to feel "intoxicated with victory." In keeping with this airy mood, Scheer, having tabulated all the wirelesses in his cabin, flatly told Weizsäcker not to cancel General Heeringen's invitation, and then ordered—as if establishing another precedent—champagne served to the bridge party as *Friedrich der Grosse* reentered the Jade.[17]

■ 13 ■
AFTERMATH

JUTLAND: LESSONS OF THE VICTORS

Unlike its anniversary namesake, Thursday, June 1, 1916, would not be a day of celebration for the Royal Navy. To be sure, every officer and sailor knew they had hit the High Seas Fleet hard, forced it to retreat back to the Jade, and prevented it, importantly, from breaking their island nation's strangling blockade of Germany. But the price had been high: three battlecruisers, three armored cruisers, and eight destroyers sunk; 6,094 officers and sailors killed; 674 wounded, many of them badly, some of these dying later from cordite and picric acid blood poisoning; and 177 taken prisoner.

The naval surgeons of the BCF and 5th BS faced the stiffest challenge. For two days they operated ceaselessly on the mutilated bodies of 422 of their comrades until the swollen feet of the doctors compelled a halt. Neither the "grim business" of muster that morning, with its alarming gaps in the ranks of those assembling topside, nor the burials at sea that forenoon of 291 victims of Germany's more properly detonating AP shells were stuff for the faint of heart. The mournful, yet somehow soothing strains of the *Sailors' Anthem* (*Eternal Father Strong to Save*), *Abide with Me*, and *The Last Post* may have helped a little. *Tiger*'s surgeon recalled, "It was a gloomy scene: the grey sky, the grey sea, the stitched up hammocks, [and] the padre with his gown blowing in the breeze. *The Last Post* was sounded by the marine buglers, and our shipmates plunged into the sullen waters."[1] At 0830 on June 2, the surviving ships of Beatty's command sailed under the Forth Bridge looking shockingly different than

246

they had when departing fifty-seven hours earlier. For royal marines like Captain Francis Jones it may have been some extra consolation after watching sixty of his comrades plunged into the "sullen waters" two-by-two that Major Francis Harvey would most certainly receive the Victoria Cross posthumously—Harvey's wife Ethel accepting for him.

Immediately, the task of replenishment, repair, and respite began in Rosyth. Colliers pulled alongside ships large and small, confirming the wisdom of the old saw that no rest will be granted to the weary. Materials and laborers for the initial fix up work struggled to find open lanes to also come on board. The walking wounded as well as the unwounded not cursed by the filthy job of coaling poured ashore by the thousands, moreover, to send telegrams to loved ones announcing they were alive and safe—only to be facially smacked by rumors of Royal Navy demise spreading from startled dock workers who had seen *Warspite*'s battered state when she arrived on June 1, and then other ships' damages as the BCF entered port the next morning. Some of these laborers provided the weary sailors with a form of welcome vastly different from previous sorties as they shouted out their "unmistakable abuse." Exacerbating all this harmful gossip and rudeness, the first misleading newspapers from London reported Germany's allegedly resounding victory at sea. Eventually, the papers got it right: "Will the shouting, flag-wagging German people get any more copper, rubber, and cotton their government so sorely needs? Not by a pound. Will meat and butter be cheaper in Berlin? Not by a pfennig. There is one test, and only one, of victory. Who held the field of battle at the end of the fight?" Meanwhile, destroyers, tenders, and drifters transported the worst casualties through this traffic jam in the anchorage to the doctors and nurses of HM Hospital Ship *Plessy*. Especially critical cases went to hospitals in Queensferry.[2]

■ ▦ ■

June 1 had also been a very tough day for Vice Admiral Sir David Beatty. The "wormwood" of not defeating the Germans Trafalgar-style, "to be so near and yet so far," rubbed at him like a saddle "gall," an especially painful sore "after the losses we had sustained." The harshly embittering reality of it all caught up to him during the burial service that morning when, choked with emotion, he had to hand the presidial duties over to Captain Ernle Chatfield. Afterward the chief stopped by *Lion*'s charthouse, where Navigation Officer William Chalmers struggled to reorder those maps and records that had survived the long battle. "Tired and depressed, he sat down on the settee, and settling himself into a corner he closed his eyes. Unable to hide his disappointment at the result of the battle, he repeated in a weary voice, 'there is something wrong with our ships,' then opening his eyes and looking at the writer, he added, 'and something wrong with our system.' Having thus unburdened himself he fell asleep."[3] Of the many things on Beatty's mind as he nodded off, attention to the BCF's inadequate armor protection and careless ammunition handling routines—those things "wrong with our ships" and "wrong with our system"—stood at the top, but they twisted and mixed emotionally with issues further down relating to the role of Jellicoe's main fleet in the battle.

First things first, however, Beatty dealt with what had caused three catastrophic battlecruiser explosions. Writing the Admiralty (copy to Jellicoe) on June 3, he concluded,

> [E]xperience of *Lion* indicates that open magazine doors in turrets are very dangerous. Present safety arrangements of flash doors are ineffective when turret armor is penetrated. Flash from shell may reach cordite in main cages and thence to handling rooms. This occurred in *Lion* when turret roof was penetrated, but magazine doors being at once closed saved magazine from catching fire. Almost certain that magazines of three lost battlecruisers exploded from such cause. Consider matter of urgent necessity to alter existing communications between magazine and handling rooms by reverting to original system of handling room supply scuttles, which should be fitted immediately. Meanwhile considered imperative to maintain small stock cordite in handling room for magazine, doors being kept closed with one clip and opened only for replenishment of handling room. Proposed handling room supply scuttles should be capable of being made watertight at will.

Beatty had just finished a long session with Commander Hubert Dannreuther, chief gunnery officer of the ill-fated *Invincible*, whose observations from that ship's foretop of what happened to the midship wing turrets weighed heavily as incontrovertible eyewitness evidence. Installation of the old system of supply scuttles as well as the reoperalization of antiflash doors got underway "immediately," in fact, along with directives drastically declining the number of full charges outside magazines in handling rooms and working chambers to only four—Grant's system would now be standard.[4]

The question of battlecruiser armor protection fell to a committee under Rear Admiral Arthur Leveson, Vice Admiral Sir Martyn Jerram's second-in-command, 2nd BS, appointed chair on June 4 by Jellicoe. His investigating committee reported inside a week that without proper antiflash doors there existed a danger of flash fires in turrets, but favored as a primary cause of the explosions enemy shells penetrating to magazines through inadequate deck and gun house roof armor. He therefore recommended the fitting of thicker plate. Jellicoe concurred on June 14: "our lightly arm[or]ed battlecruisers are not a match, ship for ship, for the Germans."[5] Beatty agreed, but the Admiralty, bristling at this criticism of their ship designs, insisted that the careless and dangerous practices of handling crews alone explained the disasters, but relented later that autumn to begin adding an extra inch of armor to decks above the magazines. Because many could play the game of shielding reputations, moreover, Beatty and Jellicoe succeeded in squashing the publication of the Admiralty's attacks on their handling crews. After all, the problem had been recognized already in Rosyth and Scapa Flow—and solved.

■ ■ ■

As witnessed by the issue of armor protection (and others discussed below), Beatty and Jellicoe continued to find ways to work together after Jutland. It is certain, however, that their relationship, while staying surface-cordial in meetings and correspondence, deteriorated due to Beatty's lowered opinion of Jellicoe as a fleet commander. Indeed the cavalier cruiser chief never forgave his C-in-C's alleged lack of charge on May 31, 1916. This had been apparent to those with him on the battle bridge and compass platform during the Run to the North before Jellicoe's arrival around 1800, but the "gall and wormwood" of the unacceptably incomplete victory that transpired in the evening hours festered during the long disappointing return voyage home on June 1—and once home it quickly became obvious that he had an axe to grind. Thus his sister recalled getting a letter describing the battle as "a famous hunt where his second horse never came up in time, and so he could not kill his fox—and if he had it would have been the most wonderful hunt in history." To others he complained about being "terribly disappointed that when Jellicoe arrived, he did not go in and take the High Seas Fleet by the scruff and sink them in line." His wife, Ethel, reflecting her husband's raging complaints, wrote, "[T]here seems to be very little to say except to *curse* Jellicoe for not going after them as the [battlecruisers] did and never stop[ping] until we had annihilated them . . . of course it makes one perfectly sick." During his session with Dannreuther shortly after dropping anchor in Rosyth, furthermore, Beatty "walked up and down talking about the [Jutland] action in a very excited manner and criticizing in strong terms the action of the commander-in-chief in not supporting him—I think he firmly believed that he had been deserted." The depth of Beatty's feeling against Jellicoe (his superior, whom he could not cross openly and remain in good form) can perhaps be plumbed by the fact that he asked, unsuccessfully, for Jerram of 2nd BS (a squadron commander whom he felt beneath him and thus more fitting to attack for not coming up to help circa 2030 on May 31) to be court-martialed.[6] If you cannot hit the donkey, the Germans would say, you hit the sack on the donkey instead.

As for Jellicoe, the battle results came down hard on him too. While in the midst of appointing investigative committees and protesting to the Admiralty about the early press attacks on the alleged incompetence of the Royal Navy, word came to his suite on *Iron Duke* that armored cruiser HMS *Hampshire* (2nd CS) while exiting a sound off Scapa Flow had hit one of the mines laid before the battle by *U-75* along a route Jellicoe had advised the armored cruiser take to avoid a nasty storm. The last German strike of the Battle of Jutland destroyed a fourth armored cruiser, killed most of the 650-man crew, and increased Britain's deaths in the battle by 10 percent, a toll that included *Hampshire*'s most important passenger, Secretary of State for War Horatio Herbert Kitchener. Enervated by two years of war, seventy sleep-deprived hours at sea, and three more days of naval postmortems and what-ifs on Jutland, the loss of *Hampshire* and Kitchener, a legend in his own time, interjected an all-encompassing sense of guilt into what was already a difficult struggle to assess his personal responsibility for the lackluster outcome of May 31–June 1. To be sure, in the analytical mix waxed many definitely mitigating factors that eventually soothed his feelings about Jutland—poor cruiser reconnaissance; smoky/foggy visibility; the threat of torpedoes; the fluky tragedy of errors during the nighttime action; and especially the long litany of the Admiralty's reporting blunders—but on June 24, while visiting Beatty at Rosyth, the heart-rending *mea culpa* factors in the equation may have weighed more heavily. "He was obviously depressed," writes Arthur Marder, "as, seated with head in hands, he made the doleful confession: 'I missed one of the greatest opportunities a man ever had.'" Could this mean that he realized, having read over all of the postbattle reports, that the action astern during the night had been shifting from west to east, and that he should have changed course accordingly to stay in contact with—and destroy—Scheer? To Beatty, not surprisingly, Jellicoe's remark amounted to a confession of "failure," while more sympathetic observers like Jellicoe biographer A. Temple Patterson believe "there was perhaps a misunderstanding here and his lament may just possibly have been that he had missed it thanks to the Admiralty."[7]

■ ▓ ■

Whatever the case may be, Beatty and Jellicoe stood on common ground when it came to the Admiralty's largely negative role in the battle. Although the C-in-C did not know the extent of Room 40's pre-Jutland intelligence that the First Sea Lord of the Admiralty's Chief of War Staff Sir Henry Oliver, Oliver's close associate, Sir Arthur Wilson, and Operations Division (OD) Director Thomas Jackson had withheld from him before Jutland, he strongly suspected, as First Lord Arthur Balfour described these suspicions, "that we possess information not supplied to you, and that you are asked to act in ignorance of the relevant facts which we have withheld from you." The most egregious error made by the Admiralty's troika, that they placed Scheer in the Jade in the early afternoon of May 31 when in actuality the High Seas Fleet neared the 56th Parallel, rankled the most. "What am I to think of OD," exclaimed Beatty to Room 40 operative William Clarke, "when I get that telegram and in three hours' time meet the whole German fleet well out at sea?" The top personnel of 5th BS, hit so hard in the Run to the North, certainly agreed. For their part, moreover, Clarke and his colleagues were understandably "horrified and furious that such gross misinformation had been sent to the [C-in-C] and to Beatty,"[8] although as argued earlier (see chapter 8, note 28, chapter 9, note 43), some of the horror and furor must also have been directed inward. After Jellicoe replaced Henry Jackson as First Sea Lord in December 1916, "one cannot but wonder what [he] thought [upon seeing] the extent of Room 40's knowledge," writes Patrick Beesly. Certainly the C-in-C's guilt-ridden assumption that it had been "my doing of course" in not "keep[ing] Beatty nearer"[9] vanished, for he would have stationed himself much closer before the battle if better informed, and the extra hour or so of daylight this provided would probably have destroyed Hipper and much, if not all, of what Sheer had left (see chapter 9, note 26, and chapter 11).

Beatty and Jellicoe demanded changes at the Admiralty. It took almost a year, but changes were made. The Admiralty initially agreed to give Jellicoe a daily summary of all intelligence on enemy movements. After he became First Sea Lord, however, the pace of change quickened initially with "the *de facto* confiscation of Room 40" from OD, and then its eventual *de jure* transfer to Captain Reginald ("Blinker") Hall as a cryptographic section of the Naval Intelligence Division. Not just passing along decrypts to OD for its use or misuse, but rather submitting detailed assessments of intercepted signals, the specialists of Room 40 "making full use of their intimate knowledge of the German navy and its procedures" became a more significant element of naval decision-making.

"The Royal Navy was learning," concludes Andrew Gordon. He, along with historian James Goldrick, buttress this observation by pointing to simultaneous (September 1916–June 1917) moves the Royal Navy made to emulate the German fleet battle turn; experiment with separate (i.e., autonomous) tactical maneuvering by squadron commanders, thereby enhancing initiative; augment shipboard flag signaling with more emphasis on wireless telegraphy to lessen communication blunders; and equip destroyers with upgraded, more potent wireless sets—all reforms that drew on important lessons from Jutland. Jellicoe also reorganized the composition of his three frontline battle squadrons to reduce the vulnerability that one of them had felt that day—his rightwing 1st BS under Burney—from sailing with so many older 12-inch gunships (five of eight). Facilitating this latter change that summer and fall, two new "R-class" dreadnoughts (*Royal Sovereign* and *Resolution*) joined *Revenge* in the Grand Fleet, with another (*Ramillies*) coming in 1917.[10]

These well-taken points also extend to the work of three additional committees appointed by Jellicoe immediately after Jutland: one chaired by Captain Frederick Dreyer of *Iron Duke* investigating British AP-shell inadequacies; and two committees examining gunnery issues headed up, respectively, by Dreyer for the battleships and Chatfield for the battlecruisers.

As for shell, while visiting Rosyth on June 24 Dreyer and Jellicoe observed the damage that German 11- and 12-inch shell had inflicted on 5th BS's HMS *Barham*. Officers told them that the enemy had some AP-shell problems of their own, mainly due to their frequently malfunctioning delayed-action fuses. However, roughly every other German shell detonated properly well behind armor plate, causing great damage to Evan-Thomas's super dreadnought.[11] Dreyer concluded that the far heavier British 13.5- and 15-inch shells, if manufactured as competently and functioning as semicorrectly, should have sunk "some half-dozen or more German capital ships." It would take over a year to push through this time, but eventually new AP shells with a superior delayed-action fuse, a more stable propellant explosive, and a thicker, less brittle metal head of better-quality steel filled British magazines.[12]

As for gunnery, Germany's remarkable Zeiss stereoscopic range finder could not be replicated, but the Royal Navy introduced vastly improved range finders along with a modified "bracket" system of fire control that borrowed substantially from the German "ladder" system (see chapter 10, note 27). Accordingly, Beatty, now C-in-C in his own right, could boast in March 1917 "that we have advanced more in our gunnery methods in the last three months than we have the previous two *years*."[13] Even the pre-Jutland cavalier panache of the battlecruiser squadrons, their predilection for rapid fire and indifference to accuracy, yielded in 1917 to a more mundane but imperative practice-makes-perfect mindset. Chatfield wrote: "Target practices were centrally controlled to carry out some particular test, some new idea, and all results were circulated and the lessons learnt. Thus procedure became standardized at a high level, according to the method tried which had produced the best results. Efficiency and confidence are bound to increase in this way. Everyone learnt from everyone else and coordination was effective." He added that he thought he "[could] say with confidence that had the enemy again ventured to sea and been brought to action in 1918, he would have found the British fleet a more terrible foe than that he had run away from in 1916, as indeed [the British fleet] ought by [1916] to have been."[14]

Mutinous conditions in the German navy would prevent that encounter from happening in 1918. Had a rematch of the world's largest naval powers occurred a few months after Jutland, however, the Grand Fleet, already awesome to be sure, would not have been the "more terrible foe" described by Chatfield. With the major exception of improved antiflash protection and handling procedures, none of the problems identified in the earlier discussion had yet been successfully resolved. Especially worrisome, wider knowledge of AP-shell deficiencies imparted a certain nagging, Jellicoe-like sense of vulnerability and inferiority. Thus in late July Dreyer decried the "many people engaged in trying to make out that our AP-shell filled with lyddite *which burst half way through the plate* are as good as the German shell filled with trotyl with delayed action fuse which burst their shell well inside the ships—it seems a pity not to be willing to learn."[15] Due to propellant and fuse issues, Chatfield also fretted "about our shell" a few weeks later when he "got a clue of the utmost importance."

> In August, David Beatty had a luncheon party on board the *Lion* for several important visitors. Among the party was a Swedish naval officer, who had been attached to the Swedish Legation in Berlin. I arranged to sit next to him to see if I could extract anything out of him. I told him a good deal about the damage to our ships when he volunteered the information that the German naval officers had told him that our shell were "laughable." . . . [Chatfield asked whether] he could tell me if our heavy shell had penetrated their armor? "No," he said, "the German officers told me they had broken to pieces on it."

Chatfield, "hardly able to restrain" himself during the remainder of the luncheon, hurried immediately afterward to inform an alarmed Beatty, who already stood in agreement with Jellicoe and Dreyer about shell propellant and fuse problems.

It soon became clear to both Chatfield and Beatty that only a scant likelihood existed of finding the German fleet at sea under circumstances conducive to a smashing victory. "We should have to pound them to pieces, and hope to find them at sea early in the day, so as to give us time to accomplish their defeat. . . . The expectation of the country that should the German fleet venture to sea again the [Grand] Fleet would gain an annihilating victory was [therefore] probably impossible of realization." Chatfield responded to the emergency by returning to his pet project of "concentrating" the fire of British squadrons on a portion of the enemy line, but now with the demoralizing provisos that the battle should somehow occur early in the day, and then that "we must press in to closer ranges where our shell would be more effective."[16] The British navy had won the Battle of Jutland, of this there could be no reasonable doubt. In the summer of 1916, however, the British navy did not wax particularly confident about the outcome of another Jutland.

SKAGERRAK: PALATABLE AND UNPALATABLE OUTCOMES

Several hours before Scheer served up champagne on June 1, frenetic preparations for the fleet's return had energized Wilhelmshaven Naval Base. Noticing this beehive of activity, locals had spread the word, and soon hundreds of civilians began to gather with telescopes and binoculars on hills, rooftops, shorelines, and riverbanks. By noon, visibility had improved enough for the growing crowd to make out the faint, distant outlines of funnels and turrets nearing the roadstead. Upon closer inspection, however, eager anticipation turned to anxious shock at the sight of two battered battlecruisers, *Derfflinger* and *Moltke*, steering for the dry docks while their sister, *Von der Tann*, also in a sorry state, anchored out in the bay—and what about *Lützow* and *Seydlitz*? The arrival of 1st Squadron an hour or so later, followed shortly by Scheer's flagship and 3rd Squadron, improved the spirits of the onlooking throng a little, for these proud ships, not as badly hurt, were perhaps victors over the once mighty Royal Navy, at least as proclaimed by excited word of mouth.

The bittersweet highlight came in the early evening as light cruiser *Regensburg* with the entire crew of *Lützow* "clinging like ants on her decks and superstructure" sailed past the fleet anchored outside the Jade and received repeated hurrahs "from the throats of thousands of rough sailors." Another hour brought the overloaded light cruiser to Wilhelmshaven. A *Lützow* midshipman recalled,

> People dressed for celebrations lined the dykes and banks. After passing through the lock, *Regensburg* made fast in the large harbor basin. The crew of *Lützow*

went ashore, lined up, counted off, and then marched to the Wilhelmshaven barracks. They marched in step and from all lips came the song *"Lützow's* Bold Audacious Hunt." Who [among the top brass] could have prevented that? The residents of Wilhelmshaven clearly heard it. There were people everywhere and in an instant the news of the fate of Battlecruiser *Lützow* spread.[17]

It would be misleading to regard the cheers shouted by "rough sailors" in the bay and the spirited marching song sung by the survivors of Hipper's sunken flagship as indications that the morale of Germany's crews soared as high as *some*—but by no means *all*—of their overseers, the officers.[18] Thus an Admiralty Staff observer recalled "the crews [being] surprised about [the news of the German victory] because they themselves had not been aware of the extent and the effect of the battle—there was no mood of victory among the crews."[19]

Even those seamen whose captains had praised "the victory we have won" reacted far more emotionally to the horrendous damage to some of their ships. A patriotic magazine handler from battleship *Helgoland* (1st Squadron) inspected a lower compartment of his ship destroyed by the lone hit she had taken, a rare penetrating British shell, and exclaimed, "Good God, how things looked down there!" The badly bashed *Derfflinger* also "looked as though a thousand devils had held an orgy there." The destruction on *Von der Tann* shocked him too: "I had never thought it possible that anything could bite through these diamond-hard walls and simply stood and gaped in astonishment at the holes and gashes." Officers laughed with good reason at the defective side of British shells and boasted that "all, down to the last seaman, believe in the strength of the fleet and look forward to further encounters with confidence," but clearly the men who "are not fools about the things they can see" wanted nothing more to do with the enemy's larger high-caliber ordnance. With their shouts and songs, therefore, German seamen honored one another and displayed solidarity after what had been an especially frightening evening and harrowing night during which their "hunt" had been transformed into the nightmare of the hunted. In particular, the "fate of Battlecruiser *Lützow*" had been an especially grisly one that killed 115 of their comrades, including the sailors doomed to drown in the dynamo room, which triggered an "outraged reaction" among the ship's survivors. As the *Helgoland* handler put it, "one could by no means describe our spirits as happy or victorious—on the contrary, we were depressed."[20]

This mood, which would become infectious throughout Germany over the next two years, had not even reached all sailors yet, to be sure, nor had things rumbled up yet to revolutionary proportions, but a tipping point had been reached in the rank and file of the Imperial German Navy, one that began to tip the common people too, beginning with those of Wilhelmshaven. On that Sunday, June 4, 1916, each German ship marched an honor guard of thirty-six sailors in the funeral procession to the naval cemetery.[21] Whereas throughout the empire the "victory" of Skagerrak gave cause to forget momentarily the mounting death toll on land, "people celebrating it with champagne, the streets gay with flags, church bells ringing, schools closed in honor of the event," in Wilhelmshaven mass death and maiming at sea—3,058 casualties—only compounded the sense of a nation bleeding from multiple wounds. "They say the sight of the procession of coffins, dead bodies, and wounded being carried through the streets was enough to suppress any feeling of rejoicing which may have been felt elsewhere."[22] No coincidence that the union of sailor and civilian discontent, magnified and exacerbated by the misery of the war's final years, marked Wilhelmshaven as one of the first towns to fall to the mutinous revolution that ended the Kaiserreich in 1918.

■ ■ ■

Monday morning, June 5, brought the Kaiser, Kaiserin, and their royal retinue to an "awful" rain-soaked Wilhelmshaven. The emperor, wearing a grey raincoat, naval officer's hat, and holding a riding crop in his good right hand, addressed sailors' units assembled on the pier beside the flagship. The first mighty hammer blow had been struck, the nimbus of English global domination had been ripped down, the tradition of Trafalgar had been torn to tatters! Admiral Scheer stood equal to Field Marshal Hindenburg, the victor of Tannenberg! A typically "excessive" performance, thought Privy Naval Cabinet Chief Georg von Müller, a show which even Scheer found "atrocious." The afternoon brought somewhat more dignity as William visited the naval hospital, where he saw a concussed Behncke and inspected damages on *Ostfriesland*, *Helgoland*, and *Von der Tann*. That evening the royal couple received visiting dignitaries, including the Kings of Saxony and Bavaria, on the gaudily exquisite imperial train.[23]

Scheer hosted another imposing group of dinner guests in the admiral's mess on *Friedrich der Grosse*. The Kaiser's brother, Prince Heinrich, and the Chief of the Admiralty Staff, Henning von Holtzendorff, headed a list of top navy officials and other officers, including one of the survivors of Graf Spee's commerce raider, light cruiser SMS *Emden*, who, like the others, had hurried from Berlin to congratulate and praise "the victor of the Skagerrak." When the conversation turned to speculation about the conclusions naval theoreticians would draw someday about the tactics that had guided Scheer to victory on May 31, he snuffed out the discussion: "What was I thinking? I wasn't thinking anything. I wanted to help the poor *Wiesbaden*. And then I wanted to have the battlecruisers lead the way [*die Kreuzer voll einsetzen*]. I came to the whole thing the way the Virgin Mary had her baby." To this, Holtzendorff raised a humorous, albeit frank objection. Would not Scheer agree that "the Virgin Mary also performed a valuable service?" Remembering this exchange, Weizsäcker thought Scheer's dinner statement had rung true to the "spur of the moment" decision-making style his admiral had exhibited at the Skagerrak.[24] In saying "I wasn't thinking anything," he had simply been getting honestly to the heart of the matter. Eventually waxing somewhat more deistic like Holtzendorff, however, Scheer would hint years later that Providence and human agency had indeed combined, cruelly and frustratingly, to play a role on May 31.

■ ■ ■

For good reasons, Scheer spun a different version of the battle when he presented his report to the Kaiser a month later. While the presentation ranged from the preparatory stages to the battle, the southern and northern Runs, the main fleet engagements, the night action, and the overall resulting claims of victory, two passages stand out in controversy.

First, Scheer asserted that the second battle turn shortly before 1900, although admittedly a very risky maneuver, aimed to surprise the enemy, drive him away with torpedo boats, and ultimately successfully retreat and disengage for the night, thereby enabling (1) setting a course for the Bight that would have been ill-advised if made earlier when a few hours of daylight remained, and (2) a last attempt to rescue the *Wiesbaden*. Both Scheer in his memoirs and the official history by Otto Groos stood by this version.[25] On several grounds discussed earlier, the report fails to convince. Scheer intended to turn back, offload the stricken light cruiser's crew, win a smashing breakthrough battle, and return home to south-southeast via Little Fisher Bank and Horns Reef, not to facilitate a delayed retreat—torpedo boats played no role in his attack plan. When visibility cleared as the range narrowed, however, he realized the mistake, unleashed the destroyers, reversed course, and retreated home circularly (i.e., from east to west to southwest to south-southeast). The report misleads with its assumption of knowingly assaulting the entire Grand Fleet. "Actually, however, the C-in-C with better visibility would neither have made the maneuver to save the *Wiesbaden*," noted Weizsäcker a few days after the battle, "nor have driven the battlecruisers into the fray."[26] In short, the report had to put the best possible light on a dubious command decision lest the Kaiser yield to his unaggressive naval instincts and search for a safer, more risk-averse fleet chief. As he had done throughout 1915 to protect his career, Scheer had chosen the safest ground with this report.

Second, in his concluding remarks Scheer stated that the fleet would be ready by mid-August "to painfully inflict heavy damage on the enemy, but nevertheless there is no doubt that even the most favorable outcome of a naval battle *in this war* will not force England to peace." Only an aggressive, unrestricted use of the U-boats could force England to her knees "in the foreseeable time" by "wrestling down English economic life." Historians like Arthur Marder take this statement at face value, implying that without unlimited use of the U-boats Scheer would continue to attack, but without his heart in it after seeing the might of the Royal Navy at Jutland. Writers like Otto Groos argue, on the other hand, that Scheer understated what he could accomplish at sea in a calculated move to enlist William for the unrestricted submarine warfare he had thus far resisted.[27]

The ever-elusive historical truth would appear in this case to fall between the two versions, but much closer to Groos' version. As Hipper's Number One Erich Raeder remembered things, for instance, Scheer knew Britain had suffered comparatively heavier losses on May 31, while the German fleet had stood up well to "the Hegemon," explaining, he felt, Jellicoe's failure to attack on June 1. By getting the German squadrons back to sea as soon as possible, therefore, hopefully before the British had completed all repairs, it was Scheer's "firm conviction" that a "well-prepared new operation aided by U-boats and airships would be able to reckon on further successes."[28] Scheer believed, without wishing to say it, in other words, that another victory was not only possible but also productive.[29] Indeed, coming amidst Britain's costly and futile Somme offensive that summer, a German "painful" infliction of "heavy damage" on the Royal Navy so close after the large losses of Jutland and the Somme, even if not followed by unrestricted U-boat warfare, would certainly have weakened Britain and made it increasingly difficult, also for fight-to-the-finishers like the ambitious and aspiring David Lloyd George, to resist the antiwar movement mounting that summer. On the other hand, the German C-in-C had to know that an all-out submarine campaign against merchant ships, if and when it came, would draw officers, men, economic resources, destroyers, and submarines away from the surface fleet, thereby limiting the frequency and power-punch of naval sorties. Scheer "hoped confidently" to take his ships, submarines, and airships to sea, achieve "[another] success," and contribute mightily to winning the war; but with pressure mounting on the Kaiser from many sides, including from Scheer, to unleash U-boats on enemy and neutral commerce, time was running out for the High Seas Fleet.

The optimistic scenario envisioned by Scheer, in other words, was a one-two knockout punch combination: first, another punishment of the Royal Navy at sea, the culminating follow-up battle envisioned by "defeat-in-detail" advocates; and second, a devastating use of the U-boats, a sort of reverse blockade of Britain, two additional blows since staggering the "blue jackets" at the Skagerrak that would beat London down to the canvas. Moreover, with the Kaiser exhibiting an increasingly "just don't bother me with it" attitude toward naval affairs that summer, understandable after loosening the reins of naval command in February, Practical/Survivor Scheer had much less disincentive to go forward with these risky designs.[30]

■ ■ ■

Scheer took the entire High Seas Fleet to sea late in the evening of August 18, 1916, on a course for enemy shores.[31] He had refined the scrubbed Sunderland plan of late May to include a better, more successful use of U-boats and Zeppelins. That morning Room 40 detected the preparatory wireless orders for this mission and the Admiralty sent the Grand Fleet out late that afternoon and Beatty early in the evening, both several hours before Hipper and Scheer.

The British operation reflected many of the lessons of Jutland. The main body sailed with a full-strength 5th BS, which Jellicoe had taken back against Beatty's objections—altogether an imposing four squadrons of thirty dreadnoughts (*Royal Sovereign* had joined the reorganized squadrons of the Grand Fleet). The BCF had been reduced to six battlecruisers, three with 13.5-inch guns (*Princess Royal, Tiger,* and *Lion* [still, however, minus Q-turret]), and three older ships with 12-inchers (*Inflexible, Australia,* and *New Zealand). Indomitable* was fitting. They steamed only twenty-eight miles ahead with strict orders to reconnoiter but not get entangled with superior enemy forces. It also remained in visual touch with the main fleet through a light cruiser chain. Thus, a harnessed Beatty advanced essentially under the C-in-C's tactical reins.

The German operation also reflected the lessons of the Skagerrak. With *Seydlitz* and *Derfflinger* still in dry dock, and the memory of 5th BS's pounding of 1st SG on May 31 fresh, Scheer reinforced *Von der Tann* and *Moltke* with three battleships, including the new, fast, 15-inch gunned *Bayern.* 1st SG's funnel smoke remained visible to 1st and 3rd Squadrons during the mission, trailing this time by only twenty miles. He augmented the main body with *König Albert,* which had missed the action in May, and *Bayern*'s sister, the new flagship *Baden,* thereby making his sixteen dreadnoughts slightly stronger than before. As he had done at Lowestoft, 2nd Squadron did not venture into British waters. Zeppelins would provide early warning and reconnaissance: four stretched across the northern North Sea; four along the coast of Britain from the Firth of Forth to the Channel (see map 1.1). Two lines of five U-boats each would form longitudinal trap lines off Blyth (northeast of Newcastle) and Flamborough Head (below Scarborough). Two U-boat trap lines off the coast of Holland would provide similar flank protection on the return. Germany's *navalis modus operandi* remained the same: to annihilate those portions of the Royal Navy that responded to the bombardment of Sunderland.

Action occurred on August 19, but no engagement of the two fleets. That morning, a British submarine off Holland hit *Westfalen* and forced her back to Wilhelmshaven. An hour later, a U-boat off Blyth sank the *Nottingham*, a light cruiser in Beatty's screen. Jellicoe, who had been hauled out of his R&R in Scotland and hurried to *Iron Duke* at sea, turned the whole fleet northward for two hours, fearing a cleverly laid mine and/or submarine trap. He reversed course two hours later, and by noon, as Hipper sailed north off Scarborough, Beatty steamed south only an hour away with Jellicoe a good hour behind him.

With Hipper and Beatty even closer to one another, Scheer received two reports at 1223 and 1230 from *L-13*, one of his Zeppelins, confidently reporting a strong force of capital ships steaming north off Yarmouth. Her captain had not sighted battleships, as it transpired, only cruisers of Tyrwhitt's Harwich flotilla, but Scheer did not know this, only that good visibility at sea level seemed to augur well for the accuracy of what *L-13* (at a cloudier thousand feet) believed it had seen. Very uncertain since war's outbreak exactly where the British stationed all of their dreadnoughts, but curious after the Lowestoft Raid in May whether the British may have moved capital ships to the south as Prime Minister Asquith had hinted (see chapter 6), Impetuous Scheer turned everything back southward, just as eager to risk victory over an as yet undetermined number of battle squadrons as he had been at 1900 on May 31.

But after no contact occurred, and having heard from a U-boat at 1413 that several British battleship squadrons steamed from the north, a sobered Scheer, the element of surprise evidently gone and the danger from enemy dreadnoughts, submarines, and/ or mines rising, turned for home at 1435. In short, the presence of prudent Jellicoe, the return of Practical Scheer, and the notorious fog of war prevented a theme variation on Jutland/Skagerrak through which would perhaps have sounded the strains of an even greater British victory when Jellicoe's armada cut off their quarry's return to base with daylight aplenty for the tactics of "concentrated" bludgeoning.[32]

Foul weather in September postponed another Sunderland mission. After this, a series of events gradually relegated the High Seas Fleet to relative passivity. In early October, the Kaiser insisted on resuming restricted U-boat warfare by attacking enemy commerce according to the prize rules the navy had repeatedly resisted. The campaign proved very successful, sinking over a million tons; but with no submarines supporting surface operations, and missing destroyers taken to escort U-boats, Scheer again scrubbed Sunderland.

Still eager for action in mid-October, however, he ordered another Skagerrak mission. With *Seydlitz* and *Derfflinger* operational again, the battleship-reinforced 1st SG and 1st and 3rd Squadrons sailed at imposing full strength toward the Fisher Banks in the hopes of bagging British victims. Although alerted by Room 40 again, the Royal Navy had recently decided not to risk action this far east: not surprising for Jellicoe, ever mindful in his cost–benefit calculations of Britain's best interests; but Beatty's agreement with this cautiousness meant something new. The "unpleasantly anxious" prospect of fighting an action far out in the North Sea with problematic ordnance, as was now known, and most probably late in the day, had humbled and slightly unnerved him to the point of thinking too much about his own death. "The old proverb that 'when you are winning risk nothing' might well be applied now," he had written in September.[33] Not sighting the enemy, Scheer steamed home.

Scheer's aggressiveness receded further in November when a battleship squadron sent to rescue two U-boats stranded on Danish shores got torpedoed, resulting in two battleships being damaged. Afterward he earned an imperial rebuke for "risking a squadron, and by so doing nearly losing two armored ships in order to save two U-boats."[34] The Kaiser, having first yielded a measure of imperial authoritativeness to Scheer in February (see chapter 8), then more to Hindenburg and Ludendorff that fall, seemed eager to save some face, at least, by hitting his fleet commander while down, for the C-in-C's ambitious summer designs had failed. William's status would take another jolt, however, when he and Chancellor Bethmann Hollweg surrendered ominously to Hindenburg and Ludendorff over the unrestricted use of submarines early the next year.

All-out U-boat warfare went into effect on February 1, 1917. As Scheer had anticipated, this drew so many resources away from the surface fleet that it now remained anchored in port. The next major sortie—another one to the Skagerrak—did not occur until April 1918.

■ ▦ ■

Politics gradually undermined the fighting effectiveness of the inactive German navy as 1916 drew on to 1917. That expiring autumn, officers began to bicker over whether or not unrestricted U-boat warfare, with its risk of triggering American entry into the Great War, boded boon or bane. Among the men, already warier of action after Jutland, transfer to the expanding submarine corps and its dangers was not attractive, but the tedium and exhausting routines of port service in the big ships, a debilitating life exacerbated by paltry rations and infrequent furloughs, festered as a worse alternative.[35] As winter yielded to spring, news of the fall of the Russian monarchy and establishment of a democracy there, coupled with U-boat warfare's provocation of the United States to declare war on Germany, made it more difficult for common people and basic seamen to support an authoritarian monarchy's war against democracies in Britain, France, Italy, and now Russia and the United States. In protest against such a seemingly unjust war, the radical faction of the Social Democratic Party seceded, declaring itself the "Independent Social Democratic Party" and demanding an end to the fighting.

That spring, naval authorities in Berlin established sailors' committees to air grievances regarding the dismal food situation. After many of the captains ignored this directive, however, these "Food Complaint Committees" came into being surreptitiously, sometimes calling themselves "Workers and Sailors Councils" in sympathy with the Russian revolution that had felled the czar in March. As spring ran its course, these radical sailors began to push for the Independent Social Democratic program, encourage hunger strikes, and even more emboldeningly, establish secret cells to organize overt political protests and peace demonstrations.

And then from early to midsummer 1917 several serious semimutinous, near-revolutionary incidents broke out in the German navy. On June 6 and July 19, sailors on battleship *Prinzregent Luitpold* organized hunger strikes; and on July 20, riotous conditions occurred in 2nd SG aboard light cruiser *Pillau*. Concerned, Hipper received a loyal petty officer from light cruiser *Bremen* on the July 24, who reported alarmingly: "There is something rotten in the fleet Excellency, and it needs clearing out."[36] The man had witnessed a "mutineers' conference" in Wilhelmshaven's Tivoli restaurant. Hipper reacted by transferring some of the most unpopular junior officers, assigning more rest during harbor duties, and raising the food allowance. When officers in 3rd Squadron canceled a recreation period on *Prinzregent Luitpold* on August 1, however, over 600 sailors bolted the ship for a nearby town and started to drink and make speeches. Sailors on four additional battleships and battlecruisers joined in, showing the same rebelliousness that would enervate the German army a year later.

Naval authorities reacted similarly to the "carrot and stick" approach the French army used that spring and summer to deal with its own disturbances. The navy made Hipper's ameliorative approach more general, but seventy-seven sailors were accused of mutiny. Of these, most got off; four were incarcerated for twelve to fifteen years; and five received death sentences. Of those, three were commuted to life imprisonment, while two sentences were not. Firing squads carried out the executions in Cologne on September 5, 1917. Among the rank and file of the German navy, these shootings "were widely regarded as a callous judicial murder and created deep resentment and hatred,"[37] completely eliminating a small morale boost that accrued from the Kaiser's mid-August visit to the fleet. For their part, Hipper and Scheer thought the affair had been dealt with properly and fairly. "Perhaps we have controlled it by [these sentences] and nipped the whole thing in the bud," observed Hipper. "If it is not too late," he added ominously.[38]

This precarious fix held for many months. No problems occurred when the fleet made its penultimate outing, a sortie toward Norwegian shores on April 23–24, 1918. During the advance of massed German army corps on Paris that spring, with German morale at home and in the army higher, and obedience in the navy holding passably, Scheer executed what one historian has labeled "perhaps the boldest operation undertaken by the German [navy] since the war began." Beatty, now C-in-C, began escorting convoys out of Scandinavia with strong guards of destroyers, cruisers, and battleships. The German navy at full strength, including the new battlecruiser *Hindenburg*, set out to destroy the naval units and capture supplies. Significantly, by this time in the war naval command had begun paying more attention to those officers who had long doubted the security of German naval codes, for prior to departing, ships' call signs had been changed, code ciphers altered, and mission orders issued by hand, not radioed. However, naval intelligence had got the convoy's departure date off by one day, such that, unfortunately for Scheer, his "powerful and secret blow was dealt in the air";[39] yet another intelligence failure in a war that had seen far too many of them for their side to have much of a chance of ultimately winning.

The final sortie of the German navy never got out of port. Scheer and Hipper planned to use the fleet to support the retreating German army off the coast of Holland and Belgium in late October 1918. By this time, however, rumors of President Woodrow Wilson's efforts to bring about an armistice had spread among the people, soldiers, and sailors. Orders to put to sea struck left-leaning as well as previously loyal sailors as suicidal. Was not the army retreating? Was not the war over anyway? With the end of the war in sight, was it a proper time to die? With hundreds of thousands of citizens dying from the malnutrition and disease related to the British blockade, why prolong the misery?[40] Hipper and Scheer had misread the mood of their men—an intelligence failure of a different but even more important sort. The sailors of Wilhelmshaven began to disobey sortie orders on October 28–29; the disturbance turned to mutiny in Kiel a few days later, where the C-in-C had moved 3rd Squadron to temper the sailors' angry mood; and from Kiel the revolt swept over other northern towns, including Wilhelmshaven on November 6. It had also spread inland and eventually reached Berlin.

On November 9, pressed by the Independent Socialists, the Social Democratic Party proclaimed a republic. Hours later, William motored into Dutch exile, nothing left now of what little had remained of his imperial authority, a revolutionary regime failure that the democracies of Britain and France, through compromise and reform—inherent, built-in advantages of their political systems—had avoided. On November 11, 1918, the victors' armistice went into effect. World War I had ended.

EPILOGUE

THE ADMIRALS

The relationship between Jellicoe and Beatty was never the same as it had been before Jutland. Occasionally, they voiced criticism of the other in private; but to the credit of these gentlemen and successive Cs-in-C, they managed to keep things very proper in public. Undoubtedly, the incomplete victory at Jutland—put differently, the avoidance of a disastrous, unacceptable defeat—when combined with Britain's victory in the Great War, kept relations mellower than they would have been otherwise. Not so, unfortunately, for other participants and commentators on Britain's great North Sea clash, who even before war's end descended into a nasty pro-Jellicoe versus pro-Beatty historiographical feud. Even Churchill jumped into the inky muck on the side of Beatty, the man he had wanted in Jellicoe's seat in 1915.

The bone-chilling weather of the motherland cut short the lives of both British admirals. Jellicoe caught a cold in November 1935 and died a few days later just short of his seventy-sixth birthday. He was buried in St. Paul's Cathedral "on a day of mist and damp not wholly unlike that of Jutland," writes his biographer, A. Temple Patterson. Beatty "may have reflected" on the similarity, continues Patterson, for "lying ill with influenza, [he] had thrust aside his doctor's expostulations and insisted on attending the funeral as pall-bearer."[1] He never fully recovered and died in March 1936 at sixty-five.

Hipper passed away in 1932 at sixty-nine, the joys that are sometimes bestowed on senior citizens having eluded the old battlecruiser commander since war's end. He had read sea adventures as a teenager, but his wartime career mutated these stories into nightmarish memories of the "hunger blockade" and the horrible deaths of valued

265

comrades. Dogger Bank, to a great extent his fault, remained especially painful, while the Skagerrak, although redeeming for him personally, nevertheless witnessed his command getting badly battered. And then came the naval mutiny, Germany's surrender, the seizure of the High Seas Fleet by the victors and its scuttling by the vanquished, the revolution and fall of the monarchy, and having to travel incognito "dead tired" in northern Germany for months to avoid capture by renegades of the Workers and Soldiers Councils who had no sympathy for the man who had tried to make sailors' lives better in the summer of 1917. Was all of this perhaps a Providential punishment for the humanitarian outrage he had inflicted on the Yorkshire coast in 1914? Hipper finally settled down in Altona, near Hamburg, not in his native Bavaria. There would be no memoirs from a man who hated paperwork, only dire financial straits, his ever-nagging sciatica, and other health problems. Ennoblement by the King of Bavaria helped only a little. When he finally passed away, his old nemesis at sea, Beatty, wrote how "very sorry" he was. "One would like to express one's regrets for the passing of a gallant officer and a great sailor."[2] The people of Scarborough, Whitby, and Hartlepool would not have agreed.

In 1919 Scheer wrote his memoir-history of the High Seas Fleet in the Great War, its 507 pages of text and charts a valuable source for historians, although obviously a carefully written apologia. As the 1910s passed to the early 1920s, however, it became clear that he had not really gotten over the Battle of the Skagerrak. His early postwar letters, unlike his history, are filled with jabs at others, mainly the suspect and allegedly less than aggressive 1st Scouting Group, which he believed had failed to lead the fleet to complete victory that late afternoon and early evening of May 31, 1916.

By the late 1920s, Scheer had been able to study many of the other histories and memoirs that flowed from scores of pens, and as he did, his critique of the battle centered more on the later moments of the pursuit of Beatty, the Run to the North circa 1800, when Hood's 3rd Battlecruiser Squadron, which bad weather had made largely invisible, hit Hipper's flank. "Luckily for England," the entire battle had then flowed to the northeast and away from "the jammed marching columns" of Jellicoe's potentially vulnerable rightwing squadrons. "The German advance that had been launched could not be sustained, the powerful German spear could no longer reach its target," thereby "[winning] time" for the British C-in-C to deploy from his port column. "Shortly before his death [in 1928]," continued Levetzow's account of his former chief's remarks, "[the sixty-five-year-old] Admiral Scheer told me in Weimar that the thought of how Providence had given [us] opportunities for a complete annihilation of the British fleet still robbed him of sleep."[3]

In Scheer's final, self-servingly convoluted, and rather deistic view of things, therefore, it was Hood's foul-weather-aided advance that, "luckily for England," destroyed a chance to achieve the even greater victory that God wanted him to have. The German had ignored Beatty's redeeming tactical role in pushing the battle eastward shortly before 6:00 p.m., Jellicoe's timely afternoon dispatching of Hood south to Little Fisher Bank to rescue the BCF, which made 3rd BCS's strike on Hipper's flank possible, and later, the British C-in-C's instinctive deployment from the leftwing column while blind to the battle raging just ahead of him, all touches of human agency brilliance. Also overlooked in Scheer's self-analytical mix, perhaps because they amounted to a painful disappointment of the wishes of Almighty Providence, were his own questionable gambles as impetuous human agent. The Victor of the Skagerrak's last thoughts about the battle had to be much kinder to an old sailor losing sleep and near death.

NOTES

INTRODUCTION

1. Eugene L. Rasor, *The Battle of Jutland: A Bibliography* (Westport, CT: Greenwood Press, 1992), 63–170.

2. For some of the recent studies, see Nicholas Black, *The British Naval Staff in the First World War* (Woodbridge, UK: Boydell, 2009); John Brooks, *The Battle of Jutland* (Cambridge, UK: Cambridge University Press, 2016); Michael Epkenhans, *Tirpitz: Architect of the High Seas Fleet* (Washington, D.C.: Potomac Books, 2008); Michael Epkenhans et al., *Jutland: World War I's Greatest Naval Battle* (Lexington: University of Kentucky Press, 2015); James Goldrick, *Before Jutland: The Naval War in Northern Waters, August 1914–February 1915* (Annapolis, MD: Naval Institute Press, 2015); James Goldrick, *After Jutland: The Naval War in Northern Waters, June 1916–November 1918* (Annapolis, MD: Naval Institute Press, 2018); Andrew Gordon, *The Rules of the Game: Jutland and British Naval Command* (Annapolis, MD: Naval Institute Press, 1996); Gerhard Granier, *Magnus von Levetzow: Seeoffizier, Monarchist und Wegbereiter Hitlers* (Boppard am Rhein: H. Boldt, 1982); Paul Halpern, *A Naval History of World War I* (London: University College London Press, 1994); Jason Hines, "Sins of Omission and Commission: A Reassessment of the Role of Intelligence in the Battle of Jutland," *Journal of Military History* 74, no. 4 (Oct. 2008): 1,117–53; Nicholas Jellicoe, *Jutland: The Unfinished Battle* (Barnsley, UK: Seaforth Publishing, 2016); Nicholas Lambert, "'Our Bloody Ships' or 'Our Bloody System': Jutland and the Loss of the Battlecruisers," *Journal of Military History* 62, no. 1 (Jan. 1998): 29–55; John C. G. Röhl, *Wilhelm II: Into the Abyss of War and Exile, 1900–1941* (Cambridge, UK: Cambridge University Press, 2014); Gary Staff, *Skagerrak: The Battle of Jutland through German Eyes* (Barnsley, UK: Pen & Sword Maritime, 2016); and Jon Tetsuro Sumida, "A Matter of Timing: The Royal Navy and the Tactics of Decisive Battle, 1912–1916," *The Journal of Military History* 67, no. 1 (Jan. 2003), 85–136. Most of these secondary sources also make valuable use of, quote at length, and often print in-full important primary sources. The same is true of the older secondary sources in note 4 below.

3. For publications of primary material in recent decades on the British side, see Eric Grove, ed., "The Autobiography of Chief Gunner Alexander Grant: HMS *Lion* at the Battle of Jutland, 1916," in *The Naval Miscellany*, ed. Susan Rose (London: Ashgate, 2008), 7: 389–404; S. M. Holloway, *From Trench and Turret: Royal Marines' Letters and Diaries* (London: Constable, 2006); Hans Joachim Koerver, *Room 40: German Naval Warfare 1914–1918* (Berlin: Schaltungsdienst Lange, 2009), 2 vols.; William Schleihauf, ed., *Jutland: The Naval Staff Appreciation* (Barnsley: Seaforth Publishing, 2016); Nigel Steel and Peter Hart, *Jutland 1916: Death in the Grey Wastes* (London: Cassel, 2003); and Julian Thompson, *The Imperial War Museum Book of The War at Sea 1914–1918* (London: Pan Books, 2005).

On the German side, see Michael Epkenhans, ed., *Albert Hopman: Das ereignisreiche Leben eines 'Wilhelminers': Tagebücher, Briefe, Aufzeichnungen 1901–1920* (Munich: Walter de Gruyter, 2004); Gerhard Granier, ed., *Die Deutsche Seekriegsleitung im Ersten Weltkrieg: Dokumentation* (Koblenz: Bundesarchiv, 1999), 2 vols.; Gerhard Granier, ed., "Eindrücke von der Skagerrakschlacht: Die Aufzeichnungen des Kapitänleutnants Ernst von Weizsäcker," *Marine Forum* 71, no. 12 (1996): 20–23; and Holger H. Herwig, ed., *Wolfgang Wegener's* The Naval Strategy of the World War (Annapolis, MD: Naval Institute Press, 1989).

4. Some of the classic older works are Geoffrey Bennett, *The Battle of Jutland* (London: B. T. Batsford, 1964); Julian S. Corbett, *Naval Operations: History of the Great War Based on Official Documents* (London: Longmans, Green, 1921, 1938), 3 vols.; Holloway H. Frost, *The Battle of Jutland* (Annapolis, MD: Naval Institute Press, 1936); Arthur J. Marder, *From Dreadnought to Scapa Flow: The Royal Navy in the Fisher Era, 1904–1919* (London: Oxford University Press, 1966), 3 vols.; and Otto Groos, *Der Krieg in der Nordsee*, vol. 1 of *Der Krieg zur See 1914–1918*, ed. Marine-Archiv (Berlin: Verlag von E. S. Mittler und Sohn, 1920–25), 7 vols. I do not include here the plethora of older biographies that are cited as used.

For some of the best-known older primary sources on the British side, see David Beatty, *The Beatty Papers: Selections from the Private and Official Correspondence of Admiral of the Fleet Earl Beatty*, ed. Bryan Ranft (Aldershot: Navy Records Society 1989–93); W. S. Chalmers, *The Life and Letters of David Earl Beatty* (London: Hodder and Stoughton, 1951); Ernle Chatfield, *The Navy and Defence: An Autobiography of Admiral of the Fleet Lord Chatfield* (London: William Heinemann, 1942); Winston S. Churchill, *The World Crisis 1911–1918*, abridged and rev. ed. (New York: Free Press, 2005); Frederic Dreyer, *The Sea Heritage* (London: Museum Press, 1955); John Arbuthnot Fisher, *Fear God and Dread Nought: The Correspondence of Admiral of the Fleet Lord Fisher of Kilverstone*, ed. Arthur J. Marder (London: Cape, 1959), 3 vols.; John Arbuthnot Fisher, *Memories and Records* (New York: Doran, 1920), 2 vols.; John Jellicoe, *The Grand Fleet 1914–1916* (London: Cassell, 1919); John Jellicoe, *The Jellicoe Papers*, ed. A. Temple Patterson (London: Navy Records Society, 1966), 2 vols.; Louise King-Hall, ed., *Sea Saga* (London: Newnes, 1935); and Filson Young, *With the Battle Cruisers* (London: Cassell, 1921).

On the German side, see Paul L. G. Behncke, *Unsere Marine im Weltkriege und ihr Zuzammenbruch* (Berlin: Verlag Karl Curtius, 1919); Walter Görlitz, ed., *Regierte Der Kaiser: Kriegstagebücher, Aufzeichnungen und Briefe des Chefs der Marine-Kabinetts Admiral Georg Alexander von Müller 1914–1918* (Göttingen: Musterschmidt, 1959); Daniel Horn, ed., *The Private War of Seaman Stumpf: The Unique Diaries of a Young German in the Great War* (London: Leslie Frewin, 1969); Günther Paschen, "SMS *Lützow* at Jutland," *Journal of the Royal United Service Institution* 72 (1927): 32–41; Erich Raeder, *Mein Leben* (Tübingen-Neckar: F. Schlichtenmayer, 1956), 2 vols.; Reinhard Scheer, *Deutschlands Hochseeflotte im Weltkrieg: Persönliche Erinnerungen* (Berlin: August Scherl, 1919); Albert Scheibe, "The Jutland Battle," *Journal of the Royal United Service Institution* 62: 31–45; Georg von Hase, *Kiel and Jutland* (London: Skeffington & Son, 1921); Eberhard von Mantey, ed., *Auf See Unbesiegt: 30 Darstellungen aus dem Seekrieg* (Munich: J. F. Lehmanns Verlag, 1921); Hugo von Pohl, *Aus Aufzeichnungen und Briefen während der Kriegszeit* (Berlin: Berlegt von Rarl Giegismund, 1920); Alfred von Tirpitz, *My Memoirs* (New York: Dodd, Meade and Company, 1919), 2 vols.; Alfred von Tirpitz, *Politische Dokumente: Deutsche Ohnmachtspolitik im Weltkriege* (Hamburg: Hanseatische Verlagsanstalt, 1926); Hugo von Waldeyer-Hartz, *Admiral von Hipper* (London: Rich & Cowan, 1933); and Ernst von Weizsäcker, *Erinnerungen* (Munich: Paul List Verlag, 1950).

5. The best examples of this point come from two of the best recent works: Gordon, *Rules of the Game*, and Staff, *Skagerrak*.

6. Frank Wilson of the editorial staff of the *Philadelphia Inquirer* to the author, September 16, 2018.

7. Grigory Rasputin to Nicholas II, n.d. (July 1914), printed in Edvard Radzinsky, *The Rasputin File* (New York: Anchor Books, 2000), 262.

8. See Tobias R. Philbin, *Admiral von Hipper: The Inconvenient Hero* (Amsterdam: R. R. Gruner, 1982).

9. For newer insights in the present work to the role of British intelligence in the strange end of his squadron, see chapter 6, note 11.

CHAPTER 1. ENGLISHMEN'S HOMES

1. For Fay Lonsdale's presence as a guest at the Grand Hotel in Scarborough in December 1914, see Robert K. Massie, *Castles of Steel: Britain, Germany, and the Winning of the War at Sea* (New York: Random House, 2003), 319–20.

2. For much of what follows here about the Admiralty's thinking at this time, see Jellicoe to the Admiralty, November 14, 1914, printed in Jellicoe, *Jellicoe Papers*, 1: 89–92; Fisher's letters of mid-to-late November 1914, printed in Fisher, *Fear God and Dread Nought*, 3: 73–74, 76–77, 83–84, 89–90; Jellicoe, *Grand Fleet*, 156–74; Young, *With the Battle Cruisers*, 45–48; Churchill, *World Crisis*, 251–53; Corbett, *Naval Operations*, 2: 1–16; and Marder, *From Dreadnought to Scapa Flow*, 2: 60–64 [NB: Volume 3 of Marder's magnum opus

appears in two 1966 printings. The second 1966 printing, which I use almost exclusively below, is slightly altered from the 1st Printing, which I also cite].

3. Corbett, *Naval Operations*, 2: 1–16. The War Group met daily.

4. For Wilson's thinking, see Corbett, *Naval Operations*, 2: 4–6, 9–10. On Oliver, see William James, *A Great Seaman: The Life of Admiral of the Fleet Sir Henry Oliver* (London: H. F. & G. Witherby, 1956).

5. On November 28, 1914, Fisher had written Jellicoe: "I see no way of preventing their coming to bombard, as we have nothing south to meet them." See Fisher, *Fear God*, 3: 81. That Fisher knew Jellicoe wanted to sortie on December 7 to stop the Germans on the 8th, see Jellicoe to Fisher, December 3, 1915, printed in Fisher, *Fear God*, 3: 85. For Fisher's general fears of harming capital ships during sweeps, see Fisher to Jellicoe, December 26, 1914, printed in Fisher, *Fear God*, 3: 111. For Fisher studies, see Reginald H. Bacon, *The Life of Lord Fisher of Kilverstone* (New York: Hodder and Stoughton, 1929), 2 vols.; and Nicholas Lambert, *Sir John Fisher's Naval Revolution* (Columbia: University of South Carolina Press, 1999).

6. On British intelligence's expectation of battle on November 24, see Young, who served on HMS *Lion*, Beatty's flagship, *With the Battle Cruisers*, 75–76; and Thompson, *Imperial War Museum Book*, 85, who cites the diary of an officer aboard the battlecruiser HMS *Queen Mary*. That Fisher doubted the worth of this intelligence, see Fisher to Jellicoe, November 21, 1914, printed in Fisher, *Fear God*, 3: 78.

7. See Churchill, *World Crisis*, 252.

8. Good discussions of Jellicoe before the war are found in the early chapters of Reginald H. Bacon, *The Life of John Rushworth, Earl Jellicoe* (London: Cassell, 1936); and A. Temple Patterson, *Jellicoe: A Biography* (London: Macmillan, 1969). Also see Cornelli Barnett, *The Swordbearers: Supreme Command in the First World War* (New York: Morrow, 1963), 101–7. Massie, *Castles of Steel*, 56–71; and especially Jellicoe, *Jutland: The Unfinished Battle*, epages 41–65.

9. Barnett, *Swordbearers*, 102.

10. Cited in Massie, *Castles of Steel*, 57.

11. Jellicoe to the Admiralty, December 4, 1914, printed in Jellicoe, *Jellicoe Papers*, 1: 102–3.

12. Jellicoe, *Grand Fleet*, 169–71. Also see Beatty to Churchill, October 17, 1914, printed in Beatty, *Beatty Papers*, 1: 139–44.

13. Citations in Fisher to Jellicoe, December 10, 1914, and Jellicoe to Beatty, December 12, 1914, printed in Jellicoe, *Jellicoe Papers*, 1: 103–5. For much of what follows in the next paragraph, see Brooks, *Battle of Jutland*, 31; Jellicoe to Churchill, July 14, 1914, and Jellicoe to Admiralty, December 4, 1914, printed in Jellicoe, *Jellicoe Papers*, 1: 37–40, 102–3; Jellicoe, *Grand Fleet*, 169–74; Barnett, *Swordbearers*, 107–20; Massie, *Castles of Steel*, 300–308; Thompson, *Imperial War Museum Book*, 90; Chalmers, *Life and Letters*, 158–59; and the fine discussion in Sumida, "Matter of Timing."

14. Scheer, *Deutschlands Hochseeflotte*, 50.

CHAPTER 2. DEATH NOTICES

1. The death notice, including Countess Spee's commentary about it, is printed in Hermann Kirchhoff, *Maximilian Graf von Spee, Der Sieger von Coronel: Das Lebensbild und die Erinnerungen eines deutschen Seemanns* (Berlin: Marinedank-Verlag, 1915), 8–9.

2. Raeder, *Mein Leben*, 1: 75.

3. The best studies of Hipper are von Waldeyer-Hartz (a member of Hipper's staff), *Admiral von Hipper*; and Philbin, *Admiral von Hipper*.

4. Citations in Eric Dorn Brose, *The Kaiser's Army: The Politics of Military Technology in Germany during the Machine Age, 1870–1918* (New York: Oxford University Press, 2001), 28; and von Tirpitz, *My Memoirs*, 1: 67.

5. Chief of the Admiralty Staff, Admiral Hugo von Pohl, wrote the following on March 23, 1915: "We know next to nothing about the presence of the enemy First Fleet. Isolated reports, which always arrive very late, indicate that it frequently changes its base, but always stays ready to strike. Not one single time since the outbreak of war has a report about its presence been received in a timely enough fashion that a sortie of our fleet can be planned accordingly." Cited in Groos, *Der Krieg in der Nordsee*, 4: 60–61. Ingenohl's "keep sharp for the decisive battle [*Entscheidungsschlacht*]" directive of August 14, 1914, is printed in Scheer, *Deutschlands Hochseeflotte*, 72–73. The best recent discussion of the German navy in the early months of the war is Michael Epkenhans, "The Imperial Navy, 1914–1915," in *Jutland*, ed. Epkenhans et al., 117–22. For a fine discussion of the Battle of the Bight, see Goldrick, *Before Jutland* [2015], 111–38.

6. The Kaiser's "no advance" marginalia of late August and standing order of October 6, 1914, are printed in Granier, *Die Deutsche Seekriegsleitung*, 2: 19, 30–31.

7. The possibility of a "Second Punic War," an allusion to the second war between Rome and sea-power Carthage, came up for discussion around the Kaiser as the war dragged on into the autumn without a smashing victory on the Western Front. See Granier, *Die Deutsche Seekriegsleitung*, 2: 524n646.

8. Diary entries of journalist Theodor Wolff, October 16 and 23, 1914, cited in Röhl, *Wilhelm II*, 1,147. For more on the state of these invasion plans in the autumn of 1914, see von Pohl to his representative in Berlin, Paul Behncke, September 6, 1914 (cited in Granier, *Die Deutsche Seekriegsleitung*, 2: 30n1), who boasts that the invasion would come after the capture of northern France to Le Harve; Hipper to Ingenohl, November 12, 1914 (printed in Philbin, *Admiral von Hipper*, 92–93), who wanted to use his battlecruisers in the South Atlantic but realized that even if the Channel ports fell to the army, "the whole fleet would be needed" for "any major planned landing in force in England" because for an invasion the whole fleet would be needed; the observations of Adolph von Trotha, captain of battleship SMS *Kaiser*, November 15, 1914 (summarized in von Tirpitz, *Politische Dokumente*, 162), who alludes to an invasion after having dealt with

France; and Evelyn Blücher's diary entry for November 1914 (*An English Wife in Berlin* [New York: E. P. Dutton, 1920], 41–42), who knew of serious preparations (including assembling transports) after the fall of Antwerp on October 10. She and her German husband were very well informed about developments in high places. On board the battleship *Helgoland*, moreover, one seaman, Richard Stumpf (see his diary printed in Horn, *Private War of Seaman Stumpf*, 83–84), recalled in April 1915 that "the fleet will be sent in" when the fall of Calais created "an operational base against England." "We were told long ago" that the fall of Antwerp or Ostend would suffice for this purpose, but neither site, once taken, had proved sufficient.

9. Tirpitz wrote Ingenohl on October 25, 1914, that he thought it unwise to engage the entire British fleet (printed in Epkenhans, *Albert Hopman*, 486–87n513). He wrote this, ostensibly, because such a stance was necessitated by the Kaiser's timidity and Chancellor Theobald von Bethmann Hollweg's desire to preserve the fleet as a bargaining chip (Röhl, *Wilhelm II*, 1,150), but privately Tirpitz wanted more, for short of charging "fatuously" into battle with the whole British navy, which the Kaiser would never approve, there were still offensive options. He believed that Ingenohl should not shrink from risking action, even "against superior forces," a gamble that appears to be what Tirpitz really wanted because in "driving the fleet out to sea" he thought the German navy would "answer" the challenge: "I believe in its success" (see von Tirpitz's notations of October 8 and 15, 1914, printed in *My Memoirs*, 2: 251, 260). Also see Hopman to Trotha, October 10, 1914 (in Epkenhans, *Albert Hopman*, 459; and Epkenhans, "Imperial Navy," *Jutland*, ed. Epkenhans et al., 122n31): "[Tirpitz] is convinced that the chances of a battle are not completely unfavorable, that we are superior in many points . . . and that consequently a great victory for us is not completely out of the question." "Deep down in his heart" (see Volker R. Berghahn, *Germany and the Approach of War in 1914* [New York: St. Martin's Press, 1973], 38–39) Tirpitz may not have wanted such action early in his career, but the need to win a war that threatened to stalemate in the late summer and early autumn of 1914, and the compounding need for the navy to prove its worth in order to prevail against competing military interests after the war, warranted a throw of the iron dice (see his notations of August 24; September 3, 14, 24, and 28; and October 6, 1914, in *My Memoirs*, 2: 219–20, 224, 233, 238–39, 243, 249).

10. See Wolfram Sauerbrei, *Ingenohl: Vier Sterne auf blauem Grund* (Neuwied: Kehrein, 1999).

11. von Tirpitz, *Politische Dokumente*, 152. For his negative impression of Ingenohl in early November, also see the diary of Tirpitz's close aide, Albert Hopman, November 7, 1914, printed in Epkenhans, *Albert Hopman*, 486–87.

12. See above, note 5.

13. In particular, see Tirpitz to Ingenohl, October 25, 1914 (printed in Epkenhans, *Albert Hopman*, 486–87n513), Epkenhans' discussion of further documentation (539–40n23), as well as Tirpitz's notations cited in note 9 above. For Pohl's running battle with Tirpitz

about committing the fleet to a major action with the Royal Navy, see Pohl's notations and letters from late summer and fall 1914 (printed in von Pohl, *Aus Aufzeichnungen*, 1–92), especially Pohl to his wife, November 21 and November 25, 1914 (pp. 89, 91).

14. On Ingenohl's initial opposition to the bombardment due to concern for civilian lives, see Philbin, *Admiral von Hipper*, 88–89.

15. Eckermann to Tirpitz, November 4, 1914 (printed in von Tirpitz, *Politische Dokumente*, 148), and Tirpitz's commentary (pp. 147, 152). For more on the navy infighting over committing to action or not, also see the diary of Georg von Müller, November 5, 1914 (printed in Görlitz, *Regierte Der Kaiser*, 68); the diary entries of Tirpitz's close aide, Captain Albert Hopman, October 29 and 30, 1914 (printed in Epkenhans, *Albert Hopman*, 480–81); Raeder, *Mein Leben*, 1: 88–89; and Philbin, *Admiral von Hipper*, 87–89.

16. Ingenohl to Tirpitz, November 9, 1914 (printed in von Tirpitz, *Politische Dokumente*, 157).

17. For the origins of this raid and details of the plan, see Groos, *Der Krieg in der Nordsee*, 3: 50–51, 56–57.

18. Philbin, *Admiral von Hipper*, 97–98.

19. There was only a little room in Hipper's plan for U-boats. Over the previous month, Scheer and the chief of the submarine corps, Hermann Bauer, had advocated a more aggressive use of U-boats (Holger H. Herwig, *"Luxury" Fleet: The Imperial German Navy 1888–1918* [London: Ashfield Press, 1980], 163). Hipper, however, had dropped submarines from an earlier proposal (Massie, *Castles of Steel*, 327), perhaps because of British progress with installing submarine booms and nets. His plan of November 25 relied almost exclusively on seven torpedo-boat flotillas that were more numerous, more maneuverable, and more capable of coordinating their movements with the main fleet than U-boats.

20. According to Corbett, *Naval Operations*, 2: 25, the coordinates lay just north of the eastern edge of the Southwestern Patch of the Dogger Bank. Scheer, *Deutschlands Hochseeflotte*, 110, puts the spot here too.

21. The "Bight" was inside the line running from Terschelling, off the far northeastern coast of Holland, to Horns Riff, off the coast of Denmark—in other words, only fifty miles out to sea from Helgoland. The Kaiser had to give his approval for any mission beyond the Bight.

22. Ingenohl to Müller, November 28, 1914 (printed in Granier, *Die Deutsche Seekriegsleitung*, 2: 37).

23. For Ingenohl's worries in late November 1914 about the code's vulnerability and Pohl's objections, see von Waldeyer-Hartz, *Admiral von Hipper*, 130–31. For Raeder's comments on this likely minority of officers, which he intimates he had favored four decades earlier, see his *Mein Leben*, 1: 96–97. In my view, Raeder's much later recollection is trustworthy, for it was consistent with his general attitude at that time, which tended to be very critical of the top brass, complaining that "we do not have any leaders," including Hipper, who trusted the codes (see Raeder's comments to Admiral Bachmann, February 14, 1915

[cited in Epkenhans, *Albert Hopman* , 552–53]). It is also interesting that Pohl, appointed C-in-C in February 1915, a man who still rejected these officers' hypothesis in late 1914, nevertheless wrote in his battle log in June 1915 in a way hinting that the minority also may have begun to influence him to be more wary of the "surprising speed" with which the British were "always more or less exactly informed of our intentions" (cited in Groos, *Der Krieg in der Nordsee*, 4: 217). Also see Chapter 4, note 21.

24. Groos, *Der Krieg in der Nordsee*, 3: 53–54.

25. Philbin, *Admiral von Hipper*, 91–95, found Hipper's proposal of November 12 to allow the battlecruisers to help Graf Spee, as well as Ingenohl's and Pohl's rejections, in German archives.

26. See Lans' letter of December 28, 1914, to Otto Lans, a relative serving under Müller in the Privy Naval Cabinet (printed in von Tirpitz, *Politische Dokumente*, 185–89), which lays out his operational views in the four months since August. He had often discussed naval strategy with his squadron captains, a few squadron commanders, and also with Ingenohl. From time to time he had worked out these views in writing. For Lans' point of view, also see Eckermann to Hopman, November 13, 1914 (printed in von Tirpitz, *Politische Dokumente*, 164); and Herwig, *"Luxury" Fleet*, 161.

27. Ingenohl to Müller, November 28, 1914 (printed in von Tirpitz, *Politische Dokumente*, 174).

28. Eckermann to Tirpitz, November 30, 1914 (printed in von Tirpitz, *Politische Dokumente*, 175).

29. von Waldeyer-Hartz, *Admiral von Hipper*, 141, a naval captain on Hipper's staff, recalled Hipper's views at this time on civilian casualties. For the "express military purpose" behind the raid, namely, to provoke the Royal Navy into a trap, see Groos, *Der Krieg in der Nordsee*, 3: 120. Also see Raeder, *Mein Leben*, 1: 89; and Scheer, *Deutschlands Hochseeflotte*, 114.

30. For Wegener's mission, see Groos, *Der Krieg in der Nordsee*, 3: 62–65.

31. It is clear from the diary of Georg von Müller, Privy Naval Counselor to the Kaiser (printed in Görlitz, *Regierte der Kaiser*, 75), that before December 15 this highly placed adviser knew nothing of Ingenohl's decision to sortie.

32. Scheer, *Deutschlands Hochseeflotte*, 107. That such sentiments helped Ingenohl make up his mind, see Goldrick, *Before Jutland* [2015], 198.

CHAPTER 3. TURNABOUT IS FOUL PLAY

1. The best sources for the positions of all British and German ships on December 15 and 16, 1914, are Groos, *Der Krieg in der Nordsee*, 3: charts 4–8; and Corbett, *Naval Operations*, 2: text chart, 48–49.

2. Good introductions to Beatty are Chalmers, *Life and Letters*, 1–106; Beatty, *Beatty Papers*, 1: 104; Stephen Roskill, *Admiral of the Fleet Earl Beatty, the Last Naval Hero: An Intimate*

Biography (London: Atheneum, 1980), 1–76; Massie, *Castles of Steel*, 83–96; and Jellicoe, *Jutland: The Unfinished Battle*, epages 46–65.

3. For his feelings, see Beatty to Ethel, October 19, 1914 (printed in Chalmers, *Life and Letters*, 178).

4. Beatty to Churchill, October 17, 1914 (printed in Beatty, *Beatty Papers*, 1: 139–44).

5. Beatty to Ethel, October 19 and 30, 1914 (printed in Chalmers, *Life and Letters*, 178–79).

6. Beatty to Ethel, November 17, 1914 (printed in Chalmers, *Life and Letters*, 162–63).

7. Jellicoe to Beatty, December 12, 1914 (printed in Jellicoe, *Jellicoe Papers*, 1: 105).

8. For its early history, see William James, *The Eyes and Ears of the Navy: A Biographical Study of Admiral Sir Reginald Hall* (London: Methuen & Co., 1955), 24–31; and especially Patrick Beesly, *Room 40: British Naval Intelligence 1914–1918* (London: Harcourt, Brace, Jovanovich, 1982), 1–51 (p. 49 for Ingenohl's messages). Also see, Koerver, *Room 40*.

9. For most of what follows, see mainly Churchill, *World Crisis*, 253–54; and Corbett, *Naval Operations*, 2: 21–25.

10. That he thought the Germans were headed toward Harwich and the Humber, see Young, *With the Battle Cruisers*, 91; and Richard Hough, *The Great War at Sea 1914–1918* (Oxford, UK: Oxford University Press, 1983), 125. That all were conceding that the German ships would probably reach the coast first, and should be intercepted on their return, see the Admiralty to Jellicoe, December 14, 1914 (printed in Churchill, *World Crisis*, 253–54).

11. Fisher to Jellicoe, December 21, 1914 (printed in Jellicoe, *Jellicoe Papers*, 1: 113; and Goldrick, *Before Jutland* [2015], 198–99).

12. Young, *With the Battle Cruisers*, 90.

13. Warrender's signal is printed in Young, *With the Battle Cruisers*, 90–91; the Admiralty's wire to Jellicoe of December 14 (sent 2130) is printed in Churchill, *World Crisis*, 253–54.

14. Churchill, *World Crisis*, 92.

15. Churchill, *World Crisis*, 48.

16. For Ingenohl's nighttime formation and placement of all eighty-five ships of the main fleet, see Groos, *Der Krieg in der Nordsee*, 3: chart 7.

17. Cited in von Waldeyer-Hartz, *Admiral von Hipper*, 133.

18. von Waldeyer-Hartz, *Admiral von Hipper*, 133.

19. For the *S-33* episode, see Goldrick, *Before Jutland* [2015], 200–201.

20. Ingenohl described his thought process after he first heard about the destroyer sighting in his after-battle report of December 18, 1914 (printed in Groos, *Der Krieg in der Nordsee*, 3: 69). For his worries about British wireless, see Philbin, *Admiral von Hipper*, 100, who draws on Ingenohl's unpublished 1918 remembrances of the first months of the war.

21. See Scheer, *Deutschlands Hochseeflotte*, 110–11.

22. For Ingenohl's worries about the British forces in the Channel, see Philbin, *Admiral von Hipper*, 100, who draws on Ingenohl's unpublished 1918 remembrances. For Ingenohl's

concern about weak destroyer protection on his northern flank, see his after-battle report of December 18, 1914 (cited in Groos, *Der Krieg in der Nordsee*, 3: 72).

23. For the skirmish, see Groos, *Der Krieg in der Nordsee*, 3: 65–69; and Corbett, *Naval Operations*, 2: 26.

24. Groos, *Der Krieg in der Nordsee*, 3: 70, quotes (indirectly) Ingenohl's after-battle report of December 18, 1914. For the signal from *V-155* and his orders of 0530 and 0620, see Groos, *Der Krieg in der Nordsee*, 3: 252–53. That Ingenohl's turn seemed temporary and not final, see Groos, *Der Krieg in der Nordsee*, 3: 72–73, 111; also see Raeder, *Mein Leben*, 1: 93–94.

25. The report is printed in von Waldeyer-Hartz, *Admiral von Hipper*, 133.

26. The Raeder–Hipper exchange is printed in von Waldeyer-Hartz, *Admiral von Hipper*, 134.

27. For the minefields off the coast, see Corbett, *Naval Operations*, 2: 23–24; and Groos, *Krieg in der Nordsee*, 3: 52–53.

28. Hipper's attitude toward the distinct possibility of civilian deaths (cited in von Waldeyer-Hartz, *Admiral von Hipper*, 141) probably applied as well to the German naval officer corps involved on December 16. They did not relish the killing of civilians but had their duty to do so in a war that was turning very ugly. The silence on this issue in so many other memoirs, however, speaks no doubt to a certain sense of guilt and the need to rationalize by exaggerating the military nature of the targets. See Scheer, *Deutschlands Hochseeflotte*, 109; Raeder, *Mein Leben*, 1: 89; Hase, *Kiel and Jutland*, 41; and even at times, von Waldeyer-Hartz, *Admiral von Hipper*, 131, 140, who argues that the raid was justified because all three towns were listed in Britain's official military lists as "defended ports" and "coast defenses." Even more transparent is Groos, *Der Krieg in der Nordsee*, 3: 117–21, who also uses the argument about the military lists, but then admits that bombarding defended ports was not the real military goal. "The express military purpose [of the German coastal shelling] was to stimulate the enemy to counterattack, for only a decision of arms at sea could break the blockade." Also see Chapter 4, note 18.

29. The best descriptions of the raid on the Yorkshire coast are Corbett, *Naval Operations*, 2: 31–35; and Massie, *Castles of Steel*, 319–36.

30. That seamen who had served in the East Asiatic Squadron made these revenge exclamations while loading shells on the battle cruisers, see von Waldeyer-Hartz, *Admiral von Hipper*, 25.

31. Corbett, *Naval Operations*, 2: 32.

32. Massie, *Castles of Steel*, 321.

33. Cited in Churchill, *World Crisis*, 255.

34. Churchill, *World Crisis*, 256.

35. For descriptions of the remainder of the day's action to about 1500, see Corbett, *Naval Operations*, 2: 35–43; von Waldeyer-Hartz, *Admiral von Hipper*, 135–38; Massie, *Castles of Steel*, 337–52; and Goldrick, *Before Jutland* [2015], 209–14.

36. Citations in Corbett, *Naval Operations*, 2: 29–30.

37. For these criticisms, see Groos, *Der Krieg in der Nordsee*, 3: 73; Raeder, *Mein Leben*, 1: 93–95; Philbin, *Admiral von Hipper*, 100; and (diplomatically understated in) Scheer, *Deutschlands Hochseeflotte*, 111, 114, who called the decision to stay on the eastward course "premature." For incoming and outgoing signals on the flagship, see Groos, *Krieg in der Nordsee*, 3: 252–53.

38. Ingenohl's rationale for not reversing course came out in his report of December 18, 1914 (cited in Groos, *Krieg in der Nordsee*, 3: 72–73, 113); and his remembrances of 1918 (cited in Philbin, *Admiral von Hipper*, 100). For his fuel worries, also see 1st Squadron Commander Lans to a relative in the Privy Naval Cabinet, December 28, 1914 (printed in von Tirpitz, *Politische Dokumente*, 189). However, Germany's prewar destroyer classes (S138, V1, and V25) had range radiuses of 900–1,200 nautical miles (at 17–20 knots), about triple the distance to Yorkshire (for technical details, see the relevant portions of Erich Gröner, *Die deutschen Kriegsschiffe 1815–1945* [Koblenz: J. F. Lehmanns, 1983], vol. 2). The same torpedo boat classes had no fuel problems covering a similar distance to the Fisher Banks and back in 1916 while engaged in frequent intense combat.

39. Churchill, *World Crisis*, 260–61.

40. According to Vice Admiral Reinhard Scheer, commander of 2nd Squadron in the van farthest away. Scheer, *Deutschlands Hochseeflotte*, 114.

41. For the citations and excerpts from battle reports of the German light forces, see Groos, *Der Krieg in der Nordsee*, 3: 91–95.

42. Cited in von Waldeyer-Hartz, *Admiral von Hipper*, 136. Also see Raeder, *Mein Leben*, 1: 93–94.

43. Cited in von Waldeyer-Hartz, *Admiral von Hipper*, 138.

44. Cited in Groos, *Der Krieg in der Nordsee*, 3: 121.

CHAPTER 4. MIGHTY HASHES

1. Young, *With the Battle Cruisers*, 112.

2. For press citations in the following paragraphs, see Massie, *Castles of Steel*, 325–26; and Groos, *Der Krieg in der Nordsee*, 3: 117–18.

3. Cited in Churchill, *World Crisis*, 263.

4. Citations in Massie, *Castles of Steel*, 148; and Jellicoe to Beatty, January 19, 1915 (printed in Jellicoe, *Jellicoe Papers*, 1: 126). Also see Chatfield, *Navy and Defence*, 128.

5. For this paragraph and citations, see Fisher to Jellicoe, December 17, and his two letters to Jellicoe of December 21, 1914 (all printed in Fisher, *Fear God*, 3: 94, 101–3; Fisher, *Memories and Records*, 2: 132; and Churchill, *World Crisis*, 263–64). Also see Goldrick, *Before Jutland* [2015], 216–20.

6. See Barnett, *Swordbearers*, 178–81, for the first citation and a discussion of Fisher's views on the problem of order- and discipline-bound officers of the predreadnought era who had been recruited from a narrow sliver of upper society, not from the deeper pool of

the whole society from whence talents like Jellicoe and Beatty had come. Similar themes abound in Andrew Gordon's long digressive run-up to the Battle of Jutland in *The Rules of the Game*, 155–399. For the second citation, see Fisher to Beatty, April 3, 1915 (printed in Fisher, *Fear God*, 3: 185). Also see Massie, *Castles of Steel*, 357.

7. For Jellicoe's controlling leadership style, see Hough, *Great War at Sea*, 59–60, 239, 267–72, 305; and Gordon, *Rules of the Game*, 397–99.

8. See Raeder, *Mein Leben*, 1: 95.

9. For Christmases aboard German ships in 1914–15, see the Richard Stumpf Diary, printed in Horn, *Private War of Seaman Stumpf*, 58, 146–48.

10. For the entire episode of the air raid on Cuxhaven Naval Air Station as well as other events related to it, see Massie, *Castles of Steel*, 361–74; and Goldrick, *Before Jutland* [2015], 236–42.

11. See Chapter 3, notes 24 and 37.

12. Printed in Groos, *Der Krieg in der Nordsee*, 3: 111.

13. Cited in Philbin, *Admiral von Hipper*, 99.

14. Scheer, *Deutschlands Hochseeflotte*, 114, 116. That this opinion was widely held at the time, also see Philbin, *Admiral von Hipper*, 100; and von Waldeyer-Hartz, *Admiral von Hipper*, 138–39. That it would remain the opinion of German naval circles, see the 1938 lecture of Kurt Assmann (cited in Epkenhans, "Imperial Navy," in *Jutland*, ed. Epkenhans et al., 139n37): "We have become accustomed to calling the day of Hartlepool a 'lost opportunity.' . . . We want to guard against exaggeration . . . [but] no one will be able to acquit Ingenohl from the charge that he retreated at the wrong time."

15. Tirpitz's notation of January 6, 1915 is printed in von Tirpitz, *My Memoirs*, 2: 285.

16. For the real possibility of German victory during the Battle of the Frontiers in late August 1914, and the prewar decisions in the German army over technology and armaments that hampered that victory, see Brose, *Kaiser's Army, passim*, but especially 183–225. In arguing that the High Seas Fleet also missed an opportunity near the SWP, I disagree with Halpern, *Naval History*, 41–42; and more recently, Epkenhans, "Imperial Navy," in *Jutland*, ed. Epkenhans et al., 123. If Ingenohl had reversed course, the limited but passable visibility circa 0800–0900 hours would have created ideal conditions for luring Beatty closer, and later probably Warrender too. Goldrick, *Before Jutland* [2015], 202, also believes that a great opportunity had been missed.

17. See Philbin, *Admiral von Hipper*, 100, who draws on Ingenohl's 1918 recollections and the minutes of the after-battle conference on December 20; and Groos, *Der Krieg in der Nordsee*, 3: 113, who cites Ingenohl's after-battle report of December 18, 1914.

18. See the reports of Tirpitz's aide, Captain Albert Hopman, December 30, 1914, and January 8, 1915 (printed in Epkenhans, *Albert Hopman*, 532–33, 541–42). He had spoken with numerous officers about Ingenohl's relations with his subordinates.

19. Citations in Lans to his cousin, Captain Otto von Lans, December 28, 1914 (printed in von Tirpitz, *Politische Dokumente*, 186–89). Also see chapter 3, note 28.

20. For the background to the two men meeting on the nineteenth and what was discussed, see Müller's diary entries for December 17, 18, and 19, 1914 (printed in Görlitz, *Regierte Der Kaiser*, 75 [including the citation]).

21. For the issue of the codes, see Chapter 2, note 23. Also see 1st Squadron chief of staff Wolfgang Wegener's treatise of July 12, 1915 (printed in Herwig, *Wolfgang Wegener's*, 183; Raeder, *Mein Leben*, 96–97; von Waldeyer-Hartz, *Admiral von Hipper*, 130–31; and Geoffrey Bennett, *Naval Battles of the First World War* (London: B. T. Batsford, 1968), 165. The admiralty staff continued to trust the German codes, assuming that the main leaks came from British submarines and merchant ships in the inner Bight as well as agents in the Wilhelmshaven-Kiel area who passed information along to the British embassy in nearby Copenhagen.

22. Müller had spoken with the Kaiser on the seventeenth (Görlitz, *Regierte Der Kaiser*, 75), reporting the Kaiser as very upset that the U-boats had not attacked, but Müller is confusing submarines with torpedo boat destroyers. For the Kaiser's reaction to the Battle of the Falklands, see Müller's diary entry for December 11, 1914 (printed in Görlitz, *Regierte Der Kaiser*, 74; and Röhl, *Wilhem II*, 1,128–29).

23. That Pohl tended to defend Ingenohl immediately after the raid, see a letter to his wife of December 23, 1914 (printed in von Pohl, *Aus Aufzeichnungen*, 93). That the C-in-C thought it unreasonable to have expected only the British 2nd Battle Squadron at sea that day, also see Ingenohl to Pohl, January 19, 1915 (printed in Groos, *Der Krieg in der Nordsee*, 3: 275–76).

24. Pohl to his wife, December 23, 1914 (printed in von Pohl, *Aus Aufzeichnungen*, 93).

25. Pohl to Ingenohl, December 23, 1914 (printed in Granier, *Die Deutsche Seekriegsleitung*, 2: 38–39). Müller had undoubtedly attended Pohl's presentation to the Kaiser, whose order to Pohl reflected his cabinet chief's views (p. 40n1). That the controversy leading to the Kaiser's order revolved not only around the midday retreat of the light forces but also around Ingenohl's lack of aggressiveness in seeking out Warrender's 2nd Battle Squadron for destruction, see Hopman's report of January 8, 1915 (printed in Epkenhans, *Albert Hopman*, 541). Hopman had spoken with Eckermann, who, perhaps beginning to change sides, sought to deflect some of this criticism by pointing out that Ingenohl could not have engaged Warrender until nightfall and his torpedo boats did not have the requisite fuel to turn back. Although Eckermann was campaigning to unseat Ingenohl, he may have felt the discipline-oriented need to stand by his chief at times (also see the uncharacteristic opening of his letter to Tirpitz of January 22, 1915 [printed in von Tirpitz, *Politische Dokumente*, 202–3]). Furthermore, see Ingenohl's letter of January 19, 1915 (cited in Groos, *Der Krieg in der Nordsee*, 3: 275–78), where he claims he could not have known whether other English squadrons would have been there.

26. The directive of December 31, 1914, is printed in Groos, *Der Krieg in der Nordsee*, 3: 120.

27. He warned them not to fight a "war against women and children. We want a decent war, whatever the others do" (cited in Röhl, *Wilhelm II*, 1,151).

28. See Tirpitz's notations of December 23–24, 1914 (printed in von Tirpitz, *My Memoirs*, 2: 276; and Görlitz, *Regierte Der Kaiser*, 75).

29. Tirpitz's conversation with Müller on January 8, 1915 (printed in von Tirpitz, *Politische Dokumente*, 189). For their conversation of December 24, 1914, see Tirpitz's notation of that day (printed in *My Memoirs*, 2: 276), and his lengthier notation (printed in *Politische Dokumente*, 178); and for the origins of Pohl's report, Tirpitz's commentary, *Politische Dokumente*, 185–86, and Müller's diary entry of December 27, 1914 (printed in Görlitz, *Regierte Der Kaiser*, 77).

30. Tirpitz notation of January 2, 1915 (printed in von Tirpitz, *My Memoirs*, 2: 282).

31. See Scheer, *Deutschlands Hochseeflotte*, 117–19.

32. On Scheer, see Eckermann to Tirpitz, January 22, 1915 (printed in von Tirpitz, *Politische Dokumente*, 203 [for first citation]); Ernst von Weizsäcker (Scheer's flag lieutenant [and Pohl's before that]), *Erinnerungen*, 34–35 (for nickname, reason for it, and *Augenblicksmensch* citation); the May 1939 notation of Adolf von Trotha, Scheer's chief of staff after 1916, cited differently in Arthur J. Marder, *From the Dreadnought to Scapa Flow: The Royal Navy in the Fisher Era, 1904–1919* 1st Printing, (London: Oxford University Press, 1966), 3: 42, and V. E. Tarrant, *Jutland: The German Perspective* (Annapolis, MD: Naval Institute Press, 1995), 44 (for unorthodox thinking); and Raeder, *Mein Leben*, 1: 105 (for nickname and anti-"quibblers" citation). Also see Friedrich Forstmeier, "Zum Bild der Persönlichkeit des Admirals Reinhard Scheer (1863–1928)," *Marine-Rundschau* 58, no. 2 (1961): 74–79.

33. It would have been protocol for Ingenohl to receive Scheer. Eckermann mentioned Ingenohl's aggressive plans to Hopman after the New Year (see Hopman's diary entry of January 8, 1915 [printed in Epkenhans, *Albert Hopman*, 541]). For details of the planned missions, see mainly Groos, *Der Krieg in der Nordsee*, 3: 161–71. Also see Scheer, *Deutschlands Hochseeflotte*, 119–20; and von Waldeyer-Hartz, *Admiral von Hipper*, 144–46. Goldrick, *Before Jutland* [1984], 255–56, states incorrectly that Hipper's sole target was the Firth of Forth.

34. For the exact location of the older fields and this new one, see Groos, *Der Krieg in der Nordsee*, 3: chart 16.

35. Scheer, *Deutschlands Hochseeflotte*, 119.

36. For the Kaiser's lifestyle during the war, see mainly Röhl, *Wilhelm II*, 1,108–34. For his front visits and talks to the wounded, see the Müller Diary for August, September, and October, in Görlitz, *Regierte Der Kaiser*, 52–67. For the Kaiser's psyche and its effect on military technology as well as his yielding to the generals in 1914, see Brose, *Kaiser's*

Army, 113–26, 181–82, 264n4 (reworks of Thomas Kohut), and 279n188–90 (reworks of Elizabeth Hull and Holger Afflerbach).

37. The best sources on the insider maneuverings prior to the meeting are von Tirpitz, *Politische Dokumente*, 185–86; and Groos, *Der Krieg in der Nordsee*, 3: 155–57.

38. For their input, see Groos, *Der Krieg in der Nordsee*, 3: 155–57, 263–65.

39. Pohl notation of January 8, 1915, (printed in von Pohl, *Aus Aufzeichnungen*, 100).

40. See Tirpitz's notations of January 2, 4, 5, and 8, 1915 (printed in von Tirpitz, *My Memoirs*, 2: 282–85).

41. For this and the following paragraph (including citations), see Müller's diary entry about the meeting, January 9, 1915 (printed in Görlitz, *Regierte Der Kaiser*, 80); Pohl's written report, January 7, 1915, including Müller's marginalia relaying the Kaiser's decisions (printed in von Tirpitz, *Politische Dokumente*, 191–92 [also printed in Groos, *Der Krieg in der Nordsee*, 3: 266–74]); and Pohl's entry of the same day (printed in von Pohl, *Aus Aufzeichnungen*, 100–101).

42. Citations in Harald Eschenburg, *Prinz Heinrich von Preussen: Der Grossadmiral im Schatten des Kaisers* (Heide: Boyens & Co., 1989), 155; and Captain Zenker's letter of January 11, 1915 (cited in von Tirpitz, *Politische Dokumente*, 194).

43. Ingenohl's letter of January 19, 1915 (printed in Groos, *Der Krieg in der Nordsee*, 3: 275–78).

44. von Tirpitz, *Politische Dokumente*, 194; Groos, *Der Krieg in der Nordsee*, 3: 159; and more recently, Barnett, *Swordbearers*, 118; and Goldrick, *Before Jutland* [2015], 221, 287. Only Epkenhans, "Imperial Navy", in *Jutland*, ed. Epkenhans et al., 128, 132, 136, has a somewhat higher and more proper regard for Ingenohl.

CHAPTER 5. MURPHY'S LAW

1. For this afternoon in Edinburgh, including their remarks here and below, see Young, *With the Battle Cruisers*, 172–74.

2. For turret loading procedures, safety regulations, and their loosening after the outbreak of war as well as various turret details, see Grove, "Autobiography of Chief Gunner Alexander Grant," 389–90 (and 390n6 for Harvey); the recollections of battlecruiser midshipman John Croome, cited in Steel and Hart, *Death in the Grey Wastes*, Chapter 5, ebook location 3087 [originally published in 2003]; N. J. M. Campbell, *Warship Special 1: Battlecruisers* (London: Conway Maritime Press, 1978), 30, as well as his *Jutland: An Analysis of the Fighting* (London: Conway Maritime Press, 1986), 371–72; Lambert, "'Our Bloody Ships,'" 29–55; and Brooks, *Battle of Jutland*, 81, 463–65.

3. The background and preliminaries to the German sortie of January 23 are not entirely clear on an hour-by-hour basis, but can be patched together from Eckermann to Tirpitz (or Hopman), January 22, 1915, and Pohl to Ingenohl, January 26, 1915 (printed in von Tirpitz, *Politische Dokumente*, 202–3, 195; Groos, *Der Krieg in der Nordsee*, 3: 189–93,

202–3; von Waldeyer-Hartz, *Admiral von Hipper*, 147–48; Raeder, *Mein Leben*, 1: 95–96; Scheer, *Deutschlands Hochseeflotte*, 121–23; Philbin, *Admiral von Hipper*, 103–4; Beesly, *Room 40*, 57–58; and Goldrick, *Before Jutland* [2015], 255–56), although I disagree with Goldrick that only Eckermann advocated and pressed for this plan—Hipper did too.

4. Churchill to Fisher, January 20, 1915 (printed in Churchill, *World Crisis*, 331).

5. Churchill, *World Crisis*, 333–34; and Corbett, *Naval Operations*, 2: 83–84. The citations (mainly Churchill), both here and the following paragraphs, draw on these two sources.

6. The first version of James Goldrick's more extensive *Before Jutland* [2015], *Before Jutland: The King's Ships Were at Sea: The War in the North Sea, August 1914–February 1915* (Annapolis, MD: Naval Institute Press, 1984), 251, cites Oliver's remembrance—emphasis in original. For the remainder of this chapter, I use this earlier version.

7. Churchill, *World Crisis*, 335.

8. Citations from Young, *With the Battle Cruisers*, 175, 177.

9. Citations from Young, *With the Battle Cruisers*, 177; and Corbett, *Naval Operations*, 2: 86.

10. Groos, *Der Krieg in der Nordsee*, 3: 198.

11. The position of all ships involved in the battle from beginning to end several hours later is best studied in Groos, *Der Krieg in der Nordsee*, 3: chart 18. Also see Scheer, *Deutschlands Hochseeflotte*, 121–30.

12. The exchange is cited in Chatfield, *Navy and Defence*, 131.

13. Citations here from Goldrick, *Before Jutland* [1984], 255; and Churchill, *World Crisis*, 335.

14. Beatty steamed throughout the evening and night at only 18 knots, while the Admiralty thought he would cruise at 20 (Goldrick, *Before Jutland* [1984], 252–53). At the latter speed, he would have been twenty-six miles farther south by first light. Moreover, he received the order to move at 1230 when his squadron was at four hours until full steam. He could have departed before 1800.

15. Cited in Massie, *Castles of Steel*, 383.

16. Citations from Young, *With the Battle Cruisers*, 179; and Chatfield, *Navy and Defence*, 132.

17. The range when the smoke clouds were sighted can be calculated from Groos, *Der Krieg in der Nordsee*, 3: chart 18.

18. See Groos, *Der Krieg in der Nordsee*, 3: 198–200, 283 (for wireless messages and citations from Hipper's postbattle report); von Waldeyer-Hartz, *Admiral von Hipper*, 151, who was on the bridge (and prints Hipper's after-battle report in near entirety, 151–54); and Raeder, *Mein Leben*, 1: 313, who prints a letter (Fritz Boie to Raeder, n.d.) describing an eyewitness account of Hipper and Raeder on the bridge during the battle.

19. Citations from Young, *With the Battle Cruisers*, 179–81; and Chatfield, *Navy and Defence*, 132.

20. Citations from Goldrick, *Before Jutland* [1984], 261; and Chatfield, *Navy and Defence*, 132.

21. See Groos, *Der Krieg in der Nordsee*, 3: 200–203, 214, 283–84 (for wireless messages); von Waldeyer-Hartz, *Admiral von Hipper*, 151–52, 158; and Philbin, *Admiral von Hipper*, 109–10.

22. Massie, *Castles of Steel*, 377, incorrectly notes the armored cruiser's allegedly slower speed hindering the battlecruisers on January 24. See Philbin, *Admiral von Hipper*, 109–10.

23. For the action between 0900 and 0940, see Corbett, *Naval Operations*, 2: 88–90; Groos, *Der Krieg in der Nordsee*, 3: 207–9, 284 (for wireless messages); Chatfield, *Navy and Defence*, 132–33; Young, *With the Battle Cruisers*, 182–85; and Goldrick, *Before Jutland* [1984], 260–63.

24. Young, *With the Battle Cruisers*, 185.

25. Cited in Corbett, *Naval Operations*, 2: 90.

26. For Ingenohl's reactions, see Groos, *Der Krieg in der Nordsee*, 3: 202–6, 283–85 (for wireless messages); and Scheer, *Deutschlands Hochseeflotte*, 125–26, 130.

27. Goldrick, *Before Jutland* (1984), 11. For Hall's method of operating, see James, *Eyes of the Navy*; Beesly, *Room 40*; and Erik Larson, *Dead Wake: The Last Crossing of the Lusitania* (New York: Crown Publishers, 2015). As for his motivation to deceive Ingenohl about British battlecruisers at Scapa Flow in late January 1915, we know that Jacky Fisher was preoccupied in December and January with the belief that Germany would send its battlecruisers raking ports in the Channel, and then return to the homeland via the north of Scotland (various letters in Fisher, *Fear God*, 3: 116–17, 141), an unlikely scenario, but out of the question if Beatty were at Scapa to block their return.

28. Citations (and diagram) in Groos, *Der Krieg in der Nordsee*, 3: 210–11. For Beatty's disappointment with their hits at long range, and desire to get closer next time (i.e., at Jutland), see Brooks, *Battle of Jutland*, 81–82.

29. Quotations in this paragraph from Young, *With the Battle Cruisers*, 186, 189; and Corbett, *Naval Operations*, 2: 92–93. For German hits and casualties on *Lion*, *Tiger*, and destroyer HMS *Meteor* during the battle, see Roskill, *Admiral of the Fleet*, 118–19 (who draws mainly on Campbell, *Warship Special 1*); and Massie, *Castles of Steel*, 413n*. For the nature of German shell/fuse deficiencies early in the war, see chapter 13, note 11.

30. For this stage of the action to 1045, see Groos, *Der Krieg in der Nordsee*, 3: 214–16; and Goldrick, *Before Jutland* [1984], 271.

31. German survivors from *Blücher* remembered this hit on their ship "materially reducing her speed" [Corbett, *Naval Operations*, 2: 90]. Because she had kept pace with the other German ships until shortly after Goodenough's cruisers and the M-class destroyers were driven off at 1010 [Groos, *Der Krieg in der Nordsee*, 3: 215], the hit they described must have happened around 1015.

32. Groos, *Der Krieg in der Nordsee*, 3: 216.

33. See Corbett, *Naval Operations*, 2: 94–95; Chalmers, *Life and Letters*, 188–89; Goldrick, *Before Jutland* [1984], 272; and Massie, *Castles of Steel*, 396–97.

34. Citations in Young, *With the Battle Cruisers*, 217, 192–93; and Harvey to Arthur Grattan, February 13, 1915 (printed in Holloway, *From Trench and Turret*, 46).

35. Citations in this and the following paragraph from Goldrick, *Before Jutland* [1984], 273–75. For signals, also see Chalmers, *Life and Letters*, 189–90.

36. For this passage, see Goldrick, *Before Jutland* [1984], 275–76; Raeder, *Mein Leben*, 1: 98–99, 313 (Fritz Boie to Raeder, n.d., who describes an eyewitness account of Hipper and Raeder on the bridge during the battle); and documentation (including Hipper's after-battle report) in Groos, *Der Krieg in der Nordsee*, 3: 218–22, 285–86 (also for wireless messages), and von Waldeyer-Hartz, *Admiral von Hipper*, 151–54, 158–59 (for the quotes on Hipper).

37. Young, *With the Battle Cruisers*, 208–9, prints a postwar article appearing in the *Times* based on the recollections of survivors.

CHAPTER 6. PRIDE COMETH

1. Young, *With the Battle Cruisers*, 220.

2. Young, *With the Battle Cruisers*, 205, for the gunroom dinner on the twenty-eighth, and that Beatty and his staff were there until being called away.

3. Chatfield, *Navy and Defence*, 136–37.

4. See Chatfield's letter to a friend shortly after the battle (printed in Thompson, *Imperial War Museum Book*, 100–101).

5. Beatty to Ethel, November 22, 1915 (cited in Chalmers, *Life and Letters*, 207).

6. See a later speech Beatty made to assembled officers (cited in Chalmers, *Life and Letters*, 208).

7. Fisher to Beatty, January 27 and 31, 1915 (printed in Fisher, *Fear God*, 3: 147, 150–51).

8. Citations from Beatty to Jellicoe, February 8, 1915 (printed in Jellicoe, *Jellicoe Papers*, 1: 144–45).

9. Jellicoe, *Jellicoe Papers*, 1: 144–45.

10. For citations, see Churchill to Jellicoe, January 26, 1915, Fisher to Jellicoe, n.d. (early February 1915) and March 25, 1915 (printed in Jellicoe, *Jellicoe Papers*, 1: 129, 141, 153). Also see Jellicoe to Beatty, February 7, 1915, and Beatty to Jellicoe, February 8, 1915 (printed in Jellicoe, *Jellicoe Papers*, 1: 142–44).

11. See Eric Dorn Brose, *Death at Sea: Graf Spee and the Flight of the German East Asiatic Naval Squadron in 1914* (Virginia Beach: Createspace/KDP Print, 2010), 269–70; and Nick Hewitt, *The Kaiser's Pirates: Hunting Germany's Raiding Cruisers 1914–1915* (Barnsley, UK: Pen & Sword Maritime, 2013), 128–29. Dannreuther's after-battle report is printed in Richard Hough, *The Pursuit of Admiral von Spee* (London: Allen & Unwin, 1969), 171–75. For German shell/fuse deficiencies early in the war, see Chapter 13, note 11.

Soon after heading NID in November 1914, it seems that Hall first employed disinformation to block Graf Spee's return to Germany. Referring after the war specifically to Spee's demise off the Falklands, Hall jotted down in lecture notes that "propaganda" served various purposes, among them "deceiving the enemy in order to lead him to take a certain course for which you are prepared" (Beesly, *Room 40*, 77). Based on this, Beesly speculated that Spee's belief in sources telling him that there were no British ships at Port Stanley resulted from a disinformational plant by Hall, but it is likely that more was involved. In his postwar, semiofficial history of the war at sea, Julian S. Corbett (*Naval Operations*, 3: 404–5), who had access to all the Admiralty sources but could not mention classified details, speculated—but it had to have been more than speculation—that Spee's turn back to the west after Coronel (November 1), which probably ruined any chance he had of making it safely back to Germany, happened because he believed two or three battlecruisers were being sent from the home fleet to escort the East Asiatic home. Some of his officers had been told this was underway, and German diplomats in Montevideo thought so too. In fact, nothing was further from the truth. Hall wrote after the war that a leading principle of intelligence work was "that of mystifying and misleading the enemy" (Larson, *Dead Wake*, 88, 377), so Spee's costly delay may well have been the result of another NID plant in Uruguay. After a while Spee probably sniffed out the truth, which only deepened his fatalistic sense of demise. If Hall was behind the ruse, he came close to outfoxing himself, for Sturdee's battlecruiser reinforcement to the South Atlantic only narrowly missed being destroyed while coaling in the very port the NID chief had "prepared." London assumed Sturdee would have time to patrol further south to block the German, but now risked getting "Copenhagened," an emergency that kept Churchill in a state of near apoplexy for several hours. Fortunately for Churchill and Sturdee, the captain of armored cruiser *Gneisenau*, sent to capture the town, refused to believe his chief gunnery officer's sighting of battlecruisers refueling in harbor, assuming these must have been older battleships. After reporting this to Spee, the chief called off the raid, thinking the East Asiatic could easily outrun slower vessels and advance closer to home, but the faster battlecruisers hunted him down that same day (see Brose, *Death at Sea*, 241–57).

12. Fisher to Beatty, March 5, 1915 (printed in Fisher, *Fear God*, 3: 163).

13. Beatty to Jellicoe, February 8, 1915 (printed in Jellicoe, *Jellicoe Papers*, 1: 144); and Beatty to Fisher, March 8, 1915 (printed in Chalmers, *Life and Letters*, 200).

14. Beatty to Ethel, May 15, 1915 (cited in Massie, *Castles of Steel*, 565).

15. For citations from 1915 (and one from 1916) in this and the following paragraph, see Jellicoe to Bethell, January 22; Jellicoe to Hamilton, January 29; Fisher to Jellicoe, February 7; Jellicoe to Beatty, February 7 and March 23; Jellicoe to Hamilton, April 14 and 26; and Beatty to Jellicoe, n.d. (late January 1915) and February 3, 1916 (printed, respectively, in Jellicoe, *Jellicoe Papers*, 1: 128, 132, 141, 142, 152, 157, 158, 131, 208). Also see Jellicoe, *Grand Fleet*, 181; and Roskill, *Admiral of the Fleet*, 117.

16. Jellicoe to Beatty, March 31, 1915 (printed in Jellicoe, *Jellicoe Papers*, 1: 155).

17. Jellicoe's postwar recollections are cited in Bacon, *Life of John Rushworth*, 162; and Brooks, *Battle of Jutland*, 79.

18. Roskill, *Admiral of the Fleet*, 191–92 (for the citation); Brooks, *Battle of Jutland*, 453–55 (for German and British explosive); and chapter 10, note 37, and chapter 13, note 11, for comparative fuse/dud issues. For European tensions over armaments, see Eric Dorn Brose, "Arms Race prior to 1914, Armament Policy," *1914–1918-online: International Encyclopedia of the First World War*, ed. Ute Daniel, Peter Gatrell, Oliver Janz, Heather Jones, Jennifer Keene, Alan Kramer, and Bill Nasson (Berlin: Freie Universität Berlin, 2014).

19. Dreyer, *Sea Heritage*, 58, 63.

20. For the Admiralty's 1914–15 tests and Jellicoe's doubts, see Brooks, *Battle of Jutland*, 76–80. For Jellicoe's continuing concern about British AP shells in 1914–15, also see Bacon, *Life of John Rushworth*, 162: the C-in-C recalled after the war that they "did not achieve the results they ought to have . . . in the *various actions* in which the shell naturally struck at oblique impact" (emphasis mine). "Various actions" would obviously include Dogger Bank and not just Jutland in 1916. Also see Marder, *Dreadnought to Scapa Flow*, 3: 171, who notes that British "shell was under suspicion after the Dogger Bank action, but nothing was done." Furthermore, Barnett, *Swordbearers*, 184, writes that problems of this sort were "of course known to Jellicoe before Jutland [in 1916]," and that he therefore went into combat at Jutland aware of these deficiencies, whereas Beatty did not. Beatty came to realize, however, that defective shells had been a problem at *both* Dogger Bank and Jutland. See his letter to Ethel, March 1917 (printed in Chalmers, *Life and Letters*, 290): "If we had had decent projectiles on the 24th January [1915], we should certainly have destroyed three of the enemy's ships instead of only *one*." On another point, that Jellicoe opted not to press during the war for a new shell did not mean, as argued by Sumida, "Matter of Timing," 115, that he leaned heavily toward fighting at shorter ranges—he just remained tempted—only that wartime conditions, as I argue above, precluded such a change. Also see below, note 24.

21. Chatfield, *Navy and Defence*, 142.

22. Young, *With the Battle Cruisers*, 222–23, 233.

23. For the citations, see Churchill to Jellicoe, January 26, 1915 (printed in Jellicoe, *Jellicoe Papers*, 1: 131); Churchill memo of January 27, 1915 (printed in Churchill, *World Crisis*, 352); Fisher to Beatty, February 12, 1915 (printed in Fisher, *Fear God*, 3: 157); Beatty to Jellicoe, (n.d., late January 1915) (printed in Jellicoe, *Jellicoe Papers*, 1: 131). For Beatty, also see Sumida, "Matter of Timing," 119; and Brooks, *Battle of Jutland*, 81–82.

24. See Brooks, *Battle of Jutland*, 74–76; and Norman Friedman, *Naval Firepower: Battleship Guns and Gunnery in the Dreadnought Era* (Annapolis, MD: Naval Institute Press, 2008), 87, 90–94, 96–97. The battle orders of late 1915 are printed in Schleihauf, *Jutland*, 271–75. Also see Dreyer, captain of HMS *Orion* (and later HMS *Iron Duke*), *Sea Heritage*,

90–91, who writes about long-range (14,000–16,000 yards) firing practice in October and December 1914. Friedman dates a change in emphasis to rapid fire descending from 10,000 yards from late 1914, a trend that was reinforced by Beatty's poor shooting at Dogger Bank in January 1915 (*Naval Firepower*, 93, 97) but never incorporated into battle orders. Sumida, "Matter of Timing," 111–15, also shows clearly that Jellicoe remained tempted by shorter-range fighting, an inclination that the reality of the North Sea's visibility issues strengthened. He remained somewhat torn, in other words; but it is doubtful, as Sumida argues elsewhere ("Expectation, Adaptation and Resignation: British Battle Fleet Tactical Planning, August 1914–April 1916," *Naval War College Review* 60, no. 3 [Summer 2007]: 117), that the C-in-C switched, even if only temporarily in early 1915, to plans for dispatching the Germans at shorter ranges, a statement that the evidence Sumida presents (pp. 113–16) sooner contradicts than supports.

25. Churchill to Beatty, November 11, 1924 (cited in Roskill, *Admiral of the Fleet*, 336 [405n63]).

26. Citations from Chatfield's letter to a friend (n.d., right after the Battle of the Dogger Bank) (printed in Thompson, *Imperial War Museum Book*, 101–2).

27. Grove, "Autobiography of Chief Gunner," 389; Lambert, "'Our Bloody Ships,'" 55; and Bennett, *Naval Battles*, 164, 166. Also see Norman Friedman, *Naval Weapons of World War One: Guns, Torpedoes, Mines and ASW Weapons of All Nations* (Barnsley, UK: Seaforth Publishing, 2011), 28; Mike Farquharson-Roberts, *A History of the Royal Navy in World War I* (London: I. B. Tauris, 2014), 97–99; and other works cited in Chapter 5, note 2.

28. Thompson, *Imperial War Museum Book*, 101.

29. Fisher to Beatty, January 31, 1915 (printed in Fisher, *Fear God*, 3: 150).

30. Thompson, *Imperial War Museum Book*, 102. I disagree with Thompson, however, that Chatfield was responsible for spreading these "highly dangerous ways" throughout the BCF.

31. This passage, including the dialogue, follows Grant's memoir, printed in Grove, "Autobiography of Chief Gunner," 383–90, and Grove's commentary, 379–83. Also see Campbell, *Warship Special 1*, 30.

32. For faulty shell testing, see Hough, *Great War at Sea*, 275–76. For the citation, see Gordon, *Rules of the Game*, 46. For comparative disadvantages of British propellant, see Brooks, *Battle of Jutland*, 460–62.

33. Chatfield, *Navy and Defence*, 154.

34. For Fisher's leaning toward Jellicoe after Dogger Bank, see the commentary and correspondence in Churchill, *World Crisis*, 347–59; for Fisher and the Baltic, see Marder, *Dreadnought to Scapa Flow*, 2: 191–98; and for the building strains between the two men, see Massie, *Castles of Steel*, 481–83.

35. For the citations in this paragraph and the rest of this passage, see the excellent discussions in Marder, *Dreadnought to Scapa Flow*, 2: 282–86; and Massie, *Castles of Steel*, 484–91.

36. Marder, *Dreadnought to Scapa Flow*, 2: 302.

CHAPTER 7. GERMAN EYES NORTH

1. The following passage (describing German seamen visiting the damaged ships) is based on the Richard Stumpf Diary, January 24–25, 1915 (printed in Horn, *Private War of Seaman Stumpf,* 59–63).

2. Citation in Horn, *Private War of Seaman Stumpf,* 62. Stumpf's diary entries from late 1914 through mid-1916 contain valuable documentation on the progressively sagging morale of German sailors, even patriotic men like Stumpf.

3. The "laughable" comment was brought to the attention of *Lion*'s captain, Ernle Chatfield, in August 1916 by a Swedish naval officer who had earlier been stationed in Berlin and heard what German officers were saying, but the shell problem, and German awareness of it, predated Jutland to the Dogger Bank battle. See Chatfield, *Navy and Defence,* 136–37, 153–55; Groos, *Der Krieg in der Nordsee,* 3: 238–39; and especially the three German postbattle reports (February–March 1915) regarding the superiority of German AP shell over the British cited below in note 14.

4. For the citations and evidence of Hipper's suffering, see Philbin, *Admiral von Hipper,* 101, 123.

5. For the citations, see von Waldeyer-Hartz, *Admiral von Hipper,* 159–60. For Raeder and codes, see chapter 2, note 23, and chapter 4, note 21.

6. Hipper's report (January 27, 1915) and journal entries are cited in Philbin, *Admiral von Hipper,* 113–14, 116–17.

7. Lans' staff chief, Wolfgang Wegener, wrote the document, dated February 1, 1915, which is printed in Herwig, *Wolfgang Wegener's,* 133–44. Also printed in von Tirpitz, *Politische Dokumente,* 209–13.

8. See Trotha to Müller, July 9, 1915 (printed in von Tirpitz, *Politische Dokumente,* 246–47); Tirpitz's letter of March 5, 1915 (printed in von Tirpitz, *My Memoirs,* 301); Hopman's diary entry of January 25, 1915, and Raeder's comments to Admiral Bachmann of February 14, 1915 (printed in Epkenhans, *Albert Hopman,* 552–53, 557–58n94); and Epkenhans, "Imperial Navy," in *Jutland,* ed. Epkenhans et al., 134. As for Raeder's comments about Scheer's lack of aggressiveness (Epkenhans, "Imperial Navy," 133), see my comments below in notes 19 and 25, as well as Chapter 8, notes 8 and 10. For further evidence of timidity among fleet commanders, also see Pohl's letters to his wife of February 24, February 27, and March 13, 1915 (printed in von Pohl, *Aus Aufzeichnungen,* 115, 117–18; and von Waldeyer-Hartz, *Admiral von Hipper,* 170, which also references Scheer's tactically prudential viewpoint at this time point).

9. See Philbin, *Admiral von Hipper,* 70–72.

10. Admiral Hugo von Pohl, who replaced Ingenohl in the first days of February, wrote two months later that "new work, which should have been done before the war, must be constantly undertaken" (Pohl to Bachmann, April 7, 1915 [printed in Groos, *Der Krieg in*

der Nordsee, 4: 59]). For safety changes made, also see Scheer, *Deutschlands Hochseeflotte*, 134; Dreyer, *Sea Heritage*, 205; and Herwig, *"Luxury" Fleet*, 153. The citation is Massie, *Castles of Steel*, 423.

11. Bennett, *Naval Battles*, 164, cites this report (n.d.), allegedly from Ingenohl or perhaps "his advisers," but the document probably dates from February 1915 when Pohl asked Hipper and others to report on these matters. For the German double asbestos flaps and other changes of this sort, see a German post-Jutland report (n.d.) summarized in Jellicoe, *Jellicoe Papers*, 1: 267–268; and Schleihauf, *Jutland*, 143n23.

12. Groos, *Der Krieg in der Nordsee*, 5: 235n1; Massie, *Castles of Steel*, 422–23; and Vincent P. O'Hara, W. David Dickson, and Richard Worth, eds., *To Crown the Waves: The Great Navies of the First World War* (Annapolis, MD: Naval Institute Press, 2013), 107.

13. Tirpitz to Trotha, March 26, 1915 (printed in von Tirpitz, *Politische Dokumente*, 233–35). Also see Tirpitz's postwar comments on p. 208. For German ship construction, see the still useful passage in von Tirpitz, *My Memoirs*, 1: 170–77.

14. For the citations, see Schaumann's report (cited in von Tirpitz, *Politische Dokumente*, 226); and the reports of Boedicker (n.d., early February 1915) and Hopman (n.d., early February 1915) (also printed in von Tirpitz, *Politische Dokumente*, 215, 218)—emphasis mine. For battlecruiser hits at Dogger Bank, see Roskill, *Admiral of the Fleet*, 118–19 (who draws mainly on Campbell, *Warship Special 1*).

15. For the views of Scheer's second-in-command, Rear Admiral Schaumann, see von Waldeyer-Hartz, *Admiral von Hipper*, 169–71; and von Tirpitz, *Politische Dokumente*, 226. In March, in fact, the Royal Navy bombarded Gallipoli with a flotilla of sixteen allied ships that included two battlecruisers and one of the newest dreadnoughts, HMS *Queen Elizabeth*.

16. For the citation, also from Schaumann's pen (n.d., March–April 1915), see von Tirpitz, *Politische Dokumente*, 226.

17. Lans circular, February 1, 1915 (cited in Herwig, *Wolfgang Wegener's*, 135.) For the issue of codes, also see chapter 2, note 23, and chapter 4, note 21.

18. Zenker's memorandum of February 1, 1915 is cited in Groos, *Der Krieg in der Nordsee*, 3: 243. Also see Bennett, *Naval Battles*, 165, 167. For Levetzow and Raeder, respectively, see Philbin, *Admiral von Hipper*, 101–3.

19. Citations in Müller Diary, February 1, 1915 (printed in Görlitz, *Regierte Der Kaiser*, 87); and Müller to Trotha, July 19, 1915 (printed in von Tirpitz, *Politische Dokumente*, 255). With regard to an ostensible plot to promote Scheer, see Eckermann to Tirpitz (or Hopman), January 22, 1915, and Hopman's notation of January 27 about his conversation a day earlier with Müller (printed in von Tirpitz, *Politische Dokumente*, 202–3, 200–201, respectively; and Epkenhans, "Imperial Navy," in *Jutland*, ed. Epkenhans et al., 133). A protégé of Tirpitz, Eckermann made his case for Scheer to Tirpitz, asking (1) that he make use of it at headquarters in Charleville, hence Hopman's visit to Müller, and (2) that Scheer, who

agreed with this (*darüber bin ich mit Scheer einig*), have him as chief of 3rd Squadron. Although Müller did not believe at this point that a replacement was warranted, he agreed that should one become necessary, only Scheer was suitable (*nur Vizeadmiral Scheer als Nachfolger in Betract kommen könne*). The cabinet chief also said, however, that a "certain caution" was what the fleet needed at the moment, and that anyone who acted "too offensively" would be "dubious under the present circumstances." He was hinting strongly, in other words, that Scheer, whom Eckermann praised in glowing terms as energetic, with backbone, and strong, was not really the man Germany needed. For the effect being passed over may have had on Scheer, see below, note 25. As for Eckermann's wishes, his illness and early retirement in July, and death on January 13, 1916, two weeks before Scheer became C-in-C, ended any hopes of taking over 3rd Squadron.

20. Another officer in the car, Captain Mann, overheard the exchange: Mann notation of February 4, 1915 (cited in von Tirpitz, *Politische Dokumente*, 207–8).

21. Pohl notation of February 4, 1915 (printed in von Pohl, *Aus Aufzeichnungen*, 106).

22. For the exchange, see Müller Diary, February 5, 1915 (printed in Görlitz, *Regierte Der Kaiser*, 88).

23. Görlitz, *Regierte Der Kaiser*, 88.

24. See the argumentation in Diana Preston, *Lusitania: An Epic Tragedy* (New York: Berkley Books, 2002), 397–99; and especially Larson, *Dead Wake*, passim.

25. For the citations in this paragraph, see Pohl to his wife, February 5, 24, 27, and March 8, 1915 (printed in von Pohl, *Aus Aufzeichnungen*, 107, 115, 117); and Bachmann's diary entry of February 14, 1915 (cited in Epkenhans, *Albert Hopman*, 557n94). As for Scheer, Epkenhans, "Imperial Navy," in *Jutland*, ed. Epkenhans et al., 124–26, provides ample evidence that in the weeks after Dogger Bank, Scheer had genuinely veered away from wanting action, taking a swipe at Tirpitz by asking Admiralty Staff Chief Bachmann if "other powers are at work that, in order to lift the navy's prestige, would push the navy into a battle at any cost, that is, even at the cost of annihilation?" However, that his own reputation as a man favoring action had undoubtedly cost him the prize promotion he desired to culminate his career (see note 19) must have factored into such statements and sentiments; in other words, Scheer's temperance, while genuine, was a complex one affected by personal factors other than Dogger Bank. Moreover, it is also probable that Scheer was torn psychically, his action-friendly urges tamped down by anxiety—but only for now. Already that March, for instance, he supported the logic behind the aggressive proposals of 3rd Squadron Number One Carl Schaumann before Pohl but urged Schaumann not to undermine the C-in-C's authority by pushing too hard (see von Waldeyer-Hartz, *Admiral von Hipper*, 169–70). That Scheer continued to shy away from openly pressing for action throughout 1915, therefore, seems to indicate that playing the lamb and not the lion was a wise tactic if he were ever to accede to the top position, overcome inner worries, and appease other-inner aggressive impulses. Also see above, notes 8 and 19, and chapter 8, notes 8 and 10.

26. On this point, see Pohl's letters to his wife, February 24, March 2, and March 24, 1915 (printed in von Pohl, *Aus Aufzeichnungen*, 115–16, 120); and Pohl's Chief of Staff, William Michaelis, to Zenker, January 16, 1916 (cited in Groos, *Der Krieg in der Nordsee*, 4: 393).

27. For the citations in this paragraph, see Pohl to his wife, March 3, 1915 (printed in von Pohl, *Aus Aufzeichnungen*, 116); Pohl to Müller, March 14, 1915 (cited in Groos, *Der Krieg in der Nordsee*, 4: 60); Michaelis to Zenker, March 21, 1915 (cited/printed in von Tirpitz, *Politische Dokumente*, 225, 231); and the Hopman Diary, March 24, 1915 (printed in Epkenhans, *Albert Hopman*, 584).

28. Pohl's report of March 23, 1915 (cited in Groos, *Der Krieg in der Nordsee*, 4: 62); and the Kaiser's outburst of March 27, 1915 (cited in Epkenhans, *Albert Hopman*, 584n165, 586).

29. Citations in the paragraph above from the Bachmann Diary, March 30, 1915 (printed in Granier, *Die Deutsche Seekriegsleitung*, 2: 62–63); and here from the Hopman Diary, March 30, 1915 (printed in Epkenhans, *Albert Hopman*, 589). Also see Pohl's derogation of German intelligence, March 23, 1915 (cited in chapter 2, note 5).

30. Pohl's orders are cited in Groos, *Der Krieg in der Nordsee*, 4: 93. For British siege intentions, see von Waldeyer-Hartz, *Admiral von Hipper*, 168; and Groos, *Der Krieg in der Nordsee*, 4: 88. Fisher's letters are cited in Sumida, "Expectation," 112; Bachmann in Epkenhans, "Imperial Navy," in *Jutland*, ed. Epkenhans et al., 125.

31. For this sortie, see Groos, *Der Krieg in der Nordsee*, 4: 92–98; and von Waldeyer-Hartz, *Admiral von Hipper*, 169.

32. Richard Stumpf Diary, April 23, 1915 (printed in Horn, *Private War of Seaman Stumpf*, 87).

33. See Trotha to Tirpitz, March 31 and April 24, 1915 (printed in von Tirpitz, *Politische Dokumente*, 237–38, 242).

34. For the position of the Grand Fleet, see Jellicoe, *Grand Fleet*, 213–14; and especially Groos, *Der Krieg in der Nordsee*, 4: chart 4.

35. Young, *With the Battle Cruisers*, 245.

36. Pohl to his wife, April 21, 1915 (printed in von Pohl, *Aus Aufzeichnungen*, 124–25).

37. Corbett, *Naval Operations*, 3: 325. For a good discussion and documentation of the operations of the 10th Cruiser Squadron, see Thompson, *Imperial War Museum Book*, 140–90.

38. See Groos, *Der Krieg in der Nordsee*, 4: charts 6–7.

39. Cited in Groos, *Der Krieg in der Nordsee*, 4: 217. Also see Pohl's comments in Chapter 2, note 5.

40. Groos' commentary, Groos, *Der Krieg in der Nordsee*, 4: 216.

41. For the disagreements between Pohl and Prince Heinrich as well as the latter's motivations, see Groos, *Der Krieg in der Nordsee*, 4: 224–29; and the Hopman Diary, July 26, 1915 (printed in Epkenhans, *Albert Hopman*, 659–60).

42. For the citation, see Michaelis to Zenker, January 13, 1916, cited in Groos, *Der Krieg in der Nordsee*, 4: 393. Also see Pohl to Müller, August 3, 1915, printed in Görlitz, *Regierte der Kaiser*, 119–120.

43. See the Bachmann Diary, July 12, 1915, printed in Granier, *Die Deutsche Seekriegsleitung*, 2: 78; and Trotha to Müller, July 9, 915, printed in von Tirpitz, *Politische Dokumente*, 246–47.

44. See Groos, *Der Krieg in der Nordsee* , 4: 214–16, 393.

45. Wegener's three treatises of June, July, and August 1915 are printed in Herwig, *Wolfgang Wegener's*, 145–98. Citations here are from the second piece, 167, and the third, 195, 197–98.

46. See Herwig's discussion in *Wolfgang Wegener's*, xxviii–xxxi; Groos, *Der Krieg in der Nordsee*, 4: 392–93; and especially Carl-Axel Gemzell, *Organization, Conflict, and Innovation: A Study of German Naval Strategic Planning, 1888–1940* (Lund, Germany: Esselte Studium, 1973), 222–25.

47. Citations from Karl von Restorff, commanding one of the destroyer flotillas, to Müller, November 6, 1915 (printed in Groos, *Der Krieg in der Nordsee*, 4: 350).

48. For the October 23/24 mission, see Groos, *Der Krieg in der Nordsee*, 4: 224–28, 339–47. For the actual and intended course of this sortie, see 4: chart 15.

49. Herwig, *Wolfgang Wegener's*, xxviii, xxx. Also see Groos, *Der Krieg in der Nordsee*, 4: 392.

50. Restorff to Müller, November 6, 1915 (printed in Groos, *Der Krieg in der Nordsee*, 4: 350).

51. For the details, see Groos, *Der Krieg in der Nordsee*, 4: 348–51.

52. Müller Diary, October 25, 1915 (printed in Görlitz, *Regierte Der Kaiser*, 138).

53. For the meeting, see Levetzow to Holtzendorff, January 7, 1916 (printed in Granier, *Magnus von Levetzow*, 212–15). Although obviously one-sided, Levetzow's description of the meeting is so lengthy and specific that an objective assessment of what transpired can be drawn from his details.

54. Jellicoe to Beatty, April 26, 1915 (printed in Jellicoe, *Jellicoe Papers*, 1: 157).

55. Müller described the illness in a postscript to his diary entry of January 9, 1916 (printed in Görlitz, *Regierte Der Kaiser*, 146). Also see Pohl to his wife, January 9, 1916 (printed in von Pohl, *Aus Aufzeichnungen*, 150), where he claimed he had *not* been suffering before the incident, which seems doubtful. That the collapse probably resulted from the meeting, see Moritz von Egidy, captain of *Seydlitz*, to Levetzow, August 1, 1916 (cited in Granier, *Magnus von Levetzow*, 15).

56. For the citations, see von Weizsäcker, *Erinnerungen*, 32–33; von Waldeyer-Hartz, *Admiral von Hipper*, 178; and Granier, *Magnus von Levetzow*, 14–15.

57. Raeder, *Mein Leben*, 1: 104.

CHAPTER 8. GIVE ME COMBAT

1. The BCF squadrons had begun to take somewhat more regular target practice in August and September at Scapa Flow and in Moray Firth for the first time in October. See Chalmers, *Life and Letters*, 211; Chatfield, *Navy and Defence*, 138; and especially Jellicoe, *Grand Fleet*, 243, 247, 253, 259. For the "bracket" method of fire, see Marder, *Dreadnought*

to Scapa Flow, 3: 166n2. For the citation, see the diary of Stephen King-Hall, n.d. (March 1916) (printed in L. King-Hall, *Sea Saga*, 436–37).

2. For the citations, see Beatty to Jellicoe, November 21, 1915, and Jellicoe to Beatty, November 18 and 21, and December 22, 1915 (printed in Jellicoe, *Jellicoe Papers*, 1: 187–90—emphasis in original); Beatty to Jellicoe, December 15, 1915 (cited in Lambert, "'Our Bloody Ships,'" 42—emphasis mine); and Chatfield, *Navy and Defence*, 158–59). Also see Jellicoe, *Grand Fleet*, 263–63; Sumida, "Matter of Timing," 111–15; and Brooks, *Battle of Jutland*, 82–83. Also see Chapter 6, notes 20 and 24 for exaggerations in Sumida's argument.

3. For the views of Jellicoe and other officers on the question of the best station for the 5th BS, see the fine discussion in Gordon, *Rules of the Game*, 42–49. Also see Jellicoe to Jackson, March 5 and 9, 1916 (printed in Jellicoe, *Jellicoe Papers*, 225–26, 227); and recollections cited in Marder, *Dreadnought to Scapa Flow*, 3: 39n3.

4. For the citations, see Jackson to Jellicoe, September 2, 1915, Balfour to Jellicoe, January 17, 1916, and Jellicoe to Balfour, January 25, 1916 (printed in Jellicoe, *Jellicoe Papers*, 184, 197, 202–3); and Jellicoe to Beatty, April 11, 1916 (printed in Marder, *Dreadnought to Scapa Flow*, 2: 422–23).

5. Scheer, *Deutschlands Hochseeflotte*, 147–48.

6. Citations, respectively, in Bogislaw von Selchow, *Hundert Tage aus meinem Leben* (Leipzig: K. F. Koehler, 1936), 262; Raeder, *Mein Leben*, 1: 105; and the first postbattle notation of Scheer's flag lieutenant, Ernst von Weizsäcker, June 6, 1916 (printed in Granier, "Eindrücke von der Skagerrakschlacht," 21). Selchow came into contact with Levetzow while serving in the Admiralty Staff in 1917–18.

7. von Waldeyer-Hartz, *Admiral von Hipper*, 169–70; and von Tirpitz, *Politische Dokumente*, 226.

8. For the Levetzow quotes on Wegener's treatises, see Levetzow to the ex-Kaiser, October 12, 1930 (printed in Herwig, *Wolfgang Wegener's*, xl; and Gemzell, *Organization*, 225). Levetzow refers to the 1916 meeting in his 1930 letter, as well as its allegedly punitive purpose, but failed to appreciate Scheer's ulterior motive of dampening friction in the naval corps. For this motive, see Forstmeier, "Zum Bild der Persönlichkeit," 77–78. For the citations on Levetzow's fiery nature, see von Selchow, *Hundert Tage*, 262. Also see Raeder, *Mein Leben*, 1: 105. That Scheer had been passed over for C-in-C in 1915, see Epkenhans, "Imperial Navy," in *Jutland*, ed. Epkenhans et al., 133. While Scheer's views, like those of many officers, were subdued by the Dogger Bank disaster, they were also tempered by being passed over as C-in-C because he was perceived as too aggressive. It is my argument that he downplayed his aggressive ideas, which he quickly revived, for ambitious political reasons. Also see chapter 7, notes 8, 19, and 25.

9. See Gemzell, *Organization*, 225–27, 234–46; and Brose, *Death at Sea*, 75–78, 228–29. Also see Chapter 6, note 11. For Trotha's imperialism and colonialism, see in particular Trotha to Tirpitz, April 24, 1915 (printed in von Tirpitz, *Politische Dokumente*, 241–42).

For Tirpitz's sudden and surprising advocacy of "cruiser warfare in the Atlantic" to force the British to disperse their ships, see Tirpitz to Pohl and Müller, January 25, 1915 (printed in *Politische Dokumente*, 196–98). It can be safely assumed that Tirpitz, always in close contact with Trotha, got the idea from him—in fact, even before the war he had been leaning toward Trotha's idea (Brose, *Death at Sea*, 77).

10. Scheer's operational plans of February 1916, quoted here and in the preceding paragraph, are cited in Granier, *Die Deutsche Seekriegsleitung*, 2: 81–85; and Groos, *Der Krieg in der Nordsee*, 5: 27–29. For evidence that Scheer was not loathe to engage the Grand Fleet itself, and never considered this prospect a likely disaster, see that he asserted vehemently in letters to Vice Admiral Carl Hollweg on May 19, 1919 (for most of the citations), and January 15, 1920 (printed at length from German archives in Staff, *Skagerrak*, 146–48). For the splendid effectiveness citation, see Scheer's letter to Holloway Frost, n.d. (1920s) (printed in Frost, *Battle of Jutland*, 328). Also see chapter 11, note 75 on Scheer at Jutland. For Falkenhayn supporting the use of U-boats to aid his Verdun offensive, see Holger H. Herwig, *The First World War: Germany and Austria-Hungary 1914–1918* (London: Arnold, 1997), 181–82; and Eric Dorn Brose, *A History of the Great War: World War One and the International Crisis of the Early Twentieth Century* (New York: Oxford University Press, 2009), 201–3.

11. See Müller's diary entries for January 29 (for the citation in the paragraph above), January 30, and February 3, 4, 5, and 23, 1916 (for this citation) (printed in Görlitz, *Regierte Der Kaiser*, 150–53, 158). Also see Groos, *Der Krieg in der Nordsee*, 4: 348–51.

12. William's remarks are printed in von Tirpitz, *Politische Dokumente*, 279. I have changed the printed statement from the impersonal third person to the first person he would have used, not the "royal we."

13. Scheer to his friend, Vice Admiral Daehnhardt, March 12, 1916 (printed in Granier, *Die Deutsche Seekriegsleitung*, 2: 89).

14. Scheer, *Deutschlands Hochseeflotte*, 169, for the citation; and Brose, *Kaiser's Army*, 181–82, 231–32, for the Kaiser as Europe went to war in 1914 and then giving in to Hindenburg and Ludendorff in 1916.

15. Citations in Röhl, *Wilhelm II*, 1,151; and the Müller Diary, September 12, 1915 (printed in Görlitz, *Regierte Der Kaiser*, 128–29). Müller's and Bethmann's views were identical. For the political wrangling in Germany over air attacks, also see Admiral Bachmann's diary entry for August 23, 1915 (printed in Granier, *Die Deutsche Seekriegsleitung*, 2: 243; and Groos, *Der Krieg in der Nordsee*, 4: 261–63, 296).

16. Citations in the Müller Diary, February 23, and January 15, 1916, respectively (printed in Görlitz, *Die Der Regierte der Kaiser*, 158, 147). Also see Scheer to Daehnhardt, March 12, 1916 (printed in Granier, *Deutsche Seekriegsleitung*, 2: 89; and Röhl, *Wilhelm II*, 1,152).

17. For one such pub brawl in Rosyth, see the letter of 1st Lieutenant Douglas King-Harman to his mother, July 1915 (printed in Thompson, *Imperial War Museum Book*, 288–89).

18. See the pre-Jutland diary entries (1915–16) of Stephen King-Hall of 2nd LCS, printed in L. King-Hall, *Sea Saga*, 412–49. Also see his *My Naval Life: 1906–1929* (London: Faber and Faber, 1951), 106.

19. For the social lives of BCF officers that spring, see Gordon, *Rules of the Game*, 30–33, 52–54, 61–63.

20. For the entire British side of this operation underway to the Bight, see Jellicoe, *Grand Fleet*, 280–83; Chalmers, *Life and Letters*, 212–14; Marder, *Dreadnought to Scapa Flow*, 2: 420–22; and especially Corbett, *Naval Operations*, 3: 290–96. For the mission Scheer was planning, the initial German naval reaction to the British mission, as well as subsequent developments that weekend on the German side, see Groos, *Der Krieg in der Nordsee*, 5: 73–100; and von Waldeyer-Hartz, *Admiral von Hipper*, 189–91.

21. William S. Chalmers, Beatty's junior navigation officer, was present when his admiral made these remarks (Chalmers, *Life and Letters*, 214).

22. Chalmers, *Life and Letters*, 214.

23. For the exchange "toward the end of March," see von Waldeyer-Hartz, *Admiral von Hipper*, 192–93.

24. Citations in Philbin, *Admiral von Hipper*, 123–24; and Raeder, *Mein Leben*, 1: 105. For Levetzow's campaign to have Hipper removed from command in early 1915, see Philbin, *Admiral von Hipper*, 101–3.

25. See Beatty to Jellicoe, April 7, 1916 (printed in Jellicoe, *Jellicoe Papers*, 1: 231–32—emphasis in original); and Jellicoe to Beatty, April 11, 1916, and Beatty to Jellicoe, April 14, 1916 (printed in Beatty, *Beatty Papers*, 1: 301–6).

26. For a detailed description of the April 2, 1916, raid, see "First Blitz—Zeppelins L14 and L20 Bomb Edinburgh and Leith in 1916," *Newbattle at War* blog, March 24, 2013, newbattleatwar.wordpress.com/2013/03/24. Also see Groos, *Der Krieg in der Nordsee*, 5: 108–9, who carefully avoids, however, any mention of harm to civilians.

27. For the raids, see Groos, *Der Krieg in der Nordsee*, 5: 101–12. For the citation, see Jellicoe to Beatty, April 11, 1916 (printed in Marder, *Dreadnought to Scapa Flow*, 2: 423).

28. For the Lowestoft Raid, see Beesly, *Room 40*, 148 (for the citation), 149, 152; Jellicoe, *Grand Fleet*, 286–89; Groos, *Der Krieg in der Nordsee*, 5: 137; Marder, *Dreadnought to Scapa Flow*, 2: 424–27; and Massie, *Castles of Steel*, 558–59. For still more distrust of the Scouting Forces around Scheer because of this raid, see the second postbattle notation of Scheer's flag lieutenant (Weizsäcker), June 11, 1916 (printed in Granier, "Eindrücke von der Skagerrakschlacht," 22). Brooks, *Battle of Jutland*, 133–34, notes correctly that Scheer had missed a good chance to destroy Beatty, but incorrectly attributes the decision to retreat to Scheer—Boedicker had presented him, on the contrary, with a fait accompli, hence the growing mistrust of 1st SG's aggressiveness.

That Room 40 did not know about the DK ruse as early as December 1914, as one top operative, William Clarke, claimed in 1922/1924, see Hines, "Sins of Omission," 1,129n72.

It also seems evident that the sixteen months between Scarborough and Lowestoft brought no breakthrough either, for Room 40 was clearly caught off guard during the raid and "it was not until later that decodes confirmed with certainty that the [High Seas Fleet] was actually at sea" (Beesly, *Room 40*, 148). Moreover, Brooks and David Ramsay (see Brooks, *Battle of Jutland*, 166n12) conducted a thorough search of all Room 40 archival logs and found no mention at all of British intelligence knowing about the DK ruse. Thus, nothing about it had gone up the chain of command to the Operations Division (OD) and COS. But Clarke's account mentioned the Lowestoft Raid (along with Scarborough) as a precedent for Room 40 knowing about Scheer's call sign switch. Beesly (*Room 40*, 152), drawing on Clarke, claims that Room 40 knew by late May that the DK ruse was German "standard procedure," which, while probably an exaggeration, points strongly to some sort of awareness. Clarke himself claimed that everyone in Room 40 knew about it prior to Jutland, which, while also perhaps a stretch, cannot be dismissed and discarded so easily. Because so much conjecture and speculation surrounds this particular controversy in the literature on the lead-up to the Battle of Jutland (e.g., Hines, "Sins of Omission," 1,130n75), permit me to conjecture that Room 40 operatives had at least a hunch after Lowestoft, and were in the process of pinning things down, but were reluctant to voice strong hunches about the ruse to Jackson five weeks later, especially given his haughty, condescending, and overbearing nature (for Jackson's unlikeability, see Brooks, *Battle of Jutland*, 165–66, 166n15). Also see Beesly, *Room 40*, 155: Jackson "was obviously not the sort of senior officer to whom one offered gratuitous advice." I find it incredible, in other words, that Clarke and others completely fabricated their claims; but given the Admiralty's costly assumption that Scheer remained in port on May 31, the overall unsatisfying outcome of the battle, and then the escalating "Jutland Controversy" of the 1920s, they may have exaggerated them. By not expressing their hunch-like opinions to the off-putting Jackson on "the Great Day," however, Clarke and others share the blame for what happened on the early afternoon of May 31, 1916. The suggestion of Hines ("Sins of Omission," 1,130n75) that they were involved in something akin to a cover-up may therefore be close to the mark: what seemed like deserving payback treatment to the Director of the Operations Division (DOD) at the time perhaps took on a more significant, tragic, and conceal-or-distort-worthy dimension after Jutland.

29. Cited in Marder, *Dreadnought to Scapa Flow*, 2: 433. For the effect and five-week aftermath of the Lowestoft Raid, see Marder, *Dreadnought to Scapa Flow*, 2: 427–35; Corbett, *Naval Operations*, 3: 309–20; Gordon, *Rules of the Game*, 48–51; and Frost, *Battle of Jutland*, 81–94.

30. Jellicoe to the Admiralty, May 10, 1916 (cited in Marder, *Dreadnought to Scapa Flow*, 2: 428). For his earlier opposition to fighting such a battle, see Jellicoe to Jackson, April 12, 1916 (printed in Jellicoe, *Jellicoe Papers*, 1: 232–33). For a good description of the operation, see Frost, *Battle of Jutland*, 81–93.

31. Citations from Beatty to Jellicoe, May 7, 1916, and Beatty to Ethel, May 7, 1916—emphasis in original (printed in Beatty, *Beatty Papers*, 1: 307–9).

32. Cited in Roskill, *Admiral of the Fleet*, 184. For historical criticism of Jellicoe's decision, see Frost, *Battle of Jutland*, 90–92.

CHAPTER 9. TO THE FISHER BANKS THITHER SAIL

1. For Jellicoe's opposition that spring to the Admiralty's "more active policy," see Jellicoe to Beatty, April 11, 1916 (printed in Marder, *Dreadnought to Scapa Flow*, 2: 422–23); and Jellicoe to Jackson, April 12, 1916 (printed in Jellicoe, *Jellicoe Papers*, 1: 232–34).

2. For Beatty's resumption of desiring to attack into the Bight, see Beatty to Jellicoe, May 18, 1916 (printed in Marder, *Dreadnought to Scapa Flow*, 2: 429–30).

3. Corbett, *Naval Operations*, 3: 320–21.

4. Hood's remarks were made at a gunnery conference at Rosyth two weeks earlier, cited in Marder, *Dreadnought to Scapa Flow*, 3: 39n3.

5. Jellicoe to Jackson, March 5, 1916 (printed in Jellicoe, *Jellicoe Papers*, 1: 225). Also see Roskill, *Admiral of the Fleet*, 184.

6. See Massie, *Castles of Steel*, 569–74.

7. Gordon, *Rules of the Game*, 121–22, 409. For details of the fleet movements and dispositions on May 4–5, see Frost, *Battle of Jutland*, 81–93; and Groos, *Der Krieg in der Nordsee*, 5: 159–74.

8. Corbett, *Naval Operations*, 3: 322.

9. Trotha's letter to Müller of mid-May is quoted indirectly in the Müller Diary, May 21, 1916 (printed in Görlitz, *Regierte Der Kaiser*, 181).

10. Citations in Herwig, *"Luxury" Fleet*, 175, 177.

11. Herwig, *"Luxury" Fleet*, 162–63.

12. Groos, *Der Krieg in der Nordsee*, 5: 189. Groos (5: 189–90, 203–8) is the best source for German planning in May 1916. Also see Frost, *Battle of Jutland*, 94–98; and chapter 2, note 5.

13. That Trotha visited Raeder shortly before the decision fell for the Skagerrak mission to learn his opinion, and for Raeder's emphatic response approving this operation, see Raeder, *Mein Leben*, 1: 111. For the plan to draw out the British and reports of the Royal Navy's reaction to the Lowestoft Raid, see Scheer's postbattle report to the Kaiser, July 4, 1916 (printed in Werner Rahn, "The Battle of Jutland from the German Perspective," in *Jutland*, ed. Epkenhans et al., 201—emphasis in original); and the Richard Stumpf Diary, June 2, 1916 (printed in Horn, *Private War of Seaman Stumpf*, 196), who recalls the comments of his captain on May 31, 1916, comments that would have come from top-down briefings ("heavy concentration of shipping," "many warships have been sighted in that area," "wireless messages," and "give them a little tickle"). For Levetzow's pressure to go out regardless of air reconnaissance, see the first postbattle notation of

Scheer's flag lieutenant (Weizsäcker), June 6, 1916 (printed in Granier, "Eindrücke von der Skagerrakschlacht," 20).

14. Hipper may or may not have been in attendance, but his "rub" comments on the Sunderland mission as well as eagerness for battle soon are cited in Philbin, *Admiral von Hipper*, 127; and Herwig, *"Luxury" Fleet*, 175, 177.

15. The most important wireless messages for the entire German operation are printed in Groos, *Der Krieg in der Nordsee*, 5: 519ff.

16. Citations (here and the following paragraph) in Scheer, *Deutschlands Hochseeflotte*, 195–96.

17. Gordon, *Rules of the Game*, 121–22, 409.

18. Scheer, *Deutschlands Hochseeflotte*, 198. Also see his postbattle report to the Kaiser, July 4, 1916 (printed in Rahn, "Battle of Jutland," in *Jutland*, ed. Epkenhans et al., 202, 201). The Scouting Groups' cruiser warfare from the late afternoon of May 31 through that night would lure the British; the main German fleet would "cover the [Scouting] Groups during the operation and pick them up on the morning of 1 June" (p. 202), and some hours later, presumably, trap "considerable *portions*" (p. 201) of the British fleet.

19. See Kameke's address to his crew on May 31, 1916, cited in the Richard Stumpf Diary, June 8, 1916 (printed in Horn, *Private War of Seaman Stumpf*, 196).

20. For Room 40 activity in May 1916 described here and in the following paragraph, see the decrypts it sent to the Operations Division (printed in Koerver, *Room 40*, 2: 600–65). Also see Beesly, *Room 40*, 151–55; and Brooks, *Battle of Jutland*, 138–42.

21. The Admiralty's orders cited here are printed in Brooks, *Battle of Jutland*, 142; and Jellicoe, *Jellicoe Papers*, 1: 254–55. Also see Chalmers, *Life and Letters*, 222. That the Admiralty suspected Scheer would continue northward, but did not inform Jellicoe, rather just confused the situation by pointing to the possible "object" of supporting returning Zeppelins, see note 26.

22. Citations in Beesly, *Room 40*, 155; and Brooks, *Battle of Jutland*, 140. Even though one top Room 40 operative, William Clarke, wrote some positive comments about relations with the Operations Division—that were inconsistent with other comments claiming negative relations—it seems clear that Thomas Jackson was all too often insensitive and off-putting (see the discussion in Brooks, *Battle of Jutland*, 166–67). For not entirely convincing attempts to rehabilitate Jackson, Oliver, and Wilson before Jutland, see chapter 8, note 28.

23. Cited in Grove, "Autobiography," 396. For the BCF readying for sea on May 30, including Zeppelin raid rumors, see Gordon, *Rules of the Game*, 52–53, 61–65.

24. This description of the BCF's departure is cited in Gordon, *Rules of the Game*, 64–65.

25. Corbett, *Naval Operations*, 3: 325.

26. According to Brooks, *Battle of Jutland*, 141, the Admiralty had concluded (but did not report to Jellicoe) "that the Germans intended to continue northwards," but had confused this picture with an earlier wire on air operations: "In view of the persistently unfavorable

weather for airships," writes Brooks, "it is a mystery why the first signal supposed that the German object might be to meet returning Zeppelins."

For varying trailing distances in 1915–16, see Corbett, *Naval Operations*, 3: 325; and especially Schleihauf, *Jutland*, 41–42n22. In this controversial "pro-Beatty" assessment of the Battle of Jutland, the Admiralty found fault with Jellicoe for not stationing his fleet closer to Beatty, believing the C-in-C should have been twenty-eight miles back, a distance that guaranteed visual contact with the BCF and 5th BS through the advance guard of armored cruisers and Hood's 3rd BCS. Not surprisingly, in this critique the Admiralty completely omitted any mention of the paltry information they had given their C-in-C. Such an admission was also absent during the meeting at the Admiralty on June 25, 1916, when this matter was discussed with Beatty and Jellicoe (see Patterson, *Jellicoe*, 139). The "control" on the speculation here about how far Jellicoe would have trailed at Jutland if he had known action was imminent is undoubtedly his reaction to Sheer's attempt to execute his Sunderland operation in August 1916: warned by the Admiralty that Scheer had come out again, the C-in-C, "with the lessons of Jutland fresh in mind" (Marder, *Dreadnought to Scapa Flow*, 3: 238), trailed Beatty *by only thirty miles*. Also see Jellicoe to First Sea Lord Jackson, June 6, 1916 (printed in Jellicoe, *Jellicoe Papers*, 1: 273–74): "When next I go out I must keep Beatty nearer so that we can start [the action] with a knowledge of each other's positions. All our difficulties arose from want of this knowledge on May 31st. It was my doing of course, but I have learned a lesson. There are many others." But after becoming First Sea Lord in late 1916, it is doubtful that Jellicoe still felt "it was my doing of course" (see chapter 13).

Moreover, it would have been entirely manageable for Jellicoe to have arranged to get closer to the BCF. If he had departed at his actual speed of 15 knots, but two and a half hours after he was ordered to raise steam at 1728 hours (i.e., leaving circa 2000), and Beatty had left when he did in actuality, the Grand Fleet would easily have been about thirty-five to forty miles from the BCF terminus by 1400 hours on the May 31. This presumes logically that Jellicoe would have kept Beatty's coordinates, a fixed spot, the same, for this is where he wanted him.

If the events of mid- to late afternoon had unfolded in *ceteris paribus* (i.e., other things being equal) fashion, the so-called Run to the North (see chapters 10–11) would have brought Jellicoe and Scheer into combat further south circa 1745—depending, that is, on what trailing distance Jellicoe had chosen, and when he had his ships with steam for 20 knots. Considering the actual time Jellicoe opened fire—*Marlborough* at 1817, *Iron Duke* at 1830—the unfolding battle into the evening would have occurred with perhaps thirty to forty-five minutes more daylight left than in actuality. For the likely result, see chapter 11.

27. See Roskill, *Admiral of the Fleet*, 184. For corroboration, see Plunkett (Drax) to Marder, April 28, 1960 (cited in Marder, *Dreadnought to Scapa Flow*, 3: 115).

28. For the citations, see the first postbattle notation, June 6, 1916, of Scheer's flag lieutenant, Weizsäcker (printed in Granier, "Skagerrakschlacht," 20–21)—for pleasure cruise mood and feeding on the English; Groos, *Der Krieg in der Nordsee*, 5: 520–21—for the scouting reports; Scheer, *Deutschlands Hochseeflotte*, 207—his reaction to the reports; and von Weizsäcker, *Erinnerungen*, 35—for the annoying sliding door.

29. The wireless is printed in Jellicoe, *Jellicoe Papers*, 1: 259. The flawed work of the German cryptanalysts with this wireless makes it difficult to understand how Hans Joachim Koerver (*Room 40*, 2: 657) can conclude that this bureau "worked with considerable success." Also see chapter 2, note 5.

30. Frost, *Battle of Jutland*, 129. His research in the archives showed that the wireless (circa midnight) was delayed, perhaps just a staff foul-up. Interestingly, when it was published decades later by Jellicoe, *Jellicoe Papers*, 1: 259, indicating the allegedly correct sending time of 2254, this was still a half hour after the entire Grand Fleet had put to sea. A risky wireless, therefore, whether dispatched at nearly 2300 at 0000, or at 0122 according to German sources (Groos, *Der Krieg in der Nordsee*, 5: 485). Oddly, neither Marder, *Dreadnought to Scapa Flow*, Gordon, *Rules of the Game*, nor Brooks, *Battle of Jutland* mention this mistake by the C-in-C's staff. None had used Frost or apparently the German version of Groos with its appendix listing British wirelesses—but all had used Jellicoe.

31. For details of the German submarine mission, see Groos, *Der Krieg in der Nordsee*, 5: 189–214; and Frost, *Battle of Jutland*, 93–134.

32. For the crowded bridge, see Gustav Frenssen, *Die Brüder* (Berlin: G. Grote, 1923), chapter 23 (*Gutenberg.spiegel.de/buch/die-bruder-8739/23*). Frenssen spent several days after the battle speaking with Hipper's officers and seamen to be able to portray the fight accurately in his remarkable novel. After the war Raeder praised Frenssen's ability to "accurately depict" not only the battle details but also the "entire atmosphere" on board the ships "as if he had been there experiencing all of this personally" (Raeder, *Mein Leben*, 1: 126).

33. Citations in von Waldeyer-Hartz, *Admiral von Hipper*, 203.

34. Cited in von Waldeyer-Hartz, *Admiral von Hipper*, 203.

35. The record of "the most important" German fleet wirelesses and signals sent since the squadrons left base in the early morning (printed in Groos, *Der Krieg in der Nordsee*, 5: 520–21) shows that Hipper's force, like Scheer's, maintained radio silence, sending messages only optically to the advance screen.

36. In his memoirs (*Mein Leben*, 1: 112), Raeder points to the morning's U-boat reports as the basis for the "definite hope" of action that day, but he and a faction of Doubting Thomases had long held the belief that German codes had been broken. See Raeder, *Mein Leben*, 1: 96–97; and chapter 2, note 23, and chapter 4, note 21.

37. Printed in Groos, *Der Krieg in der Nordsee*, 5: 521.

38. For Scheer's calm demeanor, see von Weizsäcker, *Erinnerungen*, 35; and Adolph von Trotha, "Mit Admiral Scheer auf der Kommandobrücke," in von Mantey, *Auf See Unbesiegt*, 9–11.

39. Marder, *Dreadnought to Scapa Flow*, 3: 45.

40. Oliver's recollection is cited in Marder, *Dreadnought to Scapa Flow*, 3: 45. For the legitimacy of these concerns with Channel security, see Marder, *Dreadnought to Scapa Flow*, 3: 45–46; Brooks, *Battle of Jutland*, 239; and Goldrick, *After Jutland*, 7, 68, as well as portions of later chapters.

41. Beesly, *Room 40*, 153. For the Dover Patrol, see Sir Reginald Bacon, *The Dover Patrol 1915–1917* (New York: George H. Doran Company, 1919).

42. Gordon, *Rules of the Game*, 419–20; Frost, *Battle of Jutland*, 120–21.

43. Beesly, *Room 40*, 155, for the citation. Also see Chapter 8, note 28 for Room 40's suspicions weeks earlier, after Lowestoft, that Scheer was likely using a DK harbor call sign as a ruse.

   The efforts of Andrew Gordon, *Rules of the Game*, 415; Jason Hines, "Sins of Omission," 1,127–30; Nicholas Black, *British Naval Staff*, 158–63; Jim Crossley, *Voices from Jutland: A Centenary Commemoration* (Barnsley, UK: Pen & Sword Maritime, 2016), 71–72; and John Brooks, *Battle of Jutland*, 164–67, to portray the Jackson visit episode as a myth are not entirely convincing. While it is true that Scheer's actual order to transfer his call sign to the Jade guard ship (in *III.Einfahrt*) had not been decoded at the time of Jackson's visit, Room 40 knew from another successfully deciphered wire of 1841 (6:41 p.m.) the previous evening that this ruse may have been set in motion (Beesly, *Room 40*, 152; Schleihauf, *Jutland*, 234). Even though, as Room 40's main direction-finding analyst, Herbert Hope, recalled, "there was nothing to actually show [this]" (Hines, "Sins of Omission," 1,129); nevertheless, if Jackson had asked more questions, or Room 40 operatives had properly ventured their opinions, the telegram to Jellicoe would not have been sent. Hope said as much generally in his "Admiral Hope's Narrative" of 1925 (printed in Koerver, *Room 40*, 1: xi): "I do not think that there was any occasion of anything out of the ordinary happening when we had not some kind of warning. . . . Had we been called upon by the [DOD] to do so, we could have furnished valuable information . . . but the [DOD] was obsessed by ideas of secrecy."

   Furthermore, the controversy over the Admiralty's telegram obscures the more relevant point that the sea lords should have informed Jellicoe early on that they had good reason to expect sea action, which probably would have induced the C-in-C to change his dispositions (i.e., position himself closer to Beatty). On this, see note 26.

44. Cited in Jellicoe, *Jellicoe Papers*, 1: 260; and (with a slightly different wording) Beesly, *Room 40*, 155.

45. The Great Fisher Bank is located on the same longitude (56°40′ N) as Beatty's heading. It is 4°15′ E, while his terminus was twenty-five miles farther east at 5° E. For the actual positions of Beatty and Jellicoe, the latter further from his terminus, see Corbett, *Naval Operations*, 3: 327–28, 347–48, and chart 16; and Marder, *Dreadnought to Scapa Flow*, 3: chart 1.

46. Jellicoe's 1918 remembrance is cited in Marder, *Dreadnought to Scapa Flow*, 3: 43.
47. Corbett, *Naval Operations*, 3: 347n1, and chart 16 concluded Jellicoe was roughly eighty-seven miles from Beatty at 1400. Marder's calculations put it at over seventy-seven miles, *Dreadnought to Scapa Flow*, 3: chart 1; while Brooks, *Battle of Jutland*, 167, plots it at seventy-one miles. The average of the three equals 78.5 miles.
48. Citations in Gordon, *Rules of the Game*, 74.
49. Citations in Gordon, *Rules of the Game*, 76–77.
50. Chalmers, *Lion*'s junior navigation officer, *Life and Letters*, 227. Chatfield, *Navy and Defence*, 140, recalled similarly that Beatty "immediately re-disposed [his force] . . . round to the south-eastward and increased speed to get between the enemy, whatever it was, and his base."
51. Citation in Steel and Hart, *Death in the Grey Wastes*, chapter 2, ebook location 1,035/1,043. For German fuse problems, see chapter 13, note 11. For earlier instances on the German side, see chapter 6, note 11, for the Falklands; chapter 5, note 29, for Dogger Bank; and the related text passages.

CHAPTER 10. CAVEAT EMPTOR

1. The movements of Hipper's and Beatty's forces toward one another circa 1430 hours, as well as the maneuverings of both fleets until the end of the battle during the night of May 31–June 1, can be followed in detail in the scores of charts published in Corbett, *Naval Operations*, vol. 3 (Maps); Groos, *Der Krieg in der Nordsee*, vol. 5; and Marder, *Dreadnought to Scapa Flow*, vol. 3. Also see the maps interspersed throughout the narrative texts in Schleihauf, *Jutland*; Scheer, *Deutschlands Hochseeflotte*; Dreyer, *Sea Heritage*; Frost, *Battle of Jutland*; Bennett, *Battle of Jutland*; Tarrant, *Jutland*; Gordon, *Rules of the Game*; and Staff, *Skagerrak*. Also see below, note 13, for commentary on distances at 1515–48 hours in the minutes before the battlecruiser duel.
2. Frenssen, *Die Brüder*, ch. 23.
3. For the signals, see Groos, *Der Krieg in der Nordsee*, 5: 220–22, 522. Also see Frost, *Battle of Jutland*, 153.
4. Cited in Groos, *Der Krieg in der Nordsee*, 5: 522.
5. The description is Frenssen's, *Die Brüder*, ch. 23.
6. Lieutenant Albert Schèibe, one of Hipper's officers, actually made such a statement in his memoir, "The Jutland Battle," 31.
7. For good descriptions of the day for sailors and officers on the British side before and after *Galatea*'s first shots, see Gordon, *Rules of the Game*, 69–77, 102–5; Thompson, *Imperial War Museum Book*, 293–97; and especially Steel and Hart, *Jutland 1916*, chapter 2.
8. Gordon, *Rules of the Game*, 105–6.
9. Compare Gordon, *Rules of the Game*, 54–58, 67–69, 81–101, with Roskill, *Admiral of the Fleet*, 155–56, and Brooks, *Battle of Jutland*, 170–73. The latter two are more lenient toward

Evan-Thomas and critical of Beatty and Seymour than is Gordon. Interestingly, Brooks proves that Evan-Thomas had received a copy of BCF battle orders (p. 136).

10. The gunnery officer of *Iron Duke*, cited in Marder, *Dreadnought to Scapa Flow*, 3: 55.

11. For the above citation, see Roskill, *Admiral of the Fleet*, 155. For the 30–35 minute run-up to the first shots between the battlecruisers at 1548 hours, including signals on both sides, see Schleihauf, *Jutland*, 55–60; Groos, *Der Krieg in der Nordsee*, 5: 224–26, 235–36, 524–25; Frost, *Battle of Jutland*, 169–84; Barnett, *Swordbearers*, 137–40; Gordon, *Rules of the Game*, 108–10; and especially Brooks, *Battle of Jutland*, 177–93.

12. See Brooks, *Battle of Jutland*, 175; and von Waldeyer-Hartz, *Admiral von Hipper*, 204.

13. The distances between opposing forces from 1515 or so until first shots is best determined by either (1) working backward from the best official postwar guesstimates of the British, which all agree on a distance of 14,300 yards at 1548 (see Schleihauf, *Jutland*, 53–54; Corbett, *Naval Operations*, 3 [Maps]: chart 23; and Marder, *Dreadnought to Scapa Flow*, 3: chart 4), and the closing pace of the two forces, 550 yards per minute (Brooks, *Battle of Jutland*, 184); or preferably by (2) using the same closing pace and working backward from the ranges determined by the leading German ships at first shots, 16,250–680 yards, and subtracting for the 1,750 yards they fell "over," that is, backward in time from an opening range of 14,930 yards (*Lützow*) and 14,500 yards (*Derfflinger*) (see Groos, *Der Krieg in der Nordsee*, 5: 236; and Brooks, *Battle of Jutland*, 192). Historians agree that looking west into the haze affected German range-finding less adversely at this moment than the British looking east.

14. von Hase, *Kiel and Jutland*, 74, 80–81.

15. See my estimates below in note 22.

16. Hipper stated afterward that he would not have broken off a battle running to the north, which Scheer thought would have been a mistake. See Philbin, *Admiral von Hipper*, 132–33.

17. See the recollection of Lieutenant Kienast of Hipper's staff, printed in Staff, *Skagerrak*, 45.

18. Chalmers, *Life and Letters*, 228.

19. Citations here from von Hase, *Kiel and Jutland*, 81; Groos, *Der Krieg in der Nordsee*, 5: 524; and Frenssen, *Die Brüder*, ch. 23.

20. Chatfield, *Navy and Defence*, 142, 140–41. For Beatty's 1540 wire to Jellicoe, and for effects of Dogger Bank, see Brooks, *Battle of Jutland*, 182, 81–82, 190–92.

21. Signals to and from Jellicoe are most conveniently accessed in Brooks, *Battle of Jutland*, 215–16. Also see Barnett, *Swordbearers*, 130–31; and Massie, *Castles of Steel*, 606–7.

22. For the distance of seventy-one miles at 1526 hours, see Corbett, *Naval Operations*, 3: 348. Proceeding from their relative positions at 1515/1521 (see Brooks, *Battle of Jutland*, 182, 216), my rough plotting of Jellicoe's south-southeast course at 18–19 knots from 1515 to 1548 or so, and Beatty's course alterations from northeast to east to southeast over the same time at speeds of 22–23, then 25 knots, point to Jellicoe closing about four miles.

However, had Beatty turned north at 1530 rather than east, the two forces would have closed to about fifty miles by 1600.

23. Brooks, *Battle of Jutland*, 216. For Hood's maneuvering and Jellicoe's expectations, see Corbett, *Naval Operations*, 3: 348; Frost, *Battle of Jutland*, 220–21; and especially Jellicoe, *Grand Fleet*, 323–24.

24. Beatty to Jellicoe, November 21, 1915 (printed in Jellicoe, *Jellicoe Papers*, 1: 188).

25. For the citations in this paragraph, and the argumentation, see Frost, *Battle of Jutland*, 181–82; and Brooks, *Battle of Jutland*, 188ff.

26. The succession of Hipper's orders from 1524 to 1545 are printed in Groos, *Der Krieg in der Nordsee*, 5: 524. Also see Barnett, *Swordbearers*, 138.

27. For the "bracket" and "ladder" systems of range-finding firing, see Marder, *Dreadnought to Scapa Flow*, 3: 166n2. In the German system, three salvoes fired together "in range steps several hundred yards apart (with the center step at the range-finder range), you hoped to find at once that the target was within the ladder, and little further correction would be needed to get hits." For all citations in this paragraph, see Chalmers, *Life and Letters*, 229, 231; Brooks, *Battle of Jutland*, 185; von Hase, *Kiel and Jutland*, 82, 83–84; Paschen, "SMS *Lützow* at Jutland," 33; and Groos, *Der Krieg in der Nordsee*, 5: 237, 239–40.

28. Brooks, *Battle of Jutland*, 196; Frost, *Battle of Jutland*, 204; Groos, *Der Krieg in der Nordsee*, 5: 241–42.

29. Steel and Hart, *Jutland 1916*, ch. 3, ebook location 1,558 (for the citation); and Groos, *Der Krieg in der Nordsee*, 5: 238.

30. See Frost, *Battle of Jutland*, 201; Gordon, *Rules of the Game*, 111; Groos, *Der Krieg in der Nordsee*, 5: 239; and Steel and Hart, *Jutland 1916*, ch. 3, ebook locations 1,533 and 1,490–513 (for the citations).

31. Marine private H. Willons in the handling room heard Harvey's order through the voice pipe and remembered the evacuation of the two wounded. His recollection, n.d. (circa 1919) is printed in Beatty, *Beatty Papers*, 1: 354. Historians know that Harvey's legs were not blown off, as often incorrectly reported, but I assume that he needed help to get to the voicepipe, and that could only have been from Comley.

32. Citations in Chalmers, *Life and Letters*, 231–32; and Chatfield, *Navy and Defence*, 143.

33. For German fire-control commands, see von Hase, *Kiel and Jutland*, 83. For the end of *Indefatigable*, see Gordon, *Rules of the Game*, 112–13; and Groos, *Der Krieg in der Nordsee*, 5: 240.

34. Citations in Gordon, *Rules of the Game*, 112; and Steel and Hart, *Jutland 1916*, chapter 3, ebook location 1,672.

35. Citations in von Hase, *Kiel and Jutland*, 84; Hipper's postbattle report of July 4, 1916, and the recollections of Artillery Leader Karl Groth (n.d.), printed, respectively, in Rahn, "Battle of Jutland," in *Jutland*, ed. Epkenhans et al., 216, 241. The figures in Roskill, *Admiral of the Fleet*, 164, and Brooks, *Battle of Jutland*, 193–95, indicate that, *Indefatigable*

excluded, each of the other British battlecruisers fired on average around 150 shells in the first half hour. *Indefatigable* fired 40 in eight to nine minutes before exploding. Roskill's figures for the entire Run to the South, which lasted about fifty minutes, show that each German ship fired an average of 334 shells, Beatty's four surviving ships an average of 320, but the BCF, it will be recalled, fired very haltingly in the first minutes.

36. For the German testimony, see von Hase, *Kiel and Jutland*, 85; Schèibe, "Jutland Battle," 33; Steel and Hart, *Jutland 1916*, chapter 3, ebook location 1,612; Dreyer, *Sea Heritage*, 169–70; Chatfield, *Navy and Defence*, 153; Hipper's postbattle report of July 4, 1916 (printed in Rahn, "Battle of Jutland," in *Jutland*, ed. Epkenhans et al., 216); and Paschen, "SMS *Lützow* at Jutland," 35. For British dud percentages, see Brooks, *Battle of Jutland*, 456.

37. For these hits, see the accounts of Paschen, "SMS *Lützow* at Jutland," 34; and the testimony of German officers in Steel and Hart, *Jutland 1916*, ch. 3, ebook locations 1,523 and 1,610. The most detailed description and tabulation, however, is found in Staff, *Skagerrak*, 51–62, who has meticulously combed through the archives for German ships' postbattle reports. The 40 percent figure I use for these particular nondud hits on armor, as well as nondud hits (tabulated from Staff) occurring at various points later in the battle that fall in the 0–36.4 percent range, should be placed in the context of the overall figures for the entire battle tabulated by Brooks, *Battle of Jutland*, 456: *counting duds*, he calculated that only 13 percent of British hits on German armor (5-inch+) penetrated and burst correctly inside ships, while the corresponding figure for German shells was over 47 percent. Brooks makes excellent use of the data in Campbell, *Jutland*. For German shell/fuse problems, see chapter 13, note 11.

38. Citations in this and the preceding paragraph in Groos, *Der Krieg in der Nordsee*, 5: 245, 247; Steel and Hart, *Jutland 1916*, ch. 3, ebook location 1,724; von Waldeyer-Hartz, *Admiral von Hipper*, 219–20; and Marder, *Dreadnought to Scapa Flow*, 3: 71. Also see Corbett, *Naval Operations*, 3: 336–37; and Brooks, *Battle of Jutland*, 201. For the effect of each of 5th BS's eight hits on *Moltke* and *Von der Tann*, see especially Staff, *Skagerrak*, 63–65. Also see above, note 37.

39. von Waldeyer-Hartz, *Admiral von Hipper*, 205–6—emphasis in the original—offers a good description of Hipper and many direct and indirect quotes of the chief during this stage of the battle. See Groos, *Der Krieg in der Nordsee*, 5: 525, for many of the signals and orders. Also see Brooks, *Battle of Jutland*, 203, for hits and range.

40. Citations in Chatfield, *Navy and Defence*, 141; and the journal of Second Sea Lord Admiral Frederick Hamilton, June 7, 1916 (printed in Beatty, *Beatty Papers*, 1: 321). Beatty referred to the sinking of the *Invincible*.

41. Brooks, *Battle of Jutland*, 204 (for the *New Zealand* citation), 207.

42. Frost, *Battle of Jutland*, 215. Also see Brooks, *Battle of Jutland*, 209, for Beatty's 1555 signal.

43. For the citations, see Groos, *Der Krieg in der Nordsee*, 5: 249; von Hase, *Kiel and Jutland*, 89, 85; and Chatfield's Gunnery Committee report of June 24, 1916 (printed in Beatty,

Beatty Papers, 1: 365). Also see the figures for shots fired in Roskill, *Admiral of the Fleet*, 164; and note 35 above. Brooks, *Battle of Jutland*, 203, 207, mentions only three hits, but he does not count the two hits recalled by Hase. Also see above, note 37.

44. For the hits in this paragraph, see Groos, *Der Krieg in der Nordsee*, 5: 246–49; von Hase, *Kiel and Jutland*, 92; Frost, *Battle of Jutland*, 209–14, 217; and Brooks, *Battle of Jutland*, 203–7. Roskill, *Admiral of the Fleet*, 161, concludes that the Germans scored forty-four hits during the entire Run to the South. Brooks' total of only twelve for the second phase of the run south is too low. Also see Brooks, *Battle of Jutland*, 456 (and note 37 above) for German versus British shell effectiveness percentages; and chapter 13, note 11 for German fuse issues.

45. Citation here (British gunner) and above (Hase) in von Hase, *Kiel and Jutland*, 91.

46. Recollection of telegraphist Arthur Lewis of *Lion*, cited in Steel and Hart, *Jutland 1916*, ch. 3, ebook location 1,989. Also see Chatfield, *Navy and Defence*, 143, who recalls Beatty saying: "There seems to be something wrong with our bloody ships today," but adds, apparently incorrectly, that "Beatty was ostensibly unaffected by these two serious losses."

47. For the movements of the two forces around this time (1426–30), see Gordon, *Rules of the Game*, 118–20; Groos, *Der Krieg in der Nordsee*, 5: 246–47; and Marder, *Dreadnought to Scapa Flow*, 3: chart 5.

48. von Waldeyer-Hartz, *Admiral von Hipper*, 205; and Groos, *Der Krieg in der Nordsee*, 5: 525.

49. For citations here and below, most of them the observations of contemporary witnesses, see Chalmers, *Life and Letters*, 236; von Hase, *Kiel and Jutland*, 88; Tarrant, *Jutland*, 91; Frost, *Battle of Jutland*, 227; Steel and Hart, *Jutland 1916*, chapter 3, ebook locations 2,112 and 2,153; and Corbett, *Naval Operations*, 3: 339.

50. Schèibe, "Jutland Battle," 33–34.

51. Citations in Chalmers, *Life and Letters*, 235; and Chatfield, *Navy and Defence*, 143.

52. For all signals sent to and from Scheer's flagship, 1427 to 1648 hours, see Groos, *Der Krieg in der Nordsee*, 5: 522–26.

53. For the citations, see von Weizsäcker, *Erinnerungen*, 35; and Gordon, *Rules of the Game*, 121. Also see Scheer, *Deutschlands Hochseeflotte*, 207.

54. Brooks, *Battle of Jutland*, 218; Groos, *Der Krieg in der Nordsee*, 5: 523 (for the first citation); and Corbett, *Naval Operations*, 3: 322 (for the second citation).

55. Notations of Scheer's flag lieutenant (Weizsäcker), June 6 and 11, 1916 (printed in Granier, "Eindrücke von der Skagerrakschlacht," 21–22).

56. Richard Stumpf Diary, June 3, 1916 (printed in Horn, *Private War of Seaman Stumpf*, 197–98; and Groos, *Der Krieg in der Nordsee*, 5: 252).

57. For all citations here and in the following paragraphs, see Gordon, *Rules of the Game*, 124; Tarrant, *Jutland*, 94; Scheer, *Deutschlands Hochseeflotte*, 215; Chatfield, *Navy and Defence*, 144; Chalmers, *Life and Letters*, 23; and Jellicoe, *Jutland: The Unfinished Battle*, epage 141.

Also see Beesly, *Room 40*, 156, and Roskill, *Admiral of the Fleet*, 153, who quote Beatty averring angrily to a Room 40 operative in 1918 that Scheer's arrival had been a surprise.

58. Citations in Gordon, *Rules of the Game*, 127; and Diary of Stephen King-Hall, June 30, 1916 (printed in L. King-Hall, *Sea Saga*, 454).

59. Citations here and below from Gordon, *Rules of the Game*, 137, 150, 149, 147, respectively. Also see Brooks, *Battle of Jutland*, 226–27, 485; and Staff, *Skagerrak*, 84.

60. Citations here and the subsequent paragraph in Grove, "Autobiography," 398–99; recollection of Royal Marine Private H. Willons, n.d. (circa 1916–19), printed in Beatty, *Beatty Papers*, 1: 353–56; Chatfield, *Navy and Defence*, 151; and Groos, *Der Krieg in der Nordsee*, 5: 261. For the "lull in the firing" after 1633 hours, see Brooks, *Battle of Jutland*, 208.

61. For this paragraph, see Willons' recollection, n.d. (circa 1916–19), printed in Beatty, *Beatty Papers*, 1: 354–55; the statement of a stoker who helped Willons, printed in Steel and Hart, *Jutland 1916*, ch. 7, ebook location 7,358; and Brooks, *Battle of Jutland*, 231.

62. von Hase, *Kiel and Jutland*, 96, and Paschen, "SMS *Lützow* at Jutland," 36 (for the citations). Groos, *Der Krieg in der Nordsee*, 5: 264–65; and Staff, *Skagerrak*, 87–88, for damage to German ships from other hits. Staff does not provide enough detail here for a shell effectiveness percentage.

63. For the ranges at 1735 hours, see Marder, *Dreadnought to Scapa Flow*, 3: chart 6. Groos, *Der Krieg in der Nordsee*, 5: 262–63, 267; Scheer, *Deutschlands Hochseeflotte*, 216–17; Corbett, *Naval Operations*, 3: 344; and Tarrant, *Jutland*, 103–9, also discuss the German battleships slipping back. For the citations, see Scheer, *Deutschlands Hochseeflotte*, 217; Marder, *Dreadnought to Scapa Flow*, 3: 76; Groos, *Der Krieg in der Nordsee*, 5: 527; and Staff, *Skagerrak*, 89, 121–22, 148. Brooks, *Battle of Jutland*, 245, believes Scheer's order to "pick up the chase" was a rebuke of Hipper, which can also be read between the lines of von Waldeyer-Hartz, *Admiral von Hipper*, 207–8; Raeder, *Mein Leben*, 1: 114; and Groos, *Der Krieg in der Nordsee*, 5: 265–66, who served on *Von der Tann* at Jutland.

CHAPTER 11. CLASH OF THE STEEL CASTLES

1. For changing visibility, see Scheer, *Deutschlands Hochseeflotte*, 217; Jellicoe, *Grand Fleet*, 331–33; Schèibe, "Jutland Battle," 36; and Groos, *Der Krieg in der Nordsee*, 5: 265, 269.

2. Citations in von Waldeyer-Hartz, *Admiral von Hipper*, 207–8; and Paschen, "SMS *Lützow* at Jutland," 36. Also see Brooks, *Battle of Jutland*, 245–46, 248–49; and Groos, *Der Krieg in der Nordsee*, 5: 269–70.

3. See the fine discussion of 5th BS's perilous situation in Gordon, *Rules of the Game*, 409–15, 425–29.

4. For Jellicoe's signals, see Brooks, *Battle of Jutland*, 216, 243, 245, 248–49; and Groos, *Der Krieg in der Nordsee*, 5: 268. Also see the discussion and position charts in Frost, *Battle of Jutland*, 264, 267, 269, 275; and Schleihauf, *Jutland*, 89, 91. While in actuality the two forces were only 28–30 miles apart at 1725, dead reckoning errors on *Lion* made it appear

to Beatty that Jellicoe was either 41.3 miles away (Frost, *Battle of Jutland*, 264), 42 miles away (Schleihauf, *Jutland*, 91), or ten minutes closing time less than 44 miles away (i.e., 39–40 miles) (Brooks, *Battle of Jutland*, 243). Closing at 28 miles per hour—"not 40, as has sometimes been stated; they were not heading directly for each other" (Patterson, *Jellicoe*, 117–18)—put Jellicoe over an hour away.

5. Leading signalman on *Lion*, Alec Tempest, recalled ill-feelings against the main battle squadrons around this time because "they did not make their best speed during the approach to the battle" (cited in Gordon, *Rules of the Game*, 509).

6. Barnett, *Swordbearers*, 147.

7. For Beatty's commands from 1725 to 1747 cited here, see Brooks, *Battle of Jutland*, 243, 248. His north-northeast turn at 1735 hours was earlier interpreted as an attempt to block Hipper from spotting Jellicoe's advancing main fleet (Chalmers, *Life and Letters*, 243, 245; Marder, *Dreadnought to Scapa Flow*, 3: 74; Patterson, *Jellicoe*, 114–15; and Roskill, *Admiral of the Fleet*, 163), which presumes Beatty knew circa 1735 that the main fleet was closer than he had thought. Andrew Gordon (*Rules of the Game*, 430–31) assumes that Beatty must have known at the time of his north-northeast turn that his cruiser screen had made contact with Jellicoe's cruiser screen, which it had in fact; but John Brooks (*Battle of Jutland*, 247) disputes this, showing that 1st LCS sent no report sternward to Beatty, who in his after-battle dispatch also made no mention of having had such knowledge until around 1750, while Robert Massie (*Castles of Steel*, 605) thinks he may have known at 1745. It has also been speculated that Beatty made the north-northeast turn to make contact with Jellicoe's cruiser screen (Jellicoe, *Grand Fleet*, 331–32; Dreyer, *Sea Heritage*, 125–26; Marder, *Dreadnought to Scapa Flow*, 3: 74; and Brooks, *Battle of Jutland*, 243–44), but based on where he thought the BCF was in relation to the main fleet, this would have entailed staying the northward course or even turning north-northwest, which strengthens the case that he turned north-northeast to "bag the lot" alone, for he was turning away from the south-southeast course vector/north-northwest line of bearing he assumed Jellicoe moved along. Also see especially Holloway Frost (*Battle of Jutland*, 264, 270, 276), who argues that circa 1725–30 Beatty thought, based on Jellicoe's wire of 1713 hours, that Jellicoe was away to the northwest and that by making the north-northeast turn instead he may well have intended to close with Hood, who had wired for the BCF's position.

8. Beatty twice wrote Jellicoe after the battle stating that he felt victory was "assured," a "certainty" when the main fleet finally hove into view right before 1800 hours (letters of June 6 and 9, 1916 [printed in Jellicoe, *Jellicoe Papers*, 1: 272, 277]), which implies that he considered it most unassured and uncertain before this time. This does not mean, however, that he was elated when he saw the battle squadrons. In both letters he states that Jellicoe's "move to the south" was "masterful," the "sweep south was splendid," but he probably referred here to the nighttime hours in a ploy to deflect from his own mistakes

(see chapter 12), not Jellicoe's southeasterly descent before arriving, the omission of any mention of which seems to indicate Beatty thought *that* move not masterful or splendid at all, the opposite in fact—indeed, he had been saying so (see chapter 13).

9. For the citations, see Dreyer, *Sea Heritage*, 125; and Patterson, *Jellicoe*, 116.

10. Midshipman Croome of *Indomitable*, cited in Steel and Hart, *Jutland 1916*, ch. 5, ebook location 3,151.

11. Corbett, *Naval Operations*, 3: 352–54. Also see Gordon, *Rules of the Game*, 431; and Brooks, *Battle of Jutland*, 252–55.

12. Citations here from the battle report of *Seydlitz*, printed in Staff, *Skagerrak*, 89. Also see von Hase, *Kiel and Jutland*, 96; Groos, *Der Krieg in der Nordsee*, 5: 269–70, 272, 528; Frost, *Battle of Jutland*, 278; and Brooks, *Battle of Jutland*, 245–46.

13. For this and the following paragraphs, see Frost, *Battle of Jutland*, 288; Groos, *Der Krieg in der Nordsee*, 5: 275; Staff, *Skagerrak*, 96–98; and Brooks, *Battle of Jutland*, 247–48. Also see chapter 12, note 91.

14. Petty Officer Edwin Downing is cited in Steel and Hart, *Jutland 1916*, ch. 5, ebook location 3,419 (3,395, 3,419, for the authors' citation). For the other citations, see Gordon, *Rules of the Game*, 433–34, who also cites Leading Signalman Alec Tempest, 509; and Frost, *Battle of Jutland*, 301. Furthermore, see Brooks, *Battle of Jutland*, 537–38, who is also critical of Beatty. Chalmers' attempt (*Life and Letters*, 248–49) to apologize for Beatty, who he said was busy fighting Hipper and could not see Scheer, is not convincing.

15. Citations in Gordon, *Rules of the Game*, 433 (also see 441–43); Marder, *Dreadnought to Scapa Flow*, 3: 102n24; and Brooks, *Battle of Jutland*, 264–65.

16. Jellicoe, *Grand Fleet*, 348–49. Brooks, *Battle of Jutland*, 279–80, doubts that Jellicoe ever seriously considered rightwing deployment, but then contradicts himself (p. 280n83) by writing that while heading south from 1802 to 1806, he "might have briefly contemplated a starboard deployment but he never mentioned this possibility," but the latter part of this statement also errs, for Jellicoe wrote that "my first and natural impulse was to form on the starboard wing column" (p. 348).

17. For concerns on the bridge about the fighting to the northeast, see the first postbattle notation of Scheer's flag lieutenant (Weizsäcker), June 6, 1916 (printed in Granier, "Eindrücke von der Skagerrakschlacht," 21). Also see the discussion in Scheer, *Deutschlands Hochseeflotte*, 218–19, as well as a sketch from the flagship's vantage point, which corresponds to the charts in Corbett, *Naval Operations*, 3: Maps 28–29) and Marder, *Dreadnought to Scapa Flow*, 3: chart 7). From the opposite direction somewhat earlier (1727 hours), HMS *Chester* had seen the flashes and heard the sounds of fighting in the southwest from even further away (Corbett, *Naval Operations*, 3: 352).

18. On this point, see Groos, *Der Krieg in der Nordsee*, 5: 298.

19. Scheer, *Deutschlands Hochseeflotte*, 220; and Weizsäcker's second postbattle notation, June 11, 1916 (printed in Granier, "Eindrücke von der Skagerrakschlacht," 22).

20. Scheer, *Deutschlands Hochseeflotte*, 221; Groos, *Der Krieg in der Nordsee*, 5: 528.

21. For the citations: Scheer, *Deutschlands Hochseeflotte*, 220; and the second postbattle notation of Scheer's flag lieutenant (Weizsäcker), June 11, 1916 (printed in Granier, "Eindrücke von der Skagerrakschlacht," 22).

22. For Trotha's recollections, see Trotha, "Mit Admiral Scheer," 10–11—emphasis mine.

23. Groos, *Der Krieg in der Nordsee*, 5: 529.

24. See Weizsäcker's first postbattle notation, June 6, 1916 (printed in Granier, "Eindrücke von der Skagerrakschlacht," 21).

25. Levetzow to Rudolf Hess, August 10, 1936 (cited in Marder, *Dreadnought to Scapa Flow*, 3: 76). His words described the German advance into the British fleet that he desired.

26. Trotha, "Mit Admiral Scheer," 11.

27. Scheer, *Deutschlands Hochseeflotte*, 222.

28. Trotha's recollection of May 1939 is cited in Marder, *Dreadnought to Scapa Flow*, 1st printing, 3: 42. Also see Groos, *Der Krieg in der Nordsee*, 5: 298. Groos, navigation officer on *Von der Tann*, clearly thought that the decision "to push forward," however understandable given the desire to move beyond the disappointments of 1914–15, was nevertheless a mistake by "the German leader and subordinate commanders." It is interesting, however, that to buttress his case he draws on criticism in the battle log of Captain Walther von Keyserlingk of Trotha's old ship, SMS *Kaiser*. This may have been his way of pointing the finger of blame not at Scheer and both "subordinate commanders," but just Scheer and Levetzow. Of the two, furthermore, Levetzow was the more active player, Scheer more passive for most of the day. Scheer admitted on June 5 (Weizsäcker's postbattle notation of June 11, 1916 [printed in Granier, "Eindrücke von der Skagerrakschlacht," 22]) that his only two really independent decisions of the day came later that hour. We also know that it was his *modus operandi* "to have all options presented to him" (Trotha's recollection of May 1939) before making a decision. From the "somewhat unruly" deliberations at this time, a back and forth "not coordinated" well by Trotha, whose advice did he weigh more heavily, Trotha's or Levetzow's? Who captured "the fleet chief's ear"? In his memoirs (von Weizsäcker, *Erinnerungen*, 37), Flag Lieutenant Weizsäcker gave Levetzow "a special share" in the day's "successful" outcome; Trotha, merely "a share." This sentence clearly implies that Scheer was swayed more by the advice of Levetzow than Trotha and that the former was more assertive, which stands to reason given their personality differences. However, once options were presented to him the way he liked, the admiral could move impetuously, almost as if one side of him struggled with the other. Weizsäcker continued: "Corresponding to his nature, [Scheer usually acted] not out of cool, consistent considerations, but rather as a spur-of-the-moment man" (*Augenblicksmensch*). At this point at least, he seems to have been drawn more to the heated urgings of Levetzow than the rational approach of Trotha. Also see below, note 72.

29. Scheer, *Deutschlands Hochseeflotte*, 220.

30. Groos, *Der Krieg in der Nordsee*, 5: 298. For Behncke's aggressiveness in particular, see chapter 4, note 38; and below, note 75, where his postwar book is cited.

31. A British battleship observer cited in Gordon, *Rules of the Game*, 444.

32. Frost, *Battle of Jutland*, 300, believes Beatty "assumed that Jellicoe would deploy eastward" and therefore hurried across the main fleet in that direction. Gordon, *Rules of the Game*, 440, also states that Beatty, "rather than trying to take up station ahead of the starboard wing of the cruising battle fleet," drove on "across the front of the fleet" to the leftwing column. Brooks, *Battle of Jutland*, 250, seems to agree. Others argue, however, that Beatty's initial assumption was probably that Jellicoe would deploy from the right (see the postwar Admiralty Staff assessment, Schleihauf, *Jutland*, 108, 108n8; and Marder, *Dreadnought to Scapa Flow*, 3: 85). Beatty did, in fact, initially take up station off the starboard bow of *Benbow*, flagship of the 4th Division, steering southeast (see Dreyer, *Sea Heritage*, 126–27; Roskill, *Admiral of the Fleet*, 169–71; Corbett, *Naval Operations*, 3 [Maps]: chart 30; and Marder, *Dreadnought to Scapa Flow*, 3: chart 8). Also see Chatfield, *Navy and Defence*, 145, who seems to confirm these latter historians: "when we sighted our battle fleet, we steered to take up position ahead of them on the course to which they intended to deploy." Only after *Defence* and *Warrior* barged across *Lion*'s bow did the BCF defensively jam helms over and dart to the east, that is, radically veer to port to avoid a collision, by which time Jellicoe was deploying to the east and *Lion* raced in that direction.

33. Paschen, "SMS *Lützow* at Jutland," 36.

34. Citations in Gordon, *Rules of the Game*, 448.

35. Citations in this paragraph from Jellicoe, *Grand Fleet*, 349–50; and Dreyer, *Sea Heritage*, 146. Readers find a fine technical discussion of Jellicoe's deployment in Stephen McLaughlin, "Equal Speed Charlie London: Jellicoe's Deployment at Jutland," in *Warship 2010*, ed. John Jordan (London: Conway, 2010), 122–39.

36. Jellicoe, *Grand Fleet*, 349.

37. For technical specifications of the battleships in Jellicoe's six division columns, see Jellicoe, *Grand Fleet*, 310–11, 320; Groos, *Der Krieg in der Nordsee*, 5: 460–61; and check online for each ship.

38. Dreyer, *Sea Heritage*, 130. Also see Corbett, *Naval Operations*, 3: 365; and Frost, *Battle of Jutland*, 323, 325.

39. von Hase, *Kiel and Jutland*, 102, for both citations. Also see Staff, *Skagerrak*, 111; Brooks, *Battle of Jutland*, 284–86; and Groos, *Der Krieg in der Nordsee*, 5: 293–94, 529. Hase's gunnery chart (p. 107) shows *Derfflinger* firing a distance of 10,800 yards at 1820, while *Lion* had fired from somewhat above 8,250 yards at 1819 (Brooks, *Battle of Jutland*, 285, for descending ranges of the BCF), hence the German's 2,000 yard "overs." The charts in Corbett (*Naval Operations*, 3 [maps]: chart 31) and Marder (*Dreadnought to Scapa Flow*, 3: chart 8) also indicate that Beatty was then 8,000–9,000 yards from Hipper. Hase thought he had been firing at Hood's 3rd BCS at this time, but his chart shows the

salvos going to the northwest, while Hood was then to the northeast. Groos (*Der Krieg in der Nordsee*, 5: 294) also mistakenly assumes the targets were the 3rd BCS. Paschen ("SMS *Lützow* at Jutland," 36) recalled that the two hits circa 1820 (probably right after the southeast turn) came from "port aft" (i.e., northwest) and were fired by "our old friends, Beatty's battlecruisers."

40. Chief Gunnery Officer Dannreuter in *Invincible* remembered (recollection of June 2, 1916, cited in Steel and Hart, *Jutland 1916*, ch. 5, ebook location 4,110) that 3rd BCS "turned and came into action at about [1815]," while in Beatty's postbattle dispatch (cited in Brooks, *Battle of Jutland*, 286), he observed that "at [1820] the [3rd BCS] appeared ahead, steaming southwards toward the enemy van."

41. Citation in Corbett, *Naval Operations*, 3: 366. For the hits, see Staff, *Skagerrak*, 112–14, 119. Also see chapter 10, note 37.

42. Citations in von Hase, *Kiel and Jutland*, 102–3; Paschen, "SMS *Lützow* at Jutland," 37–38; and recollections of assistant clerk Hubert Fischer (*Indomitable*) and stoker Sidney Blackman (*Inflexible*), cited in Steel and Hart, *Jutland 1916*, ch. 5, ebook locations 4,138–60.

43. von Hase, *Kiel and Jutland*, 103.

44. Blake to Marder, August 15, 1963 (printed in Marder, *Dreadnought to Scapa Flow*, 3: 100–101).

45. See Staff, *Skagerrak*, 116–17, 119; and Hugo Zenne, "Die letzten Stunden S.M.S. *Wiesbaden*," *Auf See Unbesiegt*, ed. von Mantey, 286–89 (p. 286 for the citations).

46. Frost, *Battle of Jutland*, 323.

47. The best descriptions of Jellicoe's initial engagement with the High Seas Fleet are Brooks, *Battle of Jutland*, 291–93; and Staff, *Skagerrak*, 116–19. Also see the postbattle report of SMS *Markgraf*, June 2, 1916 (printed in Rahn, "Battle of Jutland," in *Jutland*, ed. Epkenhans et al., 218, 221–22).

48. Brooks, *Battle of Jutland*, 291, reports that *Agincourt* opened fire from 10,000 yards on "what was believed to be an enemy battlecruiser," but because *Von der Tann*, the nearest, was a good 15,000 away, she had probably fired at *Wiesbaden* instead.

49. Citations here and above from the reports of Midshipman Croome and Captain Sinclair (printed in Steel and Hart, *Jutland 1916*, ch. 5, ebook locations 4,230–53).

50. Frenssen, *Die Brüder*, ch. 23.

51. Report of Midshipman Croome (printed in Steel and Hart, *Jutland 1916*, ch. 5, ebook location 4,253).

52. For the state of the flagship and the citations, see Paschen, "SMS *Lützow* at Jutland," 38–39; Frenssen, *Die Brüder*, ch. 24; the postbattle report of Gunner Karl Groth (n.d.) (printed in Rahn, "Battle of Jutland," in *Jutland*, ed. Epkenhans et al., 244–47); and Staff, *Skagerrak*, 125–26.

53. von Waldeyer-Hartz, *Admiral von Hipper*, 208. Also see Raeder, *Mein Leben*, 1: 115–16; and Groos, *Der Krieg in der Nordsee*, 5: 302, 529.

54. The following dialogue and description draw on the direct and indirect quotations, respectively, in von Waldeyer-Hartz, *Admiral von Hipper*, 208, and Raeder, *Mein Leben*, 1: 115–16. Also see Frenssen, *Die Brüder*, ch. 23 and ch. 24; the sailors' recollections in Staff, *Skagerrak*, 125–26, 138; and Groos, *Der Krieg in der Nordsee*, 5: 529–30.

55. *Rostock* ordered *G-39*'s 1st Half-Flotilla at 1855 to start sailing to Hipper (Groos, *Der Krieg in der Nordsee*, 5: 530). Closer to Hipper than Scheer farther back, they had seen the laming of 1st SG's flagship before she reported it, but they did not yet alert Scheer. A lookout on *Lützow*'s foretop recalled that "the sound of battle diminishes" (Staff, *Skagerrak*, 126) as Hipper left, which means he actually boarded *G-39* before the battle fleets reengaged and *Lützow* was hit again at 1907 (Staff, *Skagerrak*, 138). Inexplicably, Staff (*Skagerrak*, 126) places Hipper's departure incorrectly at 1845. That Hipper left his flagship when B-turret was very badly hit, as Michelsen had heard after the battle (von Waldeyer-Hartz, *Admiral von Hipper*, 209), also could not be true, for this damage occurred at 1917 (Staff, *Skagerrak*, 138) when Hipper and *G-39* were trying to close with *Moltke* while she was under heavy fire farther north.

56. Trotha, "Mit Admiral Scheer," 9–12, describes in detail the situation in the conning tower and on the bridge in the minutes leading up to and passing 1830.

57. For these signals, see Groos, *Der Krieg in der Nordsee*, 5: 528–29.

58. Scheer wrote "that now it was clear that we had a large portion of the English fleet before us" (*Deutschlands Hochseeflotte*, 221). Corbett (*Naval Operations*, 3: 368) concluded that "he did not as yet realize that he was face to face with the whole [Grand Fleet], but he could divine enough."

59. Scheer, *Deutschlands Hochseeflotte*, 221–23.

60. Scheer, *Deutschlands Hochseeflotte*, 223.

61. See a letter Scheer wrote to Vice Admiral Carl Hollweg, January 15, 1920 (printed in Staff, *Skagerrak*, 148). His comments to Hollweg came in the context of Scheer's criticism of Georg von Hase's book, *Kiel and Jutland*, 109–17. Scheer resented Hase's implication that the battlecruisers were sacrificed so that the main fleet could withdraw, when in reality it was the battlecruisers that first turned southward into a running battle around 1913–15, as if they were "glad to be able to withdraw from the battle on a southerly course with high speed," even though they had been ordered to lead the way east for the trailing—and still attacking—main fleet. In an earlier letter to Hollweg (May 19, 1919, in Staff, *Skagerrak*, 146), Scheer leveled the same criticism at the battlecruisers, this time that they "sought to retreat" circa 1845–50. It is hard to imagine, therefore, that Scheer did not have the same suspicion when Hipper veered away to the southeast after 1820. In *Deutschlands Hochseeflotte*, 226–27, Scheer observes that the battlecruisers' 1913–15 southerly turn occurred "in the same manner as earlier," that is after 1820, without publicly citing withdrawal from battle as the reason; but given the accusations mentioned earlier in this endnote, and his concerns about Hipper's combat readiness before the campaign

began (see chapter 8) as well as during earlier stages of the Run to the North (see chapter 10), the admiral must have worried about Hipper fleeing the scene in the minutes before and after 1830.

62. See Scheer's explanations, plus his sketches of his sense of Jellicoe's position at 1816 and 1835 hours, *Deutschlands Hochseeflotte*, 221–24. Also see Frost, *Battle of Jutland*, 328.

63. Scheer to Frost, n.d. (1920s) (printed in Frost, *Battle of Jutland*, 328). The "divine" quote is Corbett, *Naval Operations*, 3: 368.

64. Groos, *Der Krieg in der Nordsee*, 5: 529.

65. Trotha, "Mit Admiral Scheer," 12.

66. Groos, *Der Krieg in der Nordsee*, 5: 302.

67. Trotha, "Mit Admiral Scheer," 12.

68. Scheer to Hollweg, May 19, 1919 (printed in Staff, *Skagerrak*, 146).

69. See below, note 72.

70. Groos, *Der Krieg in der Nordsee*, 5: 301n1.

71. See Groos, *Der Krieg in der Nordsee*, 5: 310, 529 (for the citation).

72. Trotha, "Mit Admiral Scheer," 12–13, presents "the considerations from which Admiral Scheer drew his aggressive conclusions" during the "quiet moment," the "breathing spell" after British fire stopped. Scheer, the impetuous "spur of the moment man" (*Augenblicksmensch*) (von Weizsäcker, *Erinnerungen*, 37), had not yet made up his mind what to do—hence his "what now" wording in 1919 (see above, note 68). The admiral would soon act, but very spontaneously and exogenously closer to the top of the hour; therefore, these calculated "considerations" were no doubt the advice of his top two staffers. I assume here that the first part of Trotha's indirect quotation represents the cautious advice Trotha gave, while the second part quoted here is that of Levetzow. Trotha does not state this explicitly, but his pros versus cons presentation allows this to be read between the lines. Moreover, because the consistently aggressive Levetzow (see Granier, *Magnus von Levetzow*, 18–19, 18–19n59; Raeder, *Mein Leben*, 1: 105; and von Selchow, *Hundert Tage*, 262) did not desire a retreat to the Bight, it can be gleaned that this second, more aggressive group of "considerations" came from the operations chief, especially because Trotha's wording here ("push hard into the broad bend of enemy power") comes so close to Levetzow's memory of what he said: "Fall upon the enemy, jolt him, and then punch on through (*und dann die Schlacht durchschlagen*) (Levetzow to Rösling, February 4, 1943 [cited in Granier, *Magnus von Levetzow*, 18]). For some of the other "considerations" that came up (i.e., the expectation that Jellicoe would surely pursue, the realization that he was however not pursuing, and the effect of British casualties on this caution), see Scheer, *Deutschlands Hochseeflotte*, 225–26; and Groos, *Der Krieg in der Nordsee*, 5: 310. Also see especially above, note 28, and below, note 75.

Barnett (*Swordbearers*, 164) believed that Scheer "intended to steer for home, taking a passing punch at Jellicoe's rear ships as he went," while Corbett (*Naval Operations*, 3:

375) argued in more detail that Scheer wanted to cut off Evan-Thomas (5th BS) to the north, cross the stern of Jellicoe, presumably doing considerable damage in the process, pass to the east, gain gunnery advantage (i.e., front-lit not back-lit and silhouetted) and presumably do more damage, and then return to his base, driving off British attempts to stop him with damaging destroyer attacks. Scheer's rearward deployment of torpedo boats during the battle turn and charge forward supports Corbett's view (see note 91 below). Regarding Nelson and Trafalgar, it is interesting that although generally pro-Jellicoe in his presentation, Corbett seems to have been influenced by a portion of the anti-Jellicoe *Narrative of the Battle of Jutland* (1924), written by the brothers Arthur and Kenneth Dewar, who indirectly jabbed at Jellicoe by attributing Nelsonian initiative to Scheer's wanting to surprise the enemy and upset his plans, this in contrast to Jellicoe's caution. "I think it will surprise and confound the enemy, they don't know what I am about," Nelson had said. Such Nelsonian tactics as Corbett describes, however, were more probably advised by Levetzow, not divined by Scheer, who admitted later that he "wasn't thinking about anything," that he turned back with "no particular object" other than rescuing *Wiesbaden* and "seeking contact with the enemy again" (von Weizsäcker, *Erinnerungen*, 37; Report of the Austrian Naval Attaché, quoting Scheer, June 17, 1916 [cited in Schleihauf, *Jutland*, 140n11]). Angus Konstam's incorrect assertion to the contrary (*Jutland 1916: Twelve Hours to Win the War* [London: Aurum Press Limited, 2016], 177), Groos (*Der Krieg in der Nordsee*, 5: 311–12) scoffed at the notions of Dewar and Corbett, at least *as far as Scheer* wanting to emulate Nelson was concerned. But again, this was very much in character for Levetzow. In fact, having presumably read both Corbett (1923) and Groos (1925), Levetzow averred in 1926 that "the English fleet would have come into a tactically highly unfavorable situation had the German side held course. Dusk and nightfall would have been favorable for the German side" (Levetzow to Donnersmarck, October 29, 1926 [cited in Granier, *Magnus von Levetzow*, 18]). Pinning the enemy to the setting sun is such basic naval science that there is every reason to believe that Levetzow advised doing this ten years earlier. At the very least we know that he claimed that he advised Scheer near this point in the battle to do something that certainly smacked of this.

73. von Weizsäcker, *Erinnerungen*, 37; and the postwar report of the Austrian Naval Attaché in Schleihauf, *Jutland*, 140n11.

74. Citations from Scheer to Hollweg, May 19, 1919 (printed in Staff, *Skagerrak*, 146).

75. For Scheer's predilections and prejudices, see his postwar statement in "The Jutland Battle" (cited in Marder [with n.d.], *Dreadnought to Scapa Flow*, 3: 112 ["The second attack upon the British line is the most striking proof that nothing was further from our thoughts than to think of 'escape'"]); Levetzow to Hess, August 10, 1936 (cited in Marder, *Dreadnought to Scapa Flow*, 3: 76 ["Shortly before his death Scheer told me in Weimar that the thought of how Providence had given [us] the opportunities for a *complete* annihilation of the British fleet still robbed him of sleep"]); Scheer to Frost, n.d. (1920s) (printed in Frost, *Battle of*

Jutland, 328 ["In looking at the diagrams that are made subsequently, it would seem as if we must have regarded our situation as critical. In reality this was not the case. We were under the impression of the splendid effectiveness of our gunfire"]); the report of the Austrian Naval Attaché, quoting Scheer (cited in Schleihauf, *Jutland*, 140n11 ["When I noticed that the British pressure had quite ceased and that the fleet remained quite intact in my hands, I turned back under the impression that the action could not end in this way, and that I ought to seek contact with the enemy again"]); Forstmeier, "Zum Bild der Persönlichkeit," 82 ("Should he, whom the whole fleet trusted and looked to as a leader who would take them into battle, withdraw ingloriously like his predecessors? 'I cannot leave here like that' [*So gehe ich hier nicht weg*], said Scheer at this phase of the battle"); Schèibe, "Jutland Battle," 38 (Scheer "knew his weapons and his men"); and Paul L. G. Behncke, *Unsere Marine*, 18, 20, 23–25. Behncke, commanding 3rd Squadron, also made a "weapons and men" boast that tended to corroborate Scheer's "splendid effectiveness of our gunfire" assertion, but added a criticism of the inadequate penetrating power of British ordnance, a view held in the German navy since Dogger Bank. Also see Scheer to Hollweg, January 15, 1920 (printed in Staff, *Skagerrak*, 148), where he scoffs at the incredulous idea of those in the German navy who had maintained that seeking battle with the Royal Navy could not be allowed to happen; and rejected the indecisive outcome of the war's land battles: "we should avoid everything that happened on land." In short, influenced more by Levetzow than Trotha (see note 28), Scheer thought the moment of a thus far elusive victory at sea was near and turned back to get it.

Scheer claimed that it was his "conscious intention" to strike the middle of the enemy line (*Deutschlands Hochseeflotte*, 227), but this is probably an *ex post facto* defense of his actually hitting the center, unless by "middle" he meant the gap he assumed separated 5th BS and the BCF to the north from Jellicoe farther south. It certainly was not his intention at the time to strike a solid middle, for it is clear from his own maps (pp. 221, 224, 228) that he anticipated finding a gap at Jellicoe's rear, which later historians also assume to be the case (Schleihauf, *Jutland*, 140; Frost, *Battle of Jutland*, 342–43; Marder, *Dreadnought to Scapa Flow*, 3: 111; Hough, *Great War at Sea*, 252–53; Gordon, *Rules of the Game*, 458; Massie, *Castles of Steel*, 624–25; and most recently, Konstam, *Jutland*, 175–76). Only Tarrant (*Jutland*, 149–53) and Staff (*Skagerrak*, 130) reject this idea. None of these historians believe, however, that Scheer meant to fight and win, nor merely to surprise Jellicoe and disengage for the night (i.e., facilitate an escape), which is essentially what both Scheer (*Deutschlands Hochseeflotte*, 226) and Groos (*Der Krieg in der Nordsee*, 3: 311–12) alleged after the war—later echoed by Tarrant and, somewhat contradictorily, by Staff. Marder at least cites Scheer's "most striking proof" assertion—clearly there is a discrepancy between this bolder statement and the admiral's memoirs—but places little credence in it. Brooks (*Battle of Jutland*, 313–14) thinks Scheer may have returned to the fray out of a sense of duty, but mainly to rescue *Wiesbaden*, not win a victory in detail;

Rahn ("Battle of Jutland," in *Jutland*, ed. Epkenhans et al., 172) argues similarly. The sole exceptions are Barnett (*Swordbearers*, 164) and especially Corbett (*Naval Operations*, 3: 375).

76. For the preparatory turn, see Groos, *Der Krieg in der Nordsee*, 5: 529; and Brooks, *Battle of Jutland*, 311–12. For the Heinrich citation, see Staff, *Skagerrak*, 133.

77. Scheer's orders of 1855 and 1900 hours are printed in Groos, *Der Krieg in der Nordsee*, 5: 529–30. For the negativing of Heinrich's attack, see Staff, *Skagerrak*, 133. For Scheer's rescue by *G-39*, also see the sources in note 55 above. For Weizsäcker's and Scheer's recollections, see the former's postbattle notation of June 6, 1916 (printed in Granier, "Eindrücke von der Skagerrakschlacht," 21); and Scheer to Hollweg, May 19, 1919 (printed in Staff, *Skagerrak*, 146). It is significant, and an interesting corroboration, that in his battle log Scheer mentioned only the "attempt to pick up the *Wiesbaden*" to explain the turn back (cited in Rahn, "Battle of Jutland," in *Jutland*, ed. Epkenhans et al., 172). But as argued above in note 75, the conscious stimulation of seeing the hapless light cruiser combined with all sorts of other concerns that had eaten away at him for a long time. In Weizsäcker's second notation of June 11 (Granier, "Eindrücke von der Skagerrakschlacht," 23), he records Scheer saying on June 5 that turning back to rescue *Wiesbaden*, and then sending the battlecruisers "back into action," were his only really independently made decisions of the day—that is, unlike most of the day, he acted largely independent of Levetzow and Trotha. Also see Groos, *Der Krieg in der Nordsee*, 5: 311, who argued that Scheer's decision to go back was "essentially the intuition of the moment"; and Raeder, *Mein Leben*, 1: 117, who recalled that "as we correctly supposed [at the time], this order sprang from the impulsive nature of the fleet chief." von Weizsäcker, *Erinnerungen*, 37, supports this version of Scheer's rather spontaneously making up his mind by noting that for the most part the admiral did not think things through this day, but rather acted mainly as a "spur of the moment man" (*Augenblicksmensch*)—the chief later asserting that he "wasn't thinking about anything. I came to the whole thing like the Virgin Mary got her baby." Scheer also later stated that "the fact is I had no definite object . . . I thought I ought to assist the *Wiesbaden* . . . [and] turned back under the impression that the action could not end in this way, and that I ought to seek contact with the enemy again" (Report of the Austrian Naval Attaché, quoting Scheer, June 17, 1916 [cited in Schleihauf, *Jutland*, 140n11]).

78. Levetzow to Hess, August 10, 1936 (cited in Marder, *Dreadnought to Scapa Flow*, 3: 76). Also see Granier, *Magnus von Levetzow*, 18–19; and above, note 28.

79. Recollection of Midshipman John Brass, printed in Steel and Hart, *Jutland 1916*, ch. 5, ebook location 4,323

80. Diary of Stephen King-Hall, June 2, 1916 (printed in L. King-Hall, *Sea Saga*, 457).

81. Signals printed in Brooks, *Battle of Jutland*, 299. Also see Jellicoe, *Grand Fleet*, 355–58; and Corbett, *Naval Operations*, 3: 372–72.

82. The Admiralty would criticize Jellicoe for not making such a pursuit (Schleihauf, *Jutland*, 134).

83. See Brooks, *Battle of Jutland*, 299; and Frost, *Battle of Jutland*, 340.

84. Citations/signals in Jellicoe, *Grand Fleet*, 358, 357; Thompson, *Imperial War Museum Book*, 312; Frost, *Battle of Jutland*, 341; and Brooks, *Battle of Jutland*, 299.

85. Citations/signals in Brooks, *Battle of Jutland*, 299, 315 (Goodenough's postbattle report); and Diary of Stephen King-Hall, in L. King-Hall, *Sea Saga*, 456–57. These British recollections are further corroboration that *Wiesbaden*'s plight prompted Scheer to go ahead with the battle turn. Both refer to seeing "the rear" of the German line while pummeling *Wiesbaden* after 1850 hours—German ships heading west, in other words, several minutes *before* Scheer's order for the turn (1855). Goodenough also thought he had Scheer's predreadnoughts in sight, that is, the rear squadron. Chart 9 in vol. 3 of Marder, *Dreadnought to Scapa Flow*, also supports this scenario. Also see *Markgraf*'s postbattle report (in Rahn, "Battle of Jutland," in *Jutland*, ed. Epkenhans et al., 222), which has this battleship, two ships behind Behncke, in the midst of the turn at 1856 and "port side entering battle at 1857," which may indicate that she commenced firing at 2nd LCS somewhat before Groos' (*Der Krieg in der Nordsee*, 5: 312–13) stated time of "around 1905."

86. von Hase, *Kiel and Jutland*, 106 (course and timing of turns), 109 (citations). Also see Groos, *Der Krieg in der Nordsee*, 5: 313.

87. Frost, *Battle of Jutland*, 353; Brooks, *Battle of Jutland*, 317; and Staff, *Skagerrak*, 137.

88. Jellicoe says he issued the order about ten minutes after the turn to south (i.e., about 1905) (Jellicoe, *Grand Fleet*, 357–58), but it went out at 1912 (Brooks, *Battle of Jutland*, 316).

89. Midshipman Arthur James of *Royal Oak*, cited in Steel and Hart, *Jutland 1916*, ch. 5, ebook location 4,497.

90. For this paragraph, also see Frost, *Battle of Jutland*, 353; Staff, *Skagerrak*, 137; and the sources in chapter 4, note 7.

91. Further strengthening the impression that Scheer wanted to punch through, not punch and backpedal (see above, notes 72 and 75), is the fact that other than helping the crew of *Wiesbaden*, the torpedo boats had received no orders from the top. (For their position south of 1st SG, see Groos, *Der Krieg in der Nordsee*, 5: charts 22–23.) The destroyers would have been ordered to attack with the battlecruisers in the van if the intent was only to shock Jellicoe and then retreat.

92. *Derfflinger*'s navigational chart (printed in von Hase, *Kiel and Jutland*, 106) timed the southeast turn at 1913; to south at 1915.

93. Citations in Scheer to Hollweg, January 15, 1920 (printed in Staff, *Skagerrak*, 148); Weizsäcker's second postbattle notation, June 11, 1916 (printed in Granier, "Eindrücke von der Skagerrakschlacht," 23—for "did not execute" remark as well as Scheer's "I don't

care" remark); Levetzow to Rösling, February 2, 1934 (cited in Granier, *Magnus von Levetzow*, 18; and Groos, *Der Krieg in der Nordsee*, 5: 530). That Scheer made his blunt remark at this particular minute is not entirely certain. Weizsäcker's June 11 recollection placed it between 1900 and 1930.

94. Cited in von Hase, *Kiel and Jutland*, 110.

95. Citations in Levetzow to Rösling, February 2, 1934 (cited in Granier, *Magnus von Levetzow*, 18; and Groos, *Der Krieg in der Nordsee*, 5: 530).

96. Georg von Hase started what became an enduring myth in 1920 with *Two White People*, the English version of his memoir. The chief gunnery officer on *Derfflinger* claimed that Scheer signaled the fleet to retreat at 1912, and then ordered the battlecruisers to charge the enemy sacrificially at 1913 to cover this retirement (*Kiel and Jutland*, 109–10). Scheer immediately pounced on the assertion in a private letter to Vice Admiral Hollweg of January 15, 1920 (printed in Staff, *Skagerrak*, 147–48), rightly pointing out that the battlecruisers were ordered forward at 1913, the fleet to turn at 1918. Otto Groos, navigation officer on *Von der Tann*, nevertheless repeated a similar claim in 1925 (*Der Krieg in der Nordsee*, 5: 319), even though his own text shows that the battle turn order was either 1916 or 1918, and what might be dubbed "1st SG's version"—one detects anger here that the order to charge, which caused such damage, had been given by Scheer—has become a staple of most works ever since, mainly on the Anglo-American side. See Corbett, *Naval Operations*, 3: 378–79; Frost, *Battle of Jutland*, 355; Dreyer, *Sea Heritage*, 135; Barnett, *Swordbearers*, 165; Marder, *Dreadnought to Scapa Flow*, 112–13; Hough, *Great War at Sea*, 253; Massie, *Castles of Steel*, 627; and Konstam, *Jutland*, 184, 192. Remarkably enough, Staff (*Skagerrak*, 146, 148), who dredged Scheer's letters out of the archives, does not properly emphasize this much-needed historical revision of a famous part of an important naval battle. Also see above, note 61.

97. Groos, *Der Krieg in der Nordsee*, 5: 318–19, 321; Frost, *Battle of Jutland*, 353; Brooks, *Battle of Jutland*, 318.

98. Levetzow to Donnersmarck, October 29, 1926 (cited in Granier, *Magnus von Levetzow*, 18).

99. Recollection of Seaman Albert Blessman, printed in Steel and Hart, *Jutland 1916*, ch. 5, ebook location 4,520.

100. Frost, *Battle of Jutland*, 353; Schleihauf, *Jutland*, 142; Staff, *Skagerrak*, 137.

101. von Hase, *Kiel and Jutland*, 107–8; Staff, *Skagerrak*, 136. Staff incorrectly places the torpedo net repair after the turn east.

102. Citations in Gordon, *Rules of the Game*, 459; and Frenssen, *Die Brüder*, ch. 24.

103. von Hase, *Kiel and Jutland*, 109.

104. ERA Harold Wright of *King George V*, printed in Steel and Hart, *Jutland 1916*, ch. 5, ebook location 4,478.

105. von Hase, *Kiel and Jutland*, 110–11; Groos, *Der Krieg in der Nordsee*, 5: 321, 323; Gordon, *Rules of the Game*, 459; Schleihauf, *Jutland*, 166n2.

106. Using postbattle reports from the archives, Staff (*Skagerrak*, 137–41) provides the most detailed description of British hits on German ships. Also see Schleihauf, *Jutland*, 166n2; and chapter 10, note 37.

107. Staff, *Skagerrak*, 141–43. Also see Gordon, *Rules of the Game*, 459; and chapter 10, note 37.

108. Chatfield, *Navy and Defence*, 153; Behncke, *Unsere Marine*, 18, 23–25.

109. For unsuccessful German ranging at muzzle flashes as well as hits on *Colossus*, see Groos, *Der Krieg in der Nordsee*, 5: 319 (p. 530 for the third battle turn order); and Staff, *Skagerrak*, 143–44. For Scheer's tumble, see Trotha, "Mit Admiral Scheer," 13. That Trotha "jocularly" told others (e.g., the Austrian Naval Attaché) about Scheer deserving to be relieved of his command for the second battle turn, see Marder, *Dreadnought to Scapa Flow*, 3: 111n42.

110. Frost, *Battle of Jutland*, 367.

111. See charts 12 and 13 in volume 5 of Groos, *Der Krieg in der Nordsee*; and Brooks, *Battle of Jutland*, 323.

112. Cited in Staff, *Skagerrak*, 153.

113. Both quotes of Petty Officer Arthur Brister are cited in Steel and Hart, *Jutland 1916*, ch. 5, ebook locations 4,671 and 4,718.

114. Citation of Arthur Brister in Steel and Hart, *Jutland 1916*, ch. 5, ebook location 4,718.

115. Jellicoe, "Errors Made in Jutland Battle," 1932 (printed in Dreyer, *Sea Heritage*, 167). Also see Jellicoe, *Grand Fleet*, 361–62.

116. For a good description of the torpedo attack, see Frost, *Battle of Jutland*, 367–70; and Brooks, *Battle of Jutland*, 323–26, 331–39.

117. For German and British changes of course, see Brooks, *Battle of Jutland*, 339–41.

118. Groos, *Der Krieg in der Nordsee*, 5: chart 28; Frost, *Battle of Jutland*, 378.

119. Cited in Brooks, *Battle of Jutland*, 341.

120. Roskill, *Admiral of the Fleet*, 177.

121. Citations in Patterson, *Jellicoe*, 125; and Plunkett to Marder, April 28, 1960, and June 27, 1963 (cited in Marder, *Dreadnought to Scapa Flow*, 3: 115, 124).

122. Gordon, *Rules of the Game*, 520. For all British signals cited over this passage (1940–2115 hours), including changes of course, see Brooks, *Battle of Jutland*, 341–65. For distances between the opposing fleets, see Groos, *Der Krieg in der Nordsee*, 5: charts 28–32; and Marder, *Dreadnought to Scapa Flow*, 3: charts 11–12.

123. For the light forces encounters as well as the subsequent actions between battlecruiser/battleship squadrons described in following paragraphs, see mainly Groos, *Der Krieg in der Nordsee*, 5: 340–46; Corbett, *Naval Operations*, 3: 383–89; Frost, *Battle of Jutland*,

388–97; Brooks, *Battle of Jutland*, 344–53; and Staff, *Skagerrak*, 160–68, which provides much detail on the nature of hits to German ships.

124. Citations in Brooks, *Battle of Jutland*, 350; and Chalmers, *Life and Letters*, 255.

125. Citations in Brooks, *Battle of Jutland*, 349–50; and Groos, *Der Krieg in der Nordsee*, 5: 346. Brooks' research reveals that observers on the rear BCF ships saw a "burst of air underwater" along with a "large swirl of oil," but he rules out such a boiler explosion as the cause because BCF charts showed *Queen Mary's* wreck eight miles away and *Nestor's* well over twelve miles away. It is well known, however, that these charts had been many miles off their dead reckoning before 1800 hours, and since then the BCF had completed a giant circle in two and a half hours, plus its controversial lesser "circling" around 1845 (see Gordon, *Rules of the Game*, 457–58), all of this giving record keepers the impression that they were far away from *Queen Mary's* grave. German charts (Groos, *Der Krieg in der Nordsee*, 5: 346 and chart 31), however, show that the BCF was much closer to *Nestor* at 2035; although, as Brooks notes from the dispatches of both Beatty and Chatfield, the BCF course was northwest by north, not still southeast as on the German chart, that is, even closer to *Nestor*.

Research on underwater explosions, including shock waves in shallower water, is easily accessible online. See Nathan Okun, "The Effects of Underwater Explosions," *NavWeaps*, March 13, 1999, navweaps.com/index_tech/tech-026.htm; and "Underwater Explosion," Wikipedia, en.wikipedia.org/wiki/ Underwater_explosion—last consulted in 2019.

For the timing of BCF and German 2nd BS firing, courses, and turns, see Brooks, *Battle of Jutland*, 349–50, 354–55; and Groos, *Der Krieg in der Nordsee*, 5: 345–46, the latter giving more credence to the underwater explosion theory.

126. Citations in Ernst von Weizsäcker's first postbattle notation, June 6, 1916 (printed in Granier, "Eindrücke von der Skagerrakschlacht," 22; and Scheer, *Deutschlands Hochseeflotte*, 256).

127. Hawksley cited in Brooks, *Battle of Jutland*, 361.

128. Corbett, *Naval Operations*, 3: 389, errs in writing there "was nothing to suggest the error" made by Jerram. See Brooks, *Battle of Jutland*, 362.

129. Jellicoe, "Errors Made in Jutland Battle," 1932 (printed in Dreyer, *Sea Heritage*, 167).

130. Gordon, *Rules of the Game*, 468.

131. Jellicoe, *Grand Fleet*, 373.

132. Marder, *Dreadnought to Scapa Flow*, 3: 43; Gordon, *Rules of the Game*, 415.

CHAPTER 12. NIGHT, MORNING, NOONTIDE

1. Beatty sent his last signal by flags at 2130 on the May 31. The first traces of light in the eastern sky came at 0145 hours on June 1.

2. Groos, *Der Krieg in der Nordsee*, 5: 533–38, for German signals, 2106 to 0324.

3. Citation in Brooks, *Battle of Jutland*, 375. For British signals (including the Admiralty's), 2138 to 0440, see pp. 376–441.

4. The most succinct analysis of the night of May 31–June 1 is Marder, *Dreadnought to Scapa Flow*, 3: 132–62; Brooks, *Battle of Jutland*, 366–450 (see especially 408–14), 529–33, is the most detailed. Also helpful is Gordon, *Rules of the Game*, 472–99.

5. Corbett, *Naval Operations*, 3: 393.

6. The best ship-by-ship accounting of casualties during the night is Schleihauf, *Jutland*, 219–20. For the citation, see the Richard Stumpf Diary, June 8, 1916 (printed in Horn, *Private War of Seaman Stumpf*, 213): Stumpf had spoken to survivors of the ship after they came back to port.

7. For the citations, see Waller's journal article of 1935, and Gunnery Officer Blake's letter to Marder, August 15, 1963 (cited respectively in Marder, *Dreadnought to Scapa Flow*, 3: 156–57, 155; and Brooks, *Battle of Jutland*, 386).

8. Citations in Marder, *Dreadnought to Scapa Flow*, 3; 150; and Brooks, *Battle of Jutland*, 413. Chart 14 [in vol. 3 of Marder, *Dreadnought to Scapa Flow*], including its insets, is the best visualization of the relative positions of 2nd LCS, 5th BS, and the High Seas Fleet as midnight approached.

9. Marder's belief that not sending all of Room 40's nighttime reports to Jellicoe amounted to "criminal neglect" (*Dreadnought to Scapa Flow*, 3: 152) seems a sound assessment. Gordon, *Rules of the Game*, 486, who disagrees, and Brooks, *Battle of Jutland*, 410, who glosses over the Admiralty's failing, do not convince.

10. Marder, *Dreadnought to Scapa Flow*, 3: 161.

11. For the citations, see Trotha, "Mit Admiral Scheer," 14; and the addendum to Scheer's postbattle report, July 16, 1916, in Scheer, *Deutschlands Hochseeflotte*, 250.

12. Citations in Groos, *Der Krieg in der Nordsee*, 5: 533, 535, 537; and Weizsäcker's first post-battle notation, June 6, 1916 (printed in Granier, "Eindrücke von der Skagerrakschlacht," 22).

13. Citations in Weizsäcker's first postbattle notation, June 6, 1916 (printed in Granier, "Eindrücke von der Skagerrakschlacht," 22; and von Weizsäcker, *Erinnerungen*, 35).

14. Citations in von Waldeyer-Hartz, *Admiral von Hipper*, 212–13; and Groos, *Der Krieg in der Nordsee*, 5: 537.

15. Richard Stumpf Diary, June 3, 1916 (printed in Horn, *Private War of Seaman Stumpf*, 203).

16. Tarrant, *Jutland*, 233; and Groos, *Der Krieg in der Nordsee*, 5: 540.

17. For the citations, see Groos, *Der Krieg in der Nordsee*, 5: 540–50 (for ships' reports on June 1); Weizsäcker's first postbattle report, June 6, 1916 (printed in Granier, "Eindrücke von der Skagerrakschlacht," 22); von Waldeyer-Hartz, *Admiral von Hipper*, 214; and the report of the Austro-Hungarian naval attaché, June 17, 1916 (cited in Gordon, *Rules of the Game*, 514). For this paragraph, also see von Weizsäcker, *Erinnerungen*, 36.

CHAPTER 13. AFTERMATH

1. Citations in Steel and Hart, *Jutland 1916*, ch. 7, ebook locations 7,292 and 7,401–5. Also see their useful statistical appendices, ebook locations 7,892–7,905.

2. First citation in Goldrick, *After Jutland*, 53; the *Globe* editorial of June 4, 1916, is cited in Tarrant, *Jutland*, 250.

3. For the citations, see Beatty to Fisher, June 16, 1916 (printed in Fisher, *Fear God and Dreadnought*, 3: 357; and Chalmers, *Life and Letters*, 262). Also see Stoker Donald Maclachlan's memory of Beatty at the service, printed in Steel and Hart, *Jutland 1916*, ch. 7, ebook location 7,401.

4. Copy of June 3, 1916 to Jellicoe (printed in Jellicoe, *Jellicoe Papers*, 1: 265–66). Also see Marder, *Dreadnought to Scapa Flow*, 3: 216; and Lambert, "'Our Bloody Ships,'" 47.

5. Jellicoe to Jackson, June 14, 1916 (printed in Jellicoe, *Jellicoe Papers*, 1: 278). Also see Marder, *Dreadnought to Scapa Flow*, 3: 216–19; and Lambert, "'Our Bloody Ships,'" 47–52.

6. For the citations, see Roskill, *Admiral of the Fleet*, 183 (and p. 178 for Jerram); and Gordon, *Rules of the Game*, 508–9. Dannreuter's recollection is cited in Marder, *Dreadnought to Scapa Flow*, 3: 193; and Steel and Hart, *Jutland 1916*, ch. 8, ebook location 7,791.

7. Citations in Marder, *Dreadnought to Scapa Flow*, 3: 192, 192n10; and Patterson, *Jellicoe*, 135. For this paragraph, also see Gordon, *Rules of the Game*, 503–4; Goldrick, *After Jutland*, 57: a Russian naval observer found Jellicoe "rather depressed" after the battle; and Brooks, *Battle of Jutland*, 413–14, who discusses Jellicoe and postbattle reports of mid-June.

8. Citations in Beesly, *Room 40*, 168, 156, 155.

9. Beesly, *Room 40*, 168; and Jellicoe to Jackson, June 6, 1916 (printed in Jellicoe, *Jellicoe Papers*, 1: 273–74). Also see Chapter 9, note 26.

10. Citations in Marder, *Dreadnought to Scapa Flow*, 3: 220; and Gordon, *Rules of the Game*, 508. Also see Gordon, *Rules of the Game*, 507, 517–19, and Goldrick, *After Jutland*, 57–60, for other reforms.

11. According to Dannreuther, German naval shell fuses had a right-hand thread, which meant they spun in the same direction as the shell in flight and could drop off if not inserted tightly. See Hewitt, *Kaiser's Pirates*, 128–29. At Jutland, the right-hand thread and other fuse issues caused 52+ percent of German hits on armor (5-inches+ thick) either not to burst at all (26 percent duds), not to hole the plate (21 percent), or to burst while penetrating (5 percent). But 47+ percent of their remaining hits successfully penetrated and burst behind plate, while only 13 percent of British hits on this thickness of armor at Jutland did so. See Brooks, *Battle of Jutland*, 455–56.

12. Dreyer, *Sea Heritage*, 203 (for the citation), 203–4 (for his memo to Jellicoe, July 23, 1916), and 169–70, 204–7 (for further comments); Chatfield, *Navy and Defence*, 153–58; Marder, *Dreadnought to Scapa Flow*, 3: 213–16; and Brooks, *Battle of Jutland*, 454–55.

13. Beatty to his wife, Ethel, March 1917 (printed in Chalmers, *Life and Letters*, 290). Also see Beatty's letter to Ethel on December 23, 1916 (Chalmers, *Life and Letters*, 285), where he remarks that "giving the battlecruisers a spell at Scapa will be good for them."

14. Chatfield, *Navy and Defence*, 160–61.

15. Dreyer to Jellicoe, July 27, 1916 (printed in Dreyer, *Sea Heritage*, 203–4—emphasis in original).

16. Citations from Chatfield, *Navy and Defence*, 153, 156, 158, 160. Also see Marder, *Dreadnought to Scapa Flow*, 3: 215. On July 25, 1916, Jellicoe, backed by Dreyer, Beatty, and Chatfield, requested tests with trotyl propellant using delay action fuses reverse engineered from a German shell. The Admiralty was unmoved.

17. Citations in the Richard Stumpf Diary, June 8, 1916 (printed in Horn, *Private War of Seaman Stumpf*, 207; and Staff, *Skagerrak*, 238).

18. See, for instance, the negative recollection of SMS *Oldenburg* Lieutenant Fritz-Otto Busch, in Peter Cornelissen [Busch's pseudonym], *Die Hochseeflotte ist Ausgelaufen* (Munich: Lehmanns, 1930), 122.

19. Recollection of Admiralty staffer Friedrich Lützow, *Der Nordseekrieg: Doggerbank und Skagerrak 1914–1918* (Oldenburg: Stalling, 1931), 157.

20. Citations from the Richard Stumpf Diary, June 3 and 8, 1916 (printed in Horn, *Private War of Seaman Stumpf*, 204, 207, 208, 209, 213, 215); report of the Austro-Hungarian naval attaché, June 17, 1916 (cited in Marder, *Dreadnought to Scapa Flow*, 3: 189; and Gordon, *Rules of the Game*, 514).

21. For these arrangements, see the Richard Stumpf Diary, June 8, 1916 (printed in Horn, *Private War of Seaman Stumpf*, 210).

22. Blücher, *An English Wife in Berlin*, 138–40.

23. See the Müller Diary, June 5, 1916 (printed in Görlitz, *Regierte Der Kaiser*, 189); the Richard Stumpf Diary, June 8, 1916 (printed in Horn, *Private War of Seaman Stumpf*, 212); and Röhl, *Wilhelm II*, 1,154.

24. For the exchange, see Weizsäcker's second postbattle notation of June 11, 1916 (printed in Granier, "Eindrücke von der Skagerrakschlacht," 22); von Weizsäcker, *Erinnerungen*, 37; and Hopman to Vice Admiral Souchon, June 11, 1916 (printed in Epkenhans, *Albert Hopman*, 827).

25. Most of the report is printed in Rahn, "Battle of Jutland," in *Jutland*, ed. Epkenhans et al., 199–207. Also see Scheer, *Deutschlands Hochseeflotte*, 225–26; and Groos, *Der Krieg in der Nordsee*, 5: 310–11.

26. Weizsäcker's second postbattle notation, June 11, 1916 (printed in Granier, "Eindrücke von der Skagerrakschlacht," 22).

27. Marder, *Dreadnought to Scapa Flow*, 3: 206–7, 206–7n27; and Groos, *Der Krieg in der Nordsee*, 5: 451–52. The citation from Scheer's report is from Rahn, "Battle of Jutland," in *Jutland*, ed. Epkenhans et al., 206–7—emphasis in original.

28. Raeder, *Mein Leben*, 1: 125–26.

29. I disagree here with Gordon, *Rules of the Game*, 514, who finds it "tendentious, and highly questionable" that Scheer really believed another surface sortie and/or U-boat warfare could break Britain.

30. Citations in Raeder, *Mein Leben*, 1: 128; and Müller Diary, August 8, 1916 (printed in Görlitz, *Regierte Der Kaiser*, 209).

31. For August 18–19, see Scheer, *Deutschlands Hochseeflotte*, 258–68; Raeder, *Mein Leben*, 1: 127–28; Patterson, *Jellicoe*, 140–42; Frost, *Battle of Jutland*, 519–24; and especially Marder, *Dreadnought to Scapa Flow*, 3: 235–47; and Goldrick, *After Jutland*, 67–79.

32. Presumably, if Hipper and Beatty had met again (between Whitby and Hartlepool), Prudent Jellicoe would have ordered the BCF to reverse course; but given Beatty's aggressive nature, the turnabout might not have occurred before considerable destruction was wrought on Britain's six battlecruisers by Hipper's battleships. However, the degree of Beatty's aggressiveness would have depended on exactly when in August he heard from Chatfield about Britain's defective AP shell—it is not clear, in other words, whether the alarming news came before or after this sortie. But regardless of what Beatty had done, if Impetuous Scheer had held to his own northerly course, his two battle squadrons and 1st SG may well have returned to Wilhelmshaven, if at all, only a rump of a fleet, for as it was, Scheer did not hear of Jellicoe's approach until 1413 when, quite possibly, Hipper's battle was well underway, but also when Jellicoe had cut off the German's exit vector back to Germany. See the timing details in Marder, *Dreadnought to Scapa Flow*, 3: 239–243; and Goldrick, *After Jutland*, 69, 72–75. The speculation is mine.

33. See the discussion and citations in Chatfield, *Navy and Defence*, 157–58; and Marder, *Dreadnought to Scapa Flow*, 3: 251.

34. Citations in Marder, *Dreadnought to Scapa Flow*, 3: 251, 256. For this paragraph, also see the entire passage in Marder, *Dreadnought to Scapa Flow*, 3: 245–56; Raeder, *Mein Leben*, 1: 129–32; Scheer, *Deutschlands Hochseeflotte*, 270–71; and Frost, *Battle of Jutland*, 524–26.

35. For political stirrings in the navy related to U-boat warfare, see von Weizsäcker, *Erinnerungen*, 37–40; and the Richard Stumpf Diary, June 17 and 24, 1917, printed in Horn, *Private War of Seaman Stumpf*, 336–37.

36. Cited in von Waldeyer-Hartz, *Admiral von Hipper*, 251. Also see Philbin, *Admiral von Hipper*, 141–44.

37. Horn, *Private War of Seaman Stumpf*, 355n50. Also see Stumpf's diary entry (n.d.) (mid-August 1917), 351.

38. Cited in Philbin, *Admiral von Hipper*, 144. Also see Horn's editorial comments, *Private War of Seaman Stumpf*, 340n35, 343n38, 347n44, 346n46, and 353n49.

39. Henry Newbolt's *Naval Operations* is cited in Frost, *Battle of Jutland*, 531. Also see Scheer, *Deutschlands Hochseeflotte*, 447–53; and for much detail, especially Goldrick, *After Jutland*, 250–57.

EPILOGUE

1. Patterson, *Jellicoe*, 252–53.
2. Citations in Philbin, *Admiral von Hipper*, 174, 177.
3. Citations in Levetzow to Hess, August 10, 1936 (cited in Marder, *Dreadnought to Scapa Flow*, 3: 76).

BIBLIOGRAPHY

Bacon, Sir Reginald H. *The Dover Patrol 1915–1917*. New York: George H. Doran Company, 1919.

——. *The Life of John Rushworth, Earl Jellicoe*. London: Cassell, 1936.

——. *The Life of Lord Fisher of Kilverstone*. 2 vols. New York: Hodder and Stoughton, 1929.

Barnett, Cornelli. *The Swordbearers: Supreme Command in the First World War*. New York: Morrow, 1963.

Beatty, Sir David. *The Beatty Papers: Selections from the Private and Official Correspondence of Admiral of the Fleet Earl Beatty*, edited by Bryan Ranft. 2 vols. Aldershot: Navy Records Society, 1989–93.

Beesly, Patrick. *Room 40: British Naval Intelligence 1914–1918*. London: Harcourt, Brace, Jovanovich, 1982.

Behncke, Paul L. G. *Unsere Marine im Weltkriege und ihr Zuzammenbruch*. Berlin: Verlag Karl Curtius, 1919.

Bennett, Geoffrey. *The Battle of Jutland*. London: B. T. Batsford, 1964.

——. *Naval Battles of the First World War*. London: B. T. Batsford, 1968.

Berghahn, Volker R. *Der Tirpitz Plan: Genesis und Verfall einer innenpolitischen Krisenstrategie unter Wilhelm II*. Düsseldorf: Droste Verlag, 1971.

——. *Germany and the Approach of War in 1914*. New York: St. Martin's Press, 1973.

Black, Nicholas. *The British Naval Staff in the First World War*. Woodbridge, UK: Boydell, 2009.

Blücher, Evelyn. *An English Wife in Berlin*. New York: E. P. Dutton, 1920.

Brooks, John. *The Battle of Jutland*. Cambridge, UK: Cambridge University Press, 2016.

Brose, Eric Dorn. "Arms Race prior to 1914, Armament Policy." *1914–1918-online: International Encyclopedia of the First World War*, edited by Ute Daniel, Peter Gatrell, Oliver Janz, Heather Jones, Jennifer Keene, Alan Kramer, and Bill Nasson. Berlin: Freie Universität Berlin, 2014.

——. *Death at Sea: Graf Spee and the Flight of the German East Asiatic Naval Squadron in 1914*. Virginia Beach: Createspace/KDP Print, 2010.

——. *A History of the Great War: World War One and the International Crisis of the Early Twentieth Century*. New York: Oxford University Press, 2009.

——. *The Kaiser's Army: The Politics of Military Technology in Germany during the Machine Age, 1870–1918.* New York: Oxford University Press, 2001.

Campbell, N. J. M. *Jutland: An Analysis of the Fighting.* London: Conway Maritime Press, 1986.

——. *Warship Special 1: Battlecruisers.* London: Conway Maritime Press, 1978.

Chalmers, W. S. *The Life and Letters of David Earl Beatty.* London: Hodder and Stoughton, 1951.

Chatfield, Ernle. *The Navy and Defence: An Autobiography of Admiral of the Fleet Lord Chatfield.* London: William Heinemann, 1942.

Churchill, Winston S. *The World Crisis 1911–1918.* Abridged and revised edition. New York: Free Press, 2005.

Corbett, Julian S. *Naval Operations: History of the Great War Based on Official Documents.* 3 vols. London: Longmans, Green, 1921, 1938.

Cornelissen, Peter. *Die Hochseeflotte ist Ausgelaufen.* Munich: Lehmanns, 1930.

Crossley, Jim. *Voices from Jutland: A Centenary Commemoration.* Barnsley, UK: Pen & Sword Maritime, 2016.

Dreyer, Frederic. *The Sea Heritage.* London: Museum Press, 1955.

Epkenhans, Michael, ed. *Albert Hopman: Das ereignisreiche Leben eines "Wilhelminers": Tagebücher, Briefe, Aufzeichnungen 1901–1920.* Munich: Walter de Gruyter, 2004.

——. *Tirpitz: Architect of the High Seas Fleet.* Washington, D.C.: Potomac Books, 2008.

Epkenhans, Michael, Jörg Hillmann, and Frank Nägler, eds. *Jutland: World War I's Greatest Naval Battle.* Lexington: University Press of Kentucky, 2015.

Eschenburg, Harald. *Prinz Heinrich von Preussen: Der Grossadmiral im Schatten des Kaisers.* Heide: Boyens & Co., 1989.

Farquharson-Roberts, Mike. *A History of the Royal Navy in World War I.* London: I. B. Tauris, 2014.

Fisher, Sir John Arbuthnot. *Fear God and Dread Nought: The Correspondence of Admiral of the Fleet Lord Fisher of Kilverstone,* edited by Arthur J. Marder. 3 vols. London: Cape, 1959.

——. *Memories and Records.* 2 vols. New York: Doran, 1920.

Forstmeier, Friedrich. "Zum Bild der Persönlichkeit des Admirals Reinhard Scheer (1863–1928)." *Marine-Rundschau* 58, no. 2 (1961): 74–79.

Frenssen, Gustav. *Die Brüder.* Berlin: G. Grote, 1923.

Friedman, Norman. *Naval Firepower: Battleship Guns and Gunnery in the Dreadnought Era.* Annapolis, MD: Naval Institute Press, 2008.

——. *Naval Weapons of World War One: Guns, Torpedoes, Mines and ASW Weapons of All Nations.* Barnsley, UK: Seaforth Publishing, 2011.

Frost, Holloway H. *The Battle of Jutland.* Annapolis, MD: Naval Institute Press, 1936.

Gemzell, Carl-Axel. *Organization, Conflict, and Innovation: A Study of German Naval Strategic Planning, 1888–1940.* Lund, Germany: Esselte Studium, 1973.

Goldrick, James. *After Jutland: The Naval War in Northern Waters, June 1916–November 1918.* Annapolis, MD: Naval Institute Press, 2018.

———. *Before Jutland: The King's Ships Were at Sea: The War in the North Sea, August 1914–February 1915*. Annapolis, MD: Naval Institute Press, 1984.

———. *Before Jutland: The Naval War in Northern Waters, August 1914–February 1915*. Annapolis, MD: Naval Institute Press, 2015.

Gordon, Andrew. *The Rules of the Game: Jutland and British Naval Command*. Annapolis, MD: Naval Institute Press, 1996.

Görlitz, Walter, ed. *Regierte Der Kaiser: Kriegstagebücher, Aufzeichnungen und Briefe des Chefs der Marine-Kabinetts Admiral Georg Alexander von Müller 1914–1918*. Göttingen: Musterschmidt, 1959.

Granier, Gerhard, ed. *Die Deutsche Seekriegsleitung im Ersten Weltkrieg: Dokumentation*. 2 vols. Koblenz: Bundesarchiv, 1999.

———, ed. "Eindrücke von der Skagerrakschlacht: Die Aufzeichnungen des Kapitänleutnants Ernst von Weizsäcker." *Marine Forum* 71, no. 12 (1996): 20–23.

———. *Magnus von Levetzow: Seeoffizier, Monarchist und Wegbereiter Hitlers*. Boppard am Rhein: H. Boldt, 1982.

Gröner, Erich. *Die deutschen Kriegsschiffe 1815–1945*. 2 vols. Koblenz: J. F. Lehmanns, 1983.

Groos, Otto. *Der Krieg in der Nordsee*. Series 1 of *Der Krieg zur See 1914–1918*, edited by Marine-Archiv. 7 vols. Berlin: Verlag von E. S. Mittler und Sohn, 1920–25.

Grove, Eric, ed. "The Autobiography of Chief Gunner Alexander Grant: HMS *Lion* at the Battle of Jutland, 1916." In *The Naval Miscellany*, edited by Susan Rose, 379–404. Volume 7. London: Ashgate, 2008.

Halpern, Paul. *A Naval History of World War I*. London: University College London Press, 1994.

Herwig, Holger H. *The First World War: Germany and Austria-Hungary 1914–1918*. London: Arnold, 1997.

———. *"Luxury" Fleet: The Imperial German Navy 1888–1918*. London: Ashfield Press, 1980.

———, ed. *Wolfgang Wegener's The Naval Strategy of the World War*. Annapolis, MD: Naval Institute Press, 1989.

Hewitt, Nick. *The Kaiser's Pirates: Hunting Germany's Raiding Cruisers 1914–1915*. Barnsley, UK: Pen & Sword Maritime, 2013.

Hines, Jason. "Sins of Omission and Commission: A Reassessment of the Role of Intelligence in the Battle of Jutland." *Journal of Military History* 74, no. 4 (Oct. 2008): 1,117–53.

Holloway, S. M. *From Trench and Turret: Royal Marines' Letters and Diaries*. London: Constable, 2006.

Horn, Daniel, ed. *The Private War of Seaman Stumpf: The Unique Diaries of a Young German in the Great War*. London: Leslie Freewin Publishers, 1967.

Hough, Richard. *The Great War at Sea 1914–1918*. Oxford: Oxford University Press, 1983.

———. *The Pursuit of Admiral von Spee*. London: Allen & Unwin, 1969.

James, William. *The Eyes and Ears of the Navy: A Biographical Study of Admiral Sir Reginald Hall*. London: Methuen & Co., 1955.

———. *A Great Seaman: The Life of Admiral of the Fleet Sir Henry Oliver.* London: H. F. & G. Witherby, 1956.

Jellicoe, Nicholas. *Jutland: The Unfinished Battle.* Barnsley, UK: Seaforth Publishing, 2016.

Jellicoe, Sir John. *The Grand Fleet 1914–1916.* London: Cassell, 1919.

———. *The Jellicoe Papers,* edited by A. Temple Patterson. 2 vols. London: Navy Records Society, 1966.

King-Hall, Louise, ed. *Sea Saga.* London: Newnes, 1935.

King-Hall, Stephen. *My Naval Life: 1906–1929.* London: Faber and Faber, 1951.

Kirchhoff, Hermann. *Maximilian Graf von Spee, Der Sieger von Coronel: Das Lebensbild und die Erinnerungen eines deutschen Seemanns.* Berlin: Marinedank-Verlag, 1915.

Koerver, Hans Joachim. *Room 40: German Naval Warfare 1914–1918.* 2 vols. Berlin: Schaltungsdienst Lange, 2009.

Konstam, Angus. *Jutland 1916: Twelve Hours to Win the War.* London: Aurum Press Limited, 2016.

Lambert, Nicholas. "'Our Bloody Ships' or 'Our Bloody System': Jutland and the Loss of the Battlecruisers." *Journal of Military History* 62, no. 1 (Jan. 1998): 29–55.

———. *Sir John Fisher's Naval Revolution.* Columbia: University of South Carolina Press, 1999.

Larson, Erik. *Dead Wake: The Last Crossing of the Lusitania.* New York: Crown Publishers, 2015.

Lützow, Friedrich. *Der Nordseekrieg: Doggerbank und Skagerrak 1914–1918.* Oldenburg: Stalling, 1931.

Marder, Arthur J. *From Dreadnought to Scapa Flow: The Royal Navy in the Fisher Era, 1904–1919.* 3 vols. London: Oxford University Press, 1966.

Massie, Robert K. *Castles of Steel: Britain, Germany, and the Winning of the War at Sea.* New York: Random House, 2003.

McLaughlin, Stephen. "Equal Speed Charlie London: Jellicoe's Deployment at Jutland." In *Warship 2010,* edited by John Jordan, 122–39. London: Conway, 2010.

O'Hara, Vincent P., W. David Dickson, and Richard Worth, eds. *To Crown the Waves: The Great Navies of the First World War.* Annapolis, MD: Naval Institute Press, 2013.

Okun, Nathan. "The Effects of Underwater Explosions." *NavWeaps.* March 13, 1999. navweaps.com/index_tech/tech-026.htm.

Paschen, Günther. "SMS *Lützow* at Jutland." *Journal of the Royal United Service Institution* 72 (1927): 32–41.

Patterson, A. Temple. *Jellicoe: A Biography.* London: Macmillan, 1969.

Philbin, Tobias R. *Admiral von Hipper: The Inconvenient Hero.* Amsterdam: R. R. Gruner, 1982.

Preston, Diana. *Lusitania: An Epic Tragedy.* New York: Berkley Books, 2002.

Raeder, Erich. *Mein Leben.* 2 vols. Tübingen-Neckar: F. Schlichtenmayer, 1956.

Rasor, Eugene L. *The Battle of Jutland: A Bibliography.* Westport, CT: Greenwood Press, 1992.

Röhl, John C. G. *Wilhelm II: Into the Abyss of War and Exile, 1900–1941.* Cambridge, UK: Cambridge University Press, 2014.

Roskill, Stephen. *Admiral of the Fleet Earl Beatty, the Last Naval Hero: An Intimate Biography.* London: Atheneum, 1980.

Sauerbrei, Wolfram. *Ingenohl: Vier Sterne auf blauem Grund.* Neuwied: Kehrein, 1999.

Scheer, Reinhard. *Deutschlands Hochseeflotte im Weltkrieg: Persönliche Erinnerungen.* Berlin: August Scherl, 1919.

Schèibe, Albert. "The Jutland Battle." *Royal United Service Institution Journal* 62, no. 445 (1917): 31–45.

Schleihauf, William, ed. *Jutland: The Naval Staff Appreciation.* Barnsley, UK: Seaforth Publishing, 2016.

Staff, Gary. *Skagerrak: The Battle of Jutland through German Eyes.* Barnsley, UK: Pen & Sword Maritime, 2016.

Steel, Nigel, and Peter Hart. *Jutland 1916: Death in the Grey Wastes.* London: Cassel, 2003.

Sumida, Jon Tetsuro. "Expectation, Adaptation and Resignation: British Battle Fleet Tactical Planning, August 1914–April 1916." *Naval War College Review* 60, no. 3 (Summer 2007): 101–22.

———. "A Matter of Timing: The Royal Navy and the Tactics of Decisive Battle, 1912–1916." *Journal of Military History* 67, no. 1 (Jan. 2003): 85–136.

Tarrant, V. E. *Jutland: The German Perspective.* Annapolis, MD: Naval Institute Press, 1995.

Thompson, Julian. *The Imperial War Museum Book of the War at Sea 1914–1918.* London: Pan Books, 2005.

von Hase, Georg. *Kiel and Jutland.* London: Skeffington & Son, 1921.

von Mantey, Eberhard, ed. *Auf See Unbesiegt: 30 Darstellungen aus dem Seekrieg.* Munich: J. F. Lehmanns Verlag, 1921.

von Pohl, Hugo. *Aus Aufzeichnungen und Briefen während der Kriegszeit.* Berlin: K. Siegismund, 1920.

von Selchow, Bogislaw. *Hundert Tage aus meinem Leben.* Leipzig: K. F. Koehler, 1936.

von Tirpitz, Alfred. *My Memoirs.* 2 vols. New York: Dodd, Meade and Company, 1919.

———. *Politische Dokumente: Deutsche Ohnmachtspolitik im Weltkriege.* Hamburg: Hanseatische Verlagsanstalt, 1926.

von Waldeyer-Hartz, Hugo. *Admiral von Hipper.* London: Rich & Cowan, 1933.

von Weizsäcker, Ernst. *Erinnerungen.* Munich: P. List, 1950.

Young, Filson. *With the Battle Cruisers.* London: Cassell, 1921.

INDEX

ABOUT THE AUTHOR

Eric Dorn Brose grew up in Ohio, completing graduate and postgraduate degrees at Miami University of Ohio and Ohio State. He began his professorial career at Drexel University, where he was awarded special emeritus status upon retirement in 2015. His publications focus on German and European warfare in the nineteenth and twentieth centuries.

The Naval Institute Press is the book-publishing arm of the U.S. Naval Institute, a private, nonprofit, membership society for sea service professionals and others who share an interest in naval and maritime affairs. Established in 1873 at the U.S. Naval Academy in Annapolis, Maryland, where its offices remain today, the Naval Institute has members worldwide.

Members of the Naval Institute support the education programs of the society and receive the influential monthly magazine *Proceedings* or the colorful bimonthly magazine *Naval History* and discounts on fine nautical prints and on ship and aircraft photos. They also have access to the transcripts of the Institute's Oral History Program and get discounted admission to any of the Institute-sponsored seminars offered around the country.

The Naval Institute's book-publishing program, begun in 1898 with basic guides to naval practices, has broadened its scope to include books of more general interest. Now the Naval Institute Press publishes about seventy titles each year, ranging from how-to books on boating and navigation to battle histories, biographies, ship and aircraft guides, and novels. Institute members receive significant discounts on the Press' more than eight hundred books in print.

Full-time students are eligible for special half-price membership rates. Life memberships are also available.

For a free catalog describing Naval Institute Press books currently available, and for further information about joining the U.S. Naval Institute, please write to:

Member Services
U.S. Naval Institute
291 Wood Road
Annapolis, MD 21402-5034
Telephone: (800) 233-8764
Fax: (410) 571-1703
Web address: www.usni.org